THE EVOLUTION FROM STRICT LIABILITY TO FAULT IN THE LAW OF TORTS

Gradually, the law of tort has shifted away from a strict-liability approach to one where fault predominates. This book charts important case law documenting this shift. It seeks to understand how and why the shift occurred. Given that the *Rylands v Fletcher* decision is typically seen as a prime exemplar of strict liability, it focuses particularly on that case, as part of the historical development of tort law. It considers the intellectual arguments made in favour of strict liability, and for fault-based liability. Having done so, it then focuses on particular areas of the law of tort, including nuisance, defamation and trespass. It is somewhat anomalous that though most would view these as examples of torts of strict liability, fault considerations have become prominent in their application. This presents an uneasy compromise, where torts that are notionally strict in nature are infused with fault considerations, often through exceptions or defences. This book advocates for further development in the law of tort to make it more coherent, and to better reflect a primarily fault-based approach to liability, at least in the common law.

Volume 37 in the series Hart Studies in Private Law

The Evolution from Strict Liability to Fault in the Law of Torts

Anthony Gray

•HART•
OXFORD • LONDON • NEW YORK • NEW DELHI • SYDNEY

HART PUBLISHING
Bloomsbury Publishing Plc
Kemp House, Chawley Park, Cumnor Hill, Oxford, OX2 9PH, UK
1385 Broadway, New York, NY 10018, USA
29 Earlsfort Terrace, Dublin 2, Ireland

HART PUBLISHING, the Hart/Stag logo, BLOOMSBURY and the Diana logo are trademarks of Bloomsbury Publishing Plc

First published in Great Britain 2021

A catalogue record for this book is available from the British Library.

Library of Congress Cataloging-in-Publication data

Names: Gray, Anthony (Law teacher), author.

Title: The evolution from strict liability to fault in the law of torts / Anthony Gray.

Description: Oxford, UK ; New York, NY : Hart Publishing, an imprint of Bloomsbury Publishing, 2021. | Series: Hart studies in private law ; volume 37 | Includes bibliographical references and index.

Identifiers: LCCN 2020051677 (print) | LCCN 2020051678 (ebook) | ISBN 9781509940998 (hardback) | ISBN 9781509947126 (paperback) | ISBN 9781509941018 (pdf) | ISBN 9781509941001 (Epub)

Subjects: LCSH: Strict liability—Great Britain. | Torts—Great Britain.

Classification: LCC KD1983 .G73 2021 (print) | LCC KD1983 (ebook) | DDC 346.41033—dc23

LC record available at https://lccn.loc.gov/2020051677

LC ebook record available at https://lccn.loc.gov/2020051678

ISBN: HB: 978-1-50994-099-8
ePDF: 978-1-50994-101-8
ePub: 978-1-50994-100-1

Typeset by Compuscript Ltd, Shannon

CONTENTS

Introduction

This book seeks to explain and understand the broad evolution in the law of torts from a focus on the fact that the defendant caused the plaintiff injury, to a deeper focus on the extent to which the defendant ought to be regarded as culpable, blameworthy or at fault for the injury to the plaintiff. That such an evolution has occurred is undoubted. It was alluded to by the House of Lords in *Read v Lyons*. There, Lord Macmillan stated:

> The gradual development of the law in the matter of civil liability is discussed and traced by the late Sir William Holdsworth with ample learning and lucidity in his *History of English Law* and need not here be rehearsed. Suffice it to say that the process of evolution has been from the principle that every man acts at his peril and is liable for all the consequences of his acts to the principle that a man's freedom of action is subject only to the obligation not to infringe any duty of care which he owes to others. The emphasis formerly was on the injury sustained and the question was whether the case fell within one of the accepted classes of common law actions; the emphasis now is on the conduct of the person whose act occasioned the injury and the question is whether it can be characterized as negligent.[1]

Leading torts scholar Donal Nolan, speaking of case Exhibit A in any discussion of strict liability, the troubling *Rylands v Fletcher*,[2] noted that 'the decision in *Rylands* … was an important victory for the supporters of strict liability, but while they won this particular battle, their opponents eventually won the war'.[3]

To take the war analogy a little further, the thesis of this book is that 'the war is not over'. Taking the law of torts as the (admittedly very broad) battlefield, strict liability soldiers still occupy it, still fighting to apply to given types of liability. However, most unsatisfactorily of all, some torts, which commenced as soldiers for the strict liability side, seem to have crossed over, at least partly, onto the fault side of liability, so they present as some kind of weird amalgam of the two sides. This makes little sense. Further, there is often little that unites the strict liability soldiers into a coherent body. The 'fault' army is clearly endemic in the law of torts, having become extremely dominant. However, it has not been able to expunge strict liability from the battlefield, leading to a complex body of rules that no one designing the system of tort from scratch would find appealing.

[1] *Read v J Lyons and Co Ltd* [1947] AC 156, 171.
[2] *Rylands v Fletcher* (1865) LR 1 Ex 265; (1868) LR 3 HL 330.
[3] Donal Nolan, 'The Distinctiveness of *Rylands v Fletcher*' (2005) 121 *Law Quarterly Review* 421, 421.

This book will demonstrate how the law of torts has, to a very large extent, moved from a system of strict liability, taken to mean liability in the absence of fault, but not absolute liability in the sense that no defences apply, to a system whereby liability is dependent on fault, ie fault-based liability. It will also demonstrate when this occurred. Understanding when it occurred will assist in understanding why it occurred. As a general observation, the lesson is that the law needs the flexibility to be able to take the individual circumstances of a particular situation into account, weighing various interests, to deliver the best results. The lesson is that a fault-based system, considering the reasonableness of the conduct of the defendant (and the plaintiff), as well as other relevant public policy interests and values, is better able to do this than a system with a hard and fast rule that insists that when D causes P injury or loss, the law must require D to compensate P. A deeper, more sophisticated approach is needed. Fault-based principles are better able to facilitate the kind of inquiry needed. They are not perfect, but they are better than the alternative.

Part I of the book considers these historical developments in the case law. Part I comprises two chapters. Chapter 1 considers the broad evolution that occurred in the law of torts generally in this direction. It will be shown that the evolution was assisted by various factors, including changes in the form of action, statutory provision and common law precedent. Chapter 2 considers briefly the evolution in particular categories of case, including nuisance, common carriers, innkeepers, animals, liability for fire, and defamation, and documents briefly the growth of negligence, the prime exemplar of fault-based liability in the law of torts. It will be shown that in many past areas of strict liability, fault principles intruded. Perhaps juries took these issues into account from very early times. There are many examples where parliaments acted to prohibit the application of strict liability principles. And courts progressively developed the law, so that judges could take into account the full circumstances of the interaction between defendant and plaintiff, as well as public policy considerations, in a way that simplistic application of strict liability principles would evidently struggle to accommodate.

Part II of the book considers in detail Exhibit A in the strict liability regime, *Rylands v Fletcher*. Part II comprises two chapters. Chapter 3 considers the various judgments in the case, and the various explanations given for it. It considers subsequent development of the doctrine in the law of the United Kingdom and subjects that development to significant criticism. Ironically, even in application of supposedly strict liability *Rylands*, courts began to take account of the fault of the defendant, creating significant doctrinal confusion. Again, they were forced into this position by the unfairness and harshness of a system of strict liability. But rather than discard the problem (precedent and principle), they sought a 'work around', as the common law does, developing and applying principles that ultimately serve, wittingly or unwittingly, to largely neuter and sideline the harshness of the strict liability principle that would otherwise apply.

Chapter 4 then considers how *Rylands* impacted on the law in Australia, Canada and the United States. It will show how Australian law initially accepted

Rylands liability, before radically turning against it. The Australian High Court eventually rebelled against the confusion and unfairness caused by the strict liability principle. The chapter will show how Canadian law accepted the *Rylands* doctrine, including its uncertainties. And it will show the effect that *Rylands* had, and continues to have, on American tort law.

Part III considers the philosophical rationales said to support the imposition of strict liability. Part III comprises two chapters. Chapter 5 considers the various theories and rationales said to support strict liability, including efficient loss distribution, deterrence, enterprise risk theory, and non-reciprocal risk, through exponents such as Smith, James, Keating, Fletcher, Bentham, Epstein, Klemme Ehrenzweig, Beuermann, Murphy and Calabresi. It also considers theories against strict liability through exponents such as Schwartz, Perry, Holmes, Morris, Weinrib and Beever. Chapter 6 subjects the arguments in favour of strict liability to a detailed critique. They are underwhelming and do not withstand scrutiny. They demonstrably do not explain how courts actually decide cases, it is not clear at all how they will increase 'fairness', they make bold assumptions about loss spreading that would require much more significant empirical work to justify, and they seem to view courts as having a resource redistribution function that would be news to most judges, and they apparently ignore that society would generally regard parliaments, not courts, as the body better placed to engage in any redistribution of resources thought desirable. They rely on concepts that cannot be defined with any sense of certainty.

Part IV then turns to a consideration of torts that were, historically, regarded as strict liability torts, but which in varying degrees have taken on significant aspects of fault. Part IV comprises three chapters. Chapter 7 concerns nuisance. Chapter 8 concerns defamation. Chapter 9 concerns trespass. The development of each is charted, nuisance and defamation in detail, trespass briefly. It will be shown that fault principles have significantly 'intruded' into these torts, primarily through the use of defences. Principles of strict liability that apparently underlie the torts are effectively subverted by extensive use of fault considerations when defences are considered. Again, it has been found that the application of strict liability principles leads to unfair results. Innocent people are found liable for torts, when most would not agree they should be held liable because they did not do anything 'wrong'. They acted reasonably, as their peers would have. Individuals generally see the justice in being judged by their peers – witness the popularity and enduring nature of the jury system in our law. But rather than attacking the problem at its root, by reconceptualising the torts to place fault at the heart of each of them, the law does its familiar-by-now 'work around', by permitting defences to apply to innocent defendants who have acted 'reasonably'. In this way, fault again becomes relevant to resolution of a matter apparently involving a strict liability tort.

This creates significant confusion. It is not clear any more whether the tort should be regarded as strict liability or not. It is surely not how someone designing tort rules in terms of simplicity would create a system. Three significant torts in the family of torts seem to have a Jekyll and Hyde nature, simultaneously apparently embracing both strict liability and fault, when in principle these are opponents. The result is significant doctrinal confusion that infects the resolution of cases. It creates significant uncertainties for litigants, as well as academics and theoreticians, and perhaps the idealist who wishes to see coherence within a body of law. This is surely not too much to ask.

History has taught us that strict liability does not work. It is too inflexible, too insensitive to the nuances of a particular factual situation, and what the particular defendant and particular plaintiff did or did not do, and public policy questions. It ill suits a common law system of justice, based on a collective set of past precedents resulting from a multitude of different factual situations. In contrast, a fault-based system of liability is much better able to do so, thus delivering 'better' outcomes in terms of justice and fairness. Individuals are liable for things they ought reasonably to have foreseen, where they did not act in a way that a reasonable person would have done. People generally accept the fairness of being judged by, and against the standards of, their peers. This is much fairer than applying unrealistic standards of behaviour that pay no regard to moral culpability. Yet, we stubbornly hold on to vestiges of strict liability in some of our torts, while at the same time trying to water it down through piecemeal statutory reforms and developments in the case law.

The evolution has a way to play out yet.

PART I

Strict Liability and Legal History

1

Strict Liability and the Common Law

Ancient Times

It is important to consider the development of strict liability[1] for personal injuries in the context of the blood feud. Traditionally, those who believed that another had wronged them would resort to self-help, including violence against the one thought to have been responsible. In other words, a system of vengeance was in operation. There is evidence of this in a range of early legal systems, including the Babylonian *Code of Hammurabi* (circa 1900 BC) and *Assyrian Code* (circa 1500 BC).[2] Wigmore refers to an 'instinctive impulse, guided by superstition, to visit with vengeance the visible source … of the evil result'.[3]

Malone describes it thus:

> The primordial seed from which both crime and tort were to germinate was the blood feud that was characteristic of any barbaric society organized along the lines of blood kinship. The defence of the honour of the clan by resort to warfare against the harm-inflicting outsider and his entire kin was a traditional practice with roots deep in the need for survival of the family unit. The outrage that cried for revenge lay not so much in the desire to enforce atonement for the bodily harm inflicted upon the wounded family member as in the humiliation that was suffered by his entire kin group.[4]

Decision makers determined that individuals should not resort to the blood feud in order to 'resolve' disputes among members of society. The law had a role

[1] The phrase strict liability is used in contrast with the phrase absolute liability. Absolute liability is taken to mean liability in all circumstances where it is shown that a defendant's actions caused loss to the plaintiff, with no defences, exceptions or justifications. In contrast, strict liability is taken to mean liability in the absence of fault, but with the possibility that a defence might apply, for example that of 'inevitable accident', 'inevitable necessity' or Act of God (all of which will be discussed below). This reflects an orthodox view of the meaning of, and difference between, strict and absolute liability: Percy Winfield, 'The Myth of Absolute Liability' (1926) 42 *Law Quarterly Review* 37, 51. Fault here is taken to mean the failure to live up to an objective standard of conduct. See for discussion of different meanings of strict liability and fault in this context Allan Beever, *A Theory of Tort Liability* (Hart Publishing, 2016) 29–37.

[2] R Wyse Jackson, 'The Evolution of the Law of Accident' (1938) 26(51) *Hermathena* 49, 57–58.

[3] John Wigmore, 'Responsibility for Tortious Acts: Its History I' (1894) 7 *Harvard Law Review* 315, 316.

[4] Wex Malone, 'Ruminations on the Role of Fault in the History of the Common Law of Torts' (1970) 31 *Louisiana Law Review* 1, 1. This desire for revenge also contained a spiritual element.

to play here.[5] In order that individuals would be dissuaded from such an action, it was determined that a payment system ought to be introduced. Under this system, the wrongdoer would pay a specified amount to the person they had wronged. This system appears in the *Code of Hammurabi*, *Laws of Eshnunna* and in Greek texts.[6]

It is also evidenced in Roman times in the *Twelve Tables* (circa 450 BC). These Tables contained precise amounts to be paid for particular injuries. The Tables reflect absolute liability for loss that the defendant causes to another. They do differentiate between cases where the loss was caused inadvertently or deliberately, with punishment in the latter case, and payment of compensation in the former case. The amount of compensation payable depended on the status of the victim,[7] reflecting the irrelevance of the culpability of the alleged wrongdoer.

The *Lex Aquilia* (circa 287 BC) also reflected this. Under it, for example, anyone causing wrongful loss to another by 'burning, smashing or maiming unlawfully' would have to pay the injured person compensation. This reflects concepts of *injuria* and *damnum*, but not culpa.[8] Compensation was independent of either intention or negligence. Jansen says that Roman law only embraced notions of culpa (fault) a century-and-a-half later.[9] Ibbetson refers to the Roman law as 'result oriented' rather than based on notions of fault.[10] It was primarily punishment and revenge oriented, rather than compensatory.[11]

Some vestiges of (physical) vengeance would remain. For example, where the 'wrongdoer' was an inanimate object, the person wronged could exact revenge against such an object by demanding its destruction, forfeiture or removal from the jurisdiction. This ancient right continues today in the form of the deodand.[12] And if the wrong were caused by a person's slave or animal, the law might require

[5] Wex Malone, 'Ruminations on the Role of Fault in the History of the Common Law of Torts' (1970) 31 *Louisiana Law Review* 1, 1: 'the primary object of law was to provide a substitute for the feud'.

[6] David Ibbetson, 'How the Romans Did for Us: Ancient Roots of the Tort of Negligence' (2003) 26 *University of New South Wales Law Journal* 475, 489, who, writing of legal systems of the Ancient Near East, concludes that 'in ordinary situations of causing injury by one's own act, the legal collections point to liability being based primarily on bringing about the result, with no suggestion that any additional element of fault or blameworthiness might be required', though he documents limited examples of recognition of fault as being relevant to liability (489–91); similarly Vernon Palmer, 'General Theory of the Inner Structure of Strict Liability, Common Law, Civil Law and Comparative Law' (1988) 62 *Tulane Law Review* 1303, 1311–13.

[7] R Wyse Jackson, 'The Evolution of the Law of Accident' (1938)(51) 26 *Hermathena* 49, 59–60.

[8] Vernon Palmer, 'General Theory of the Inner Structure of Strict Liability, Common Law, Civil Law and Comparative Law' (1988) 62 *Tulane Law Review* 1303, 1315.

[9] Nils Jansen, 'Duties and Rights in Negligence: A Comparative and Historical Perspective on the European Law of Extra-Contractual Liability' (2004) 24(3) *Oxford Journal of Legal Studies* 443, 448. Jansen adds that culpa was introduced as part of the *mores maiorum* of Roman society.

[10] David Ibbetson, 'How the Romans Did for Us: Ancient Roots of the Tort of Negligence' (2003) 26 *University of New South Wales Law Journal* 475, 494: 'both in the *Twelve Tables* and in the *Lex Aquilina*, liability is expressed in straightforward result-oriented terms'; see also David Ibbetson, *A Historical Introduction to the Law of Obligations* (Oxford University Press, 1999) 7.

[11] Nils Jansen, 'Duties and Rights in Negligence: A Comparative and Historical Perspective on the European Law of Extra-Contractual Liability' (2004) 24(3) *Oxford Journal of Legal Studies* 443, 448.

[12] Jacob Finkelstein, *The Goring Ox: Some Historical Perspectives on Deodands, Forfeitures, Wrongful Death and the Western Notion of Sovereignty* (Temple University, 1973).

its relinquishment to the person injured.[13] These rights existed despite the absence of any fault on the part of the owner of the thing (or person) forfeited.[14]

Because these systems were designed to avoid the blood feud, they were understandably quite generous, and compensation was relatively easy to obtain. Specifically, all that the plaintiff was required to show was that the defendant had caused the plaintiff's injuries. It was not necessary for the plaintiff to show that the defendant was at fault or was to blame for the plaintiff's injuries. This observation is succinctly captured by Sayre:

> The law, which was seeking to supplant the blood feud by inducing the victim or his kin to accept money payments in place of taking violent revenge, seemed to concentrate its gaze rather upon the outraged victims or would-be avengers who must be brought under control than upon the actual blameworthiness of the accused … the law thus set forth smacks strongly of liability without fault.[15]

Pollock makes the same point:

> [I]n a rude state of society the desire of vengeance is measured by the harm actually suffered and not by any consideration of the actor's intention; hence the archaic law of injuries is a law of absolute liability for the direct consequences of a man's acts, tempered only by partial exemption in the hardest cases.[16]

However, Roman law would evolve. Its concept of *injuria* began to evolve from mere unlawfulness to embrace culpa. Ibbetson notes that by the second century AD (civil) liability depended on the culpa (fault) of the alleged wrongdoer.[17] Gaius' *Institutes* of the second century reflects evolution of the Roman law, away from automatic (civil) liability for loss caused to another, to embrace notions of culpa (fault). Civil liability was defined thus: 'A person is understood to kill wrongfully when it occurs by his deliberate act or his fault. And loss caused without wrongfulness is not condemned by any other lex; hence a person who causes some loss without fault or deliberate intent, but by accident, is not punished'.[18]

[13] Oliver Wendell Holmes, *The Common Law* (Little, Brown & Co, 1881) 20.

[14] *Doctor and Student* (circa 1530): 'where a man killeth another with the sword of John at Stile, the sword shall be forfeit as deodand, and yet no default is in the owner'; Wex Malone, 'Ruminations on the Role of Fault in the History of the Common Law of Torts' (1970) 31 *Louisiana Law Review* 1, 5.

[15] Francis Bowes Sayre, 'Mens Rea' (1932) 45 *Harvard Law Review* 974, 977, 979. See similarly Jeremiah Smith, 'Tort and Absolute Liability Suggested Changes in Classification' (1917) 30 *Harvard Law Review* 241, 248: 'in very early times there was no occasion to discuss the essential elements of a tort or wrong. Wrong was then not essential to liability. It was enough that the defendant's conduct, although perfectly blameless, has occasioned harm to the plaintiff'.

[16] Frederick Pollock, *The Law of Torts: A Treatise on the Principles of Obligations Arising from Civil Wrongs in the Common Law* (4th edn, Steven and Sons, 1886).

[17] David Ibbetson, 'How the Romans Did for Us: Ancient Roots of the Tort of Negligence' (2003) 26 *University of New South Wales Law Journal* 475, 477.

[18] G 3.2.11. David Ibbetson, 'How the Romans Did for Us: Ancient Roots of the Tort of Negligence' (2003) 26 *University of New South Wales Law Journal* 475, 495, notes that 'for Gaius … culpa (in conjunction with dolus) had come wholly to displace injuria as the test of whether or not the person who brought about the harm should be liable under the lex'. He says it is not entirely clear what led to the evolution of Roman law away from absolute liability for injury caused to liability depending on fault, but speculates about various possible factors, including the need to resolve ambiguities around

English Law

There is substantial evidence of the reception of these ideas and trends into English law. Initially, a strict liability approach seems to be evident,[19] similarly with a view to suppressing the blood feud.[20] One example is found in the laws of Alfred. Alfred 16 states that 'if a man have a spear over his shoulder and any man stake himself on it, then he (the man with the spear) pays (compensation to the victim)'.[21] So the *Leges Henrici Prima* of circa 1118, Chapter 8 s6, notes *qui inscienter peccat scienter emendet*. In other words, that a person who commits wrong unknowingly must pay for it knowingly. The law at this time contains various examples of cases where a defendant will be liable:

- misfortunes taking place by accident, rather than by design;
- a person engaged in a mission for the defendant meeting death while so engaged;
- the defendant asks another to visit them, and the would-be visitor is killed on the way;
- the defendant lends their horse to another, and the other is injured while engaged with the horse.[22]

causation and the fact that culpa had been developed as a principle applicable originally to particular kinds of relationships (495–96). Roman (and Spanish) influences are evident in Hugo Grotius' *De Jure Belli ac Pacis II* where he states that 'by a wrong we mean any fault, whether of commission or of omission, which is in conflict with what men ought to do, either generally or by reason of a special quality. From such a fault, if damage has been caused, by the law of nature an obligation arises, namely, that the damage should be made good' (17.1): quotes from Francis Kelsey (trans), *The Law of War and Peace* (Bobbs-Merrill Company, 1925).

[19] R Wyse Jackson, 'The Evolution of the Law of Accident' (1938)(51) 26 *Hermathena* 49, 49–50: 'it will be found that as we go back further into the realms of early English law, we approach closely to a rule of absolute liability – that a man acts at his peril … these are the surviving relics of a more primitive stratum of law, when liability for actions was measured, not by motive or intention, but solely and simply by the amount of injury inflicted'; Jeremiah Smith, 'Tort and Absolute Liability Suggested Changes in Classification' (1917) 30 *Harvard Law Review* 241, 248: 'in very early times there was no occasion to discuss the essential elements of a tort or wrong. Wrong was then not essential to liability. It was enough that the defendant's conduct, although perfectly blameless, had occasioned harm to the plaintiff'; Charles Gregory, 'Trespass to Negligence to Absolute Liability' (1951) 37 *Virginia Law Review* 359, 362: 'in the early days of the King's Court the only available writ was that of trespass … and it made no difference whether or not the defendant was negligent or otherwise at fault'.

[20] Francis Bowes Sayre, 'Mens Rea' (1931–32) 45 *Harvard Law Review* 974, 977: 'English law started from a basis bordering on absolute liability. The law, which was seeking to supplant the blood feud by inducing the victim or his kin to accept money payments in place of taking violent revenge, seemed to concentrate its gaze rather upon the outraged victims or would-be avengers who must be brought under control rather than upon the actual blameworthiness of the accused. The wer (amount of compensation payable) varied according to the rank of the former; the latter may be liable even for purely accidental injuries, once causation is proved'.

[21] R Wyse Jackson, 'The Evolution of the Law of Accident' (1938) 26(51) *Hermathena* 49, 51–52.

[22] See the English translation of the relevant provisions of the *Leges Henrici Primi* contained in Francis Bowes Sayre, 'Mens Rea' (1931–32) 45 *Harvard Law Review* 974, 978–79, and his conclusion thereafter: 'the law thus set forth smacks strongly of liability without fault and certainly without criminal intent'.

There is no suggestion in any of these cases that the defendant is only liable when they are shown to have been at fault in relation to these accidents. The mere fact that the plaintiff suffered injury in such circumstances is apparently sufficient to place liability on a defendant who caused it.[23] Legal historians William Holdsworth,[24] and Frederic Pollock and Frederick Maitland,[25] make the same point. Henry II maintained this position, again seeking to suppress the blood duel and private vengeance.[26] The wrongdoer would pay *bot* (compensation) to the person injured and *wite* (a penalty) to the monarch.[27] Legislation of the day also reflects notions of strict liability.[28] Wigmore states that 'in the thirteenth century … in England … in probably all torts the harmdoer paid some compensation to the injured party'.[29]

There are examples of this position in the English case law of the time. One is provided in 1466's *Case of Thorns*. There it was stated that 'though a man doth a lawful thing, yet if any damage do thereby befall another, he shall answer for it, if he could have avoided it', and that 'where a man does a thing, he is held to do it in such a way that through his act no prejudice, or damage, shall happen to others' (Brian J).[30] Littleton J states that 'if a man is damaged he ought to be recompensed … if your cattle come on my land and eat my grass, notwithstanding you come freshly and drive them out, you ought to make amends for what your cattle have done'.

[23] Francis Bowes Sayre, 'Mens Rea' (1932) 45 *Harvard Law Review* 974, 979, who, after quoting from the list, concludes: 'the law thus set forth smacks strongly of liability without fault'; Wex Malone, 'Ruminations on the Role of Fault in the History of the Common Law of Torts' (1970) 31 *Louisiana Law Review* 1, 3.

[24] William Holdsworth, 2 *History of English Law* (Methuen, 1927) 50: 'the doer of feed was responsible whether he acted innocently or inadvertently, because he was the doer'.

[25] Frederic Pollock and Frederick Maitland, *The History of English Law Vol 2: Before the Time of Edward I* (Cambridge University Press, 1895) 468: 'law in its earliest days tries to make men answer for all the ills of an obvious kind that their deeds bring upon their fellows'; *cf* Percy Winfield, 'The Myth of Absolute Liability' (1926) 42 *Law Quarterly Review* 37, 40: 'we respectfully urge that it is putting the case too strongly to say that, if harm ensued even by pure accident from a distinct voluntary act, the actor, however innocent his intention, is liable, and that the question of negligence is not considered at all' (citing the work of Pollock and Maitland).

[26] Janet Loengard, 'The Assize of Nuisance: Origins of an Action at Common Law' (1978) 37(1) *Cambridge Law Journal* 144, 145: 'no strong king could tolerate the spasmodic upheaval and unjust results of private quarrels and Henry II, when he came to the throne in 1154, intended to be a strong king'.

[27] Frederick Pollock and Frederic Maitland, *The History of English Law 2: Before the Time of Edward I* (1895) 449.

[28] For example, the Statute of Gloucester (1278) provided that a person who killed another in self-defence or through misadventure was liable, unless the monarch pardoned them.

[29] John Wigmore, 'Responsibility for Tortious Acts: Its History I' (1894) 7 *Harvard Law Review* 315, 325.

[30] *Hull v Orynge* (1466) B & M 327 (KB). Ames discusses a case, not named, where the defendant admitted he had struck the plaintiff, but claimed it was in self-defence. The court rejected the suggestion that such a defence existed: JB Ames, 'Law and Morals' (1909) 22 *Harvard Law Review* 97, 97. See also Jeremiah Smith, 'Torts and Absolute Liability – Suggested Changes in Classification' (1916) 30 *Harvard Law Review* 241, 248 and John Wigmore, 'Responsibility for Tortious Acts: Its History' (1894) 7 *Harvard Law Review* 315, 319.

The orthodox view is that Brian and Littleton JJ were expressing a strict liability standard.[31] On the other hand, Choke J suggested a possible defence if the defendant could show that he had done all he could reasonably could to avoid the damage to the defendant's interests. Some view this as a crude early example of what would later be regarded as a negligence principle. Others regard it as an early example of the defence of inevitable accident, which they regard as different to a negligence principle.[32] This is discussed in more detail below.

Though the context of the *Case of Thorns* was a case of trespass to land, the comments appear to state a general principle that is not confined to that particular scenario.[33] Subsequent case examples would demonstrate the applicability of the principle to personal injury, not just interference with land interests.

In the 1506 *Tithe Case*, Rede J states:

> Although the defendant's intent here was good, yet the intent is not to be construed, though in felony it shall be, as where one shoots at the butts and kills a man, this is not a felony, since he had not intend to kill him; and so of a tiler on a house where against his knowledge a stone kills a man, it is not felony. But where one shoots at the butts and wounds a man, although it be against his will, yet he shall be called a trespasser against his will.[34]

Another appears in the 1681 decision of *Lambert & Olliot v Bessey*.[35] There the reporter states that civil liability did 'not so much regard the intent of the actor, as the loss and damage of the party suffering', suggesting that culpability or fault was not relevant to liability at this time. They gave an example: 'if a man assault me, and I lift up my staff to defend myself, and in lifting it up hit another, an action lies against me, and yet I did a lawful thing. And the reason of all these cases is because he that is damaged ought to be recompensed'. In other words, individuals take (legal) responsibility for the consequences of their actions, whether or not they were intended or, whether it was negligent for them to act as they did.

Another example appears in the 1705 decision in *Tenant v Goldwin*.[36] There Holt CJ states that 'every one must so use his own, as not to do damage to another'. He refers in particular to cases of nuisance and cattle trespass. He appears to be applying a (general) principle of strict liability.[37]

[31] Stephen Gilles, 'Inevitable Accident in Classic English Tort Law' (1994) 43 *Emory Law Journal* 575, 596.

[32] Stephen Gilles, 'Inevitable Accident in Classic English Tort Law' (1994) 43 *Emory Law Journal* 575, 597.

[33] Francis Bohlen, 'Rule in *Rylands v Fletcher*' (1911) 59 *University of Pennsylvania Law Review* 298, 308. At 309: 'the original conception was that legal liability for injury *of all kinds* depended not upon the actor's fault, but upon the fact his act had directly caused harm to the plaintiff' (emphasis added).

[34] See similarly *Weaver v Ward* (1617) Hob. 134; 80 ER 284: 'trespass … tends only to give damages according to hurt or loss'.

[35] *Lambert & Olliot v Bessey* (1681) Sir T. Raym. 467, 467; 83 ER 244, 244.

[36] *Tenant v Goldwin* (1705) 2 Ld. Raym. 1089, 1092; 92 ER 222, 224.

[37] Though in some of these cases the courts refer to intention, it has been observed that this was because what we would today regard as criminal consequences could also flow from the defendant's conduct, if shown. For instance, they could be required to pay an amercement (fine), and in more

Another example appears in the 1803 decision in *Leame v Bray*[38] where Grose J states that

> looking into all the cases from the Year Book in the 21 H: VII down to the latest decision on the subject, I find the principle to be; that if the injury be done by the act of the party himself at the time, or he be the immediate cause of it, though it happens accidentally or by misfortune, yet he is answerable in trespass.[39]

Importance of Forms of Action

Further evidence appears in the forms of action. They initially clearly focus on the kind of harm done, not the culpability or otherwise of the defendant's actions or omissions.[40] It is possible that the origins of the writ of trespass are relevant here. It has been suggested, for instance, that the writ of trespass was derived from the actions for novel disseisin and replevin.[41] Violence tended to characterise such actions as displacement from land and dispossession of goods. The derivative trespass action was originally trespass *vi et armis* (with force). The historical link with disseisin and replevin explains why trespass actions were conceived in this way, though the aspect of force increasingly became redundant in the trespass action.[42] This is important because it is said that the court's focus on the use of force in the trespass alleged blinded it to other aspects of the defendant's behaviour, including questions of fault and blameworthiness.[43]

Another way in which the forms of action were relevant is that the action in trespass did not permit the plaintiff to discuss much by way of the facts.[44] They would simply state that the defendant had done the act about which complaint was made, or would recite hackneyed and/or tired phrases which typically described the action about which complaint was made, and claim that the defendant caused the plaintiff injury.[45] They would not typically allege blame on the defendant's part.

serious cases, they may face imprisonment. The question of intention related to criminal culpability, not civil liability: Morris Arnold, 'Accident, Mistake and Rules of Liability in the Fourteenth-Century Law of Torts' (1979) 128 *University of Pennsylvania Law Review* 361, 370.

[38] *Leame v Bray* (1803) 3 East 593; 102 ER 724.

[39] ibid, 600; 727.

[40] Eltjo Schrage, 'A Comparative Historical Introduction to a Legal Concept' in Eltjo Schrage (ed), *Negligence: The Comparative Legal History of the Law of Torts* (Duncker & Humblot, 2001); JH Baker, 'Trespass, Case and the Common Law of Negligence 1500–1700' in Eltjo Schrage (ed), *Negligence: The Comparative Legal History of the Law of Torts* (Duncker & Humblot, 2001) 52.

[41] George Woodbine, 'The Origins of the Action of Trespass' (1924) 33 *Yale Law Journal* 806.

[42] JH Baker, *An Introduction to English Legal History* (Butterworths, 2002) 61–62.

[43] Wex Malone, 'Ruminations on the Role of Fault in the History of the Common Law of Torts' (1970) 3 *Louisiana Law Review* 1, 10. Malone states that because a trespass *vi et armis* 'imported of necessity the element of transgression or wrong. It is not surprising therefore that no further showing of blameworthiness or fault on the part of the defendant was necessary in order to warrant a recovery in trespass' (11).

[44] JH Baker, *An Introduction to English Legal History* (Butterworths, 2002) 405.

[45] Robert Kaczorowski, 'The Common Law Background of Nineteenth-Century Tort Law' (1990) 51 *Ohio State Law Journal* 1127, 1175.

The plaintiff's focus was on showing that the defendant had done that which was alleged.[46] In turn, the defendant was highly constrained in how they expressed their defence. They could deny that they did the acts alleged, or they could argue that they were caused by an exceptional event for which they should not be held responsible, for instance the acts of a third party, or Act of God. They could not specifically plead that they should not be held liable because they were not at fault. If they wished to argue this, they would simply plead 'not guilty' and plead their case before the jury.[47] The question of defences, which might include that they were not at fault for what happened, was left for the jury. The jury would determine whether any defences applied on the facts, and, even if the defendant could show they were not at fault, whether this was an acceptable defence to the action. Obviously, since their deliberations are confidential, we cannot know the extent to which juries did in fact take into account questions of the defendant's blameworthiness in assessing their possible liability.

Baker points to a handful of cases for the proposition that in the fourteenth century defendants were able to avoid liability by showing the plaintiff's loss was caused by an accident and was not their fault.[48] He says they would typically do this by pleading not guilty under the general issue, rather than by way of defence of justification. In contrast, Gilles says the defence of inevitable accident was pleaded specifically by way of confession and avoidance.[49]

The other important feature of the forms of action was the development of the action on the case in the second half of the fourteenth century. It sharply contrasted with the trespass action. While the trespass action was primarily focused on whether the defendant's actions (directly) caused the plaintiff's injuries, with fault considerations possibly considered by a jury in a factual inquiry, the action on the case was much more clearly focused on the question of the fault of the defendant for the plaintiff's injuries.[50] This impact on the law was initially modest. Actions on

[46] JH Baker, *An Introduction to English Legal History* (Butterworths, 2002) 403.

[47] David Ibbetson, 'How the Romans Did for Us: Ancient Roots of the Tort of Negligence' (2003) 26 *University of New South Wales Law Journal* 475, 500. For some, this justifies their description of liability at the time as being 'strict': Morris Arnold, *Select Cases in Trespass from the King's Courts 1307–1399* (Selden Society, 1985) 375.

[48] JH Baker, *An Introduction to English Legal History* (2002), though Baker acknowledges that in all three of the cases he cites, the defendant relied on a lack of intention, as opposed to lack of fault. Nevertheless, and after referring to seventeenth-century precedents such as *Weaver v Ward*, Baker concludes that 'what the judges wanted to know was whether the defendant could have taken steps to avoid the accident; in other words, whether it was inevitable … in that there was no reasonable opportunity of avoidance' (405).

[49] Stephen Gilles, 'Inevitable Accident in Classical English Tort Law' (1994) 43 *Emory Law Journal* 575, 621.

[50] Charles Gregory, 'Trespass to Negligence to Absolute Liability' (1951) 37 *Virginia Law Review* 359, 363: 'those who sued in case, therefore, because they could not show a trespassory contact, had to submit some item of illegality or fault to take the place of the missing element of trespass in order to establish liability. In actions on the case for inadvertently caused harm to person or property, this new items of illegality or fault ultimately became what we now speak of as negligence'.

the case were originally confined to cases of indirect, as opposed to direct, injury[51] and (relatedly) could not be used when a case of trespass lay. It was very important that the plaintiff chose the correct form of action, and many lost cases because they brought the action in the wrong form. This position was exacerbated by the fact that, originally, joinder of actions was forbidden.[52]

Actions on the case, at least those alleging negligence, were mostly used in assumpsit where the plaintiff and defendant were in a pre-existing relationship, such as a bailment, innkeeper situation, or professional/tradesperson and client/customer. Again, as with the trespass action, the form of the pleadings meant that the question of fault was usually suppressed. Again, the defendant would enter a general plea of guilty and then attempt to convince the jury that they were not to blame for the plaintiff's loss.

However, by the late seventeenth century actions on the case were becoming more popular, at the expense of the older action for trespass,[53] for reasons including possible longer limitation periods, possible increased damages in case, the availability of costs in such cases, and because vicarious liability was only available in case, not trespass. Juries might reduce the amount of damages in an action for trespass if they believed the defendant's actions were unintentional. For these reasons, pleaders sought to bring claims in case rather than trespass.[54] This placed the issue of fault more squarely before the courts because case was inherently a fault-based jurisdiction.[55] The subsequent abolition of the distinction between direct and indirect harm also made actions on the case more attractive.

Though liability in trespass was traditionally strict, it was not absolute. The defendant could raise defences which might absolve them of legal responsibility for the plaintiff's loss. Noteworthy here are the references to a defence of 'inevitable accident' or 'unavoidable necessity'[56] or 'inevitable necessity'.[57] Defendants might avoid liability by demonstrating that the injury to the plaintiff was caused by such inevitability or necessity. The relationship between these defences, if they may be grouped together as one for current purposes, and the concept of fault is not entirely clear in the cases and academic writings. Sometimes, attempts are made

[51] *Scott v Shepherd* (1773) 3 Wils. 403; 95 ER 1124 (KB). This position was reformed in *Williams v Holland* (1833) 2 LJCP (NS) 190; 131 ER 848, the court permitting an action on the case for a direct injury, provided it was not intentional. This greatly expanded the potential to bring an action on the case, removing it from the shackles of merely consequential injury.

[52] Michael Pritchard, 'Trespass, Case and the Rule in *Williams v Holland*' [1964] *Cambridge Law Journal* 234.

[53] David Ibbetson, 'How the Romans Did for Us: Ancient Roots of the Tort of Negligence' (2003) 26 *University of New South Wales Law Journal* 475, 478.

[54] JH Baker, *An Introduction to English Legal History* (2007) 410.

[55] David Ibbetson, 'How the Romans Did for Us: Ancient Roots of the Tort of Negligence' (2003) 26 *University of New South Wales Law Journal* 475, 499: 'more complex situations fell within the action on the case; in these, fault of some sort seems to always have been necessary', and 'the action on the case … was inherently fault-based' (501).

[56] *Dickenson v Watson* (1682) Sir T Jones. 337.

[57] *Barker v Braham* (1773) 3 Wils. 368 (De Grey CJ).

to relate this defence to issues of lack of fault or blameworthiness.[58] This seems to be the orthodox position.[59] Sometimes it appears that issues of inevitable accident and fault are separate.[60] Ibbetson says it was not clear until 1891 (*Stanley v Powell*) that a defendant could establish a defence based on lack of fault if they could not (perhaps, also) demonstrate that the events reflected an 'inevitable accident'.[61]

Academic View that the Liability at this Time was Strict

Arnold studied English decisions of the fourteenth century and attempted to draw conclusions on the extent to which liability at this time was strict or fault based.

[58] Baker seems to take this position. Referring to some late seventeenth-century decisions, he states that 'what the judges wanted to know was whether the defendant could have taken steps to avoid the accident – in other words, whether it was inevitable … in that there was no reasonable opportunity of avoidance': *An Introduction to English Legal History* (Butterworths, 2002) 405. This appears to contain elements of negligence. It is also possible that the meaning given to 'inevitable accident' evolved. Baker states that by the mid-nineteenth century inevitable accident was effectively a proxy for questions of fault. See also John Wigmore, 'Responsibility for Tortious Acts: Its History III' (1894) 7 *Harvard Law Review* 441, 461, who, discussing the decision in *Wakeman v Robinson*, states: 'note how "unavoidable" here as elsewhere before and afterwards is loosely taken as synonymous with "not occasioned by the defendant's default"'. Other examples of this include *Cotterill v Starkey* (1837) 8 C & P 691.

[59] David Kretzmer, 'Transformation of Tort Liability in the Nineteenth-Century: The Visible Hand' (1984) 4 *Oxford Journal of Legal Studies* 46, 74, refers to the 'generally accepted view that a loss which is "inevitable" is not inevitable in any metaphysical sense, but is merely a loss that could not have been avoided by reasonable care', and (86–87): 'this defence of inevitable accident is … part and parcel of the notion of reasonable care which forms the backbone of the modern notion of negligence'.

[60] One example of an acceptance of a distinction between the two appears in *Weaver v Ward* (1616) B & M 331 where it is said that the defendant was absolved from liability for the plaintiff's loss where the injury was 'inevitable and that the defendant had committed no negligence'. Speaking of *Weaver v Ward*, Percy Winfield states that 'the case is instructive as showing that the court thought that negligence included everything that *cannot be reckoned* as inevitable accident', 'The History of Negligence in the Law of Torts' (1926) 42 *Law Quarterly Review* 184, 194 (emphasis added); similarly *Hall v Fearnley* (1842) 3 QB 919, where Wightman J 'told the jury that the question for them was whether the injury was occasioned by unavoidable accident or by the defendant's default' (Lord Diplock cites *Hall v Fearnley* for the view that inevitable accident and lack of negligence were distinct concepts in *Fowler v Lanning* [1959] QB 427, 433); Percy Winfield, 'The Myth of Absolute Liability' (1926) 42 *Law Quarterly Review* 37, 41, refers with evident disapproval to the list of situations cited in *Leges Henrici* as apparently attracting strict liability, calling them a 'queer collection, and show to a modern eye a good deal of muddling on intent with negligence, or perhaps even with inevitable accident'. He says that the meaning of negligence, though contested, excluded cases of inevitable accident (49). Baker states that 'by 1700 lawyers were beginning to perceive a new general principle: that a man was answerable for all mischief proceeding from his neglect or his actions unless they were of unavoidable necessity'. This statement appears to distinguish negligence from unavoidable necessity, contrary to the references in the previous footnote. At least two explanations for this are considered possible – (a) that when Baker uses the word 'neglect' in the sentence just quoted, he does not mean negligence as we understand it; or (b) Baker is effectively pointing out a change in how the concepts of unavoidable necessity/inevitable accident are being interpreted, from originally meaning something different from fault and negligence to eventually embracing it. Stephen Gilles' thesis is that inevitable accident means something in addition to negligence: 'Inevitable Accident in Classical English Tort Law' (1994) 43 *Emory Law Journal* 575.

[61] David Ibbetson, 'How the Romans Did for Us: Ancient Roots of the Tort of Negligence' (2003) 26 *University of New South Wales Law Journal* 475, 503.

He notes the limitations caused by the form of action, as has been discussed above. He adds that under the early pleading rules, there was no effective way for the defendant to raise a defence of accident (no negligence). He says that when a defendant was accused of trespass, they had (only) two defences available to them. Either they had to deny that their actions caused the plaintiff's injuries, or they had to admit that they did so, but claim that the actions were done 'with cause' (something like self-defence). There was no formal mechanism for them to effectively claim that it was an accident for which they should not be liable. Arnold thus points out that the defendant would have to raise the relevant facts during the trial, as discussed above. According to other scholars who take a different view from that of Arnold, discussed presently, this explains why there is no record of negligence being utilised in decision making – because it was something that juries took into account.

However, Arnold notes that if a materiality rule were enforced at trial, it is odd that there is little record of the defendant raising this kind of defence:

> It is odd that no trace of an attempt to plead them is to be found in the Year Books in light of the fact that serjeants expended so much energy in attempting to plead evidence in so many other kinds of case. The absence of such an effort seems, therefore, to argue for the immateriality of the facts and thus for a rule of strict liability.[62]

Arnold says it is sensible that questions of negligence did not arise in cases involving trespass because the tort of trespass is (and was at the relevant time) a tort of intention. In torts of intention, questions of negligence or otherwise do not affect liability.[63] Arnold also cites the Rochester Townhouse case of 1378 as evidence that at this time civil liability was strict,[64] and the 1401 decision in *Beaulieu v Finglam* for the same principle.

Schrage concludes that

> [i]n both actions [trespass and case] the plaintiff who had suffered harm caused by the defendant sought compensation. Throughout the medieval and early modern periods there is a strong focus on the loss suffered by the plaintiff rather than on the wrongful conduct of the defendant – plaintiffs in trespass did not alleged fault on the part of the defendants but – what is even more important – defendants hardly ever pleaded that the injury had been caused without their fault or negligence. Defendants simply denied that they were guilty … the jury came to their conclusion … without disclosing

[62] Morris Arnold, 'Accident, Mistake and Rules of Liability in the Fourteenth-Century Law of Torts' (1979) 128 *University of Pennsylvania Law Review* 361, 375.

[63] ibid, 376. He discusses a 1382 decision that he says makes clear that the tort of trespass required intention in order to be committed; if the tort were unintentional, the relevant action was in case (375–76).

[64] *Jankyn v Anon* (1378); Morris Arnold (ed), *Yearbooks of Richard II: 2 Richard II 1378–1379* (The Ames Foundation, 1975) 69; Morris Arnold, 'Accident, Mistake and Rules of Liability in the Fourteenth-Century Law of Torts' (1979) 128 *University of Pennsylvania Law Review* 361, 376: 'the few judicial dicta concerning the nature of liability rules in the Middle Ages all seem to support the view that the rule of strict liability was a favoured principle'; 'the inference to be drawn from all the available evidence is that in fourteenth-century trespass actions civil liability was strict' (378).

why. Approaching the question without the preconception that liability must have been fault-based it is hard to avoid the conclusion that liability in the *writs of trespass and trespass on the case* was prima facie strict (emphasis added).[65]

Academic View that Fault was Relevant

Scholars such as Oliver Wendell Holmes,[66] Peter Birks,[67] David Ibbetson,[68] Donal Nolan,[69] JH Baker,[70] SFC Milsom[71] and John Wigmore[72] have claimed that the formal record noted above, which seems to determine issues of liability without having regard to the culpability of the alleged wrongdoer other than the mere fact of causation, does not reflect reality. Holmes claims that juries (and, prior to their introduction, judges) tasked with making determinations of fact did in fact take into account the question of the defendant's culpability in deciding on liability. Obviously, given that juror deliberations are strictly confidential and are not on the public record, this assertion is difficult to assess.[73] Further, that case reporting is somewhat haphazard, brief and sometimes incomplete. We are relying on accurate reporting of cases, which may not always be the case. Perhaps the best way to summarise this evidence is that liability was generally strict, in the sense that the question of the defendant's culpability beyond causation was not something

[65] Eltjo Schrage, 'A Comparative and Historical Introduction to a Legal Concept' in Eltjo Schrage (ed), *Negligence: The Comparative Legal History of the Law of Torts* (Duncker & Humblot, 2001) 28; see also Charles Gregory, 'Trespass to Negligence to Absolute Liability' (1951) 37 *Virginia Law Review* 359.

[66] Oliver Wendell Holmes, *The Common Law* (Little, Brown & Co, 1881) 64: 'a more exact scrutiny of the early books will show that liability in general, then and later, was founded on the opinion of the tribunal that the defendant ought to have acted otherwise, or, in other words, that he was to blame'.

[67] Peter Birks, 'Negligence in the Eighteenth Century Common Law' in Eltjo Schrage (ed), *Negligence: The Comparative Legal History of the Law of Torts* (Duncker & Humblot, 2001) 183–87.

[68] David Ibbetson, *A Historical Introduction to the Law of Obligations* (Oxford University Press, 1999) 58–63. He states that juries did sometimes depart from strict liability, but this was not systematic (58). Sometimes, issues of fault are concealed in the discussion of causation (59). He concludes that 'liability in tort in the Middle Ages … was suffused by some idea of fault' (63).

[69] Donal Nolan, 'The Distinctiveness of *Rylands v Fletcher*' (2005) 121 *Law Quarterly Review* 421, 446.

[70] JH Baker, 'Trespass, Case, and the Common Law of Negligence 1500–1700' in Eltjo Schrage (ed), *Negligence: The Comparative Legal History of the Law of Torts* (Duncker & Humblot, 2001) 65.

[71] SFC Milsom, *Historical Foundations of the Common Law* (LexisNexis, 1981) 298.

[72] John Wigmore, 'Responsibility for Tortious Acts: Its History III' (1894) 7 *Harvard Law Review* 441, 443–44: 'there has never been a time, in English law, since (say) the early 1500s, when the defendant in an action for trespass was not allowed to appeal to some standard of blame or fault in addition to and beyond the mere question of his act having been voluntary … somewhere about 1500 a decided sloughing-off of the last stage of the primitive action took place, and a defendant could exempt himself in this sort of an action if his act, though voluntary, had been without blame'.

[73] Robert Kaczorowski, 'The Common Law Background of Nineteenth-Century Tort Law' (1990) 51 *Ohio State Law Journal* 1127, 1169–70: 'Charles Wigmore and John Baker and S Milsom argued that as early as the sixteenth century, fault or negligence was a factual circumstance plaintiffs had to prove before juries would find defendants guilty. These authors have suggested that the defendant's negligence may have become relevant if he pleaded the general issue of "not guilty" and tried to explain his action by explaining the circumstances to the jury. However, lacking records of trial proceedings and jury deliberations, conclusive evidence supporting this view is non-existent and hence the view itself will never advance beyond an unprovable hypothesis'.

decision makers needed to consider, in terms of the relevant law. This comment is subject to the acknowledgment that it is possible that some decision makers did take such matters into account. There is some limited evidence on the public record to support such assertions.[74] Baker cites a few cases for the proposition that in the fourteenth century defendants were able to avoid liability by showing the plaintiff's loss was caused by an accident and was not their fault.[75] Perhaps the classic decision of the *Case of Thorns* (1466) is an example, and in particular the judgment of Choke CJ. Choke CJ suggests that the defendant 'ought to show that he could not act in any other way (analogous perhaps to "inevitable accident") or that he did all that was in the power to [prevent the damage to the plaintiff's property]'.[76] Ibbetson distinguishes between trespass and case, stating in contrast to Schrage above that case was (always) 'inherently fault-based'.[77]

Others state that at least until the seventeenth century, it is just not possible to know the extent to which fault was or could be taken into account by juries in deciding cases.[78]

It is also important to consider how the concept of 'fault' changed over time in how it was used in cases. Fletcher says that, when originally utilised in the cases, fault was an excuse. This confined it to particular factual circumstances – the defendant being able to show in an individual case that he or she was not at fault for the fact of the plaintiff's loss. He says that, in time, fault moved from being an excuse, potentially applicable to a given case, to a justification. This gave it far broader application, beyond the confines of a particular case, and into a general principle based around notions of reasonableness.[79]

[74] One of the few seventeenth-century examples is *Weaver v Ward* (1616) Hob. 134, 134; 80 ER 284, 294 where it is stated that 'no man shall be excused of a trespass … except it may be judged utterly without his fault'.

[75] JH Baker, *An Introduction to English Legal History* (2007), though Baker acknowledges that in all three of the cases he cites (404), the defendant relied on a lack of intention, as opposed to lack of fault. Nevertheless, and after referring to seventeenth-century precedents such as *Weaver v Ward*, Baker concludes that 'what the judges wanted to know was whether the defendant could have taken steps to avoid the accident; in other words, whether it was inevitable … in that there was no reasonable opportunity of avoidance' (405).

[76] *Hull v Orynge* (1466) B & M 327 (KB).

[77] David Ibbetson, 'How the Romans Did for Us: Ancient Roots of the Tort of Negligence' (2003) 26 *University of New South Wales Law Journal* 475, 501.

[78] David Kretzmer, 'Transformation of Tort Liability in the Nineteenth-Century: The Visible Hand' (1984) 4 *Oxford Journal of Legal Studies* 46, 69.

[79] George Fletcher, 'Fairness and Utility in Tort Theory' (1972) 85 *Harvard Law Review* 537, 556–58: 'the core of this revolutionary change was a shift in the meaning of the word "fault". At its origins in the common law of torts, the concept of fault served to unify the medley of excuses available to defendants who would otherwise be liable in trespass for directly causing harm. As the new paradigm emerged, fault came to be an inquiry about the context and the reasonableness of the defendant's risk-creating conduct. Recasting fault from an inquiry about excuses into an inquiry about the reasonableness of risk-taking laid the foundation for the new paradigm of liability. It provided the medium for tying the determination of liability to maximization of social utility, and it led to the conceptual connection between the issue of fault and the victim's right to recover. The essence of the shift is that the claim of faultlessness ceased being an excuse and became a justification … (they) have different relationships to the rule of liability. To justify conduct is to say that in the future, conduct under similar circumstances will not be regarded as wrongful or illegal. Excusing conduct, however, leaves intact the imperative not to engage in the excused act'.

A Third Way: Something between Strict Liability and Negligence

Stephen Gilles disagrees with both of the above theories. He advances a third theory – that, as a result of the availability of the doctrine of 'inevitable accident', liability during the period of the fourteenth to eighteenth centuries was neither strict nor fault based, but rather something in between.[80] He says that the word 'accident' was a synonym for negligence. He says the fact that mere accident was not sufficient to avoid a defendant who had caused the plaintiff loss being held liable means that it was not a fault-based system during this time, as other scholars have argued. He says the question was not in fact whether the defendant acted reasonably – this was not sufficient for them to avoid liability.[81] In addition, they were also required to demonstrate that the accident was 'inevitable'. He says that inevitably meant practical impossibility. In other words, that the defendant had to show they had done everything they reasonably could have done to avoid injury to the plaintiff. He says this is why it is not correct to state that liability at this time was strict – the fact that the defendant caused the plaintiff injury was not sufficient to attract liability if the defendant could show that they had taken reasonable care (in the parlance of the day, what happened was an 'accident') and that there was nothing else practically they could have done to avoid it occurring. In the view of Gilles, both of these requirements would have to be shown for the defendant to avoid liability for the plaintiff's injuries. He says the standard expected was higher than just non-negligence, but lower than strict liability, because if strict liability were applied, the defendant would have to show literal physical impossibility of avoiding the injury to the plaintiff. In the view of strict liability theorists, Gilles says, mere practical impossibility would not be sufficient. He says that the defence (or excuse) of inevitable accident morphed into something like a principle of negligence similar to what we would recognise today, but this involved a change in principle. He rejects the view of Baker and others that the defence of inevitable accident and non-negligence are two sides of the same coin. He seems to place practical impossibility as being very close to a denial of causation, which might explain the confusion which leads some strict liability scholars to maintain that liability at this time was non-fault based.

Influence of Criminal Law on the Civil Law

Some light may be shed on this matter by the historical links between tort and crime. Obviously, at one time, criminal law as we now understand it as a discrete

[80] Stephen Gilles, 'Inevitable Accident in Classical English Tort Law' (1994) 43 *Emory Law Journal* 575.

[81] A similar point is made by Lewis Klar, 'Intentional and Negligent Trespass: It Is Time to Clarify the Law' (2004) 28 *Advocate Quarterly* 410, 426.

area of law did not exist. Those kinds of wrongs were dealt with in the civil law system as those for which compensation was paid. Then a primitive form of criminal law developed. At first, it reflected the kind of strict liability approach evident in the civil law from whence it had emanated,[82] as noted above.

However, agitation began in the criminal law realm.[83] Part of the explanation might involve Bracton. Obviously he was steeped in and heavily influenced by Roman civil law.[84] He would have been familiar with the recognition of the concept of culpa (fault) in Roman civil law, as well as *dolus* (acting contrary to good conscience). Bracton began to suggest that the *animo* (mind) and *voluntate* (intent) of a person accused of breaching the criminal law might be a relevant consideration.[85] Canon law might also have had an influence. It regularly distinguished between acts that were morally blameworthy (deliberate wrongdoing) from innocent wrongdoing. Religious figures conducted the trials by ordeal, and religious figures typically educated the young. Ames also refers to the concept of the 'moral sense of the community'. He states that it could not tolerate forever the notion of punishing those who were morally innocent.[86]

Arnold refers to a 1368 decision which apparently makes a distinction between liability in what we would today regard in a criminal sense, and liability in what we would today regard in a civil sense.[87] This is the earliest decision to which I have seen reference in this regard. The plaintiff in the case claimed his goods had been stolen while staying with the defendant innkeeper. The defendant innkeeper claimed the premises had been solidly constructed, the plaintiff's room was sound, and that the theft occurred without fault on the defendant's part. The plaintiff apparently sought a *capias*, which was an order to arrest and jail the defendant. The court refused such an order, and also declined to fine the defendant. The court explained that because there was no fault on the part of the defendant, criminal penalties such as fines and jail were not appropriate. It ordered the defendant to compensate the plaintiff for his loss. The case is thus evidence of at least two points – the distinction between criminal and civil consequences for the one series of events, based on questions of fault/intent, and secondly, the strict liability in civil law imposed on innkeepers.

Criminal statutes of the late fifteenth and early sixteenth centuries seemed to accept these factors as relevant considerations. For example the *Yearbook Mich*

[82] Francis Bowes Sayre, 'Mens Rea' (1932) 45 *Harvard Law Review* 974, 981.

[83] Wex Malone, 'Ruminations on the Role of Fault in the History of the Common Law of Torts' (1970) 31 *Louisiana Law Review* 1, 7: 'it is in the criminal appeal of felony that we find the first indication that some regard for the moral aspect of the prosecution might be manifested by the courts'.

[84] Francis Bowes Sayre, 'Mens Rea' (1932) 45 *Harvard Law Review* 974, 983.

[85] 'We must consider with what mind (animo) or with what intent (voluntate) a thing is done … in order that it may be determined what action should follow and what punishment … a crime is not committed unless the intent to injure intervene': *De Legibus et Consuetudinibus Angliae* 101b.

[86] James Barr Ames, 'Law and Morals' (1909) 22 *Harvard Law Review* 97, 98.

[87] Morris Arnold, 'Accident, Mistake and Rules of Liability in the Fourteenth-Century Law of Torts' (1979) 128 *University of Pennsylvania Law Review* 361, 372. The case he refers to is found in YB Pasch. 42 Edw. 3, f.11, pl. 13, 42 Liner Assisarum, f. 260, pl. 17 (1368), and he quotes the Chief Judge.

(1466) records the following statement: 'there is no felony, for felony is of malice propense'. The *Yearbook 1498* states: 'the question was whether [what happened] should be called mayhem or not … and it seems that it was, because he had a bad intent at the beginning'. It also appears in *Yearbook 1506*, that a person who accidentally shot another while aiming at another target did not commit a felony because 'he had no intent to kill him'.[88] This position in the English criminal law was subsequently observed by Matthew Hale[89] and William Blackstone.[90] This is partly also explained by ecclesiastical influences on the law. For example, there are many examples of trial by ordeal being conducted by priests. As a result, it is not really surprising that intention became particularly important, given that the moral blameworthiness attached to a deliberate act is likely much worse than that attached to neglect in act or omission.[91]

For a time, the clear differences in the civil law and criminal law pertaining to fault were quite stark. The court made the distinction very clearly in *Weaver v Ward*. There the court explained that if a person with mental illness killed another, they would not be liable in the criminal law. However, they would be liable in civil law for the same wrongdoing.[92] Similarly in *Lambert & Olliot v Bessey* the court stated:

> If a man assault me and I lift up my staff to defend myself and in lifting it up hit another, an action lies by that person, and yet I did a lawful thing … and the reason is because he that is damaged ought to be recompensed. But otherwise it is in criminal cases, for there *actus non facit reum, nisi mens sit rea*.[93]

Sir Francis Bacon alludes to the stark difference between the approach of the civil and the criminal law:

> In capital cases … The law will not punish in so high a degree, except the malice of the will and intention appear; but in civil trespasses and injuries that are of an inferior nature, the law doth rather consider the damage of the party wronged, than the malice of him who was the wrongdoer … if a man be hurt or maimed … an action of trespass lieth, though it be done against the party's mind and will, and he shall be punished in

[88] These references are gathered in Francis Bowes Sayre 'Mens Rea' (1932) 45 *Harvard Law Review* 974, 990–91.

[89] Matthew Hale, *Pleas of the Crown* (Atkyns and Atkyns trans, 1682) 38: 'if the act that is committed be simply casual and per infortunium, regularly that act, if it were done ex animi intentione, were punishable by death, is not by the laws of England to undergo that punishment, for it is the will and intention, that regularity is required, as well as the act and event, to make the offense capital'.

[90] William Blackstone, *Commentaries on the Laws of England 1765–1769* (1768) 21: 'to make a complete crime, cognizable by human laws, there must be both a will and an act … as a vicious will without a vicious act is not civil crime; so, on the other hand, an unwarrantable act without a vicious will is not crime at all. So that to constitute a crime against human laws, there must be, first, a vicious will, and secondly, an unlawful act consequent upon such vicious will'; see also Sir Edward Coke, *Third Institute* (1641) 6.

[91] Francis Bowes Sayre, 'Public Welfare Offences' (1933) 33 *Columbia Law Review* 55, 68; Francis Bowes Sayre, 'Mens Rea' (1932) 45 *Harvard Law Review* 974, 983.

[92] *Weaver v Ward* (1616) Hob. 135; 80 ER 284.

[93] *Lambert & Olliot v Bessey* (1681) Raym. Sir T. 421, 423; 80 ER 220, 221.

> the law, as deeply as if he had done it of malice … so if an infant within years of discretion, or a madman, kill another, he shall not be impeached thereof; but if they put a man's eye, or do him like corporal hurt, he shall be punished in trespass.[94]

Interestingly, this sharp distinction between how the criminal law viewed issues such as intent, and how they were viewed in the civil law, began to soften. Pollock and Maitland note that in relation to the civil law, the amount of compensation the victim received began to depend on the particular factual scenario, including whether the defendant had acted intentionally or unintentionally. If they had acted intentionally, both *wer* and *wite* would be paid. If they had acted unintentionally, only *wer* would be paid.[95]

Development of the action on the case also practically encouraged the consideration of fault in resolving cases. The form of the action permitted more detail of the alleged incident to be explained. Naturally, this permitted a more expansive consideration of matters, including those pertaining to the possible fault of the defendant.[96]

Fault becomes More (Expressly) Prominent in the Civil Law

The cases began to expressly consider 'fault' in determining civil claims. As discussed above, it is possible that fault was being considered by juries at a much earlier time than this, but the evidence is scant. One of the earliest examples where it is on the record is *Weaver v Ward*.[97] The plaintiff was a soldier. He was accidentally injured by another soldier during horseplay. The defendant claimed it was an

[94] Sir Francis Bacon, *Maxims of the Common Law* (1630) Reg. 7; to like effect Sir Thomas Erskine (*Speeches of the Honourable Sir Thomas Erskine*, James Ridgway ed, 1813) 208: 'if the proprietor of a York coach, though asleep in his bed in that city, has a drunken servant on the box at London, who drives over my leg and breaks it, he is responsible to me in damages for the accident; but I cannot indict him as the criminal author of my misfortune – what distinction can be more obvious and simple?'. To like effect James Barr Ames, 'Law and Morals' (1909) 22 *Harvard Law Review* 97, 98: 'criminal liability (for actions committed in self-defence or through misadventure) disappeared comparatively early … but the doctrine of civil liability for accidental damage caused by a morally innocent actors was very persistent'.

[95] See similarly Wex Malone, 'Ruminations on the Role of Fault in the History of the Common Law of Torts' (1970) 31 *Louisiana Law Review* 1, 6, who, commenting on the distinctions between the criminal and the civil law realm, noted that 'each of the two reparations begins to acquire its own peculiar characteristics. It is with reference to these newly emerging distinctions that we find the first clear suggestion that fault, or absence of fault, may have a role to play … the full wer must still be paid to the outraged family irrespective of whether the homicide was the intended or unintended … however … if the (defendant) … succeeded in establishing there was a misadventure, he may escape the payment of wite … (but) … There is no tendency to relax the traditional requirement that the wer (civil reparation) must be paid irrespective of moral innocence on the part of the accused'.

[96] David Ibbetson, 'How the Romans Did for Us: Ancient Roots of the Tort of Negligence' (2003) 26(2) *University of New South Wales Law Journal* 475, 499.

[97] *Weaver v Ward* (1616) Hob. 134, 135; 80 ER 284, 284.

accident, and thus he should not be held responsible for it. The court concluded that 'no man shall be excused of a trespass … except it may be judged utterly *without his fault*' (emphasis added).

The court elaborated on what it meant by this:

> As if a man by force take my hand and strike you, or if here the defendant had said that the plaintiff ran across his piece when it was discharging, or had set forth the case with the circumstances, so as it had appeared to the court that it had been inevitable, and that the defendant had committed no negligence to give occasion to the tort.

While the first example can be ignored for present purposes because it points to a lack of volition on the defendant's part,[98] the other examples clearly raise the question of the defendant's culpability or fault.[99] This clearly represents a departure from past cases which had suggested that liability for personal injuries existed in the absence of fault. We should be careful, however, not to conflate the question of 'utterly without fault' with the mention of negligence, to reach a conclusion (which would make sense to today's eyes) that here is an early example of the court accepting that where a defendant had taken reasonable steps to avoid the risk of harm, they would be judged to be without fault and would hence not be liable. The reference to 'committed no negligence' was not a reference to how we would today regard negligence.[100]

Further, it is submitted that the inclusion of the concept of 'inevitability' is important or, at least, that it *may* be important. It is used in contrast to and in addition to the concept of negligence. This can suggest that it means something different from a lack of negligence, on the assumption that the phrase used by the court is not tautological and/or compendious. As explained above, Gilles opines there was in fact a significant reason for the court's phrasing here – that the judges were indicating that mere non-negligence would not be sufficient to avoid liability; that the defendant would also have to demonstrate that they had taken all practically reasonable precautions to avoid injury to the plaintiff in order to avoid liability.[101]

Gilles says this is clear when the full context of the decision is taken into account. He states that the defendant's defence in the case was of accident. In other words, the defendant was pleading lack of negligence. He reads the decision as a

[98] Though even here, contrast the decision in *Gilbert v Stone* (1703) Aleyn. 35; 82 ER 902, where a defendant was held liable for trespass although he claimed that 12 armed men had threatened to kill him if he did not break in to the plaintiff's premises. He was held liable nonetheless.

[99] This interpretation of the case is supported in the secondary materials. Sir John Comyns included *Weaver v Ward* in his Digest under the heading 'Action upon the Case for Negligence'. He interchanged the words 'committed no negligence' in the judgment with the phrase 'without his fault': *A Digest of the Laws of England* (1762) 295.

[100] Somewhat confusingly, and counterintuitively, negligence in this context could actually be equated with strict liability. Malone points out that in cases where strict liability had been imposed, including for the damage caused by fire, the courts sometimes expressed the liability of the defendant for 'neglect' although the damage was not caused by their fault at all: Wex Malone, 'Ruminations on the Role of Fault in the History of the Common Law of Torts' (1970) 31 *Louisiana Law Review* 1, 18.

[101] Stephen Gilles, 'Inevitable Accident in Classical English Tort Law' (1994) 34 *Emory Law Journal* 575.

further affirmation of the fact that mere lack of negligence was not a defence in itself; the defendant would also need to show the 'inevitability' of the accident. This required consideration of whether the defendant had taken all reasonably practicable steps to avoid the injury to the plaintiff. Gilles says this is a higher standard than mere negligence. He says the *Weaver v Ward* case is in fact unremarkable, since from the thirteenth century the courts had actually been taking into account the 'inevitability' or otherwise of the defendant's injuries. However, he acknowledges this is obscure and difficult to quantity. He concedes it is typically not on the judicial record; but he says it was largely an implicit understanding underlying the proceedings.[102] While the 'inevitable' nature of the accident suggests this is a higher standard than merely showing a lack of negligence, there is some relation between the two – the fact that a defendant took all reasonable precautions would surely tend to indicate a lack of negligence on their part.

It should be acknowledged that views differ on this. Baker and others view *Weaver v Ward* as a landmark decision which specifically recognises fault as a defence, in contrast to the view of Gilles. Lord Diplock in *Fowler v Lanning* adopted a very different position from that of Gilles. Far from attributing particular significance to use of the word 'inevitable' in the case, as Gilles does, Lord Diplock says 'the word "inevitable" is superfluous, and … the phrase meant no more than that the accident could not have been avoided by the exercise of reasonable care'.[103]

Further, it is clearly a case of *trespass*, the injuries being directly inflicted, as opposed to *case*. Baker states that 'there is no reason to suppose that the standard of liability was any different as between trespass and case, since in either action it was left to the jury to decide according to current notions of culpability'.[104] In contrast, Ibbetson says there is a difference, with case more readily accepting notions of negligence, whereas it came more slowly to trespass.

The case is important as establishing that in cases of trespass, proof of either intention or negligence on the defendant's part is required in order to make them liable. Lord Diplock would note the significance of the case three-and-a-half centuries later: 'the strict liability principle that every man acts at his peril was not applied in case of trespass to the person as long ago as 1617'.[105]

An example may be drawn from the late seventeenth century. The case of *Michell v Allestry*[106] involved a defendant whose employee brought his horse to a busy public place. It escaped from his control, causing injury to others. An original action against the servant in trespass failed on the basis that the employee was not

[102] ibid, 608.
[103] *Fowler v Lanning* [1959] 1 QB 426, 428.
[104] JH Baker, *An Introduction to English Legal History* (2007) 405. Robert Kaczorowski states that 'by the eighteenth century tort principles underlying the writ of trespass were the same principles of culpability associated with actions on the case for personal injury': 'The Common Law Background of Nineteenth-Century Tort Law' (1990) 51 *Ohio State Law Journal* 1127, 1173.
[105] *Fowler v Lanning* [1959] QB 427, 433.
[106] *Michell v Allestry* (1676) 1 Vent. 295; 86 ER 190.

at fault for the plaintiff's injuries.[107] There was nothing to suggest negligence in how the employee handled the horse.

The plaintiff then, at the court's suggestion, brought action against the defendant themselves. As an example of vicarious liability, this could only be brought in case. The new action alleged the defendant was liable for the injuries because they were his fault. He had decided to bring an untamed animal to a place where he knew injury would likely arise if it were to break loose. The court concluded that 'it was the defendant's fault, to bring a wild horse into such a place where mischief might probably be done, by reason of the concourse of people'.[108] Wylde J analogised it to the liability of a person who has a horse in their stable. They would be liable if they left open the stable door and as a result, the horse escaped and did mischief. Similarly, Twisden J states that one who owned a tame fox which escaped would not be liable for any injuries caused by the fox once it had resumed its 'wild' nature.

The judgments are extremely brief, and it is dangerous to extrapolate too much from a seven-line summary of what the judges stated in the case, but they seem to reflect a trend towards considering the fault of the defendant for the plaintiff's injuries, other than the simple fact that the defendant caused the injuries. The court found against the defendant in *Michell* not simply because the plaintiff was injured by the defendant's horse, but because it was due to the fault of the defendant in bringing the horse into a crowded public area that the injury occurred. Similarly, in views attributed to Wylde J, the owner of a horse in stables would be liable if it escaped and did injury to others, but he qualified the observation by explaining how the horse escaped – the owner left the stable door open. This observation again points to fault in how the accident happened, rather than the mere fact that it did. And in contrast, where a tamed (usually wild) animal escaped (though Twisden J did not elaborate how this occurred), the former owner would not be liable for any subsequent injury the animal caused once it became wild again. Twisden J did not explain why this was, so to some extent we are left to speculate. It is possible that it would have been because such injuries were too far removed from any fault committed by the owner in permitting the animal to be released, and the fact it had become wild might mean that the accident was not to be considered to be the former owner's fault.[109] Baker traces the effective birth of the tort of negligence, as a distinct tort, with an essential basis in fault, to this decision.[110]

While these cases expressly use the term 'fault' and suggest a move away from the strict liability principles of the past, some scholars caution against this. It is said

[107] Robert Kaczorowski 'The Common Law Background of Nineteenth-Century Tort Law' (1990) 51 *Ohio State Law Journal* 1127, 1176 (I have not been able to locate a report of this original decision in trespass).

[108] *Michell v Allestry* (1676) 1 Vent. 295; 86 ER 190.

[109] See also *Gibbons v Pepper* (1695) 1 Ld. Raym. 39; 91 ER 922.

[110] JH Baker, *An Introduction to English Legal History* (2007) 411.

that the words 'fault' and 'negligence' are used in a different sense from what we would regard them to mean today.[111] Winfield, for instance, says that these cases are merely further examples of strict liability, despite the way in which the judgments are expressed:

> One or two other cases on the borderland between commission and omission are perhaps referable to the germs of that very rationale strict liability for dangerous things which is now typified by the *Rylands v Fletcher* rule, and is independent of negligence, though subject to some half-dozen important qualifications. Men who handle deadly weapons, or who took unruly horses into public places, or who infuriated bulls, or let filth escape from privies, could no more complain if the law took a stern view of their carelessness in the seventeenth century than their descendants can at the present day.[112]

In the footnote accompanying this footnote, Winfield cites *Weaver v Ward*, stating that 'The case is instructive as showing that the Court thought that negligence included everything that cannot be reckoned as inevitable accident: the latter seemed to have been proved in (citing various cases, including *Michell v Allestree*)'.[113]

Further illustrations of resort to issues of blame in relation to personal injury include *Davis v Saunders*,[114] and *Wakeman v Robinson*. There Dallas CJ states that 'if the accident happened entirely without default on the part of the defendant, or blame imputable to him, the action does not lie'.[115]

There is also apparently some consideration of fault, albeit obliquely, in cases that consider the intention of the defendant, if intention can be somewhat analogised to fault. So, for example, in the trespass case of *Cole v Turner*,[116] Holt CJ states that an action for trespass would not lie if the plaintiff and defendant bumped into one another in a narrow passage 'without any evidence or design of harm'. Arnold discusses a 1381 decision where a plaintiff sued a defendant for causing the plaintiff's house to burn down. It was agreed the fire was unintentional. The court dismissed the case in trespass, telling the plaintiff his only action was in case, due to the lack of intention on the defendant's part.[117]

[111] *Fowler v Lanning* [1959] QB 427, 433 (Diplock LJ).

[112] Percy Winfield, 'The History of Negligence in the Law of Torts' (1926) 42 *Law Quarterly Review* 184, 193–94. See also Wex Malone, 'Ruminations on the Role of Fault in the History of the Common Law and Torts' (1970) 31 *Louisiana Law Review* 1, 28: 'terms such as driving "negligently" or "needlessly and carelessly" appear even in the early proceedings. Yet there is nothing to indicate that any finding of fault was made or even suggested'.

[113] Percy Winfield, 'The History of Negligence in the Law of Torts' (1926) 42 *Law Quarterly Review* 184, 194.

[114] *Davis v Saunders*, (1771) 2 Chit. 639.

[115] *Wakeman v Robinson* (1823) 1 Bing. 213.

[116] *Cole v Turner* (1704) 6 Mod. 149; 90 ER 958.

[117] Morris Arnold, 'Accident, Mistake and Rules of Liability in the Fourteenth-Century Law of Torts' (1979) 128 *University of Pennsylvania Law Review* 361, 375–76.

Full Acceptance of Fault

The late nineteenth-century case law suggests a different approach has been adopted. For example, *Holmes v Mather* involved another accident involving a horse.[118] There a carriage driven by the defendant's servant struck the plaintiff. The horses had been startled by a barking dog. The Court of Exchequer rejected the plaintiff's case against the defendant. Bramwell B classified the action as one in trespass. He said that in such cases, injuries were only actionable where the defendant's actions were either wilful or negligent.[119] Clearly, the defendant's actions were not deliberate. Further, they were not negligent. The court found the defendant's driver was 'absolutely free from all blame in the matter … he endeavours to do what is best to be done under the circumstances'.[120] The law has clearly moved away from strict liability for personal injuries. Interestingly, Bramwell B refers to the concept of reasonable care that would later be the hallmark of the generalised negligence principle: 'for the convenience of mankind in carrying on the affairs of life, people as they go along roads must expect, or put up with, such mischief as reasonable care on the part of others cannot avoid'.[121]

A similar approach is evident in *Stanley v Powell*.[122] There the defendant was a member of a shooting party. He shot at a bird, but one of his pellets ricocheted from a tree, striking the plaintiff. The jury had found there was no negligence on the defendant's part. The court determined, following *Holmes*, that no action in either trespass or case arose. An action in trespass required proof of wilfulness or negligence; neither existed on the facts.[123] An action in case required proof of negligence, thus was similarly not maintainable.[124] It is interesting to contrast this decision with that of *Underwood v Hewson*, where the court had found that an action in trespass to the person lay although the defendant had not intended to cause injury,[125] and that of *Sharrod v London and North Western Railway Co*,[126] which had found similarly.

[118] *Holmes v Mather* (1875) Law Rep 10 Ex. 261. Writing in this period, US Supreme Court Justice Oliver Wendell Holmes Jr in *The Common Law* (Little, Brown & Co, 1881) states the law 'does not adopt the coarse and impolitic principle that a man acts always at his peril'.

[119] *Holmes v Mather* (1875) Law Rep 10 Ex.261, 269.

[120] ibid, 267.

[121] ibid, 267.

[122] *Stanley v Powell* [1891] 1 QB 86 (Denman J).

[123] Subsequently, UK law would move to a position that the trespass action was appropriate for intentional acts, and the negligence action appropriate for unintentional acts: *Letang v Cooper* [1964] 2 All ER 929.

[124] This decision lies in sharp contrast with the earlier decision *Underwood v Hewson* (1724) 1 Str. 596; 93 ER 722 where the (very brief) report suggests that where a defendant is uncocking a gun, with the plaintiff observing, and the gun goes off, injuring the plaintiff, the plaintiff might claim compensation. The report of the case summarises the finding as 'trespass lies for an accidental hurt'. It is obviously difficult to reconcile this finding with the decisions in *Holmes v Mather* and *Stanley v Powell*.

[125] *Underwood v Hewson* (1723) 1 Stra. 596.

[126] *Sharrod v London and North Western Railway Co* (1849) 4 Ex. 581, 585; 154 ER 1345, 1347.

There is obviously much conjecture as to why the law relating to personal injuries moved from a strict liability approach to one requiring either intent or negligence. Some have drawn attention to the possible influence, unacknowledged in the case law though it might be, of the Industrial Revolution: 'The principle eliminating the unintended trespass as a substantive tort and establishing a consistent theory of liability based on fault was developed to confer on industrial enterprise an immunity from liability for accidental harm to others'.[127] This is where timing becomes very important. Obviously, if authors such as Baker and others are correct and fault was being taken into account centuries earlier,[128] it is not actually correct to connect development of fault doctrine with the nineteenth-century Industrial Revolution.[129]

The Important Influence of Statute on Development of the Common Law

Another feature of the nineteenth century, in particular, is the use of statute to authorise particular commercial activities, including the railways, but also things like reservoirs, canals, roads and bridges, which obviously facilitated trade and commerce during the Industrial Revolution. Parliament would typically create legislation under which the companies that would build and run this infrastructure operated. Originally the legislation would relate to construction of a particular piece of infrastructure, however over time standardised clauses would develop with respect to particular types of activity.[130]

Prior to a consideration of how the cases developed, it is important to briefly consider the significance of the fact that Parliament had authorised companies to perform tasks. There was in the past a strong debate as to whether monarchs were bound by law. At one time it was believed they were immune from the law.[131]

[127] Charles Gregory, 'Trespass to Negligence to Absolute Liability' (1951) 37 *Virginia Law Review* 359, 382.

[128] Robert Kaczorowski, 'The Common Law Background of Nineteenth Century Tort Law' (1990) 51 *Ohio State Law Journal* 1127, 1169: 'Charles Wigmore, and more recently John Baker and SFC Milsom, argued that as early as the sixteenth century, fault or negligence was a factual circumstance plaintiffs had to prove before juries would find defendants guilty'. Earlier, it was noted Baker cited fourteenth-century cases for this proposition. The judgment of Choke J in the *Case of Thorns* (1466) seems to contain elements of a no-fault defence. Obviously, case records during the Middle Ages can be difficult to access.

[129] Robert Kaczorowski, 'The Common Law Background of Nineteenth Century Tort Law' (1990) 51 *Ohio State Law Journal* 1127, 1128: 'the fault-based system of tort law was established by the eighteenth century, before the industrial revolution in England and the United States. This article is a corrective to the prevailing views of legal historians who argue that negligence was a nineteenth-century by-product of the industrial revolution'.

[130] AW Brian Simpson, 'Coase v Pigou Reexamined' (1996) 25 *Journal of Legal Studies* 53, 79.

[131] Bracton's 1235 *Law and Customs of England* noted 'quod Rex non debet esse sub homine, sed sub Deb et Lege' (that the king should not be under man, but God and the law). In the famous 1615

Today, this is known as 'crown immunity'. Partly, this was because the courts were seen as those of the monarch, and a monarch could not be sued in their own court. In addition, the monarch was seen as sitting above Parliament. As parliaments progressively gained ascendancy over the Crown in the sixteenth and seventeenth century, the idea gained momentum that some of this immunity should be extended to the work that Parliament had authorised. It extended to government bodies. Immunity from the law had two important facets for current purposes – it was suggested that the government, including government bodies, should not be bound by parliamentary statute. It was further suggested that the government enjoyed an immunity from suit.[132] Subsequently the former doctrine would evolve into a principle that the Crown should not be held bound by a statute, in the absence of express words or necessary implication.[133] These doctrines would long persist in the common law,[134] and certainly existed at the time during which the cases now to be discussed fell for consideration. It is important to interpret these cases in light of the background just described.

An important decision in this regard is *Rex v Pease* of 1832.[135] It concerned two statutes which concerned the construction of a particular railway. The railway ran close to a public thoroughfare, and the complaint was that the noise, smoke, sparks and explosions from the railway presented a danger to the public. Importantly, the action against Pease, who was principally involved in its construction, was for criminal liability on the basis of public nuisance. Pollock was the advocate for Pease, arguing they should not be held liable because the activity benefitted the public. Section 8 of the relevant legislation under which the railway had been constructed stated:

> it shall and may be lawful for the said company … to make and erect such and so many locomotive or movable engines as the said company shall from time to time think proper and expedient, and to use and employ the same in and upon the said railway and tramroads.

The section did not refer to any criminal (or civil) liability for operation of the railway. The judge interpreted this section as being incompatible with an offence

Magdalen College case, Lord Coke famously stated that 'the King cannot do a wrong': (1615) 11 Co. Rep 66, 72a; 77 ER 1235, 1243; Anthony Gray, 'Immunity of the Crown from Statute and Suit' (2010) 1 *Canberra Law Review* 1.

[132] It was said to be a logical circularity that the monarch would enforce a writ in the royal courts against themselves: *Case of Prohibitions* (1607) 12 Co. Rep. 64; 77 ER 1342; *Byrne v Ireland* [1972] Irish Reports 241, 265–66 (Walsh J); Allen Linden, 'Strict Liability, Nuisance and Legislative Authorization' (1966) 4 *Osgoode Hall Law Journal* 196, 197.

[133] *Attorney-General v Donaldson* (1842) 10 M & W 117, 124 (Alderson B); *Ex Parte Postmaster-General; in re Bonham* (1879) 10 Ch D 595, 601 (Jessel MR); *Coomber v Berks Justices* (1883) 9 App Cas 61, 76 (Lord Watson).

[134] Crown immunity from statute was re-confirmed in *Province of Bombay v Municipal Council of the City of Bombay and Another* [1947] AC 58, 61 (PC); *M v Home Office* [1994] 1 AC 377. Crown immunity from suit was limited in 1860 (Petition of Rights Act 1860 (UK)) and abolished in 1947 (Crown Proceedings Act 1947 (UK)).

[135] *Rex v Pease* (1832) 4 B & Ad. 30; 110 ER 366. See for discussion AW Brian Simpson, 'Coase v Pigou Reexamined' (1996) 25 *Journal of Legal Studies* 53, 79–84.

of public nuisance. It could hardly be said that an activity was both lawful, as the legislation stated, and unlawful, which conviction for public nuisance would suggest. Another interpretation of the case is a utilitarian one, that the court thought that the benefit to the public of having access to the railway line was 'worth' the negative side-effects to users of the nearby road.

One of the issues left unclear as a result was the implications, if any, of this decision in the civil context. This came to the court for consideration in *Vaughan v Taff Vale Railway*.[136] Here sparks emanating from the defendant's railway ignited trees nearby, causing the plaintiff damage. Legislation had authorised the construction and operation of the railway. It is interesting to follow this case through the courts. At first instance, the judge was Baron Bramwell. He applied strict liability principles, just as he had done in the Court of Exchequer decision, in dissent, in *Fletcher v Rylands*,[137] as we will see in the next chapter. He said the railway company was liable for the damage caused, irrespective of fault.

However, this was overturned by the full Court of Exchequer. Chief Baron Pollock rejected the strict liability argument, seeking to make an analogy between the keeping of a dangerous animal and the running of a railway. He did so by stating that the running of a railway was authorised by statute, unlike the case of the animal. Relying on the precedent of *Rex v Pease*, he said that in cases where the activity had been authorised by statute, the defendant would only be liable in the case of negligence. As will be seen in the next chapter, this was consistent with the position he took on the *Fletcher v Rylands* case, applying a principle of no liability without fault in that case in the Court of Exchequer.[138] As noted above, Chief Baron Pollock was counsel for the successful defendant in the *Rex v Pease* case.

In applying the *Rex v Pease* precedent to the facts in *Vaughan v Taff Vale Railway*, Chief Baron Pollock did not consider whether the precedent was in fact applicable to the different civil context in which *Vaughan* fell to be considered. Clearly, it is one thing, in a criminal action, to say that the action for public nuisance could not lie for something authorised by statute, since it would be impossible for the law to say on the one hand that something was lawful (authorised by statute), but then say it was unlawful (an offence of public nuisance). However, similar issues do not arise in the civil context. There is no necessary inconsistency in saying, on the one hand, that an action is lawful, but also holding that a person who does the action is liable to pay compensation to someone injured by the action in a civil law action.

On appeal to the Court of Exchequer Chamber, all members of the court simply endorsed the position of Chief Baron Pollock below, that the precedent of *Rex v Pease* governed the matter, such that no civil liability could arise with respect to activity that had been authorised by statute, in the absence of

[136] *Vaughan v Taff Vale Railway* (1860) 5 H & N 679; 156 ER 667.
[137] *Fletcher v Rylands* (1865) 3 H & C 774, 791 (dissenting).
[138] ibid, 798 (agreeing with Martin B).

proven negligence.[139] Again, no member of the court even discussed the argument that *Rex v Pease* may not have been applicable to a civil context, for the reasons just explained. Even after *Rylands v Fletcher* was decided by the Court of Exchequer Chamber and confirmed by the House of Lords within a decade after the decision in *Vaughan*, the House of Lords affirmed the line of cases commencing with *Rex v Pease*.[140] The way the courts reconciled the two lines was to say that where statute had authorised the particular activity, the defendants would only be liable for damage they caused others as a result of negligence.[141] However, if statute had not authorised the particular activity, the defendants could be liable on the basis of strict liability as per *Rylands*, in the absence of negligence.[142] This effectively placed great emphasis on statutory interpretation, and the decision whether or not a particular activity of the defendant was authorised by the statute or not and/or whether Parliament intended that those in the position of a given plaintiff should be entitled to compensation. Obviously, this could also depend on the level of abstraction at which the statute was expressed, and how judges interpreted it.

For instance, judges in the *Hammersmith and City Railway Co v Brand*[143] litigation had very different views as to the meaning of particular statutory provisions. The legislation there enabled a company to acquire land with a view to construction of a railway line. The plaintiff, an owner of property near the constructed railway line, suffered damage from the use of the line, including smoke and noise. The relevant legislation apparently provided for a right to compensation for those adversely affected by the work.[144] The judges who interpreted the legislation did so quite differently. There were two particular interpretation questions – whether the legislation removed the common law right of action in nuisance, and whether the legislation conferred someone such as the plaintiff a claim for compensation here. Some said that the legislation provided the plaintiff with a right to compensation for her injuries;[145] some said that the legislation did not provide the plaintiff with a right to compensation for her injuries on the basis that its compensation

[139] *Vaughan v Taff Vale Railway* (1860) 5 H & N 679; 157 ER 1351 (Cockburn CJ Williams Crompton Willes Byles and Blackburn JJ). Acceptance of this point by Blackburn J is particularly notable, given his significant judgment five years later in *Rylands* that strongly advocated adoption of strict liability principles for damage to land interests (though in a non-statutory context).

[140] *Hammersmith and City Railway Co v Brand* (1869) LR 4 HL 171.

[141] David Kretzmer, 'Transformation of Tort Liability in the Nineteenth Century: The Visible Hand' (1984) 4 *Oxford Journal of Legal Studies* 46, 77–80.

[142] Examples include *Powell v Fall* (1880) 5 QBD 597 (CA) (steam locomotive on the highway held not statutorily authorised, so strict liability applied); and *Jones v Festiniog Railway* (1867) LR 3 QB 733.

[143] *Hammersmith and City Railway Co v Brand* (1869) LR 4 HL 171.

[144] The relevant section was s6 of the Railway Clauses Consolidation Act 1845 (UK): 'in exercising the powers given by the special act to construct the railway and to take lands for that purpose, the company shall … make to the owners and occupiers of … any land taken or used for the purposes of the railway or injuriously affected by the construction thereof, full compensation for the value of the lands so taken or used, and for all damage sustained by such owners'. Section 16 authorised various works, before adding that 'the company shall do as little damage as can be, and shall make full satisfaction in manner herein and in the special acts, provided to all parties interested for all damage by them sustained by reason of the exercise of such powers'.

[145] *Hammersmith and City Railway Co v Brand* (1869) LR 4 HL 171, Willes and Lush JJ.

entitlements were limited to injury that occurred during construction, not use after construction.[146] Some said a right to compensation did not exist unless conferred by statute;[147] others said that a right to compensation did exist unless taken away by statute.[148] All judges except Baron Bramwell found that the legislation extinguished the common law action for nuisance that would otherwise apply.[149] In so finding, they cited and followed *Rex v Pease* and *Vaughan v Taff Vale Railway*. The reasoning for this position is best exemplified in the judgment of Lord Cairns:

> The effect of the legislation on this subject is to take away any right of action on the part of the landowner against the railway company for damage that the landowner has sustained. It must be taken … from the statements in this case that the railway could not be used for the purposes for which it was intended without vibration … it was the intention of parliament … that the railway should be used. If therefore it could not be used without vibration, and if vibration necessarily caused damage to the adjacent landowner, and if it was intended to preserve to the adjacent landowner his right of action, the consequence would be that the action after action would be maintainable against the railway company for the damage that the landowner sustained, and after some actions had been brought and succeeded, the Court of Chancery would interfere by injunction and would prevent the railway being worked – which of course is a reductio ad absurdeum and would defeat the intention of the legislature. I … therefore … conclu[de] that no action would be maintainable against the railway company.[150]

For his part, Baron Bramwell vehemently disagreed, in terms with which Blackburn J clearly had sympathy.[151] He conceded that the precedents *Rex v Pease* and *Vaughan v Taff Vale Railway Company* supported the view of the majority that the legislation here abrogated the common law action. However, he expressed strong disagreement with these decisions, holding that they were 'clearly wrong … proceedings on an inadvertent misapprehension of the object and effect of the clauses in question'.[152] He said that if the argument were that legislation had taken away common law rights, it was incumbent on those making the argument to show so. He said the legislation made no reference to an intention to abrogate the right to bring a common law action in nuisance, and he refused to imply it.[153]

[146] ibid, Blackburn J, and Lords Chelmsford and Colonsay.

[147] ibid, 198 (Blackburn J).

[148] ibid, 189 (Baron Bramwell).

[149] ibid, 183 (Willes J), 185 (Lush J), 197 (Blackburn J), 202 (Lord Chelmsford), 215 (Lord Cairns).

[150] ibid, 215; to like effect Lord Chelmsford (202): 'if such locomotives cannot possibly (be) used without occasioning vibration and consequent injury to neighbouring houses … it must be taken that power is given to cause that vibration without liability to an action. The right given to use the locomotive would otherwise be nugatory … I therefore think that the cases of *R v Pease and Vaughan v Taff Vale Railway Company* were rightly decided'.

[151] Blackburn J said that if the matter were being considered anew, Baron Bramwell's approach had much to commend it. However, he held the matter was settled by *R v Pease*, even if it had been an 'error', and that reliance had subsequently been placed upon it, such that it could not now be overturned (196–97).

[152] *Hammersmith and City Railway Co v Brand* (1869) LR 4 HL 171 (1869) LR 4 HL 171, 189.

[153] ibid, 190–93; he also pointed out that the original decision in *R v Pease* was an action for public, as opposed to private, nuisance, and different considerations might well be applied there in terms of weighing up public benefit considerations (193).

While it is understood as a matter of precedent setting and following, it is more difficult to accept this position on the basis of principle. Why, on the basis of principle, should it determine whether or not strict liability or negligence principles are applied, that the particular activity was or was not authorised by statute? Clearly, if the legislation had specifically stated that the defendant conducting the activity would only be liable for damage caused by it due to negligence, that would be one thing. However, the legislation was typically much fuzzier than this, not specifically precluding strict liability.[154] For example, the legislation at issue in the House of Lords decision in *Hammersmith and City Railway Co v Brand* was silent as to whether strict liability applied or not.[155] As the facts in *Rylands v Fletcher* tell us, the fact that an activity was lawful does not necessarily preclude the imposition of strict liability for the defendant who undertook it. The construction of the reservoir in that case was entirely lawful. The court was not correct, with respect, in *Vaughan v Taff Vale Railway* to simply apply *Rex v Pease*, determined in a criminal context, to the civil context, without a serious consideration as to whether the important differences between a criminal and civil context might caution against such an application. There might be some exception with respect to situations where the authorised action inevitably and on all occasions caused the nuisance about which complaint had been made, as Lords Cairns and Chelmsford noted, but it is certainly not every case in which activity is authorised that such consequences are inevitable, or if they do occur, always accompanied by negligence.

Another example of the judges using principles of statutory interpretation to sideline strict liability from the law occurred in *Hammond v The Vestry of St Pancras*.[156] There the defendant was charged with maintaining sewers that were vested in it. The sewer became choked because it had not been cleaned out. As a result, the muck escaped from the defendant's property onto that of the plaintiff, causing the plaintiff damage. At first blush, one would have thought the facts to be very similar to those in *Rylands*, decided nearly a decade prior to this decision. The court considered the legislation under which the defendant operated. As with earlier examples, the relevant provision was silent as to whether strict or fault-based liability was imposed on the defendant.[157] Brett J, the same judge that would

[154] AW Brian Simpson, 'Coase v Pigou Reexamined' (1996) 25 *Journal of Legal Studies* 53, 80, notes that 'neither special acts nor clause acts (which set out standardized clauses which would apply to legislation dealing with a particular kind of infrastructure) clearly spelled out how the operations of authorized undertakings fitted into the scheme of common law liability'; Allen Linden, 'Strict Liability, Nuisance and Legislative Authorization' (1966) 4 *Osgoode Hall Law Journal* 196, 202: 'the basis of the immunity is said to rest on the intention of the legislature. This approach is acceptable where there is an express intention set out in the legislation; seldom, however, is this the case. The legislation is normally silent on the effect of the legislation on tort liability. Undaunted, the courts continue to speculate about the mythical and non-existent legislative intention in their quest for a solution to these problems'.

[155] *Hammersmith and City Railway Co v Brand* (1869) LR 4 HL 171.

[156] *Hammond v The Vestry of St Pancras* (1874) LR 9 CP 316.

[157] Section 72 of the relevant legislation stated that vestries should 'cause the sewers vested in them to be constructed, covered and kept so as not to be a nuisance or injurious to health, and to be properly cleared, cleansed and emptied' and authorised them to perform works such they would not present a risk to others.

commence the process of ushering in the general principle of generalised duty of care based on reasonable care in *Heaven v Pender*,[158] stated:

> [I]t would seem to me to be contrary to natural justice to say that parliament intended to impose upon a public body a liability for a thing which no reasonable care or skill could obviate. The duty may notwithstanding be absolute: but if so, it ought to be imposed in the clearest possible terms … where the language used [in the legislation] is consistent with either view [strict liability or fault-based liability] it should not be construed as to inflict a liability unless the party sought to be charged has been wanting in the exercise of due and reasonable care in the performance of the duty imposed.[159]

Subsequent decisions would have to grapple with interpretations of statute, to determine whether or not Parliament intended to alter common law rights. At some points, the cases are contradictory. In some cases, a narrow view of the possible statutory defence is taken. It is said in these cases that it is necessary for the defendant who wishes to take advantage of a statutory defence to what would otherwise be an actionable nuisance to demonstrate that the only way in which the activity could be conducted involved the commission of a nuisance.[160] In such cases, the courts generally say that strict liability (whether on the basis of *Rylands* or nuisance) does not apply, and the organisation can only be liable, if at all, in negligence. According to some, this is only when the activity is mandatory. If it is merely discretionary, the ordinary common law rules would still apply.[161] Sometimes, the immunity might be removed by holding that although the activity was authorised, it took place in an unauthorised way, whether by way of location, for example, or how the activity was conducted.[162]

Other judgments seem to suggest that it is sufficient, in order for the defence to apply, that the activity is authorised by the statute.[163] The court simply considers whether the legislature has authorised the doing of a particular thing. If it has, the court will determine that strict liability cannot apply. The reasoning that it applied here is that where Parliament has authorised a particular activity to occur, a person affected by it cannot be heard to complain of a legal wrong.[164]

[158] *Heaven v Pender* (1883) 11 QBD 503, 509.

[159] *Hammond v The Vestry of St Pancras* (1874) LR 9 CP 316, 322. Denman J reached the same conclusion.

[160] *Metropolitan Asylum District v Hill* (1881) 6 HL 193, 213 (Lord Watson); *Ogston v Aberdeen District Tramways* [1897] AC 111, 118–19 (Lord Watson); *Manchester Corporation v Farnworth* [1930] AC 171, 183 (Viscount Dunedin) (meaning what is practically, not theoretically, possible), 200–01 (Viscount Sumner).

[161] *Metropolitan Asylum District v Hill* (1881) 6 HL 193, 213 (Lord Watson).

[162] *Porter and Co v Bell* [1955] 1 DLR 62, 72 (MacDonald J); *West v Bristol Tramways* [1908] 2 KB 14; *Sadlier v Staffordshire Tramway* (1889) 23 QBD 17, 21 (Lord Esher).

[163] *Mersey Docks Trustees v Gibbs* (1866) LR 1 HL 93, 112 (Lord Blackburn, for the Court); *Dunn v Birmingham Canal Navigation* (1872) LR 8 QB 42, 52 (Pigott J); *Geddis v Proprietors of the Bann Reservoir* (1878) 3 App Cas. 430, 438 (HL) ('authorised or directed' (Lord Hatherley), 455–56 ('authorised') (Lord Blackburn).

[164] *Mersey Docks Trustees v Gibbs* (1866) LR 1 HL 93, 112 (Lord Blackburn, for the Court); *Canadian Pacific Railway Coy v Roy* [1902] AC 220, 231 (Lord Chancellor, for the Privy Council): 'the legislature is supreme, and if it has enacted that a thing is lawful, such a thing cannot be a fault or an actionable wrong'.

Sometimes, it is apparently enough that the legislature was aware that a 'possible or probable' effect of the activity legislated that a nuisance would be caused.[165] At times, the requirement that a particular activity be shown to inevitably, or by necessity, cause a nuisance appears to be overlooked entirely, as if it is superfluous.[166]

In some cases, the principle is expressed that the law should as far as possible apply the same principles to statutory authorities as it would apply to other defendants.[167] This would obviously suggest a narrow defence based on statutory authority. However, in other cases the courts appear to be very willing to interpret legislation so as to count out the common law of strict liability. For example the Privy Council readily interpreted from a simple provision stating that a company such as the defendant would compensate anyone injured as a result of the activities authorised by statute to mean that strict liability would not apply, the company being liable only for proven cases of negligence.[168] The legislation was completely silent on the question of whether the statutory authority holder should be held liable according to principles of strict liability or only on the basis of proven fault.

Reflecting on these precedents, Linden points out that typically such legislation did not specify an intention to immunise organisations from ordinary principles of common law liability, including strict liability.[169] He suggests that the courts in these cases had an (unspoken policy) agenda:

> The most important policy reason for the creation of the immunity was the desire to promote industrial expansion and to refrain from saddling infant industries with legal responsibility for their non-negligent conduct. Legislative authority was generally used in cases involving semi-public activities such as railways, roadbuilding, canals and hospitals. These types of enterprises were even more vital to the economy than were other industries and thus deserving of additional protection from civil liability.[170]

The effect of the courts' subsequent attempts to reconcile the *Vaughan* line with the *Rylands* line is to place great strain on interpretation of the words in the relevant statute. It is not immediately obvious to me that the words in some of these statutes,

[165] *Dunn v Birmingham Canal Navigation* (1872) LR 8 QB 42, 51 (Baron Bramwell).

[166] *Canadian Pacific Railway Co v Roy* [1902] AC 220, 231 (Lord Chancellor, for the Privy Council).

[167] *Mersey Docks Trustees v Gibbs* (1866) LR 1 HL 93, 110 (Lord Blackburn, for the Court).

[168] *Northwestern Utilities Ltd v London Guarantee and Accident Co Ltd* [1936] AC 108, where Lord Wright (for the Privy Council) stated (120) it was a 'question of construction, depending on the language of the statute' as to whether fault-based or strict liability should apply. With respect, in that case, the statute was silent as to that issue.

[169] Allen Linden, 'Strict Liability, Nuisance and Legislative Authorization' (1966) 4 *Osgoode Hall Law Journal* 196, 201: 'there is seldom evident any legislative intention to immunize from liability the authorized activity and it is questionable whether the policy of the legislature is advanced by protecting authorized activities from ordinary tort liability'. He laments that the courts 'continue to speculate about the mythical and non-existent legislative intention in their quest for a solution to these problems' (202).

[170] ibid, 199. He cites other policy rationales, including the fact that many of the municipalities given these infrastructure building responsibilities were short of funds, such that (strict) legal liability could bankrupt them, as well as utilitarian principles (200). He also refers to the 'considerable judicial antipathy towards strict liability' (199).

often quite vague on the liability question, can bear such a strain. But this ended up becoming yet another 'way out' of the strict liability principle,[171] at a time when fault-based liability was gaining the ascendancy in the nineteenth-century law of tort. Linden concludes that 'there was and is considerable judicial antipathy toward strict liability. The defence of legislative authority was one weapon that could be used in a counter-attack on this doctrine'.[172]

In terms of reconciling *Rylands* with these developments in statute-authorised activity, Carroll claims a cause and effect relationship: 'it is more likely that the absence of legislative intervention to safeguard people's rights from development in industry was responsible for this radical restatement of the law'.[173]

Conclusion

This chapter has documented the gradual shift in the law of tort from principles of strict liability to fault-based principles. The original attachment to strict liability is understandable in light of the law's concern with the blood feud, and an effort to persuade individuals to resort to the legal system instead to resolve their conflicts. In this light, a plaintiff-friendly system of strict liability was appealing. However, perhaps at first within juries, and later in the case law itself, courts in non-criminal cases began to take account of the moral blameworthiness, or fault, if any, of the defendant, just as the criminal law had done. This trend was encouraged by changes to the forms of action, in particular the growth of the action on the case. It was also encouraged by statutory reforms, often taken to reflect an intention by Parliament that principles of strict liability ought not to apply. In Chapter 2 specific torts will briefly be considered in relation to these trends.

[171] The Pennsylvania Supreme Court noted of *Rylands v Fletcher* that 'the later decisions in the English courts seem to encourage rather than discourage exceptions to it': *Pennsylvania Coal Company v Sanderson* 113 Pa. 126, 150 (1886).

[172] Allen Linden, 'Strict Liability, Nuisance and Legislative Authorisation' (1966) 4 *Osgoode Hall Law Journal* 196, 199.

[173] Declan Carroll, 'The Rule in *Rylands v Fletcher*: A Re-assessment' (1973) 8 *Irish Jurist* 208, 210.

2

Strict Liability and Particular Torts in Legal History

In this chapter the application of strict liability principles in particular factual scenarios within the law of tort will be considered, as well as the rapid development of the negligence action in the late nineteenth century and early twentieth. Some reasons for this growth will be considered. Examples will also be noted of occasions where strict liability was ameliorated by statutory reform, reflecting dissatisfaction with the rigidity and unfairness of strict liability principle.

Strict Liability and Damage to Property Interests

Nuisance

Concerns about the blood feud were not confined to personal injury. They extended to damage to property interests. Loengard observes:

> No strong king could tolerate the spasmodic upheaval and unjust results of private quarrels and Henry II, when he came to the throne in 1154, intended to be a strong king. Thus the same considerations which gave the impetus to expanded royal protection of peaceable possession of real property – culminating in the Assize of Novel Dissseisin – no doubt lay behind the extension of royal jurisdiction to offending acts which later generations characterised as nuisances; the need for securing weaker subjects in the enjoyment of their property and the need for keeping the peace.[1]

The term 'nuisance' is derived from the Latin word for harm, *nocumentum*. Early nuisance cases also evidence concern for the loss or injury suffered by the plaintiff, as opposed to the culpability or otherwise of the defendant. One example appears in *Tenant v Goldwin*, where Holt CJ states:

> Every man must so use his own, as not to do damage to another. And as every man is bound so to look to his cattle, as to keep them out of his neighbour's ground, that so he may receive no damage; so he must keep in the filth of his house of office, that it may

[1] Janet Loengard, 'The Assize of Nuisance: Origins of an Action at Common Law' (1978) 37(1) *Cambridge Law Journal* 144, 145.

> not flow in upon and damnify his neighbour … a man shall not leave his dung so high as to damage his neighbour, and the reason of these cases is, because every man must so use his own as not to damnify another.[2]

This case involved adjoining landowners. The plaintiff's property was inundated by muck which flowed from the defendant's premises through a faulty wall. There was no suggestion that the defendant was aware, or should have been aware, of the condition of the wall, or that it required attention. The defendant was held liable to the plaintiff.[3]

Yet the concept of reasonableness started to seep into the law of nuisance. The case of *Hole v Barlow* involved a defendant who burned bricks on his own property, near the boundary with that of the plaintiff.[4] Rather than a strict rule, which would have made the defendant liable for their interference with the plaintiff's property rights, concepts of reasonableness appear. Willes J states that individuals had a right to quiet enjoyment of their property. However, this was subject to the use by others of their land, provided it was 'conducted in a reasonable and proper manner, and in a reasonable and proper place'.[5] The significant use of the notion of reasonableness in this nuisance case has been observed elsewhere.[6]

A few years after *Hole v Barlow*, confusion as to whether liability in nuisance is strict or is subject to reasonableness-type principles appears in the decision in *Tarry v Ashton*.[7] The plaintiff was injured while walking along a public thoroughfare. A lamp attached to the defendant's premises fell on her, causing her injuries. The defendant was aware of the deteriorating condition of the lamp and had taken steps towards getting it repaired at the time of the accident. The jury found the defendant was not guilty of negligence. The remaining question was his liability for public nuisance. All judges found in favour of the plaintiff in this regard. Of most interest for current purposes are the clearly divergent views in relation to the scope of an action for nuisance.

Some judgments clearly favour a strict liability view of nuisance liability. So Lush J referred to a duty upon the defendant to keep their premises in such a state so as not to be dangerous. He said that the defendant had 'put the public safety in peril' with his actions in mounting the lamp in that position.[8] Quain J similarly

[2] *Tenant v Goldwin* (1702) 2 Ld. Raym. 1090; 21 ER 222.

[3] Francis Bohlen, 'Rule in Rylands v Fletcher' (1911) 59 *University of Pennsylvania Law Review* 298, 301 discussing *Tenant v Goldwin*: 'the point of view is still wholly objective, purely external to the defendant, his conduct is judged solely by its result, not by his subjective attitude, his deliberate disregard of his neighbour's safety, nor even by his omission to diligently take those steps necessary to secure it'.

[4] *Hole v Barlow* (1858) 4 C.B (N.S) 334; 140 ER 1113.

[5] ibid, 345; 1118.

[6] FH Newark, 'The Boundaries of Nuisance' (1949) 65 *Law Quarterly Review* 480, 487, notes that 'there was a tendency for cross-infection to take place, and notions of negligence began to make an appearance in the realm of nuisance proper. We note an endeavour to introduce the element of reasonableness in *Hole v Barlow*'.

[7] *Tarry v Ashton* (1876) 1 QBD 314.

[8] ibid, 320.

referred to an obligation on someone such as the defendant to ensure the lamp was kept in such a state so as not to injure the public.[9] These judgments tend to suggest that the liability of a person in the position of the defendant is strict in nature.

On the other hand, the position of Blackburn J differed substantially. His comments seem to reflect his view of an underlying requirement of fault in such circumstances:

> If there were a latent defect in the premises, or something done to them without the knowledge of the owner or occupier by a wrongdoer, such as digging out the coals underneath and so leaving a house near the highway in a dangerous condition, I doubt … whether or not the occupier would be liable. But if he did know of the defect, and neglects to put the premises in order, he would be liable. He would be responsible to this extent, that as soon as he knew of the danger he would be bound to put the premises in repair or pull them down.[10]

The Court of Appeal seemed to lean towards a strict liability view of nuisance in *Rapier v London Tramways Co*,[11] stating that 'at common law, if I am sued for a nuisance, and the nuisance is proved, it is no defence on my part to say, and to prove, that I have taken all reasonable care to prevent it'.[12]

Subsequent decisions appeared to vindicate the position taken by Blackburn J. Evidence of this is to be found in *Sedleigh-Denfield v O'Callaghan*[13] in the judgments of Lords Atkin,[14] Wright[15] and Porter,[16] and in *Caminer and Another v Northern and London Investment Trust*,[17] in the judgments of Lords Porter,[18] Oaksey[19] and Reid.[20] However, more recent times seem to suggest that, once again,

[9] ibid, 320.

[10] ibid, 319; this point is also made by FH, Newark, 'The Boundaries of Nuisance' (1949) 65 *Law Quarterly Review* 480, 486–87.

[11] *Rapier v London Tramways Co* (1893) 2 Ch 588.

[12] ibid, 599–600 (Lindley LJ, with whom Bowen and Kay LLJ agreed); see also *Ware v Garston Haulage Co Ltd* [1944] 1 KB 30, 31 (Scott J, with whom Mackinnon and Goddard LLJ agreed) (CA).

[13] *Sedleigh-Denfield v O'Callaghan* [1940] AC 880.

[14] 'The occupier or owner is not an insurer; there must be something more than the mere harm done to the neighbour's property to make the party responsible … some degree of personal responsibility is required', ibid, 897.

[15] 'An occupier is not prima facie responsible for a nuisance created without his knowledge and consent. If he is to be liable, a further condition is necessary, namely, that he had knowledge or means of knowledge, that he knew or should have known of the nuisance in time to correct it and obviate its mischievous effect. The liability for a nuisance is not, at least in modern law, a strict or absolute liability', ibid, 920.

[16] Lord Porter noted that the defendants 'ought to have had knowledge of the danger, and could have prevented the danger if they had acted reasonably'.

[17] *Caminer and Another v Northern and London Investment Trust* [1951] AC 88.

[18] He noted the defendants 'were free from blame whether the case against them is framed in negligence or nuisance', ibid, 99.

[19] ibid, 104.

[20] ibid, 105. See also *British Road Services v Slater* [1964] 1 WLR 498, where Lord Parker CJ stated that 'the present tendency of the law is not only to move further and further away from absolute liability but more and more to assimilate nuisance and negligence', and *Maitland v Raisbeck and R T and J Hewitt Limited* [1944] 1 KB 689, 691–92. In fairness, there is also evidence during this time of a strict liability view of nuisance: *Read v J Lyons and Co Ltd* [1947] AC 156, 183 (Lord Simonds): 'if a man commits a legal nuisance it is not answer to his injured neighbour that he took the utmost care not to commit it … there the liability is strict'.

a strict liability view of nuisance is being taken.[21] These developments will be considered in more detail in Chapter 7.

Rylands v Fletcher

The famous case of *Rylands v Fletcher* involved the escape of water from a reservoir which contractors had built on the defendant's land.[22] The water escaped from the defendant's property and flooded the neighbouring property and mine owned by the plaintiff. The evidence suggested that there was no negligence in how the mine was constructed. The soil on the defendant's property apparently contained latent defects of which the defendant was unaware. The plaintiff brought legal action against the defendant. Interestingly, all three of the heads of claim nominated by the plaintiff allege negligence on the part of the defendant.

All members of the Court of Appeal found for the plaintiff. However, in contrast to the content of the statement of claim, the judgment was not based on principles of negligence. The court specifically found that the defendants were 'free from all blame'. Notwithstanding this finding, the Court of Appeal found the defendants were liable. It could not do so in negligence, but found an alternative path on the basis of strict liability. It referred to other examples of strict liability in seeking to justify its position:

> We think that the true rule of law is, that, the person who for his own purposes brings on his lands and collect and keeps there anything likely to do mischief if it escapes, must keep it at his peril, and if he does not do so, is prima facie answerable for all the damage which is the natural consequence of its escape. He can excuse himself by shewing that the escape was owing to the plaintiff's default, or perhaps that the escape was the consequence of vis major, or the Act of God … the general rule seems, on principle, just. The person whose grass or corn is eaten down by the escaping cattle of his neighbour, or whose mine is flooded by the water from his neighbour's reservoir, or whose cellar is invaded by the filth of his neighbour's privy, or whose habitation is made unhealthy by the fumes and noisome vapours of his neighbour's alkali works, is damnified without any fault of his own, and it seems but reasonable and just that the neighbour, who has brought something on his own property which was not naturally there, harmless to others so long as it is confined to his own property, but which he knows to be mischievous if it gets on his neighbour's, should be obliged to make good the damage which ensues if he does not succeed in confining it to his own property … the case that has most commonly occurred, and which is most frequently to be found in the books, is as to the obligation of the owner of cattle which he has brought on his land, to prevent

[21] *Cambridge Water Co v Eastern Counties* [1994] 2 AC 264, 299: 'liability for nuisance has generally been regarded as strict' (Lord Goff, for the Court); *Hunter v Canary Wharf Ltd* [1997] AC 655, 724: 'the tort of nuisance is a tort of strict liability in the sense that it is no defence to say that the defendant took all reasonable care to prevent it' (Lord Hope); FH Newark, 'The Boundaries of Nuisance' (1949) 65 *Law Quarterly Review* 480, 486–87.

[22] *Fletcher v Rylands* (1865) LR 1 Ex. 265 (Court of Appeal).

> their escaping and doing mischief. The law as to them seems to be perfectly settled from early times; the owner must keep them *at his peril*, or he will be answerable for the natural consequences of their escape (emphasis added).[23]

Two judges in the House of Lords dismissed an appeal from the decision of the Court of Appeal.[24] Of the two, Lord Cranworth's judgment reflects a classic strict liability position:

> In considering whether a defendant is liable to a plaintiff for damage which the plaintiff may have sustained, the question in general is not whether the defendant has acted with due care and caution, but whether his acts have occasioned the damage … and the doctrine is founded on good sense. For when one person, in managing his own affairs, however innocently, damages to another, it is obviously only just that he should be the party to suffer.[25]

The precedent was applied for a time, for instance, to make railway companies liable for damage caused by sparks emitting from their locomotives, in the absence of any proof of negligence.[26] However, it was found that in cases of specific statutory authority to conduct that transport, the defendant would only be liable if negligence were proven.[27]

Of course, subsequent courts would have great difficulty interpreting and applying concepts such as 'not naturally there', 'likely to do mischief' and 'escape'. United Kingdom courts would at first sideline the decision, creating exceptions to its general rules, and denying that it stood for a universal broad proposition,[28] before eventually re-interpreting it as a subset of the tort of private nuisance.[29] It has refused to overrule it, however.[30] In contrast, it would be swept into the law of negligence in Australia.[31] These principles will be considered in more detail in Chapters 3 and 4.

Common Carriers

A common carrier carries goods or personal property as part of a business and for reward. An early decision involved an action by the owner against a common carrier for theft of the goods while in transit. The court found in favour of the plaintiff.

[23] ibid, 279–80 (Blackburn J, for Willes, Keating, Mellor, Montague Smith and Lush JJ).
[24] *Rylands v Fletcher* (1868) LR 3 AC 330.
[25] ibid, 341.
[26] *Jones v Festiniog Railway Co* (1868) LR 3 QB 733.
[27] *Vaughan v Taff Vale Railway Co* (1860) 5 H & N 679; 157 ER 1351.
[28] *Read v J Lyons and Co Ltd* [1947] AC 156, 165–66 (Viscount Simon), 172 (Lord Macmillan) and 182 (Lord Uthwatt).
[29] *Cambridge Water Co Ltd v Eastern Counties Leather Co* [1994] 2 AC 264.
[30] *Transco Plc v Stockport Metropolitan Borough Council* [2004] 2 AC 1.
[31] *Burnie Port Authority v General Jones Pty Ltd* (1994) 179 CLR 520.

However, the case records that the theft took place due to the negligent custodianship of the common carrier.[32]

In 1672 the strict liability of a common carrier appears to be established.[33] In a very short summary of the case and decision (one paragraph), it appears the plaintiff brought suit against the defendant. They had entrusted the defendant with possession of their goods, delivering them to the defendant's ship. Apparently, thieves stole the goods. The question was the liability of the defendants. There is no suggestion of any negligence on their part in the storage or handling of the goods, or that they were a party to the theft. The record states that the matter was resolved in the plaintiff's favour.

Holt CJ confirms this position in *Coggs v Bernard*,[34] stating that a common carrier, if they are to receive a reward for their work, are strictly liable for the goods carried, except in cases of Act of God or the actions of enemies of the king. Holt CJ grounds this rule in public policy:

> This is a political establishment, contrived by the policy of the law, for the safety of all persons, the necessity of whose affairs oblige them to trust these sorts of persons, that they may be safe in their ways of dealing; for else these carriers might have an opportunity for undoing all persons that had any dealings with them, by combining with thieves, and yet doing it in such a clandestine manner, as would not be possible to be discovered.[35]

The strict liability of a common carrier for loss caused to the goods carried was specifically noted by two judges in *Gibbon v Paynton*.[36] It was also noted in *Dale v Hall*, where the court noted the strict liability of 'a carrier or hoyman'.[37]

A similar conclusion is reached in *Forward v Pittard*.[38] There the defendant agreed to transport the goods of the plaintiff between two towns. While in transit, the goods were stored temporarily in a barn. A fire started near the barn, through no fault of the defendant, and the plaintiff's goods were destroyed. The question was whether the carrier was liable for the loss.

[32] *Rich v Kneeland* (1613) Cro. Jac. 330; 79 ER 282.

[33] *Mors v Slue* (1672) 1 Vent. 190, 238.

[34] *Coggs v Bernard* (1703) 2 Ld. Raym. 909.

[35] 918. See also Ezra Ripley Thayer, 'Liability Without Fault' (1916) 29 *Harvard Law Review* 801, 806: 'this stringent liability of the carrier is not due to his public calling, but to the nature of the agencies he uses, the helplessness of the passengers, and the peril to life and limb'; see Robert Kaczorowski, 'The Common Law Background of Nineteenth-Century Tort Law' (1990) 51 *Ohio State Law Journal* 1127, 1129–69.

[36] *Gibbon v Paynton* (1769) 4 Burr. 2298, 2301 (Lord Mansfield) and 2302 (Yates J); 98 ER 199, 200 and 201.

[37] *Dale v Hall* (1750) 1 Wils. 281; 95 ER 619 (KB) per Lee CJ: 'every thing is a negligence in a carrier or hoyman that the law does not excuse, and he is answerable for goods the instant he receives them into his custody, and in all events, except they happen to be damaged by the act of God, or the King's enemies and a promise to carry safely, is a promise to keep safely'. The use of the word 'negligence' in this passage is an example of the use of the word in a different sense from that applicable today. Clearly Lee CJ was not referring to negligence in terms of the legal tort we know today, which was clearly not part of the legal landscape until later.

[38] *Forward v Pittard* (1785) 1 T.R. 28; 99 ER 953.

All members of the court found that it was. Mansfield CJ for the Court stated that the common carrier had an obligation under contract (assumpsit) to provide reasonable care and skill. However, their liability went further:

> There is a further degree of responsibility by the custom of the realm, that is, by the common law; a carrier is in the nature of an insurer. It is laid down that he is liable for every accident except by the Act of God[39] or the king's enemies ... if an armed force come to rob the carrier of the goods, he is liable ... the true reason is, for fear it may give room for collusion, that the master may contrive to be robbed on purpose, and share the spoil.[40]

It has been suggested that the reason for the imposition of strict liability in cases of common carriers was the trust and confidence which individuals using the service necessarily reposed in such carriers.[41] Lord Mansfield said it was sourced in fear that concepts of negligence would not sufficiently protect customers from possible collusion between carriers and thieves.[42] Elsewhere, Lord Ashurst claimed it would lead to carriers being more careful with the products they carried.[43]

The strictness of the liability in relation to common carriers did not apply to cases of passengers, only in respect to goods.[44] This has been explained on the basis that individuals, unlike inanimate objects, could and were expected to take their own precautions to avoid injury.[45] In relation to passengers, common carriers were liable in cases of negligence (only) in an action for assumpsit.

It is interesting to note how the requirement of Act of God, the exception to the strict liability otherwise attaching to common carriers, was interpreted. This was considered in a case concerning the loss of a horse.[46] The plaintiff had agreed that the defendant would carry his horse via boat. Due to rough seas, and the horse's anxiety, the horse perished during the journey. The plaintiff sought to make the defendant liable for the loss. The defendant argued that the facts involved an Act of God, and thus they were absolved of responsibility.

There appears to be an initial attempt in this case to confine its meaning very strictly, to mean only situations of a sudden and irresistible act of nature as could

[39] Lord Mansfield said that an Act of God was something that could not happen by the intervention of man, including storms and tempests ibid, 33, 957.

[40] ibid, 33–34.

[41] Oliver Wendell Holmes, *The Common Law* (Little, Brown & Co, 1881) 9.

[42] *Forward v Pittard* (1785) 1 T.R. 28, 33; 99 ER 953, 956. This suggestion finds support in the rationale for the ancient Roman laws on the liability of innkeepers and common carriers: David Bogen, 'Ignoring History: The Liability of Ships' Masters, Innkeepers and Stablekeepers Under Roman Law' (1992) 36 *American Journal of Legal History* 326, 351.

[43] *Proprietors of Trent Navigation v Ward* (1785) 3 Esp. 127, 132; 170 ER 562, 563–64 (KB): 'it will naturally lead to make carriers more careful in general. If this sort of negligence were to excuse the carrier, when he finds that an accident has happened to goods from the misconduct of a third person, he would give himself no further trouble about the recovery of them'.

[44] *Aston v Heaven* (1797) 2 Esp. 533; Ezra Ripley Thayer, 'Liability Without Fault' (1916) 29 *Harvard Law Review* 801, 813.

[45] Robert Kaczorowski, 'The Common Law Background of Nineteenth-Century Tort Law' (1990) 51 *Ohio State Law Journal* 1127, 1157.

[46] *Nugent v Smith* (1875) 1 CPD 19; (1876) 1 CPD 423.

not have been foreseen, or if foreseen, not by any degree of human care and skill have been resisted.[47] However, this was overturned on appeal. The Court of Appeal adopted a liberalised test very similar to ordinary negligence principles. An Act of God could exist where there was a perilous act of nature, as occurred on the facts, where the defendant could not have avoided the accident through the use of reasonable care and skill.[48] In this circumstance, the defendant would not be liable. Thus, we see in this case an attempt to circumvent the otherwise strictness of the liability of a common carrier, by recognising an exception relating to due care and skill, at least to the limited extent of cases involving Acts of God.

Other examples exist of the courts limiting the scope of the strict liability position of common carriers. In *Nugent v Smith*,[49] Cockburn CJ rejects the mooted extension of that situation to all carriers. Further, it was accepted that where the thing being transported by a common carrier was lost or damaged during the journey for reasons inherent to its nature, the defendant should not be held liable for it, in the absence of any negligence on their part.[50]

Common carriers also took steps to attempt to limit their liability through contractual provision. They commonly included a clause in their contracts of carriage stating that they would only be liable for loss or damage to the goods carried if the owner of the goods paid in full for the carriage prior to its occurring, and had fully insured the goods. They needed to bring this clause to the attention of the public through public notice. The courts permitted such clauses to be enforced, ameliorating the strict liability to which common carriers might otherwise be subject.[51] It held that, where either or both conditions were not met, common carriers would not be strictly liable for the loss or damage of the goods to be carried, except where the owner could show that the carrier had been guilty of negligence.[52] Here is another example of the intrusion of fault-based principles into the supposed domain of strict liability.

Subsequently the Carriers Act 1830 (UK) would reform the common law, limiting the customers' ability to claim to situations where they had declared the value of the goods to be transported to the carrier, and permitting the carrier to charge an increased fee on the basis they would act as an effective insurer of the goods to be transported. Note also that common carriers could also be liable for what we would today regard as negligence in the action of assumpsit, discussed below, as one of those businesses pursuing a common calling.

[47] *Nugent v Smith* (1875) 1 CPD 19, 34 (Brett and Denman JJ).

[48] *Nugent v Smith* (1876) 1 CPD 423, 437 (Cockburn CJ), 439 (Mellish LJ), 443 (Cleasby B), 444 (Mellish and James LLJ).

[49] Cockburn CJ also rejected the attempt by the lower court to apply the strict liability position of common carriers to all carriers, ibid, 434.

[50] *Blower v Great Western Railway Co* (1872) 7 CP 655, 664–65 (Willes J), to like effect Keating J (665).

[51] *Wyld v Pickford* (1841) 8 M & W 443.

[52] ibid, 461 (Baron Parke, for the Court).

Innkeepers

The first evidence of the strictness of an innkeeper's liability in English law appears in the 1360s,[53] reflecting the Roman position. The strict nature of an innkeeper's liability for loss or damage to the goods of a tenant was established in 1604 in *Calye's Case*.[54] It was subsequently applied in cases such as *Bennett v Mellor*.[55] There the plaintiff arrived at the defendant's inn, intending to stay there. While seated in the bar area as a guest of the inn, the plaintiff placed some of his items on the floor. When he determined to leave the bar area, he noticed that his items had been taken. He brought action against the innkeeper. All judges found in his favour. One specifically noted the strict nature of the liability of the innkeeper in such cases.[56]

The courts would subsequently create exceptions to this strict liability position, for instance in cases involving Acts of God or actions of the monarch's enemies, or where the plaintiff had been negligent.[57] Legislation would eventually severely curtail the scope of the innkeeper's strict liability for loss suffered by guests. As with common carriers, the strict liability that the common law applied to innkeepers was explained by the high trust and confidence which users of the service necessarily reposed in the service provider.[58]

Fire

Bracton apparently recognises strict civil liability in the case of fire.[59] The common law recognised from the late fourteenth century[60] and early fifteenth the liability of a defendant for damage caused by fire commencing on their property and then engulfing that of another.[61] Although the words 'negligence' and 'neglect'

[53] *Navenby v Lascelles* (1368) B & M 552, 554 (Knyvet CJ); (1368) YB 42, Edw III, No 13.

[54] *Calye's Case* (1604) 8 Co. Rep. 321; 77 ER 520.

[55] *Bennett v Mellor* (1793) TR 273; 101 ER 154.

[56] ibid, 276; 155: 'all the authorities agree that it is not necessary to prove negligence in the innkeeper' (Buller J).

[57] *Morgan v Ravey* (1861) 6 H & N 265, 278; 158 ER 109, 114.

[58] Oliver Wendell Holmes, *The Common Law* (Little, Brown & Co, 1881) 9; Percy Winfield, 'The History of Negligence in the Law of Torts' (1926) 42 *Law Quarterly Review* 184, 186.

[59] Percy Winfield, 'The Myth of Absolute Liability' (1926) 42 *Law Quarterly Review* 37, 47 (he cites Fol. 146 b of Bracton's work, presumably *De Legibus et Consuetudinibus Angliae*).

[60] *Cok v Durant* (1377) CPMR 1364–81; *Berden v Burton* (1382) YB Trin. 6 Ric. II, p. 22, pl. 9 (Belknap CJ).

[61] *Beaulieu v Finglam* (1401) B & M 557; though note that the court suggested some exceptions where a defendant might not be liable for fire, for instance where the King's enemies had caused the fire, or it had been started by sudden tempest or by a stranger (Choke CJ). Note the serjeant in the case had argued that it was 'hard' to hold the defendant responsible for the fire when there was no fault on his part. The Court rejected this argument, stating 'what is that to us. It is the better that (the defendant) be totally ruined than that the law be changed for him'. This indicates strictness of liability for fire.

appear in some of these early judgments, it is a mistake to equate those words with our current understanding of the concept of negligence.[62] Liability for fire was apparently strict in nature.[63] Exceptionally, it could include omissions to act or non-feasance, as opposed to misfeasance. Generally, the common law had not recognised non-feasance as a wrong.[64] Though liability was strict, some exceptions began to appear.[65] One example occurs in a 1582 decision, where a defendant is held liable for shooting at a fowl, causing fire in his own premises and that of his neighbour. The court concludes there is no negligence on the defendant's part, yet he is liable 'for the injury is the same, though this mischance was not by common negligence but by misadventure'.[66] Further evidence of this appears in the decision in *Turberville v Stampe*.[67]

Unfortunately it is tied in to some extent with vicarious liability concepts, yet the strictness of the liability is evident. There Holt CJ opines that 'if the defendant's servant kindled the fire in the way of husbandry and proper for his employment … his master shall be liable to an action for damage done to another by the fire'.[68] It is confirmed by Lord Denman CJ (for the Court) in *Filliter v Phippard*,[69] where he explains that 'the ancient law, or rather custom of England, appears to have been that a person in whose house a fire originated, which afterwards spread to his neighbour's property and destroyed it, must make good the loss'.[70] That case dealt with legislation that had amended the original common law, by providing that where such an 'accidental' event occurred, the owner of the property from whence the fire had emanated would not be liable.[71] The court in *Filliter* interpreted this legislation so as not to apply to cases where a defendant had deliberately lit a fire which, owing to negligence attributable to them, damaged the

[62] *Hargrave v Goldman* (1963) 110 CLR 40, 57 where Windeyer J, speaking of the use of the word 'negligently' in *Beaulieu v Finglam*, commented that 'whatever it meant, the word did not import the modern idea of tortious negligence'; *Burnie Port Authority v General Jones Pty Ltd* (1994) 179 CLR 520, 529, where the joint reasons (Mason CJ, Deane, Dawson, Toohey, and Gaudron JJ) noted the word 'negligenter' in these actions was a 'pleader's adverb which originally did no more than reflect the perception that it was the strict duty of the occupier of premises to prevent the spread of "his fire" from those premises'.

[63] John Wigmore, 'Responsibility for Tortious Acts: Its History III' (1894) 7 *Harvard Law Review* 441, 448–49 (citing *Beaulieu v Finglam* and *Turberville v Stamp* (1698) 1 Salk. 13); A Ogus, 'Vagaries in Liability for the Escape of Fire' (1969) 27(1) *Cambridge Law Journal* 104, 105–06.

[64] Percy Winfield, 'The History of Negligence in the Law of Torts' (1926) 42 *Law Quarterly Review* 184, 192.

[65] An Act of God may have provided a defence, with the court in *Turberville* observing that it would be 'relevant' in assessing liability that a storm or tempest had arisen to carry the fire from the defendant's premises to that of the plaintiff.

[66] *Anon*, Cro. Elizabeth, 10 (1582).

[67] *Turberville v Stampe* (1697) 1 Ld. Raym. 264, though as in *Beaulieu*, a possible exception for cases of fire caused by a sudden storm is suggested.

[68] ibid, 265.

[69] *Filliter v Phippard* (1847) 11 QBD 347.

[70] ibid, 354.

[71] This was originally in 6 Ann. C 31, re-enacted in stat. 12 G. 3, c.73 and stat. 14 G.3, c.78(a); this position is still reflected in the Fire Prevention (Metropolis) Act 1774 (UK), s86.

plaintiff. In effect, the court interpreted the legislation so as to confine the defendant's liability in such a situation to cases where the loss to the plaintiff caused by the fire was a result of the defendant's negligence.

Subsequently, consideration of negligence appeared to infiltrate the common law principles. Evidence of this appears in *Vaughan v Menlove*.[72] There the defendant had left a stack of hay on his property. He had been warned that the stack might ignite and cause damage to others, but he did not act to reduce the risk. The stack ignited and caused damage to a neighbouring property of the defendant. The interesting aspect for present purposes was not the finding in favour of the plaintiff, but the reasoning. The court did not apply the strict liability principles regarding fire apparently established in the cases above. Rather, it spoke in negligence-like terms, in terms of what a prudent person in the position of the defendant would have done to ameliorate the risk of which they were aware.[73]

Firearms

The courts would sometimes deal with cases against the owners of firearms for injury caused to others through their use. One such case is *Dixon v Bell*.[74] The owner requested one of his servants to fetch his gun. He specifically instructed that the gun should be rendered harmless prior to its delivery. The gun was duly delivered but for some reason had not been rendered harmless. The servant aimed the gun at a child and fired it. She did not intend or expect that this would be dangerous but the child was seriously injured. The court found the owner of the gun was liable, although he had taken reasonable precautions. It specifically determined the owner had not been negligent.

Animals

Some principles of the liability for animals exhibit features of strict liability. For example, the owner of certain species of animal will be strictly liable for the damage caused when the animal strays onto the property of another. Negligence is not relevant to such cases.[75] This doctrine is typically known as 'cattle trespass' but extends to a wide range of animals. It contains traces of the ancient deodand action described above.

Secondly, the law distinguishes between animals not known to be dangerous, on the one hand, and animals that are wild or animals that are known to have vicious propensities, on the other. If I am responsible for an animal in the latter

[72] *Vaughan v Menlove* (1837) 3 Bing. (NC) 468; 132 ER 490.

[73] ibid, 475; 493 (Tindal CJ); 477, 494 (Park J and Vaughan J); Gaselee J concurring in the judgment.

[74] *Dixon v Bell* (1816) 5 M & S 198.

[75] *Cox v Burbidge* (1863) 13 CB (NS) 430, 438; 143 ER 171, 174 (Williams J).

of the two categories, I am liable for injuries it causes another. Again, here proof of negligence is not relevant. Rather, it is the knowledge of the vicious propensity that attracts the liability.[76] In this respect, it has been observed that liability here 'straddles' both strict liability and negligence.[77] In contrast, if I am responsible for an animal in the former category, I am only liable for injuries it causes another where I have been negligent.[78] This position is largely reflected in the Animals Act 1971 (UK).

Unifying Factors, if Any, in Cases of Continued Strict Liability

It is natural, but ultimately frustrating, to seek to identify those factors which unify the areas in which the courts continued to insist upon strict liability, well after fault had become deeply established. In the case of the original examples of fire and animals, the risk of injury caused by these was a very real prospect in medieval times. In the case of common carriers and innkeepers, the rationale was said to be based on the trust and dependence that the plaintiff necessarily placed in defendants, and perhaps experience that this trust had sometimes been abused. In the case of *Rylands*, it seemed to be a notion of awareness of danger, and this might also explain the strict liability for animals known to be dangerous, as imperfect a criterion as 'dangerousness' might be in terms of a discrete category of case.

In the case of common carriers, it was also suggested that the strictness of the liability was 'for the public benefit, as tending to make carriers more careful and diligent'.[79]

It has also been suggested that it was English law's fascination with protection of property rights that explained imposition of strict liability, after negligence and fault had become established. Ibbetson argues that a person should only be liable for damage caused by failure to take reasonable care was 'counterbalanced by an equally strong view that property rights should be protected'.[80] Jansen takes a similar view. He notes the strictness of liability for defamation as being based on analogising rights to reputation with property rights,[81] as with the decision in *Rylands v Fletcher*.[82]

[76] *Smith v Pelah* (1795) 2 Stra. 1264; 93 ER 1171; *May v Burdett* (1846) 9 QBD 101; 115 ER 1213.

[77] Prue Vines, 'Animals' in Carolyn Sappideen and Prue Vines (eds), *Fleming's Law of Torts* (10th edn, Lawbook Co, 2011) 412.

[78] *Lee v Riley* (1865) 18 CB (NS) 722; 144 ER 629; *Singleton v Williamson* (1861) 7 H & N 410; 158 ER 533.

[79] *Proprietors of the Trent Navigation v Wood* (1785) 3 Esp. 127, 131; 170 ER 562, 563 (Ashurst J).

[80] David Ibbetson, *A Historical Introduction to the Law of Obligations* (Oxford University Press, 1999) 185.

[81] *De Crespigny v Wellesley* (1829) 5 Bing. 392, 406 (Best CJ).

[82] Nils Jansen, 'Duties and Rights in Negligence: A Comparative and Historical Perspective on the European Law of Extracontractual Liability' (2004) 24 *Oxford Journal of Legal Studies* 443, 465.

Malone attempts to explain a rationale underpinning strict liability in pockets of the law as follows:

> Strict liability is the public response that is to be expected whenever the society of a given time and place must deal with specific perils which it has come to recognize as serious threats to its welfare. This was true of the hazards of fire, the depredations of animals and the risks of misconduct by carriers, innkeepers and others engaged in public callings.[83]

Pollock stated:

> There seems to be this common point in all of them, that a man has for his own convenience brought about or maintained some state of things which in the ordinary course of nature may work mischief to his neighbours. Whether his property be cattle grazing in his field or water stored in a reservoir, or a structure crossing or overhanging a public road, there is a certain risk of adjoining owners or to the public which necessarily accompanies the state of things so kept up ... whoever thus exposes others to risk should abide the consequences if the risk ripens into actual harm.[84]

On the other hand, Beuermann says that the law has moved away from attempting to use something like dangerousness as an organising and justifying principle for the imposition of strict liability.[85]

Strict Liability and the Law of Defamation

Initially the tort of defamation is seen to be fault based, requiring proof of malice on the part of the defendant publisher.[86] This reflected a time when defamation proceedings were heard in ecclesiastical courts. As a result, it is not perhaps surprising that questions of (moral) blameworthiness were important. However, as the royal courts began to take over defamation actions, the question of fault on the part of the defendant waned in importance.[87] The question of publication, a key ingredient in any defamation action, did not involve any issue regarding the defendant's culpability in doing so. It was sufficient that they had done so. A classic illustration of the strictness of the law of defamation is *E Hulton & Co v Jones*. There the defendant created a poem involving a supposedly fictional person, Artemis Jones. As luck would have it, a real Artemis Jones existed, and he

[83] Wex Malone, 'Ruminations on the Role of Fault in the History of the Common Law of Torts' (1970) 31 *Louisiana Law Review* 1, 26–27.

[84] Frederick Pollock, *Essays in Jurisprudence and Ethics* (Macmillan and Co, 1882) 122, 128.

[85] Christine Beuermann, *Reconceptualising Strict Liability for the Tort of Another* (Hart Publishing, 2019) 187.

[86] *Brook v Sir Henry Montague, Recorder of London* (1605) Cro. Jac. 90, 91; 79 ER 77, 78, referring to the earlier case of *Greenwood v Prick* 8 Cro. Jac. 91. Ibbetson cites this case as *Grymwood v Prike* (1585) Ro Abr 1.87 (*A Historical Introduction to the Law of Obligations* (Oxford University Press, 1999) 115).

[87] *Day v Bream* (1837) 2 Mood. & R 54; 174 ER 212.

sued the defendant for what he claimed was the defamation involved in the poem. The Court of Appeal found in favour of the plaintiff, concluding that

> [i]t makes no difference whether the writer of the article inserted the name or description unintentionally, by accident, or believing that no person existed corresponding with the name or answering the description. If upon the evidence the jury is of the opinion that ordinary sensible readers, knowing the plaintiff, would be of the opinion that the article referred to him, the plaintiff's case is made out.[88]

The courts sometimes analogised liability in defamation with liability for breach of another's property rights.[89] This is particularly important, given the evolution in the way in which liability for breach of property rights has evolved over time (as summarised above, and further discussed in Chapters 3, 4 and 7). I will discuss strict liability and defamation in more detail in Chapter 8.

Strict Liability and Trespass to the Person

The above discussion demonstrates a clear shift in the law with respect to actions brought in trespass. Initially, a defendant who causes injury to the plaintiff is liable in trespass. Liability is strict in nature. However, in 1616's *Weaver v Ward* it is suggested that a defendant is not liable in trespass where they are not at fault for the plaintiff's injuries.[90] In 1704's *Cole v Turner* it is suggested that a defendant is not liable in trespass where they did not intend to cause the plaintiff injury.[91] By the time of 1891's *Holmes v Mather*, it had become axiomatic that liability for trespass to the person required either intention or negligence.[92] On the basis that intention can be somewhat analogised to fault, in that a person who intends to cause another injury, and does so, can be said to be at fault for causing the injury, we see the movement in the law of trespass to the person away from strict, no-fault-based liability to a system of liability where fault plays a significant role. I will discuss the consequences of this for the ongoing development of trespass to the person in Chapter 9.

[88] *E Hulton & Co v Jones* [1909] 2 KB 444. This was affirmed by the House of Lords [1910] AC 20, 23–24 (Loreburn LC, the other Lords concurring), noting 'a person charged with libel cannot defend himself by showing that he intended in his own heart not to defame or that he intended not to defame the plaintiff. If in fact he did both … a man in good faith may publish a libel, believing it to be true, and it may be found by the jury that he acted in good faith, believing it to be true, and reasonably believing it to be true, but that in fact the statement was false. Under those circumstances he has no defence to the action, no matter how excellent his intention'.

[89] *De Crespigny v Wellesley* (1829) 5 Bing. 392, 406; 130 ER 1112, 1117–18, stating that the defendant 'had no more right to take away the character of the plaintiff … than to take his property without being able to justify the act by which he possessed himself of it' (Best CJ).

[90] *Weaver v Ward* (1616) Hob. 134, 135; 80 ER 284, 285.

[91] *Cole v Turner* (1704) 6 Mod. 149; 90 ER 958.

[92] *Holmes v Mather* (1875) LR 10 Ex. 261.

Development of the Tort of Negligence

It has been documented above that increasingly the courts were considering the question of the defendant's blameworthiness or fault in determining whether they were liable for injury or damage that the plaintiff had suffered. Pleadings would sometimes use the word 'negligently' or 'negligence' in describing the case. This should not be equated with current views of that term. However, there was at this time no actual independent tort of negligence. The concept of negligence was used in assessing whether other torts had been committed; negligence was not a tort of its own.

However, the courts began to accept that where there was a contractual relationship involving the provision of particular kinds of service an obligation would be imposed on the service provider which we would today recognise as something like a duty to take reasonable care. This was originally an action in assumpsit, an allegation that the service provider had assumed a responsibility to the customer or client to perform the required service at a certain standard or quality. An early example may be *The Humber Ferry Case* of 1348,[93] and an action against a surgeon for misfeasance in 1374.[94] This obligation would be applied to what the law considered to be a 'common calling' or 'public calling'.[95] Examples of the former include attorney and client, surgeon and patient, pharmacist and customer, and veterinarians and farriers. Examples of the latter include court personnel such as sheriffs.[96] There were doubts as to whether this action based on assumpsit applied to cases of non-feasance as well as misfeasance.[97] What we would now recognise as the 'tort' element of these obligations tended to grow in importance relative to what we would now recognise as the 'contract' basis of these obligations, for reasons such as that in tort, liability was several, while in contract, it was joint; longer limitation periods; and potentially higher damages payouts.[98]

Ibbetson notes that the concept of fault had been prominent in the Roman notion of culpa and that these ideas were carried forward by natural

[93] *Bukton v Townsend* YB 22 Lib. Ass. Pl. 41; JH Baker and SFC Milsom, *Sources of English Legal History: Private Law to 1750* (Butterworths, 1986) 358–77.

[94] *Stratton v Swanlone*, YB 48 Edw. III, fo. 6, pl. 11 (1374) (KB) 362 (Cavendish CJ): 'if a farrier undertakes to heal my horse, and by his negligence or failure to cure it within a reasonable time the horse is made worse, it is right that he should be held guilty. But if he does all he can, or puts all his diligence into the cure, it is not right that he should be held guilty, even though the horse is not healed. There is a great difference between the two cases' (reprinted in JH Baker and SFC Milsom, *Sources of English Legal History: Private Law to 1750* (Butterworths, 1986) 362.

[95] Percy Winfield, 'Duty in Tortious Negligence' (1934) 34 *Columbia Law Review* 41, 44–48.

[96] Percy Winfield, 'The History of Negligence in the Law of Torts' (1926) 42 *Law Quarterly Review* 184, 186–88. Blackstone casts it in broader terms: 'every one who undertakes any office, employment, trust or duty, contracts with those who employ or entrust him to perform it with integrity, diligence and skill': Sir William Blackstone, 3 *Commentaries on the Laws of England 1765–1769*, 164.

[97] Percy Winfield, 'The History of Negligence in Torts' (1926) 42 *Law Quarterly Review* 184, 188.

[98] James Plunkett, *The Duty of Care in Negligence* (Hart Publishing, 2018) 11.

law scholars of the seventeenth century.[99] Among these were Samuel Pufendorf, who noted that

> [w]henever we hurt or endamage another, we do it either out of full purpose and premeditated guilt, or by negligence only and not of design (and this negligence, as it is more or less gross or supine, is more or less culpable). Or lastly we may do it by mere chance, so that the injury cannot rightly be imputed to us.[100]

The law of bailment deserves special mention here. It was the judgment of Holt CJ in *Coggs v Barnard*[101] that pushed the law towards a fault basis. This was reinforced in Sir William Jones's *Essays on the Law of Bailments* (1781), and discussion of it in broader context was attributed to Francis Buller in 1772.[102]

Inevitably, pressure grew to extend this nascent concept of a duty to take reasonable care to circumstances where the parties were not in a pre-existing contractual relationship. This had been effectively suggested by cases in which the plaintiff had recovered against a defendant in an action in assumpsit for negligence, where the actual contract (as we would now call it) between the parties was not enforceable, for example because of lack of consideration.[103] At this time, the judges framed the action as one for deceit.[104] It would be more than a century before it would be recognised as an action in negligence proper. But assumpsit was a fault-based action.[105]

The development of the tort of deceit also played a part. Some of the cases which today would be brought under the rubric of negligence were in the past dealt with under an action for deceit. This tort was crimped by the House of Lords in *Derry v Peek*, when it confined it to cases where the defendant either knew what they had said was wrong, or were reckless as to whether it was

[99] David Ibbetson, *A Historical Introduction to the Law of Obligations* (Oxford University Press, 1999) 158.

[100] Samuel Pufendorf, *Of the Law of Nature and Nations* (1672) 3.1.6.

[101] *Coggs v Barnard* (1703) 2 Ld. Raym. 909; 92 ER 107.

[102] Francis Buller, *Introduction to the Law of Trials at Nisi Prius* (1772): 'every man ought to take reasonable care that he does not injure his neighbour; therefore when a man receives hurt through default of another, though the same were not wilful, yet if it be occasioned by negligence or folly the law gives him an action to recover damages for the injury so sustained' (noted by David Ibbetson, *A Historical Introduction to the Law of Obligations* (Oxford University Press, 1999) 165.

[103] *Coggs v Bernard* (1703) 2 Ld. Raym. 909, 915–16, 92 ER 107, 111–12 (KB): 'assumpsit does not only signify a future agreement, but in a case such as this, it signifies an actual entry upon the thing, and taking the trust upon himself. And if a man will do that, and miscarries in the performance of his trust, an action will lie against him for that, though no body could have compelled him to do the thing … a neglect is a deceit to the bailor. For when he entrusts the bailee upon his undertaking to be careful, he has put a fraud upon the plaintiff by being negligent, his pretence of care being the persuasion that induced the plaintiff to trust him. And a breach of trust undertaken voluntarily will be a good ground for an action'. See Robert Kaczorowski, 'The Common Law Background of Nineteenth-Century Tort Law' (1990) 51 *Ohio State Law Journal* 1127, 1133.

[104] Percy Winfield, 'The History of Negligence in the Law of Torts' (1926) 42 *Law Quarterly Review* 184, 187; *Derry v Peak* (1889) 14 App Cas 337.

[105] Robert Kaczorowski, 'The Common Law Background of Nineteenth-Century Tort Law' (1990) 51 *Ohio State Law Journal* 1127, 1132.

correct or not.[106] This overturned the position of the Court of Appeal that mere negligence was sufficient to engage the tort of deceit. The decision of the House of Lords left plaintiffs without a remedy in cases of merely negligent misstatement, an anomaly some were keen to remedy.[107]

The Industrial Revolution accelerated this pressure; the vast increase in industrial activity exponentially increased the risk that victims would be injured through the possible negligence of a stranger. The court originally resisted these arguments in the mid-nineteenth century,[108] with an apparent exception in *Vaughan v Menlove*.[109] This hesitation would be overcome. A generalised duty of care, quite independent of a pre-existing contractual relationship, would crystallise in *Heaven v Pender*[110] and *Donoghue v Stevenson*.[111]

The question of the possible cause-and-effect connection between the Industrial Revolution and acceptance of fault as the primary basis for tortious liability is an interesting one. Certainly, we see in the nineteenth-century case law, at the time of the Industrial Revolution, greater acceptance of fault, rather than strict, liability for injury caused to another. This was beneficial to commercial interests, reducing the circumstances in which they would be found liable for injuries they caused others. A utilitarian perspective may support this view, that greater numbers in society benefitted from all of the industrial enterprise, in terms of employment, expansion in the type and level of services available, and in terms of contribution to government revenue, from which further services could be provided.[112] Evidence of a sympathy for business and commercial interests is evident elsewhere in the tort law of this period, including in relation to limits on the liability of occupiers for injury caused by visitors to the premises,[113] the doctrine of common employment,[114] and the way in which defences such as contributory negligence and *volenti non fit injuria*[115] were applied as complete defences to an action in tort against a defendant.

Malone might be relating the development of the negligence tort with the Industrial Revolution when he notes:

> The conception of negligence or liability upon a flexible standard of care is not likely to come into being until society has reached a stage where diverse economic and social

[106] *Derry v Peek* (1887) 37 Ch D 541; (1889) 14 App Cas 337.

[107] Paul Mitchell, 'Duties, Interests and Motives: Privileged Occasions in Defamation' (1998) 18 *Oxford Journal of Legal Studies* 381, 404–05.

[108] *Langridge v Levy* (1838) 4 M & W 337; *Winterbottom v Wright* (1842) 10 M & W 109; see Percy Winfield, 'Duty in Tortious Negligence' (1934) 34 *Columbia Law Review* 41, 51–54.

[109] *Vaughan v Menlove* (1837) 3 Bing. NC 468; 132 ER 490.

[110] *Heaven v Pender* (1883) 11 QBD 503, 506–07 (Lord Esher, MR).

[111] *Donoghue v Stevenson* [1932] AC 562. See for discussion James Plunkett, *The Duty of Care in Negligence* (Hart Publishing, 2018) ch 2.

[112] Cornelius Peck, 'Negligence and Liability Without Fault in Tort Law' (1971) 46 *Washington Law Review* 225, 231: 'the entire population stood to benefit from the workings of an industrial economy, and society could not afford to burden itself with compensating those individuals who were so unfortunate as to be injured accidentally by an instrument of progress'.

[113] *Indermaur v Dames* (1866) LR 1 CP 274.

[114] *Priestley v Fowler* (1837) 3 M & W 1; 150 ER 1030.

[115] *Butterfield v Forrester* (1809) 11 East. 60; 103 ER 926.

> needs have emerged and are in lively competition with each other. The formation of a mature set of values of this kind must await the appearance of certain clearly definable human activities in each of which an appreciable number of human beings are engaged. Only as society becomes clustered into meaningful activity groups whose respective needs come into conflict can a situation arise in which a court is faced with a dilemma that obliges it to venture the opinion that the claims of those who are engaged in one activity are to be weighed against the claims of others engaged in another activity, and one activity given preference over the other.[116]

Elsewhere, he points out the value of particular activity only being recognised by courts when engaged in by a large number of people. He says it was only when industry, transportation and commerce became highly organised in the Industrial Revolution that courts began to realise their value, and understood the need to weigh them against other interests that had been recognised for much longer, in particular property rights.[117] This rendered the past focus on the simple fact that the defendant had caused the plaintiff injury insufficient. This led to the exponential growth in the tort of negligence in the nineteenth century:

> The juxtaposition of conflicting claims between plaintiff and defendant assumed an entirely different aspect once the courts came to recognise the fact that there was a pressing interest in the full utilization of the highways. Decisions mechanically rendered in favour of victims under the trespass theory would have a serious adverse effect on highway users. A group interest had emerged and courts were impelled to take it into account … under the strict trespass action, no traveller could afford to risk his fortune by making use of the highways. Thus the idea of negligence emerged as an inviting compromise … in these early 19th century traffic cases, the courts faced up to the fact that they were called upon to do more than consider the claims of isolated individuals … the negligence theory triumphed (over strict liability) because of its capacity to accommodate conflicting group demands and to afford some sort of reconciliation between them.[118]

Another development during the eighteenth and nineteenth centuries, in particular, occurred in relation to roads. Technological advances in the late eighteenth century facilitated significant upgrades to the quality of road surfaces. Of course the Industrial Revolution of the nineteenth century contemplated significant use of these road surfaces to move produce, workers and businesses. In a way, this again placed some pressure on the previous rules regarding strict liability. Utilitarian theory of the likes of Jeremy Bentham might question the consequences of a strict degree of liability for every accident that occurred on these new roadways.

[116] Wex Malone, 'Ruminations on the Role of Fault in the History of the Common Law of Torts' (1970) 31 *Louisiana Law Review* 1, 27.

[117] Wex Malone, 'Ruminations on Group Interests and the Law of Torts' (1959) 13 *Rutgers Law Review* 565, 568.

[118] Wex Malone, 'Ruminations on Group Interests and the Law of Tort' (1959) 13 *Rutgers Law Review* 565, 569–70.

Such an approach might deter or discourage the use of such highways and roadways, inhibiting efficiencies. Malone again sagely observes:

> The liberality towards the defendant's predicament in the traffic cases was an outgrowth of the practical dilemma for litigation that was shaping up as the roads of nineteenth century England were gradually improved. Courts were faced with the fact that there was a pressing interest in the full utilization of the highways and that decisions mechanically rendered in favour of victims under the trespass theory would have a serious adverse effect on highway users. An impressive group interest in travel had emerged and courts were impelled to take it into account. Hence the plaintiff, if he were to recover, must make a presentation with greater appeal than a mere showing that his injury was directly inflicted. It became apparent that under the strict trespass action, no traveller could afford to risk his fortune by making use of the highways. Thus the idea of negligence emerged as an inviting compromise in these cases … in the early 19th century cases the courts faced upon to the fact that they were called upon to do more than consider the claims of isolated individuals. The task of the law was to adjust conflicts between members of a group of highway users, and the interests of all highway users … were at stake.[119]

Other scholars see in the highway cases that a concept of assumption of risk is being utilised. They argue that the theory was that road users, by using the roadways, had in effect accepted the risks associated with non-negligent use of the highways by others. This was why their ability to claim compensation for injury sustained on the highway was limited to circumstances in which they could demonstrate that the defendant owed, and had breached, a duty of care to them. In other words, this was why a negligence standard was applied in such cases, as opposed to others.[120] There is some support for Kretzmer's theory in the judgment of Blackburn J in *Fletcher v Rylands*:

> Traffic on the highways, whether by land or sea, cannot be conducted without exposing those whose persons or property are near to it some inevitable risk, and that being so, those who go on the highway or have their property adjacent to it may well be held to do so subject to their taking upon themselves the risk of injury from that inevitable danger … it is believed that all the cases in which inevitable accident has been held an excuse for what prima facie was a trespass can be explained on the same principle, viz, that the circumstances were such as to show that the plaintiff had taken that risk upon himself.[121]

Bohlen says it was the vast increase in human-to-human contact caused by the Industrial Revolution that placed strain on the law of tort, giving it opportunities and at the same time pressuring it to adapt to new situations. This occurred quickly:

> Injuries to the person, to personal property and to business interests had come to occupy an altogether preponderant part of the field covered by the law of torts.

[119] Wex Malone, 'Ruminations on the Role of Fault in the History of the Common Law of Torts' (1970) 31 *Louisiana Law Review* 1, 33–34.

[120] David Kretzmer, 'Transformation of Tort Liability in the Nineteenth-Century: The Visible Hand' (1984) 4 *Oxford Journal of Legal Studies* 46, 80–83.

[121] *Fletcher v Rylands* (1865) LR 1 Ex. 265, 286–87.

> As civilization advanced and society became more complex, the points of contact between man and man multiplied rapidly and an almost infinite number of novel situations arose in which the activities of one person might injuriously affect the personal interests of others … the attention of the courts was concentrated in the field of tort law on solving the new problems of liability for personal injuries constantly arising. In this field, they were forced to generalise, to discover general principles of liability to govern novel cases.

He contrasts this with cases involving property interests. He said that the volume of such cases did not markedly rise during the Industrial Revolution period. As a result, it maintained its past position favouring strict liability in many contexts, including trespass, nuisance, cattle trespass and fire.[122] He uses this theory to explain the decision in *Rylands v Fletcher*, to be discussed in more detail in Chapter 3.

Bohlen reflects more broadly on the shift from strict liability to fault-based liability in terms of increased societal sophistication and awareness of notions of the common good:

> So long as society could preserve its peace only by the satisfaction of grievances which would otherwise lead to private feuds, it is evident that the conception of the limits of legal liability must coincide with the individual sense of grievance against those who in fact cause harm, and as it could not be expected that an individual would placidly best an injury because the act which caused it was beneficial to the general interest of the community, it follows that the extent of legal liability could not be determined by its effect upon the common good. But when the state became more powerful, it became able to preserve its peace by pressure placed upon its citizens to respect it, and so was no longer forced to secure it by removing the incentive to private reprisals. And as the state, as it were, became more self-conscious, it would come to have regard to the effect of its laws upon the wellbeing of the community. Being then able to preserve its peace without satisfying what such individuals regarded as their just grievance, it seems inevitable that the state should lay down rules which would have regard primarily to the public good and which may be said to embody the collective sense of what is right and convenient, as on the whole best tending to advance the interests of all members of the community as a group, which may well be radically divergent from what each individual regards as just as between himself and his fellow. The natural tendency in any advancing civilization, to regard the utmost possible freedom of individual activity as essential to the general good, would therefore cause its encouragement to be regarded as paramount to the preservation of the interests of the merely passive citizen; and would tend to the abandonment of a rule of liability which, by making the actor answerable for all the harm he causes, would appear to unduly burden and so discourage individual initiative, and to the adoption in place thereof of a rule which relieved him from liability so long as he in his activities showed a due regard for the interests of others.[123]

[122] Francis Bohlen, 'Rule in *Rylands v Fletcher*' (1911) 59 *University of Pennsylvania Law Review* 298, 316.

[123] Francis Bohlen, 'The Rule in *Rylands v Fletcher* III' (1911) 59 *University of Pennsylvania Law Review* 423, 450–51.

Of course, this theory assumes that the position in England prior to *Rylands v Fletcher* was that liability for interference with interests to land was in fact strict. In fact, as shown above, concepts of reasonableness had crept into cases involving such cases by the mid-nineteenth century, and the legislature had moved liability in circumstances involving common carriers, innkeepers and fire towards a fault-based approach and away from a strict liability approach by that time as well.

Many have observed the exponential growth in the tort of negligence from relatively recent origins[124] and speculated as to the implications for other torts. It is a tort quite unlike many of the other torts. Traditionally, torts protected identified interests. For example, the tort of trespass to the person protected interests in bodily integrity. The tort of nuisance, and that of trespass to land and goods, protected property interests. The tort of defamation protected interests in reputation. The tort of negligence differs in that it is not focused on a particular interest, but on particular behaviour, and especially behaviour through the prism of fault.[125] Millner noted that

> [t]he growth of the tort of negligence has proceeded by way of infiltration into the causes of action of other torts, sometimes modifying the rules of those torts, sometimes ousting them entirely from particular situations. In either event the outcome is the annexation of more territory by the tort of negligence at the cost of the other torts, which are either diminished in importance or undergo certain changes in character.[126]

The potential of the tort of negligence to cut across virtually all other torts, sweeping away their focus on particular interests in favour of a universal standard of behaviour has been noted:

> The now ultra-dominant tort of negligence should in principle be capable of redressing all injuries, provided they were caused negligently: this is in the nature of its being a transversal wrong defined by reference to a degree of fault rather than a particular right or type of loss.[127]

Conclusions

Much territory has been covered in this part. The following points might be made by way of summary:

- Legal systems designed to compensate victims for injuries caused by another should be seen in the context of the blood feud in primitive society.

[124] Tony Weir observed the 'staggering march of negligence': 'The Staggering March of Negligence' in Peter Cane and Jane Stapleton (eds), *The Law of Obligations: Essays in Celebration of John Fleming* (Clarendon Press, 1998) 97; James Plunkett, *The Duty of Care in Negligence* (Hart Publishing, 2018) 39–43; James Henderson, 'Why Negligence Dominates Tort' (2002) 50 *UCLA Law Review* 377.

[125] Eric Descheemaeker, 'Protecting Reputation: Defamation and Negligence' (2009) 29 *Oxford Journal of Legal Studies* 603, 603–05.

[126] Maurice Millner, *Negligence in Modern Law* (Butterworths, 1967) 15.

[127] Eric Descheemaeker, '"A Man Must Take Care Not to Defame his Neighbour": The Origins and Significance of the Defence of Responsible Publication' (2015) 34 *University of Queensland Law Journal* 239, 261–62.

- This context helps to explain why such systems were relatively generous, requiring plaintiffs to demonstrate that the defendant's actions caused them injury, without the necessity to prove fault.
- there is ample evidence that English law accepted these principles from more ancient legal systems;
- What we would now regard as the criminal law began to consider fault, or notions of moral blameworthiness, before the civil law did – with influences from ecclesiastical courts and more general society norms and values.
- The law then sharply distinguished between liability in criminal law and liability in civil law, maintaining that fault and blame (often through the prism of intention) was relevant in the criminal law context but not the civil law context.
- As initially comprised, the trespass action was a strict liability action, focused on the force used and not the question of the fault or culpability of the defendant who used it, though with some exceptional cases where the courts found that a defendant could not be liable in trespass if they did not intend to cause injury.
- There is some conjecture that fault may have been relevant in trespass cases, either through the defendant explaining their actions to the jury, or through defences such as inevitable accident which may have involved notions of fault.
- The development of the action on the case in the late fourteenth century did encourage the consideration of fault in such cases, and may have influenced increased acceptance of the relevance of fault in trespass cases.
- The court recognised that in particular categories of case characterised by pre-existing relationships, the party providing the service had an obligation to use reasonable care and skill in their provision – originally this action was based on assumpsit but it came to be recognised as a tort in an action on the case.
- By the seventeenth century there is much more consideration of questions of fault and blame in determining liability both for trespass and case, and an increased use of case.
- There remained particular categories of case where strict liability principles continued to be applied, including in relation to animals, fires, innkeepers and common carriers, though in some cases these principles were modified by statute.
- The growth of negligence increased exponentially in the nineteenth century, coinciding with, and perhaps being explained by, the Industrial Revolution.
- Somewhat anomalously, given these nineteenth-century developments, in 1865 the court decided the landmark case of *Rylands v Fletcher* on the basis of a supposed general principle of strict liability.
- Nevertheless, further steps were taken in terms of a generalised negligence principle in the late nineteenth century, culminating in its general acceptance by 1932.

PART II

Rylands v Fletcher Strict Liability in the Common Law World

3

Rylands v Fletcher in the United Kingdom

Introduction

It is appropriate to devote substantial attention to the (in)famous decision in *Rylands v Fletcher*. It is Exhibit A in any analysis of strict liability, a clear example of its acceptance by the highest courts in the United Kingdom, at a relatively late time in the development of UK law. It might be seen as a proxy for broader acceptance of strict liability within tort. It remains (at least technically) part of the law of the United Kingdom and Canada, and has significantly impacted the law in the United States. The case itself, and its progeny, provide an excellent example of the kinds of difficulties that principles of strict liability can cause, by its rigid application of doctrines of imprecise meaning. As will be seen, it forced the courts into unlikely findings, extremely fine distinctions of questionable utility, and in attempting to give meaning to vague concepts, inevitably led the courts to apply fault principles to the heart of a doctrine loudly lauded as an exemplar of how strict, no-fault liability can do 'justice'. Its talismanic potential of a unifying principle of strict liability was scotched by the UK courts, but the unsatisfactory doctrine it represents lives on (if only just) in the jurisdiction of its birth and in Canada.

As we saw in Chapter 1, the law relating to the liability of a person for damage or injury caused to another had undergone significant change. While at first the position seems to have been one of strict liability, sometimes abbreviated to the phrase that a person acts at their own peril, there had gradually been more acceptance that liability should not be automatically applied simply by proving that the defendant caused the plaintiff injury, that the question of fault or moral blameworthiness should be taken into account. This was particularly noticeable with respect to highway accidents. Notwithstanding this, pockets of strict liability remained, for instance in relation to so-called cattle trespass and fire.

The question for the court was how, if at all, to reconcile these clearly competing philosophies. Was the general rule one of strict liability, with negligence applied in exceptional cases? Or was the general rule one of fault-based liability, with strict liability applied in exceptional cases? The courts dealing with the great case of *Rylands v Fletcher* were required to grapple with this key issue. The showdown between strict liability and fault-based liability had arrived. Not surprisingly, different views were evident in the various judgments. It is essential to discuss the great case, and the judgments, before considering how it was applied in subsequent cases and in various jurisdictions.

Facts

The facts were relatively simple. The plaintiff and defendant owned adjoining mines. The defendant decided to construct a reservoir upon their property. They engaged competent engineers and builders to design and construct the reservoir. Construction was completed. Unknown to anyone, an old mine passage connected the defendant's land to that of the plaintiff. A few days after construction was completed, water escaped from the reservoir into the old mine passage, and water entered the plaintiff's mine, causing him loss. The question was whether the defendant was legally liable for this loss. Trespass would not traditionally have been available on the facts because the damage was not direct. Nuisance would not traditionally have been available on the facts because the event was a one-off, rather than continual in nature.[1]

Judgment of the Court of Exchequer

A majority of the Court of Exchequer dismissed the claim.[2] It is clear that the majority saw the general principle of liability as fault based, with exceptional strict liability in limited cases. For example, Baron Martin referred to the position with personal injury or damage to personal property. He said that in such cases, the general position was that there was no liability in the absence of proof of negligence. There was no reason why this position should not extend to damage to real property of the kind with which this case was concerned. He vehemently disagreed with holding the defendant liable here because to do so 'would make them insurers against the consequences of a lawful act upon their own land when they had no reason to believe or suspect that any damage was likely to ensue'.[3] Chief Baron Pollock agreed. The third judge did not render a decision. The fourth judge, Barton Bramwell, dissented. He accepted the 'at peril' doctrine – the defendant's actions were at his peril, and he was liable for any injury or damage they caused to another. He acknowledged the amoral dimension of his view: 'I think that the defendants' innocence, whatever may be its moral bearing on the case, is immaterial in

[1] JH Baker, *An Introduction to English Legal History* (Butterworths, 2002) 432: 'the essence of nuisance was an interference with the enjoyment of property … it was usually a continuing wrong', though acknowledging precedents such as *Tenant v Goldwin* (1704) 2 Ld. Raym. 1089; 92 ER 222, where a one-off incident was held to be actionable as a nuisance.

[2] *Fletcher v Rylands* (1865) 3 H & C 774; 159 ER 737.

[3] ibid, 793; 745.

point of law'.[4] In other words, the fact that the defendant acted unwittingly, and without negligence or fault, did not absolve him of liability.

Judgment of the Exchequer Chamber

All members of the Exchequer Chamber allowed an appeal from this decision.[5] The Chamber comprised Willes, Blackburn, Keating, Mellor, Montague Smith and Lush JJ, obviously including some luminaries of the English common law, which helps to explain some of the reverence accorded to the decision. The Chamber's decision was delivered in one judgment delivered by Blackburn J.

The Exchequer Chamber placed importance on previous cases that had determined that the owner of cattle was strictly liable for damage caused by their escaped animal,[6] cases that had determined that one neighbour was liable to another for filth escaping from their premises onto that of the neighbour,[7] and cases where a factory was held liable for damage caused by escaping fumes.[8] The Exchequer Chamber sought to assimilate these cases into a 'true rule':

> We think that the true rule of law is, that the person who for his own purposes brings on his lands and collects and keeps there anything likely to do mischief it if it escapes, must keep it in at his peril, and if he does not do so, is prima facie answerable for all the damage which is the natural consequence of its escape. He can excuse himself by showing that the escape was owing to the plaintiff's default; or perhaps that the escape was the consequence of vis major, or the act of God; but nothing of his sort exists here, it is unnecessary to inquire what excuse would be sufficient. The general rule … seems on principle just. The person whose grass or corn is eaten down by the escaping cattle of his neighbour, or whose mine is flooded by the water from his neighbour's reservoir, or whose cellar is invaded by the filth of his neighbour's privy, or whose habitation is made unhealthy by the fumes and noisome vapours of his neighbour's alkali works, is damnified without any fault of his own, and it seems but reasonable and just that the neighbour, who was brought something on his own property which was not naturally there, harmless to others so long as it is confined to his own property, but which he knows to be mischievous if it gets on his neighbour's, should be obliged to make good the damage which ensues if he does not succeed in confining it to his own property. But for his act in bringing it there no mischief could have accrued, and it seems but just

[4] ibid, 790; 744.

[5] *Fletcher v Rylands* (1865) LR 1 Ex. 265.

[6] 'The law as to them seems to be perfectly settled from early times; the owner must keep them at his peril, or he will be answerable for the natural consequences of their escape', (1865) LR 1 Ex. 265, 280, 'whether or not the escape of the animal is due to my negligence is altogether immaterial' (281).

[7] The judgment cites *Tenant v Goldwin* (1704) 6 Mod. Rep. 311; 91 ER 20, where it is stated that 'one must use his own so as thereby not to hurt another', (1865) LR 1 Ex. 265, 283.

[8] The judgment refers to several cases where juries had found factories liable for damage caused by escaping chlorine, adding that no question of negligence or want of care had been raised in these cases. However, had it been, the judgment states that it would have been irrelevant because of the 'at peril' doctrine, (1865) LR 1 Ex. 265, 285–86.

> that he should at his peril keep it there so that no mischief may accrue, or answer for the natural and anticipated consequences. And upon authority, this we think is established to be the law, whether the things so brought be beasts, or water, or filth, or stenches.[9]

The judgment acknowledges that there are circumstances in which questions of negligence and fault are relevant in determining cases.[10] It refers particularly to highway and seaway accidents. It deals with such cases by treating them as exceptions to a general rule of strict liability. It justifies this by suggesting that in the highway and seaway cases, there are inherent risks. Traffic inherently creates risks to those who are physically nearby, or who own property nearby. It is something of a voluntary assumption of risk argument. In that category of case, the Chamber states that proof of negligence should be required in order to obtain compensation. The judgment sharply distinguishes the present case. In the current case, the plaintiff did not know of the risk, and had no control over it. He could not control whether or how the defendant constructed the reservoir.[11]

Judgment of the House of Lords

Only two Law Lords decided the appeal, both dismissing it.[12] Lord Cairns emphasised the non-natural use aspect of the Exchequer Chamber judgment. He determined that it was that factor that attracted the 'at peril' doctrine. In contrast, if what had escaped was 'natural', the defendant from whose property it emanated would only be liable upon proof they had been negligent.[13] He referred to the 'natural user of the land', or in other words something that was already on the land. He also referred to the use of premises for a purpose for which it might 'in the ordinary course of the enjoyment of land be used'. This proved critical. While Lord Cairns may have been attempting to explain away an earlier decision where water escaped from a defendant's premises when they mined coal from it,[14] and seemed to use interchangeably concepts of non-natural use and ordinary use,

[9] ibid, 279–80.

[10] The judgment has also been criticised for utilising fault elements in a judgment that is ostensibly based on strict liability: see Allan Beever, *The Law of Private Nuisance* (Hart Publishing, 2013) 110–11, 115–16.

[11] *Fletcher v Rylands* (1865) LR 1 Ex. 265, 286–87.

[12] *Rylands v Fletcher* (1868) LR 3 HL 330.

[13] ibid, 338–39.

[14] *Smith v Kenrick* (1849) 7 C.B. 515; 137 ER 205. The case was extensively discussed in *Rylands*. The case involved a lake of subterranean rain water. It was held on the defendant's premises by coal. When the defendant mined the coal, the water escaped onto the plaintiff's premises nearby. This eventuality could have been foreseen by the defendant, but he nevertheless conducted the mining activity. The court found he was not liable for the damage caused to the defendant, on the basis that a landowner had the right to use their premises as they wished. It was necessary for the plaintiff in *Rylands v Fletcher* to distinguish this precedent, and one way in which they successfully did so was to contrast the non-natural construction of the reservoir in *Rylands* with the naturally pooling rainwater at issue in *Smith v Kenrick*.

the decision introduced into the law a confusion between the concept of what was not naturally there, on the one hand, and what might have been an ordinary use of land.[15] He praised the rule established in the Exchequer Chamber as just. It was fair that someone who brought a thing onto their property that was not naturally there, in circumstances where they knew it would be mischievous if it escaped, should be held liable for the damage it caused another.[16]

Lord Cranworth agreed. He also adopted the distinction between injury or loss caused by a natural cause, and damage caused by an event or thing which was not naturally on the land. He discussed two situations – one in which the plaintiff had suffered damage due to the natural flow of water from the defendant's premises, and one in which the flow of water from the defendant's premises was caused by water that he had specifically pumped up. In the first case, the defendant would not be liable; in the second case, he would be. He specifically connected this distinction with the long-established principle of 'act of God'.[17] If something had occurred through a natural cause, it was not something for which a defendant would be responsible. There would be related issues about causation.[18]

However, it is not entirely clear how broad he believed the scope of the doctrine to be. He began by discussing liability for the escape of something from one neighbour's land to that of another. He indicated that in such circumstances the defendant would be strictly liable, regardless of what precautions they may have taken to avoid damage to another. However, shortly after he framed the relevant principle more broadly:

> In considering whether a defendant is liable to a plaintiff for damage which the plaintiff may have sustained, the question in general is not whether the defendant has acted with this care and caution, but whether his acts have occasioned the damage [he referred to

[15] Debate raged as to whether the formulation by Lord Cairns was, or was intended to be, essentially the same as that of Blackburn J. For example, in *J P Porter Co v Bell* [1955] 1 DLR 62, 66 MacDonald J for the Nova Scotia Court of Appeal referred to them as two different rules. In *Burnie Port Authority v General Jones Pty Ltd* (1994) 179 CLR 520 Mason CJ, Deane, Dawson Toohey and Gaudron JJ said that Lord Cairns' formulation of non-natural use may have been intended to simply use different words to explain Blackburn J's 'not naturally there' (538), but in any event the concept was narrowed in subsequent cases. At 544 the High Court said that Lord Cairns, in an 'unexplained and conceivably inadvertent [way] judicial[ly] transform[ed] Blackburn J's qualification "not naturally there"'. One subsequent decision which neatly shows the different meanings of the phrases is *Stearn v Prentice Bros* [1919] 1 KB 394. The case involved the defendant collecting a pile of bones on their premises for use in their bone manure factory. Rats attracted to the pile of bones then escaped onto the plaintiff's premises. The plaintiff's claim against the defendant on the basis of *Rylands v Fletcher* failed on the basis that the defendant's use of their premises was an 'ordinary user' of their land. It is submitted that a different result may have occurred if the court had considered whether the defendant's use of their land was 'natural'.

[16] William Stallybrass criticised Lord Cairns' judgment for confusing the distinction between natural and non-natural user, on the one hand, and that between things that were brought onto the land and those which were already there. He said the two concepts were logically distinct: 'Dangerous Things and the Non-Natural User of Land' (1929) 3 *Cambridge Law Journal* 376, 395.

[17] 'The damage in the former case may be treated as having arisen from the act of God; in the latter, from the act of the defendant', *Rylands v Fletcher* (1868) LR 3 HL 330, 342.

[18] ibid, 341–42.

> *Lambert v Bessey*] … for when one person, in managing his own affairs, causes, however innocently, damage to another, it is obviously only just that he should be the party to suffer.[19]

The judgments of the Exchequer Chamber and House of Lords seem to be designed to impose a principle of strict liability. Its precise ambit is not entirely clear; all members of the Exchequer Chamber and Lord Cairns seem to confine it to cases of escape from land, but Lord Cranworth's judgment seems to be broader, reflecting a general principle of liability of very broad ambit. Eminent legal historian Frederick Pollock noted this. He stated that while the case might be confined to the special circumstances of liability between neighbouring landowners, 'it was certainly intended to enunciate something much wider'.[20]

Reflections

The judgments appear to draw this broad principle of strict liability by referring to other cases of it in the law, particularly liability for so-called cattle trespass. In this light, it is somewhat strange that the judgments do not also attempt to bring in other examples of strict liability traditionally recognised in the law and discussed in Chapter 2, including liability for fire and that of common carriers and innkeepers.

The judgments place significant emphasis on the concept of a 'non-natural' user of land. The Exchequer Chamber and House of Lords decisions emphasise that the strict liability envisaged applies only in cases of a non-natural use of land. Of course, it is not entirely clear what a non-natural use of land is, as subsequent cases would demonstrate. Further, it is not entirely clear why such a distinction should be made. The cases discussed in Part I do not purport to make a distinction between a natural and a non-natural use of land, in terms of distinguishing liability, at least in those terms.

The House of Lords judgments are most illuminating in this light. In particular, Lord Cranworth makes clear that his understanding, at least, of the distinction is really another way of expressing the age-old principle of Act of God. After drawing the distinction between water flowing naturally from land, and water pumped by the act of an individual which then flows from land, he specifically relates this to the concept of 'Act of God'. As explained in Chapter 1, this was recognised as an

[19] ibid, 341.

[20] Frederick Pollock, 'Duties of Insuring Safety: The Rule in *Rylands v Fletcher*' (1886) 2 *Law Quarterly Review* 52, 56; see likewise Robert Thomas Molloy, '*Fletcher v Rylands*: A Re-examination of Juristic Origins' (1942) 9 *University of Chicago Law Review* 266, 267: 'the importance of *Fletcher v Rylands* lies in its reaffirmation of the medieval principle of action at peril'; AWB Simpson, 'Legal Liability for Bursting Reservoirs: The Historical Context of *Rylands v Fletcher*' (1984) 13 *Journal of Legal Studies* 209, 213, stating that Blackburn J 'was quite clearly contending that the basic common-law principle of tortious liability was liability without fault'.

exception to tort liability for many centuries by the time that *Rylands* was decided. In hindsight, it might have been better to continue to recognise the defence of Act of God, without attempting to rephrase it in the form of a distinction between something that was not naturally there and something that was. The defence of Act of God was understood reasonably well in the case law, and the distinction between things that were naturally there and things that were not is not a precise copy of, though somewhat analogous to Acts of God, compared with other events. The concept of non-natural user would become a favoured target for critics of the decision.[21]

Further, it is not entirely clear, in reading the judgment of Blackburn J, that his distinction between something that was not naturally there and something that was, in fact was another way of expressing the Act of God defence. This is because he draws the distinction between things not naturally there and things that were, and then suggests defences including Act of God which might apply. This seems to suggest that he does not link the concept of an Act of God with natural user, but Lord Cranworth assimilated them. Another aspect of contention is the insistence that the principle applies to something that is 'known to be mischievous' if it escapes. It is not entirely clear why knowledge of the possible dangerousness of the particular thing concerned should be necessary. It seems to have some relation to the *scienter* requirement of liability for some non-wild animals – that the owner is liable for acts of the animal when they have specific knowledge of the animal's vicious propensities. In contrast, this kind of *scienter* was not required for other categories of case in which strict liability was imposed, including fire, common carriers and innkeepers. It is not entirely clear therefore why the judges sought to limit the instance of strict liability in relation to land to things that were known to be mischievous.

Pollock criticised the decision for apparently imposing a duty of insurer upon innocent persons. He noted that was a 'hard' rule, though it may be just.[22] However, it required careful explanation and justification. He criticised the decision for failing to do so.[23] He notes that at times, liability seems to rest on the dangerousness of the activity, at times it seems to relate to traditional (strict) liability in nuisance, and at times it seems to hark back to primitive days when liability

[21] Sir John Salmond, *The Law of Torts* (7th edn, Sweet and Maxwell, 1928): 'such a distinction (that between natural and non-natural user) has little in principle to recommend it. What is the natural use of land? Is it natural to build a house on it, or to light a fire? Almost all use of land involves some alteration of its natural condition, and it seems impossible to say how far this alteration may go before the use of the land becomes non-natural or extraordinary, so as to bring the rule in *Rylands v Fletcher* into operation. Moreover, if there is one kind of use more natural than another it is the keeping of cattle; yet cattle trespass is a typical instance of the application of this rule of strict responsibility, and is indeed the historical source of the general principle'.

[22] Frederick Pollock, 'Duties of Insuring Safety: The Rule in *Rylands v Fletcher* (1886) 2 *Law Quarterly Review* 52, 55.

[23] 'The judgment *in Rylands v Fletcher*, carefully prepared as it evidently was, hardly seems to make such grounds clear enough for universal acceptance', ibid, 55.

in such circumstance was based on the general 'act at peril' doctrine, which had waned to a large extent in English law by the time of the 1860s.

There is of course a healthy literature doubting the extent to which dangerousness can operate as a defensible differentiator to explain cases where strict liability is or should be applied, and cases where negligence and fault are or should be applied. It can be difficult to determine whether or not a particular activity might pass the threshold of required dangerousness or ultra-hazardous, and the threshold might move over time. Nolan observes that

> [t]he modern tendency is towards generalisation, perhaps, because the concept of dangerousness has been overtaken by the complexity of contemporary industrial society, perhaps because technological advances have in fact rendered many previously dangerous activities much safer, both in the eyes of the public and n fact, or perhaps because the original appeal of 'dangerousness' lay in an outmoded perception of technology as alien and threatening.[24]

Most things could create a danger if they 'escape', depending how they are utilised.[25] Nolan lists the various things that have been deemed to be dangerous in this context, including water, electricity, gas, oil, fire, poisonous trees, flagpoles, house roofs, vibrations and even people. He concludes that 'one would look in vain at the long list of included objects for a clue as to why strict liability was imposed'.[26]

Pollock also noted resulting anomalies of the decision. In the result, it set up a sharp distinction between liability for damage to property interests, and liability for personal injury. By the mid-1890s negligence had become the dominant way in which liability for personal injury would be established. Yet, if *Rylands* were taken to amount to a general rule imposing strict liability on liability for interference with property interests, an anomaly would result. Pollock gave an example where a train is involved in an accident. If passengers were injured as a result, they would have to prove fault against the railway company in order to obtain compensation. However, if, as a result of the accident, there was damage to the plaintiff's land (through subsidence or water disturbance, for example), the plaintiff would be entitled to obtain compensation for this without proof of fault on the part of the defendant railway company.[27] It may be argued to be anomalous that the law should protect property interests to a greater extent than it protects interests in personal safety.[28]

[24] Donal Nolan, 'The Distinctiveness of *Rylands v Fletcher*' (2005) 121 *Law Quarterly Review* 421, 448.

[25] Donal Nolan, 'The Principle of *Rylands v Fletcher*' in Carolyn Sappideen and Prue Vines (eds), *Fleming's Law of Torts* (10th edn, Lawbook Co, 2011) 390.

[26] ibid.

[27] Frederick Pollock, 'Duties of Insuring Safety: The Rule in *Rylands v Fletcher*' (1886) 2 *Law Quarterly Review* 52, 59.

[28] Donal Nolan calls this 'indefensible': 'The Distinctiveness of *Rylands v Fletcher*' (2005) 121 *Law Quarterly Review* 421, 440.

Leading torts scholar Sir John Salmond was scathing of the decision. Writing in the preface to the fourth edition of his classic torts work he opined:

> Had the law been content to adopt the uniform principle that liability for accidental harm depended in all cases on the existence of negligence on the part of the defendant or his servants, most of the serious difficulties and complexities which now exist would have been eliminated. Unfortunately, however, for the simplicity an intelligibility of our legal system, it has been found necessary to recognize a number of cases of absolute liability, that is to say liability for accidental harm independent of any negligence on the part of the defendant or his servants, and the scope and limits of these exceptional rules still remain largely covered with doubt and darkness … [speaking of *Rylands*] … no decision in the law of torts has done more to prevent the establishment of a simple and uniform system of civil responsibility, and its true meaning and limitations remain to this day the subject of dispute and uncertainty.[29]

Further anomalies exist. In *Rylands* itself Blackburn J briefly noted that recovery for damage to personal property required proof of negligence on the part of the defendant, in apparent contrast to the position he took in the case itself regarding damage to land. Then a decade later in *River Wear Commissioners v Adamson*,[30] the case involved the defendant's vessel striking the plaintiff's pier during a storm. While the case might have been brought within the 'act of God' exception, and indeed it was so decided by Lord Cairns in that case,[31] (now) Lord Blackburn seemed to turn against the principle of strict liability for damage to property:

> The common law is, I think, as follows: property adjoining to a spot on which the public have a right to carry on traffic is liable to be injured by that traffic. In this respect there is no difference between a shop, the railings or windows of which may be broken by a carriage on the road, and a pier adjoining to a harbour or a navigable river or the sea, which is liable to be injured by a ship. In either case the owner of the injured property must bear his own loss, unless he can establish that some other person is in fault, and liable to make it good. And he does not establish this against a person merely by shewing that he is owner of the carriage or ship which did the mischief, for the owner incurs no liability merely because he is owner. But he does establish such a liability against any person who either wilfully did the damage, or neglected that duty which the law casts upon those in charge of a carriage on land, and a ship … to take reasonable care and use reasonable skill to prevent it doing injury, and that this wilfulness or neglect caused the damage.[32]

Though the factual scenario clearly differs from that in *Rylands*, there is certainly no mention here of strict liability for damage to property interests. Liability for damage to property interests in this context is placed by Lord Blackburn on notions of either wilfulness or negligence, rather than strict liability. It is not entirely clear why 'escape' of something not naturally there from land, damaging

[29] Sir John Salmond, *The Law of Torts* (4th edn, Stevens and Haynes, 1916) v.
[30] *River Wear Commissioners v Adamson* (1877) 2 AC 743.
[31] ibid, 751.
[32] ibid, 767.

property interests of another, warrants the imposition of strict liability, whereas damage to property interests in a similarly inadvertent, non-negligent way, does not. Past suggestions of special rules relating to highway accidents are, of course, no longer tenable.

Possible Explanations for the Decision in *Rylands v Fletcher*

Critical Legal Theory

Bohlen articulated an explanation of *Rylands v Fletcher* that would today be regarded as reflecting a classic critical legal theory position. This is interesting because he was writing 60 years prior to the recognition of such a theory by that moniker. Basically, critical legal theorists states that legal principles are not derived from the ways of nature, or based on strict logic or reason, but reflect the political and social values of the decision makers, whether they be legislators, or judges in the common law tradition.

Bohlen first set out the apparent anomaly in the English common law, made more prominent by the decision of *Rylands v Fletcher*. He noted that by this stage, the law of personal injuries was moving to a strongly fault-based position. In contrast, the law continued to recognise particular situations where liability would exist in the absence of fault. He recognised these as including cases involving trespass, nuisance, cattle trespass and fire. He noted that all of these cases involved damage to property interests. This is clearly correct. Notably, he also omitted to include the strict liability of common carriers and of innkeepers at common law. That of the former would have strongly supported the position he took because, as was explained in Chapter 2, the liability of common carriers was strict in respect of cargo, but fault based in respect of personal injury.

He drew a conclusion from the law in its then bifurcated state, imposing strict liability for damage to property interests but imposing only fault-based liability for personal injury. He said it was based not on any sound or defensible difference in principle, but upon some kind of bias favouring property interests, reflecting the background of judges, or the circles in which they hoped to find themselves:

> In England, the dominant class was the landed gentry, whose opinion the judges, who either sprang from this class or hoped to establish themselves and their families therein – naturally reflected. To such a class it was inevitable, that the right of exclusive dominion over land should appear paramount to its commercial utilization – to them, commerce and manufacture, in which they had little or no direct interest, appeared comparatively unimportant.[33]

[33] Francis Bohlen, 'Rule in *Rylands v Fletcher*' (1911) 59 *University of Pennsylvania Law Review* 298, 318–19.

Bohlen says that, at the time, the 'dominant class' were not interested in the commercial development of the country – they looked down with disdain on mercantilists and artisans – and people in those categories had little political power.[34]

He says landholding had an ancient history in the customs and law of England. It was not then surprising that it should be regarded with sanctity. In contrast, large-scale industrial enterprise was relatively new in the nineteenth century; it lacked the deep historical roots of landholding.[35]

Bohlen uses this theory to explain his perception that the rule in *Rylands v Fletcher* did not particularly catch on as a general principle in American law. He says this reflects fundamental differences in society and culture. He says the *Rylands* decision did not match well with American society – a heavily capitalist-oriented economy living in a country that had rebelled against what they saw as an anachronistic, aristocratic government structure in England.[36]

He uses this theory to explain the use of the concept of 'non-natural use' in *Rylands*. He opines that the English law traditionally protected natural uses of land, particularly agriculture and farming, as part of its reification of property rights. This is why, Bohlen states, the court in *Rylands* confined the principle of liability for escape from land to situations involving 'non-natural use'.[37] Others have drawn similar conclusions.[38]

In contrast, Molloy flatly denies the Bohlen thesis. Acknowledging that it had been 'almost universally accepted both at home and abroad', Molloy proceeds to dismantle it:

> Bohlen's thesis … that the English judges were drawn from the upper landed aristocracy is not true of the judges in this particular case [*Rylands v Fletcher*], nor indeed of the bar at a whole, either during the period immediately in question, namely the 1960s, or during the entire Victorian era at the very least. English barristers as a class have not been recruited from the landed gentry but rather from the middle and lower middle classes … offices in the army, the church and the state, particularly in the diplomatic corps, have attracted members of the aristocracy. Judges, on the other hand, have traditionally been recruited from those barristers who have achieved especial success and prominence at the bar.[39]

[34] ibid, 325.

[35] ibid, 323.

[36] ibid, 319.

[37] Francis Bohlen, 'Rule in *Rylands v Fletcher*' (1911) 59 *University of Pennsylvania Law Review* 423, 444. Earlier, I posited that the concept of non-natural use related to the traditional defence of Act of God because that had traditionally been defined in terms of natural events, for which a defendant would not generally be held responsible.

[38] W Friedmann, 'Modern Trends in the Law of Torts' (1937) 1 *Modern Law Review* 39, 51, states that *Rylands v Fletcher* was 'decided in a period of social development when the predominance of a landed gentry was already on the wane but the standard of social values as applied by the judges was still that of the vanishing society'.

[39] Robert Thomas Molloy, '*Fletcher v Rylands* – A Re-examination of Juristic Origins' (1942) 9 *University of Chicago Law Review* 266, 271. He accuses Bohlen and others of 'generalizing on the basis of insufficient evidence' (289), before stating that Dean Pound exhibits a 'not unusual proclivity for brilliant generalization without due regard for the necessary factual basis' (290).

Molloy then proceeds to consider the life circumstances and careers of the 11 judges who rendered a decision in the *Rylands* litigation. He says no conclusions can be drawn about the favouring of pastoral interests over other interests based on family wealth or circumstances, social connections, or indeed religion or career history. He concludes that, in direct contrast with Bohlen's theory, the English judiciary of the mid-nineteenth century was filled with 'patently self-made men'.[40]

It is easy to assert that particular judges were influenced by their upbringing, their class, or social networks or connections. The problem with such assertions is in obtaining the proof of such influences.[41] Thus, it is considered that Bohlen's suggestions do merit serious consideration, especially in the context of a class-based society inherent in England in the nineteenth century. However, it is very difficult to see, in the actual decisions themselves in this area, evidence that this was actually a factor in how cases were decided. If the bias does in fact exist, it exists at the subconscious level, and there is little textual basis to support the assertion. Now, a wider look at the tort liability of landholders might have been instructive. In particular, the past reluctance of courts to find property owners liable to any trespassers, even when the trespassers were children who had ventured onto (unfenced) land, only to be struck by trains running through the land, might provide support for an assertion that (some) judges might have been overly defensive of the rights of property owners because they were in that class themselves.[42]

In the end, the road of a critical legal scholar is a hard one. It is hard to go beyond the record and seek to determine rationales and motivating influences that are unexpressed and for which little evidence is available, one way or the other. It is simplistic to draw conclusions about all judges of a particular era. Then, as now, judges are highly individual, each with their own life experiences, circumstances, values, influences and principles. In the end, an assertion that judges of a particular era were sympathetic to property interests can amount to little more than conjecture. And Molloy's work is significant in terms of exploding stereotypes about judges coming from well-to-do backgrounds, including the particular individuals involved in determining the *Rylands* litigation, and that this explained their reverence for property rights.

Further, the suggestion that the nineteenth-century courts preferred landowners and had disdain for mercantile activity is somewhat hard to square with some very harsh doctrines of tort law in the nineteenth century clearly favouring business, for instance the so-called 'unholy trinity' of common employment,

[40] ibid, 285; see for similar criticism GHL Fridman, 'The Rise and Fall of *Rylands v Fletcher*' (1956) 34 *Canadian Bar Review* 810, 812: 'Bohlen's approach is in fact a fanciful attempt at recreating or re-interpreting legal history'.

[41] Donal Nolan says there is no evidence to support Bohlen's theory: 'The Principle of *Rylands v Fletcher*' in Carolyn Sappideen and Prue Vines (eds), *Fleming's Law of Torts* (10th edn, Lawbook Co, 2011) 386.

[42] eg *Robert Addie & Sons Collieries v Dumbreck* [1929] AC 358 (HL).

volenti non fit injuria and contributory negligence as providing (originally) a complete defence to any action by an injured worker against a business.[43]

Then-Recent Disasters Involving Collapsing Dams

AWB Simpson posits quite a different theory regarding the decision in *Rylands v Fletcher*.[44] His theory is that it was disasters involving failing dams that had occurred in the years leading up to the *Rylands* litigation that explain the courts' application of strict liability to find in favour of the plaintiff. His views have attracted judicial support.[45]

He documents the failure of a dam in Holmfirth, Yorkshire, in 1852. The dam had been constructed under a private Act of Parliament, apparently to service various woollen mills in the area. Simpson notes 105 commissioners were appointed to raise the money necessary to construct eight dams, and to carry out the construction. At least one of the dams had been poorly designed and maintained, and after heavy rain a wall of the dam collapsed. As a result, a nearby valley was flooded, resulting in the loss of 78 lives and significant damage to property and livelihoods. No civil litigation arose as a result of this disaster; the public raised money to pay some compensation to affected families.

A second disaster occurred in 1863, after the *Rylands* litigation had been commenced, but prior to it being determined in the Exchequer Chamber. The Dale Dyke embankment, including the Bradfield reservoir, had been constructed by the Sheffield Waterworks Company under private legislation in 1830, with extensions to it authorised by subsequent enactment in 1845 and 1853. The 1853 enactment, made after the Holmfirth disaster, stated that the company constructing the reservoir would pay compensation to those who were injured or otherwise suffered damage as a result of the failure of the dam. It did not specifically state whether such liability was strict or based on negligence. As the dam began to fill, cracks began to appear in its walls, and it failed. The resulting torrent of water that was released killed at least 238 people and also caused significant property damage. Those injured sought legal advice as to whether they could obtain compensation. There was media and parliamentary pressure in relation to providing relief for victims. As a result, legislation was passed in 1864 making it clear that those injured by the disaster could obtain compensation without regard to proof of fault. There were also attempts to introduce legislation applicable to reservoir owners generally, effectively imposing strict liability upon them, but these attempts failed.

[43] *Priestly v Fowler* (1837) 3 M & W 1; 150 ER 1030; *Butterfield v Forrester* (1809) 11 East 60; 103 ER 926.

[44] AWB Simpson, 'Legal Liability for Bursting Reservoirs: The Historical Context of *Rylands v Fletcher*' (1984) 13 *Journal of Legal Studies* 209.

[45] *Transco Plc v Stockport Metropolitan Borough Council* [2004] 2 AC 1, 7 (Lord Bingham), 16 (Lord Hoffmann) and 38 (Lord Walker).

Simpson summarises his position thus:

> The position reached by the common law [in *Rylands*] coincided with that imposed by parliament in the Acts of 1863 and 1864 on the Sheffield Waterworks Company at least in relation to the Dale Dyke dam … the coincidence between the position at common law and the position under these and other statutes containing strict liability clauses was, I should suggest, not accidental, and in the context in which *Rylands v Fletcher* was decided, must have seemed to make good sense. The legislation of 1853 and 1864, though relating only to a particular Waterworks Company, may well have been viewed by the judges who favoured Fletcher's claim as expressing a general legislative policy.[46]

This is an interesting, and potentially plausible, explanation for the decision. Again, we need to test the hypothesis with evidence, to try to take the idea beyond that of mere conjecture. Simpson presents one express part of the judgment that might be supportive. Blackburn J is explaining the liability of the owners of an alkali works, and how they had been held liable for the health consequences of an escape of chlorine from their premises, although they had taken reasonable steps to prevent it. He was seeking to analogise it with the case before him. But his choice of words is interesting, as *Simpson* notes. He says that

> there is no difference in this respect between chlorine and water; both will, if they escape, do damage, the one by scorching, *and the other by drowning*, and he who brings them there must at his peril see that they do not escape and do that mischief (emphasis added).[47]

Of course, that passage is interesting because of its reference to drowning, when the facts of *Rylands* clearly did not involve such an event, yet the earlier reservoir collapses did. Thus, there is some textual support in the judgment for the thesis of Simpson.

Further, the subsequent course of events might also support Simpson's theory. His article documents how Justice Blackburn and Baron Bramwell would turn away from principles of strict liability in later decisions.[48] This might again suggest that there were immediate imperatives at the time they rendered their decisions in 1865 and 1866 which had faded in importance somewhat in later years, minimising their adherence to and support for strict liability principles in the face of different factual contexts.

A detailed consideration of the extent to which statute law has and does influence the common law is clearly beyond the scope of the present work.

[46] AWB Simpson, 'Legal Liability for Bursting Reservoirs: The Historical Context of *Rylands v Fletcher*' (1984) 13 *Journal of Legal Studies* 209, 251–52.

[47] *Fletcher v Rylands* (1866) LR 1 Ex. 265, 286 (Blackburn J, for the Court).

[48] AWB Simpson, 'Legal Liability for Bursting Reservoirs: The Historical Context of *Rylands v Fletcher*' (1984) 13 *Journal of Legal Studies* 209, 258–60.

However, evidently the common law has been, and continues to be, influenced by statute law, as seen in case law.[49] There is significant conjecture and discussion in the literature.[50]

Dangerousness

Another theory arising from the decision in *Rylands v Fletcher* was that it was the concept of dangerousness that animated the particular rule. There is some basis for this in the wording of the decision. Blackburn J did not use the word dangerous, instead preferring the concept of something 'likely to do mischief if it escapes'.[51] Lord Cairns also uses the phrasing of something the defendant 'knows will be mischievous if it gets on his neighbour's (property)'.[52]

It is not precisely known from whence this concept of something likely to do mischief if it escapes emanated. This phrasing is not evident in the cases which

[49] eg *Erven Warnink Besloten Vennootschap v J Townsend & Sons (Hull) Ltd* [1979] AC 731, 743: 'where over a period of years there can be discerned a steady trend in legislation which reflects the view of successive parliaments as to what the public interest demands in a particular field of law, development of the common law in that part of the same field which has been left to it ought to proceed upon a parallel rather than a diverging course' (Lord Diplock); *Malik v Bank of Credit & Commerce International SA* [1998] AC 20, 52–53 (Lord Steyn); *Johnson v Unisys Ltd* [2003] 1 AC 518, 539: 'the common law has adapted itself to the new attitudes, proceeding sometimes by analogy with statutory rights' (Lord Hoffmann). The High Court of Australia has referred to the 'symbiotic' relationship between statute and the common law (*Commonwealth Bank of Australia v Barker* (2014) 253 CLR 169, 183 (French CJ, Bell and Keane JJ)). In seeking to justify, in my respectful view unpersuasively, a new view of the common law doctrine regarding penalties in contracts, the High Court of Australia referred to remedial consumer law legislation, before adding that 'this pattern of remedial legislation suggests the need for caution in dealing with the unwritten law as if laissez faire notions of an untrammelled "freedom of contract" provide a universal legal value': *Andrews v ANZ Banking Group Ltd* (2012) 247 CLR 205, 215–16 (French CJ, Gummow, Crennan, Kiefel and Bell JJ). The suggestion seems to be that the common law should be influenced by statute law in that broad area of law, though elsewhere the High Court has determinedly clung to common law principles clearly at variance with relevant statutory provisions: *Voth v Manildra Flour Mills Pty Ltd* (1991) 171 CLR 538.

[50] Robert Williams, 'Statutes as Sources of Law Beyond Their Terms in Common-Law Cases' (1982) 50 *George Washington Law Review* 554, 599: 'the common law [should be understood] not as a body of law whose change is impeded or blocked by a static body of statutory rules, but as a process best served by the rational integration of judge-made and legislative law'; see for further discussion Jack Beatson, 'The Role of Statute in the Development of Common Law Doctrine' (2001) 117 *Law Quarterly Review* 247; JF Burrows, 'The Interrelation Between Common Law and Statute' (1976) 3 *Otago Law Review* 583; Roscoe Pound, 'Common Law and Legislation' (1908) 21 *Harvard Law Review* 383; Harlan Stone, 'The Common Law in the United States' (1936) 50 *Harvard Law Review* 4; Caleb Nelson, 'State and Federal Models of the Interaction Between Statutes and Unwritten Law' (2013) 80 *University of Chicago Law Review* 657.

[51] *Fletcher v Rylands* (1866) LR 1 Ex. 265, 279.

[52] *Rylands v Fletcher* (1868) 3 HL 330, 340. William Stallybrass, 'Dangerous Things and the Non-Natural User of Land' (1929) 3 *Cambridge Law Journal* 376, 387–88: 'in every case the question really is: was the risk one which the defendant was entitled to take only on condition of paying compensation to those injured thereby irrespective of any negligence on his part? And the answer to that question will not depend on whether the thing in question was dangerous per se, but upon whether it was dangerous in the circumstance of the particular case'.

might be compared with the factual scenario in *Rylands*, such as cattle trespass or fire. In any event, it seemed to have been taken to indicate that if activity were considered 'dangerous', then a special rule of strict liability might be applied. This is somewhat difficult to defend. The decision occurred at a time when the courts were readily viewing legislation authorising railway activity, for example, to mean that their owners would only be liable for 'escaping' sparks in cases of negligence.[53] Evidently, the concept of 'dangerousness' had not maintained a strict liability principle there. It would be difficult to apply to cases involving personal injury. Further, many cases at the time involved highway accidents. Was using the highway a 'dangerous' activity, which justified the imposition of *Rylands* strict liability? Most would surely accept that the use of a public thoroughfare was, or could be, dangerous. If the response is that the concept of 'dangerousness' was to be confined to escape from land, there are two responses. The first is that, as noted above, many took the *Rylands* case to be establishing a general principle, not one confined to damage to property interests. The second is that it can be hard to defend at a conceptual level why dangerousness is relevant to determining cases involving property interests, but it is apparently not relevant to determining cases involving personal injury.[54] Surely, if anything, dangerousness is more likely to be relevant to factual circumstances involving personal injury than property, rather than the other way around.

Fridman's theory is that the concept of 'dangerousness' in effect accommodated growing trends in the late nineteenth century to base liability on fault concepts.[55] In other words, it was in a sense blameworthy for the landowner to bring something dangerous onto their land. Though there was no suggestion they were negligent in the escape of the dangerous thing from their land, it was their introduction of the thing that was not naturally there that meant their actions were to some extent blameworthy and worthy of legal sanction. Fridman says that this idea is behind Lord Cairns' judgment in *Rylands* and its references to 'non-natural user', though it is less evident in the judgment of Blackburn J, with which the House of Lords agreed.

Nolan states that while at one time the concept of dangerousness was appealing in tort law, it became dated as the complexity of industrial society grew, where advances in technology generally made activity safer. He opines that the concept might betray an outmoded view of technological advance as 'alien and threatening'.[56]

[53] *Vaughan v Taff Vale Railway Co* (1860) 5 H & N 679; 157 ER 1351.

[54] Donal Nolan, 'The Distinctiveness of *Rylands v Fletcher*' (2005) 121 *Law Quarterly Review* 421, 440, calls it 'indefensible'.

[55] GHL Fridman, 'The Rise and Fall of *Rylands v Fletcher*' (1956) 34 *Canadian Bar Review* 810, 815. Some support for this position appears in *Read v J Lyons and Co Limited* [1947] AC 156, 174 where Lord Macmillan, noting Blackburn J's statement that the plaintiff must bear the loss unless they can point to some default on the part of the defendant, said 'his decision for the plaintiff would thus logically seem to imply that he found some default on the part of the defendants in bringing on their land and failing to confine there an exceptional quantity of water'.

[56] Donal Nolan, 'The Distinctiveness of *Rylands v Fletcher*' (2005) 121 *Law Quarterly Review* 421, 448.

It is a matter of record that in *Read v J Lyons and Co Ltd*,[57] members of the House of Lords would turn against any suggestion that *Rylands v Fletcher* supported imposition of strict liability on a general basis in respect of particular instances where a defendant was engaged in 'dangerous' or 'extra-hazardous' activity.[58] This decision will be discussed below. To some extent Lord Bingham again seemed to revive this concept as being of critical importance in *Rylands* liability in *Transco Plc v Stockport Metropolitan Borough Council*,[59] also to be discussed below.

It would seem that these suggestions of a broader principle based on such notions would find acceptance only in the United States. This will also be considered in more detail in Chapter 4.

Precedent-Based Throwback, Traditional Privileging of Property Interests Over Protection from Personal Injury

Others proffer a simpler explanation. They say that the decision simply reflects a throwback to an earlier, medieval, time of strict liability. We saw in Part I many examples in many areas of the law of tort where liability in the absence of fault was imposed. Some simply regard *Rylands* as an application of these old rules. Fridman, for instance, states that the precedent was not designed to inhibit industrial growth. Rather, it was simply based on the 'medieval idea that a man acts at his peril. It was a moral idea, not an economic one'.[60] Nolan agrees with this analysis.[61] Fridman says that at least until near the end of the nineteenth century, the law privileged property interests over protection for personal injury, and this explains the differential treatment of damage to property interests,[62] including liability for cattle trespass, common carrier strict liability for cargo and for fire, in contrast to how the law treated personal injury damage, where proof of fault was typically required.[63]

There is considered to be some truth in Fridman's comments. It is somewhat anomalous that the liability of common carriers was strict in respect of cargo, but not in respect of personal injury. This doctrine clearly supports Fridman's view. On the other hand, contrary to Fridman's assertions, as noted in Chapter 1, there were numerous suggestions prior to *Rylands* that damage to property interests was

[57] *Read v J Lyons and Co Ltd* [1947] AC 156.

[58] ibid, 172 (Lord Macmillan), 181–82 (Lord Simonds) and 186 (Lord Uthwatt).

[59] *Transco Plc v Stockport Metropolitan Borough Council* [2004] 2 AC 1, 11 (with whom Lord Walker agreed) (39).

[60] GHL Fridman, 'The Rise and Fall of *Rylands v Fletcher*' (1956) 34 *Canadian Bar Review* 810, 812.

[61] Donal Nolan, 'The Distinctiveness of *Rylands v Fletcher*' (2005) 121 *Law Quarterly Review* 421, 445: 'the decision in the original case is most plausibly explained as a survival of the general principle of liability recognised by the medieval common law, namely that a man acts at his peril'.

[62] GHL Fridman, 'The Rise and Fall of *Rylands v Fletcher*' (1956) 34 *Canadian Bar Review* 810, 813.

[63] In *Benning v Wong* (1969) 122 CLR 249, 319 Windeyer J noted 'the movement of the common law … away from any preoccupation it may once have had with the protection of rights in land'.

only actionable on proof of fault. And there were numerous suggestions prior to *Rylands* that liability for causing personal injury was actionable without proof of fault. Liability for animals known to be dangerous was strict – this was personal injury. The liability of innkeepers was strict, and this could be for damage to property or to person. Thus, though there is some truth in what Fridman says, there is also historical evidence to the contrary of what he asserts.

The New Hampshire Supreme Court proffered the following explanation of the rules of strict liability:

> They were certainly introduced in England at an immature stage of English jurisprudence, and an undeveloped state of agriculture, manufacture and commerce, when the nation had not settled down to those modern, progressive, industrial pursuits which the spirit of the common law adapted to all conditions of society, encourages and defends. They were introduced when the development of many of the rational rules now universally recognized as principles of the common law had not been demanded by the growth of intelligence, trade and productive enterprise – when the common law had not been set forth in the precedents, as a coherent and logical system on many subjects other than the tenures of real estate.[64]

Enterprise Risk-Type Philosophy

Some who apparently support the imposition of strict liability of the type exemplified by *Rylands v Fletcher* seem to do so on the basis of a kind of enterprise risk philosophy. This is the sentiment that a business organisation should be liable for the risks that it creates, regardless of proof of negligence.[65] Lord Hoffmann alludes to this rationale:

> It is tempting to see, beneath the surface of the rule, a policy of requiring the costs of a commercial enterprise to be internalised; to require the entrepreneur to provide, by insurance or otherwise, for the risks to others which his enterprise creates. That was certainly the opinion of Bramwell B [in the Exchequer Chamber decision] … others … considered that the public interest in promoting economic development made it unreasonable to hold an entrepreneur liable when he had not been negligent … with hindsight *Rylands v Fletcher* can be seen as an isolated victory for the internalisers. The following century saw a steady refusal to treat it as laying down any broad principle of liability.[66]

As Lord Hoffmann pointed out in *Transco*, the enterprise risk theory possibly buttressing *Rylands* was not comprehensive. It could not explain why defendants

[64] *Brown v Collins* 53 NH 442 (1873) (Doe J).

[65] John Murphy, 'The Merits of *Rylands v Fletcher*' (2004) 24(4) *Oxford Journal of Legal Studies* 643, 665, who, after asking whether the rule in *Rylands* was 'positively a good thing', stated that 'those who create risks by means of activities undertaken with a view to personal gain should, on principle, be held strictly accountable for any harm thereby caused'.

[66] *Transco Plc v Stockport Metropolitan Borough Council* [2004] 2 AC 1, 16.

in such cases could rely on defences like Act of God or, subsequently to the original decision, acts of a third party. Under a true enterprise risk model, such defences would be irrelevant. He noted that in UK legislation imposing strict liability, neither of these was a good defence.[67] Nolan agrees, stating that if an enterprise risk model were taken to its logical conclusion the result would be absolute, rather than merely strict, liability.[68]

This theory will be considered in more detail in Part III of the book.

Reciprocal Risks

For completeness, it should be noted that some American scholars argue in favour of strict liability in cases where one party imposes a non-reciprocal risk upon another.[69] They agree with negligence principles where parties impose roughly equal risks upon another, but claim that in cases of unbalanced imposition of risks, strict liability is preferable. They support the decision in *Rylands* on the basis that the defendant was imposing a non-reciprocal risk upon the plaintiff.[70] This concept is explored more in Chapter 5. It has not been the express basis of any court decision of which I am aware.

Subsequent UK Decisions

The limits of the liability of a defendant for something that escaped from their land would soon be tested. One early example was *Nichols v Marsland*.[71] There the defendant kept a number of ornamental pools on their property. The pools had been created by the damming of a natural watercourse that flowed through the defendant's property, and subsequently onto the plaintiff's property. After a heavy rainfall event, the walls of the pools collapsed, and a large volume of water descended into the watercourse and onto the plaintiff's land, flooding it. The plaintiff brought an action against the defendant. There was no allegation of negligence in how the ornamental pools were constructed or maintained.

All members of the court rejected the plaintiff's case. With respect, the reasoning is somewhat convoluted and confused. The court needed to distinguish the case from *Rylands* in order to dismiss the case. The Court of Exchequer did this

[67] ibid, 17.

[68] Donal Nolan, 'The Distinctiveness of *Rylands v Fletcher*' (2005) 121 *Law Quarterly Review* 421, 445.

[69] George Fletcher, 'Fairness and Utility in Tort Theory' (1972) 85 *Harvard Law Review* 537.

[70] Keith Hylton, 'The Theory of Tort Doctrine and the *Restatement (Third) of Torts*' (2001) 54 *Vanderbilt Law Review* 1413, 'Fletcher's reciprocal risk theory seems to … provide a good explanation of the *Rylands* doctrine'.

[71] *Nichols v Marsland* (1875) LR 10 Ex. 255; (1876) 2 Ex. 1.

in a different way from the Court of Appeal. The Court of Exchequer judgment seemed at times to be grappling with fault issues: 'what has the defendant done wrong … it is not the defendant who let loose the water and sent it to destroy the bridges … why is the defendant liable if some agent over which she has no control lets the water out?'[72]

Obviously, this is somewhat anomalous in a factual scenario with clear similarities to the actual situation in *Rylands*, when strict liability principles, rather than fault-based principles, were at play. The court's mention of *control* is also interesting. That concept does not appear in the judgment of the Court of Exchequer or the House of Lords decision in *Rylands*. The court deals with the *Rylands* precedent curtly, claiming that in that case 'the defendant poured the water into the plaintiff's mine'.[73] The judgment also refers to the question of the reasonableness of the defendant's use of their property, and whether it was 'beneficial to the community'.[74]

On appeal, the language is quite different, though the decision is the same. The Court of Appeal applies the 'Act of God' defence – the severity of the downpour was an Act of God, and this was the effective cause of the plaintiff's loss. As the Court of Appeal pithily put it, 'it is the last drop which makes the cup overflow'.[75] There is no recognition of the fact that if the cup had not been full prior to the downpour, it may not have overflowed. Or that the cup being there in the first place perhaps led to a greater volume of water within a given time frame than if the only water on the plaintiff's premises had been that from the watercourse flowing. There is some sense in this decision of a pulling back from the inflexibility of strict liability, particularly in the Court of Exchequer judgment. The court could simply have based the decision purely on the concept of Act of God, as the Court of Appeal did, which would have been well within the *Rylands* reasoning. It was one of the exceptions to the strict liability rule specifically acknowledged by Blackburn J, after all. However, the decision of the Court of Exchequer in *Nichols* was clearly broader than a strict liability approach of *Rylands* would contemplate, asking what the defendant had done wrong, and referring to concepts of control. It also seemed to incorporate a requirement of reasonable foreseeability[76] not expressly evident in *Rylands* itself.[77]

Similar reasoning is found in a contemporaneous decision involving a third party's reservoir flooding the property of the defendant, which in turn then flooded that of the plaintiff.[78] The court found for the defendant on the basis of an

[72] (1875) LR 10 Ex. 255, 259 (Baron Bramwell, for Kelly CB and Cleasby BB).

[73] ibid, 260.

[74] ibid, 260.

[75] (1876) 2 Ex. 1, 6 (Mellish LJ, for Cockburn CJ James and Baggallay JJ).

[76] Mellish LJ, for the Court of Appeal, noted that the flood 'could not reasonably have been anticipated': ibid, 6.

[77] Blackburn J had referred to liability for the 'natural consequences' of the escape: *Fletcher v Rylands* (1866) LR 1 Ex. 265, 285.

[78] *Box v Jubb* (1879) 4 Ex. 76.

exception to *Rylands* (which did not appear in the *Rylands* judgment itself) based on acts of a third party effectively causing the plaintiff's loss. Again, the court rhetorically asks: 'what is the cause of the overflow? Was it anything for which the defendants are responsible – did it proceed from their act or default, or from that of a stranger over which they had no control?'[79] The court held the defendant was guilty of no relevant act or default, and they had no control over the third party, so they should not be held responsible.

The concept of what a non-natural use was would also become strained. So in *Wilson v Waddell*,[80] the case involved the lessees of adjoining coal mines. The defendant's mine was situated much higher than the plaintiff's. As a result, water from the defendant's mine would naturally descend onto the plaintiff's land, unless prevented from doing so by soil or other material. Originally, the soil above the coal in the ground on the defendant's land was hard, such that water which fell upon it would typically run off, causing no damage to the plaintiff's premises. However, in the course of the defendant mining their land, this soil was removed. As a result of this activity, the surface of the land sank. When rain fell, it then ran quickly from the defendant's land onto that of the plaintiff. It would not have done so if the defendant had not mined the land in the way outlined.

The House of Lords rejected the plaintiff's claim. It found that the only way in which the defendant could access the coal on its premises was to remove the soil. There was no legal obligation on them to replace it once removed. The House reasoned that the defendant's activity amounted to a 'natural course of user of minerals'. Some might be perplexed about mining being considered to be a 'natural' use of land. Perhaps the case highlighted the difficulties in trying to distinguish between what was a natural use of land and what was a non-natural use.

In contrast, the court found that a defendant's construction of a mound on their property comprising soil, clay, limestone and refuse was an 'artificial work'. The mound had the effect of causing rainfall falling onto the defendant's property to seep into that of the neighbouring plaintiff's property. The court found the defendant liable for this on the basis of *Rylands*, on the basis their mound was an 'artificial' work, presumably making it a non-natural use and thus attracting *Rylands* strict liability.[81]

The House of Lords reconsidered *Rylands v Fletcher* liability in *Rickards v Lothian*.[82] There the plaintiff suffered damage when water flowed from the defendant's portion of a building. There was evidence that an unknown person had for some reason turned on a tap on the defendant's premises and blocked up other pathways by which the water might have escaped, leading to the plaintiff's premises being flooded. The factual scenario appears somewhat similar to that in *Box v Jubb*, involving the actions of a third party in effect causing damage to the

[79] ibid, 79 (Kelly CB).
[80] *Wilson v Waddell* (1876) 2 AC 95.
[81] *Hurdman v North Eastern Railway Company* (1878) 3 CPD 168 (CA).
[82] *Rickards v Lothian* [1913] AC 263.

plaintiff, though the menacing 'thing' which escaped (in both cases water) came from the defendant's premises. As in *Box*, the court rejected the plaintiff's claim. Again, it is noted that the decision of Blackburn J did not on terms express an exception in relation to acts of a third party; it referred merely to 'acts of God or vis major', which are taken to refer to acts of nature. Clearly, what occurred here was not an Act of God or vis major, as those terms are commonly understood.

Yet the House of Lords denied that the defendant was liable. It expressly distinguished the current case from the *Rylands* precedent.[83] In so stating its view, it again referred to concepts of fault in considering a matter of supposedly strict liability: 'A defendant cannot … be properly said to have caused or allowed the water to escape if the malicious act of a third person was the real cause of its escaping without any fault on the part of the defendant'.[84] With respect, these passages are somewhat confusing in discussing concepts of fault in relation to a doctrine of supposedly strict liability. Surely, the thrust of *Rylands* was that the owner of the property from which the dangerous thing 'escaped' was liable regardless of 'fault', or (at least, according to Fridman), fault only in the sense that they brought the dangerous 'thing' onto their land. Water supply through pipes was clearly not naturally there. The defendant did not construct the actual water pipes themselves, so did not personally bring the dangerous thing onto the property. However, they might have been said to have taken on this responsibility/liability by purchasing the property. In other words, there were significant analogies between the facts of this case and that in *Rylands*, which might have justified application of the *Rylands* principle. It may have been that the House of Lords thought it unjust to impose liability upon the defendant in this particular case. In hindsight, the court might have seen a larger point – that application of strict liability principles of the kind espoused in *Rylands* does, or can, lead to outcomes that are unacceptably unjust – by imposing liability on a defendant who in no sensible way is to blame for the injury or damage suffered by the defendant. This might have led the House of Lords in 1913 to make a stand, rejecting the strict liability for which *Rylands* apparently stood as the leading contemporary authority, apparently espousing a broad principle, though of uncertain scope. Instead, the House of Lords did not tackle the problem 'head on'; rather it found an escape route by distinguishing the factual scenario from that in *Rylands*. However, in the process it muddied the waters considerably, by introducing fault into a concept that was said to be no-fault.

With respect, the comments of the House of Lords in *Rickards* regarding the concept of non-natural use are also confusing. Recall that the judgment of

[83] 'The present case is distinguished from that of *Rylands v Fletcher* in this, that it is not the act of the defendant in keeping this reservoir, an act in itself lawful, which alone leads to the escape of the water, and so renders wrongful that which but for such escape would have been lawful. It is the supervening vis major of the water caused by the flood, which, superadded to the water in the reservoir (which of itself would have been innocuous) causes the disaster. A defendant cannot … be properly said to have caused or allowed the water to escape, if the Act of God or the Queen's enemies was the real cause of its escaping without any fault on the part of the defendant' (277–78, Lord Moulton, for the House).

[84] ibid, 278 (Lord Moulton, for the House).

Blackburn J in *Rylands* had applied strict liability to cases involving something on the defendant's land that was not naturally there. In the House of Lords, Lord Cairns distinguished between natural and non-natural uses of the land. Lord Cranworth connected a natural use with the traditional tort defence of Act of God, though it is not entirely clear that Lord Cairns or the Court of Exchequer Chamber meant it in that sense in *Rylands*.

In *Rickards*, the House of Lords states that the *Rylands* principle only applies 'To some special use (of land) bringing with it increased danger to others, and must not merely be the ordinary use of the land or such as is proper for the general benefit of the community'.[85] This is considered to be an attempted significant refinement of the *Rylands* principle. As noted above, none of the decisions in *Rylands* actually refer to the word 'dangerous' or 'dangerousness'. Virtually anything can be dangerous in at least some circumstances.[86] A person who builds a house on their land brings increased danger to others because the house might collapse. A person who plants a tree on their land brings increased danger to others because the tree might fall. A person who builds a pool or a reservoir, or who dams water on a watercourse, brings increased danger to others because they might fail, or they might cause pooling of water in such a way as is dangerous. Thus, (no pun intended) it is dangerous to try to construct a generalised principle of strict liability, after the event at that, on the basis of whether or not an activity is dangerous.[87]

Further, reference to both of the concepts of dangerousness and non-ordinary use of the land within the one sentence above leads to the danger of conflating the two concepts. To be clear, they are and must remain separate requirements.[88] The fact something is dangerous says nothing about whether it is an ordinary use or not.

The House of Lords refers to an 'ordinary use of the land'. With respect, this is confusing and uncertain. Is the construction of a reservoir on a rural property an ordinary use of the land? One might have thought so. Is mining an ordinary use to be determined? When a commercial building is constructed, is this an ordinary use? Does it matter that at one time, the land was used for agricultural purposes? Or can the 'ordinary use' of land change over time? Whether or not something is an ordinary use of the land is arguably quite distinct from the question of whether something was 'not naturally there', which was the phrasing used in *Rylands v Fletcher*.[89] It is perhaps unfortunate and significant that the headnote of

[85] ibid, 280 (Lord Moulton, for the House).

[86] *Read v J Lyons and Co Limited* [1947] AC 156, 172 (Lord Macmillan).

[87] *cf* John Murphy, 'The Merits of *Rylands v Fletcher*' (2004) 24(4) *Oxford Journal of Legal Studies* 643, 659: 'there is a good deal to commend the contention that whoever undertakes or authorizes potentially injurious activities should be strictly liable for any ensuing mishaps'.

[88] WTS Stallybrass, 'Dangerous Things and the Non-Natural User of Land' (1929) 3 *Cambridge Law Journal* 376, 395–96.

[89] FH Newark, 'Non-Natural User and *Rylands v Fletcher*' (1961) 24 *Modern Law Review* 557, 569–71 discussing a number of cases prior to *Rickards v Lothian* where the requirement of non-natural use had apparently been substituted by a requirement of non-ordinary use.

the *Rylands* decision in the House of Lords uses the phrase 'ordinary use' without an apparent awareness that what is an ordinary use may be broader in scope than something that was not naturally on the defendant's premises. The two concepts may overlap, but occupy different spheres.

We also see some utilitarian-type reasoning creeping in, with the House of Lords' reference to whether activity is for the 'general benefit of the community'. Again, there is no reference to this at all in the judgments in *Rylands*. There is a reference to it in the Exchequer judgment in *Nicholas v Marsland*, though not the Court of Appeal decision in that case. Would this mean that, in the factual context in *Rylands*, if the same facts held the landowner would be liable on the basis of strict liability, but if they permitted nearby landowners to also take water from their reservoir (as was the case with some of the reservoirs built in England in the nineteenth century), they might not be, because the reservoir was for the 'general benefit of the community'. It is not clear that a principle of supposedly strict liability can accommodate such notions. But again, this is an example of the judges trying to introduce flexibility into a strict liability doctrine that does not readily yield such flexibility. Again, in hindsight it appears to be the court straining against the kind of strait-jacketing into which strict liability doctrines force them. However, the courts have the power, but decline to exercise it, to simply overthrow the doctrine altogether. Instead, (respectfully) they take the low road of introducing distinctions and exceptions which simply create more uncertainty and confusion into an already muddy pool. The underlying tension between the forces of strict liability, and the forces of fault-based liability, is not resolved.

In contrast, the factual scenario in *Read v J Lyons and Company Limited*[90] was relatively easy to resolve, in terms of the applicability of the *Rylands* doctrine. Of more interest in this case were the obiter dicta comments about the *Rylands* principle. The case involved the plaintiff being injured while engaged in a government inspection of a munitions factory. A shell exploded while in the course of manufacture, injuring her. She brought an action against the owners of the factory. This was primarily based on *Rylands v Fletcher*. There was no evidence that the explosion was caused by the negligence of the owners of the factory or their employees. All judges determined that the *Rylands* principle did not apply to the facts because there had been no 'escape' from the premises of the defendant, which was the factual context for the *Rylands* precedent, and was important in how the judgments in this case had espoused the general principle for which the case was (in)famous.

That said, several of the judgments clearly reflect dissatisfaction with the *Rylands v Fletcher* principle. Several pointed out the difficulties with the concept of the meaning of a non-natural use of land.[91] Viscount Simon pointed out the

[90] *Read v J Lyons and Company Limited* [1947] AC 156.
[91] ibid, 166 (Viscount Simon).

anomaly where Blackburn J had sought to deduce a general principle of strict liability from cases such as cattle trespass that was supposedly based on things not naturally there, whereas the grazing of livestock was clearly an ordinary, not non-natural, use of land.[92] He denied there was any general principle that united the disparate pockets of strict liability in the law. He agreed with another judge that if the principle in *Rylands* were taken to its logical conclusion 'it would be a very oppressive decision'.[93] Several of the judges left open the question whether *Rylands* liability could attach with respect to personal injury, as opposed to damage to property interests.[94] Several judges denied that the *Rylands* case should stand as a general principle favouring the imposition of strict liability in situations involving activity that was 'dangerous' or 'ultra-hazardous'.[95] This has been noted as the most important feature of the decision.[96] The judgments also reflect difficulties with interpretation to be given to non-natural use, with some judges suggesting that a munitions factories might not meet the definition of such a use.[97] Their Honours might have felt, but resisted, a temptation to reform this area of the law.[98]

Further dissatisfaction with the *Rylands* doctrine appeared in the judgment of Megaw LJ in *Leakey v National Trust for Places of Historic Interest or Natural Beauty*.[99] The Law Commission investigated, and rejected, a suggestion that English law should adopt a general principle of strict liability for the consequences of activities considered to be 'dangerous' or 'ultra-hazardous'. It described the existing state of the law in this area in unflattering terms.[100]

[92] ibid, 166.

[93] ibid, 167.

[94] ibid, 178 (Lord Porter) and 181 (Lord Simonds); Lord Macmillan denied this (170–71) (though acknowledging an exception in relation to animals).

[95] ibid, 172 (Lord Macmillan) ('every activity in which man engages is fraught with some possible element of danger to others. Experience shows that even from acts apparently innocuous injury to others may result … it would be impractical to frame a legal classification of things as things dangerous and things not dangerous, attaching absolute liability in the case of the former but not in the case of the latter'); Lord Simonds (181–82): 'I would reject the idea that, if a man carries on a so-called ultra-hazardous activity on his premises, the line must be drawn so as to bring him within the limit of strict liability for its consequences to all men everywhere'; Lord Uthwatt (186): 'I do not think that the invitee, any more than the occupier, would assume that, by reason only of the dangerous nature of the business carried on, the occupier guaranteed him freedom from harm … I do not regard Rylands v Fletcher as laying down any principle other than a principle applicable between occupiers in respect of their land or as reflecting an aspect of some wider principle applicable to dangerous businesses or dangerous things'.

[96] John Fleming, *The Law of Torts* (8th edn, Lawbook Co, 1992) noted that 'the most damaging effect of the decision in *Read v J Lyons & Co Ltd* is that it prematurely stunted the development of a general theory of strict liability for ultrahazardous activities'. Of course, use of the word 'damaging' in that passage depends on one's perspective; see also Donal Nolan, 'The Principle of *Rylands v Fletcher*' in Carolyn Sappideen and Prue Vines (eds), *Fleming's Law of Torts* (10th edn, Lawbook Co, 2011) 392.

[97] *Read v J Lyons and Company Limited* [1947] AC 156, 170 (Viscount Simon) and 174 (Lord Macmillan).

[98] 'Your Lordships are not called upon to rationalize the law of England' (ibid, 175, Lord Macmillan).

[99] *Leakey v National Trust for Places of Historic Interest or Natural Beauty* [1980] QB 485, 519.

[100] Report of the Law Commission on Civil Liability for Dangerous Things and Activities (1970) (Law Commission No 32) p12, para 20(a).

Then came the important House of Lords decision in *Cambridge Water Co v Eastern Counties Leather Co.*[101] In that case a chemical used by the defendant in the course of treating leather seeped into the ground beneath. It was not known at the time that this chemical was dangerous to the environment. Further, unknown to anyone, it seeped into an aquifer beneath the defendant's premises. Eventually, it infected the water from which the plaintiff drew water through a bore almost two kilometres away. The plaintiff brought legal action against the defendant, making, among other claims, a claim based on *Rylands v Fletcher*. The claim succeeded in the Court of Appeal but was rejected by all members of the House of Lords.[102] Most importantly, in doing so the House reformulated the rule in *Rylands v Fletcher* as a sub-species of the tort of nuisance.[103] As such, it found that it was necessary for a plaintiff to succeed on this basis to demonstrate that the injury they suffered was of a kind that was reasonably foreseeable.[104] This would also have the effect of harmonising common law principle in this area. The court noted that this sentiment was apparent in the judgment of Blackburn J in that case.[105] Because in the view of the House the plaintiff's loss here was not of a kind that was reasonably foreseeable by someone in the position of the defendant, the plaintiff's claim on this basis failed. Lord Goff attempted to justify his assimilation of *Rylands v Fletcher* into the tort of private nuisance by arguing that the concepts of 'non-natural' user, in the context of *Rylands*, and the concept of 'reasonable user', in the context of private nuisance, shared a 'similarity of function'.[106]

Lord Goff considered and rejected a suggestion that a general principle could or should be deduced from *Rylands* based on the character of an activity being dangerous or ultra-hazardous, as had by then occurred in the United States. He said such a position was untenable in England[107] because the House of Lords

[101] *Cambridge Water Co v Eastern Counties Leather Co* [1994] 2 AC 264.

[102] ibid. Lord Goff delivered the judgment, with which all other Lords agreed (Lord Templeman, Lord Jauncey, Lord Lowry and Lord Woolf).

[103] ibid, 306. For criticism see Donal Nolan, 'The Distinctiveness of *Rylands v Fletcher*' (2005) 121 *Law Quarterly Review* 421; John Murphy, *The Law of Nuisance* (Oxford University Press, 2010) 7–12. Murphy says it is 'highly questionable' whether Blackburn J saw the rule in *Rylands* as an example of private nuisance: 8; John Murphy, 'The Merits of *Rylands v Fletcher*' (2004) 24 *Oxford Journal of Legal Studies* 643; Allan Beever, *The Law of Private Nuisance* (Hart Publishing, 2013) 107–08: 'we can only say that nothing definitive can be said about the relationship between *Rylands v Fletcher* and nuisance'. This move had been foreshadowed in the academic commentary: see FH Newark, 'The Boundaries of Nuisance' (1949) 65 *Law Quarterly Review* 480, 487–88; Declan Carroll, 'The Rule in *Rylands v Fletcher*: A Re-Assessment' (1973) 8 *Irish Jurist* 208, 214: 'the element of unreasonableness in nuisance is somewhat analogous to the requirement of non-natural user'.

[104] *Cambridge Water Co v Eastern Counties Leather Co* [1994] 2 AC 264, 306.

[105] *Fletcher v Rylands* (1866) LR 1 Ex. 265, 280 where Blackburn J said that in cases where the principle of the case applied, the defendant would be liable for the 'natural and anticipated consequences' of the escape.

[106] ibid, 299. This observation has been the subject of trenchant criticism: Maria Lee, 'What Is Private Nuisance?' (2003) 119 *Law Quarterly Review* 298, 313; John Murphy, *The Law of Nuisance* (Oxford University Press, 2010) 11–12.

[107] England, rather than the United Kingdom, is appropriate here, since Scottish law has not accepted *Rylands v Fletcher*: *RHM Bakeries (Scotland) Ltd v Strathclyde Regional Council* (1985) SC (HL) 17, 41 (Lord Fraser).

had rejected such a suggestion in *Read v Lyons*. Lord Goff noted the position of the Law Commission. In its *Report on Civil Liability for Dangerous Things and Activities*, it had rejected the suggestion of strict liability for dangerous or ultra-hazardous activity as uncertain and impractical.[108] Lord Goff said it was not for the courts to develop such a general principle. If Parliament wished to impose strict liability in particular cases, it was of course free so to legislate. Given that the House of Lords had decided that a requirement of a successful *Rylands* claim was the existence of reasonable foreseeability by the defendant of the kind of injury suffered by the plaintiff, and that such foreseeability did not exist on the facts, that was sufficient to decide the case. However, Lord Goff went on to make some obiter dicta remarks about the concept of 'non-natural user'.

Lord Goff noted that the meaning of the concept had evolved substantially over time. As originally conceived by Blackburn J in *Rylands*, it seemed to mean something brought onto the land that was not naturally there. However, Lord Goff said that this concept was 'redolent of a different age' and noted that in *Rickard*, Lord Moulton had discussed the concept of an ordinary use and whether the activity was for the benefit of the community.

Lord Goff criticised this aspect of the House's reasoning in *Rickards*. He said the concept of 'ordinary use' lacked precision. He said that the concept of whether something was for the benefit of the community was similarly open ended and it was difficult to restrain it within meaningful limits. He seemed to express disagreement with the suggestion of Viscount Simon and Lord Macmillan in *Read v Lyons* that a munitions factory could amount to a 'natural' use of premises. He rejected a suggestion in lower court judgments that the fact that an activity created employment in a particular area helped to establish that a particular use of land was 'ordinary' for the purposes of the *Rylands* rule.[109] He declined to attempt to formulate an acceptable definition of what should be considered to be an ordinary or natural use because, in his view, the storage of substantial quantities of chemicals was a non-natural or non-ordinary use.[110] He concluded it was not objectionable to impose strict liability for the consequences of escape of such chemicals.[111] This attempted reset of the meaning of non-natural use, as compared to the somewhat extreme interpretation given to it in *Read*, has been welcomed, notwithstanding it came nearly 50 years later.[112]

The House of Lords again considered the question of the continued vitality of *Rylands v Fletcher* in *Transco Plc v Stockport Metropolitan Borough Council*.[113]

[108] Report of the Law Commission on Civil Liability for Dangerous Things and Activities (1970) (Law Commission No 32) paras 14–16.
[109] *Cambridge Water Co v Eastern Counties Leather Co* [1994] 2 AC 264, 309.
[110] ibid, 309.
[111] ibid, 309.
[112] Tim Wood, 'Sticks and Carrots: *Rylands v Fletcher*, CSR and Accountability for Environmental Harm in Common Law Jurisdictions' (2012) 91 *Canadian Bar Review* 275, 286.
[113] *Transco Plc v Stockport Metropolitan Borough Council* [2004] 2 AC 1.

By this stage, the High Court of Australia had subsumed *Rylands* into the tort of negligence, and one of the submissions of the respondent in *Transco* asked the House of Lords to do the same. All members of the House of Lords rejected this suggestion, upholding *Rylands* as a viable cause of action as part of the tort of private nuisance.

Transco had an easement permitting it to construct a gas main along a stretch of disused railway line. The respondent had constructed an apartment building nearby. It also constructed a water pipe from the apartment building to the nearby water main. Some years after construction, it purchased the land on which both the water pipe and gas main lay, subject to the plaintiff's easement with respect to its gas main. Twenty years later, the water main the respondent had constructed ruptured. This was not due to any negligence on its part. The rupture caused damage to the plaintiff's gas main. It brought legal action against the respondent for the costs associated with fixing it. The trial judge found for the plaintiff on the basis of *Rylands v Fletcher*, but this decision was overturned by the Court of Appeal, a decision which was confirmed by the House of Lords.

As with cases like *Read v Lyons* and *Cambridge Water Co*, the dispute could be resolved relatively simply, without substantial excursis on the metes and bounds of the *Rylands* doctrine. In *Read v Lyons*, there simply had been no 'escape' of something from the defendant's premises. In *Cambridge*, the damage to the plaintiff was not reasonably foreseeable. Yet, the courts embarked on a lengthy obiter dicta discussion of the *Rylands* doctrine. With respect, it is not always entirely clear that these unnecessary comments reduce the confusion and uncertainty surrounding the scope of the doctrine (to put it as kindly as possible). With respect, the same might be said of the five separate judgments issued in the *Transco* case. All judges were agreed that, because the damage to the plaintiff actually occurred on the defendant's land, there had been no 'escape' and thus *Rylands* liability could not exist. Anything else was superfluous. Now, one could understand a lengthy obiter dicta excursis in an effort to provide much-needed clarity in an area that continues to be riven by uncertainty and ambiguity. This would be difficult to achieve when five different judgments are issued, all with obvious differences in emphasis and focus, and in some cases further manifestations of disagreement among members of the court.

In any event, the decision in *Transco* did make some things very clear. First, it was necessary in order to attract *Rylands* liability that there be an escape from the defendant's land.[114] Secondly, the court reiterated that *Rylands* should be seen as a sub-species of the tort of private nuisance and should continue to exist as a recognised principle of that area of law.[115] Thirdly, the court rejected the decision of the High Court of Australia (which will be discussed in Chapter 4) to subsume *Rylands*-type actions into the tort of negligence.[116] Fourthly, all members of the

[114] ibid, 10 (Lord Bingham), 18 (Lord Hoffmann), 23 (Lord Hobhouse), 30 (Lord Scott).
[115] ibid, 10 (Lord Bingham), 20 (Lord Hoffmann), 22 (Lord Hobhouse), 30 (Lord Scott).
[116] ibid, 20 (Lord Bingham), 31 (Lord Scott) and 36 (Lord Walker).

court rejected earlier suggestions that a *Rylands* action might be available in cases of personal injury.[117] None of them sought to explain why liability for property damage should in some circumstances be strict, but not liability for personal injury.[118] Beyond that, there is substantial difference in views, which I will now turn to tease out.

Lord Bingham stated that there was a category of case in which 'it seems just to impose liability even in the absence of fault'.[119] He cited the facts in *Rylands* itself, and referred to the factual scenario in *Cambridge Water Co* (if there had been foreseeability), as being some of such factual scenarios, but did not purport to explain a succinct description of the ambit of such a liability. He noted that French and German law also recognised forms of strict liability in disputes between neighbouring landowners (obviously, a statement which might have less significance now than it once did).

Lord Bingham accepted that notions of dangerousness or mischief should be applied to cases arguably involving *Rylands* liability, but should be applied strictly:

> It must be shown that the defendant has done something which he recognized (or ought to have recognized) as giving rise to an exceptionally high risk of danger or mischief if there should be an escape, however unlikely an escape may have been thought to be.[120]

Applying this to the facts, Lord Bingham stated that while water in large quantities could cause damage, piping of water was routine activity which would 'not have struck anyone as raising any special hazard'.[121]

Lord Bingham adopted the test of 'ordinary user' in terms of one of the defences to *Rylands* liability, as earlier cases had done, as opposed to 'non-natural user'. He said that this test should also be applied strictly, confined to use that was 'extraordinary and unusual', or 'quite out of the ordinary in the place and at the time when he does it'.[122] However, this was to be also applied flexibly so that what was extraordinary and/or unusual at one time may not be at another time.[123] He doubted the suggestions of Viscount Simon and Lord Macmillan in *Read* that a munitions factory could ever amount to an ordinary use.[124] He also doubted the view in *Rickards* that whether the activity was useful to the community was relevant in assessing whether the use was ordinary or not, saying it was not helpful and could engender confusion.[125] Here the respondent's use of the land was not extraordinary or unusual.[126]

[117] ibid, 10 (Lord Bingham), 18 (Lord Hoffmann), 22 (Lord Hobhouse).
[118] Donal Nolan, 'The Distinctiveness of *Rylands v Fletcher*' (2005) 121 *Law Quarterly Review* 421, 449–50.
[119] *Transco Plc v Stockport Metropolitan Borough Council* [2004] 2 AC 1, 8 (Lord Bingham).
[120] ibid, 11.
[121] ibid, 12.
[122] ibid, 11–12. Lord Walker agreed with Lord Bingham's comments regarding the meaning of non-natural use (39).
[123] ibid, 11.
[124] ibid, 11.
[125] ibid, 12.
[126] ibid, 12.

Lord Hoffmann focused on the extent of exceptions to the rule in *Rylands v Fletcher*. He noted that within a year of the House of Lords decision in that case, Blackburn J determined that where an Act of Parliament enabled the defendant's activity to take place, strict liability did not apply, and they could only be held liable for damage or injury caused to another on proof of negligence.[127] Then the defence of Act of God was stretched, said to include a rat gnawing on timber.[128] Then the concept of non-natural user was closely considered, leading to attempts to determine what was an ordinary use of land and what was not. The social utility of the defendant's conduct was considered. Lord Hoffmann stated that the law veered into incoherence, making distinctions that were increasingly difficult to discern.[129] Lord Hoffmann concluded this part of his judgment by stating that, given the extent of the exceptions, the intellectual effort devoted to the rule by judges and writers had 'brought forth a mouse'.[130] He stated it was 'difficult to find any rational principle which explains the rule and its exceptions'.[131]

Notwithstanding these significant difficulties, Lord Hoffmann declined to abolish the rule, on the basis this would be too radical a step.[132]

Lord Hoffmann then proceeded to attempt to provide clarity on the meaning of the concept of 'non-natural use'. This might be seen to be very 'brave', in the old *Yes Minister* sense;[133] alternatively, Lord Hoffmann was venturing into territory on which angels feared to tread. He stated that in determining whether or not a use should be deemed to be a non-natural use for the purposes of *Rylands*, it would be useful to consider whether or not the damage that resulted was something against which someone in the plaintiff's position might have been expected to insure. Lord Walker expressed agreement with Lord Hoffmann's comments about non-natural use.[134]

With respect, this is confusing and confused for at least three reasons. First, no case prior to this one of which I am aware had ever considered the question of whether or not a particular loss was 'insurable' was relevant to determining the question of whether a use was 'natural' or not. So in an area already bedevilled with uncertainty and confusion, the utility of introducing a brand new concept to try to explain and give meaning to a doctrine decided more than 150 years ago is not, with respect, clear. Secondly, the concept of non-natural use is typically applied to the use of the land by the defendant. It is somewhat strange, with respect, to attempt to give meaning to this phrase by asking whether the plaintiff could have insured against the loss. And it is clear Lord Hoffmann means to ask whether the plaintiff might have insured against the loss, not the defendant. While his first

[127] *Hammersmith and City Railway Co v Brand* (1869) LR 4 HL 171, 196 (*Transco*, 16).
[128] *Carstairs v Taylor* (1871) LR 6 Ex. 217.
[129] *Transco Plc v Stockport Metropolitan Borough Council* [2004] 2 AC 1, 19.
[130] ibid, 19
[131] ibid, 20.
[132] ibid, 20.
[133] For younger readers, an alternative term might be 'ill-advised' and/or 'dangerous'.
[134] ibid, 39.

discussion of the insurance point is not clear on whether he means the defendant or the plaintiff, his second discussion leaves no doubt. He states that 'Transco can be expected to have insured against any form of damage to its pipe'.[135] As indicated, it is not at all clear that relevant to whether the defendant's use of their land is a non-natural use or not is whether the plaintiff should have insured against the loss which eventuated. Thirdly, the orthodox position is that the availability of insurance does not and should not determine legal principle.[136] Insurance might follow legal principle, but it must not lead it or influence it. I wholeheartedly agree with this orthodoxy. For this reason, too, Lord Hoffmann's judgment here is open to serious criticism.[137]

Lord Hobhouse defended the rule in *Rylands v Fletcher*. He asserted that it was based on notions of control. In other words, that an owner of a property who 'creates the relevant risk and has … control of how he uses his land should bear the risk. It would be unjust to deny the other a risk-based remedy and introduce a requirement of proving fault'.[138] With respect, 'control' is an unpromising candidate in terms of justifying or rationalising strict liability. If I am driving a motor vehicle, I certainly control it. However, liability for road accidents is clearly fault based.

Lord Hobhouse disagreed with Lord Hoffmann that the availability or otherwise of insurance affected the question of whether *Rylands* principles should be applied.[139] He seemed to be talking, though, of a broader concept that 'he who creates the risk must bear the risk'.[140] Clearly, this phrase could be applied to all kinds of accidents, injury and damage. He defined non-natural use as meaning something involving 'some positive use of the land by the landowner', focused on what the occupier has done – what they brought onto the land. He said the 'normal use of the land in the course of agriculture' was not included.[141] Lord Hobhouse spoke of *Rylands* liability in terms of creation of a risk, and failure to control the thing that escaped.[142] Questions remain – whether, for example, mining activity is a natural or non-natural use of the land (held to be natural use in

[135] ibid, 22.

[136] *Lister v Romford Ice and Cold Storage Co Ltd* [1957] AC 555, 576–77: 'as a general proposition it has not, I think, been questioned for nearly 200 years that in determining the rights inter se of A and B the fact that one or other of them is insured is to be disregarded' (Viscount Simonds); Jane Stapleton, 'Tort, Insurance and Ideology' (1995) 58(6) *Modern Law Review* 820, 829; Stelios Tofaris, 'Rylands v Fletcher Restricted Further' (2013) *Cambridge Law Journal* 11, 13: 'insurability is a complex issue and using it to determine liability is fraught with difficulties'; *cf Nettleship v Weston* [1971] 2 QB 691, 703 (Lord Denning MR); *Lamb v Camden London Borough Council* [1981] 1 QB 625, 635 (Lord Denning MR).

[137] Donal Nolan, 'The Principle of *Rylands v Fletcher*' in Carolyn Sappideen and Prue Vines (eds), *Fleming's The Law of Torts* (10th edn, Lawbook Co, 2011), called Lord Hoffmann's suggestion in this regard 'wrong-headed' (389).

[138] *Transco Plc v Stockport Metropolitan Borough Council* [2004] 2 AC 1, 24.

[139] ibid, 25.

[140] ibid, 25.

[141] ibid, 26.

[142] ibid, 27.

Williams v Waddell), and whether ornamental ponds constructed by the defendant were 'brought onto the land' by the occupier. Yet the court in *Nicholas v Marsland* found no *Rylands* liability there on the basis of Act of God.

Lord Hobhouse also determined that the strict liability rule in *Rylands v Fletcher* did not apply to cases of the spread of fire.[143] In this respect, the decision was inconsistent with the old case of *Jones v Festiniog Railway*,[144] involving sparks from a defendant's railway burning items on the plaintiff's land. This was held to be a proper subject for the application of *Rylands* type liability.[145]

Lord Scott issued a short judgment. He determined that *Rylands* could not apply here because the supply by the council of water to premises could not be regarded as a non-natural use. Thus, *Rylands* did not apply. However, he went on to discuss the supposed rule that where a particular organisation is authorised by statute in some way, whether or not to specifically undertake the works that are the subject of the case, this was relevant in determining that a particular use was natural or not. In other words, the fact that a statute established the organisation and/or authorised it to undertake particular activities could provide support to the suggestion that the organisation was engaged in a natural, rather than non-natural, use and could thus be exempt from *Rylands* strict liability. He sought to summarise the reasoning upon which such a rule was based:

> The reason … is that members of the public are expected to put up with any adverse side-effects of such an activity provided always that it is carried on with due care. The use of the land for carrying on the activity cannot be characterised as *unreasonable* if it has been authorised or required by statute. Viewed against the fact of the statutory authority the user is a natural and ordinary use of the land (emphasis added).[146]

It is the use of the word unreasonable here that is considered noteworthy. While the question of reasonable user of land is of course relevant to questions of liability in nuisance, Lord Scott seems to suggest that it will also be relevant to whether a use is to be considered non-natural for the purposes of *Rylands* liability. It is acknowledged that the House of Lords has by this point stated that *Rylands* is to be regarded as a sub-species of the tort of nuisance. In that way, it may not be totally remarkable. However, I am not aware of a previous case when the concept of a natural/ordinary use of land for the purposes of *Rylands* has been assimilated to the concept of a *reasonable* use of land. Rather, the language of 'not naturally there' is typically used. Clearly, there is a difference between saying that something was not naturally on the land, and saying that its presence on the land is unreasonable.[147] Elsewhere too, the difficult practical consequences of assimilating *Rylands* liability

[143] ibid, 26.

[144] *Jones v Festiniog Railway* [1868] LR 3 QB 733.

[145] Subsequently the Court of Appeal would further restrict the application of *Rylands* to fire-related injury, holding it inapplicable where the plaintiff had suffered loss from smoke which emanated from a fire on the defendant's premises: *Stannard t/a Wyvern Tyres v Gore* [2012] EWCA Civ 1248.

[146] *Transco Plc v Stockport Metropolitan Borough Council* [2004] 2 AC 1, 33.

[147] John Murphy, *The Law of Nuisance* (Oxford University Press, 2010) 11.

into the law of nuisance, and in particular the resulting confusing mix of principles, has been noted.[148]

As noted above, Lord Walker expressed agreement with the views of both Lord Bingham and Lord Hoffmann in relation to what was to be considered a non-natural use. He stated that the court was not in a position to undertake some utilitarian balancing exercise between the common good and individual risk.[149] Though not expressly stated, this seems to be a reaction to those aspects of the House of Lords judgments in *Rickards v Lothian* and *Read v Lyons* which appeared to take into account whether or not the defendant's activities were useful to the community in determining whether or not they should be considered to be a non-natural use.

Lord Walker also agreed that the defendant's use of land here was not unusual. The water pipe in itself was not 'dangerous'. He acknowledged that a significant quantity of water had obviously escaped to cause the fracture in the pipe, and cause the level of saturation in the ground. However, he said the 'gradual and invisible saturation of the adjacent ground cannot be described as an accumulation made by deliberate human design, in the way that Mr Rylands planned, constructed and started to fill his reservoir'.[150]

With respect, these distinctions risk arbitrariness. The defendant Transco here did build the water pipe from which the water escaped, just as Mr Rylands built the reservoir from which the water escaped. In that sense, both involved 'deliberate human design'. The attempted distinguishing of *Rylands* on the facts is unconvincing. However, at a broader level it appears to show clear uneasiness at the highest level with the concept of strict liability. Unfortunately, this is accompanied by clear reticence to abandon the case from which the unattractive principle emanates, resorting to ever more attempted explanations and distinctions, adding further complexity. The benefit to the body of legal principle is not at all clear.

In the result, this decision is highly unsatisfactory. As noted at the commencement of the discussion, the actual case could have been resolved very simply by concluding that as there had been no escape from the defendant's property, the *Rylands* principle had no application. The court might also have reconsidered the utility of the principle at a more fundamental level, but that did not occur. Significant academic calls that this should occur have been ignored to date.[151]

[148] Donal Nolan, 'The Distinctiveness of *Rylands v Fletcher*' (2005) 121 *Law Quarterly Review* 421, 436–37.

[149] *Transco Plc v Stockport Metropolitan Borough Council* [2004] 2 AC 1, 38.

[150] ibid, 40.

[151] Donal Nolan, 'The Distinctiveness of *Rylands v Fletcher*' (2005) 121 *Law Quarterly Review* 421, 450–51, noting that 'sometimes it is better simply to extinguish the flickering flame that remains when legal developments leave past doctrines behind. In the case of *Rylands v Fletcher*, the reluctance to take this step may be down in part to legal sentimentalism … [but] the new orthodoxy has left the rule in *Rylands v Fletcher* a shadow of its former self, lacking either rationale or practical significance, and hedged about with arcane and indefensible restrictions … [referring to Lord Hoffmann's description of Rylands in *Transco* as a mouse] … would not putting this poor creature down have been more merciful than leaving it in the legal equivalent of a persistent vegetative state?' There are express calls for the UK

However, regretfully each member of the House of Lords attempted then to provide further clarity on the operation of the *Rylands* principle. Unfortunately, in this process they merely added to the uncertainty and complexity as noted above. In sum, more and divergent rationales and explanations have now appeared in the context of *Rylands*. Some think it only applies to exceptionally dangerous uses of land (Lord Bingham), some think it applies to situations involving land that the defendant can control (Lord Hobhouse), some think it applies when the land use is unreasonable (Lord Scott), and some think it applies in cases of deliberate act, and maintain that construction of a reservoir which leaks is apparently a deliberate act, but construction of a water pipe that fractures and leaks is not (Lord Walker). And one (Lord Hoffmann, with whom Lord Walker agrees) states that the availability of insurance helps determine whether or not a user is 'natural' or not, but focuses on whether the plaintiff could have obtained insurance, whereas the concept of 'non-natural use' was typically applied to the defendant's use of premises. Far from assisting in resolving ambiguity, the House of Lords decision in *Transco* amplified it.

Conclusion

The *Rylands v Fletcher* precedent has not enjoyed a happy time in the common law since the 1860s. It represented something of an outlier, even then, for its apparent reassertion of strict liability principles at a time when fault-based liability was developing strongly in the United Kingdom. It may well be best explained by some disasters at the time, and a clamour for 'justice' for victims of such disasters, together with the legal system's traditional deference to and protection of property interests.

Even so, it did not take long for this line of cases to become precarious. Within ten years of its inception, judges were already considering whether the defendant was at fault for what occurred, in purporting to apply a strict liability, no-fault principle. This anomaly at the heart of *Rylands* has continued up to the present day, with the most recent House of Lords decision again referring to fault principles in purporting to consider its application to given facts.

This incoherence at the heart of the principle is not all. It is heavily dependent on concepts of 'dangerousness' and 'not naturally there', but these sound anachronistic and there is chronic disagreement and uncertainty about what they mean. The second concept has morphed into 'ordinary use' of land, but this too is uncertain. There are no convincing reasons for persisting with this rationale for the

courts to act on the *Rylands* principle by 'put(ting) it out of its misery by abolishing it altogether': Stelios Tofaris, '*Rylands v Fletcher* Restricted Further' (2013) *Cambridge Law Journal* 11, 14; Robert Stevens, *Torts and Rights* (Oxford University Press, 2007) 113, but these seem destined to fall on deaf ears. For a contrary view see John Murphy, 'The Merits of *Rylands v Fletcher*' (2004) 24(4) *Oxford Journal of Legal Studies* 643.

imposition of strict liability. Judges, even when there is no necessity to do so on the facts in front of them, purport to assist in making the doctrine clearer, usually only serving to do the opposite. And new red herrings such as insurance and 'control' are thrown about in the most recent judgment. Judges frankly acknowledge that the doctrine is not 'worth the effort', but timorously refuse to take the decision to get rid of it, once and for all. I can but agree with the conclusion of Robert Stevens that it is time to put the doctrine out of its misery[152] but, frankly, this requires judges with the courage to make hard but necessary decisions, rather than exacerbate the problem.

The United Kingdom has provided many countries around the world with the model for good governance, including a robust legal system, and many sound legal principles. *Rylands v Fletcher* was not one of them. In the next chapter, its reception elsewhere in the common law world is considered.

[152] Robert Stevens, *Torts and Rights* (Oxford University Press, 2007) 113.

4

Comparative Approach to *Rylands v Fletcher* Liability

This chapter considers the adoption of the *Rylands v Fletcher* principle into comparable common law jurisdictions Australia, Canada and the United States. It will be shown that the fate of the case, and the principles for which it apparently stands, has been quite different.

Australia

Prior to a discussion of the relevant Australian authorities, one point must first be noted. This is that the Australian High Court considered itself bound by decisions of the House of Lords until the decision of *Parker v The Queen* in 1963.[1] Thus, for the first 60 years of the existence of the High Court of Australia, it considered itself bound by the House of Lords decision in *Rylands v Fletcher*, and bound to apply it. As will be seen, it did so. However, in 1994 it would finally move to abolish the rule, controversially deciding to subsume it within the tort of negligence.[2] This development, and the precedents leading to this pivotal decision, will now be discussed.

The High Court of Australia first considered the *Rylands* precedent in the 1908 decision in *Sparkes v Osborne*.[3] There a bush known as prickly pear, a pest, grew from the defendant's land onto that of the plaintiff. The plaintiff brought an action against the defendant on the basis of *Rylands v Fletcher*. The claim failed. The court stated that the defendant had not brought the bush onto their land, and had done nothing to cultivate it. As such, the case did not fall within the *Rylands* principle.

The second occasion for the Australian High Court to consider *Rylands* was in the case of *Whinfield v Lands Purchase and Management Board of Victoria and State Rivers and Water Supply Commission of Victoria*.[4] The case involved

[1] *Parker v The Queen* (1963) 111 CLR 610, 632 (Dixon CJ, for the Court). Appeals from the High Court of Australia to the Privy Council were terminated in 1975 and from State Supreme Courts to the Council in 1986, in both cases by legislation.

[2] *Burnie Port Authority v General Jones Pty Ltd* (1994) 179 CLR 520.

[3] *Sparkes v Osborne* (1908) 7 CLR 51.

[4] *Whinfield v Lands Purchase and Management Board of Victoria and State Rivers and Water Supply Commission of Victoria* (1914) 18 CLR 606.

a fire which escaped from land on which the Commission was doing work, causing damage to the plaintiff's nearby property. The fire was started by a contractor employed by the Commission to construct a water pipe. He had apparently started the fire to cook some food. It got out of control and spread over grass and onto the plaintiff's property. Neither of the two judgments delivered found that the rule in *Rylands* applied to this case. Griffith CJ, with whom Powers J agreed, stated that the *Rylands* principle did not apply to 'fire lawfully lighted for domestic purposes or other ordinary purposes of occupation of land',[5] which accidentally spread without negligence. This may have been a reference to a non-natural use of land, but Griffith CJ did not choose to use those terms. Isaacs J did place his judgment in those terms, stating that the *Rylands* principle only applied to cases involving a special use of land bringing with it increased danger to others, and not an ordinary use of land or use as was proper for the general benefit to the community[6] (clearly, paraphrasing the judgment of the Privy Council in *Rickards v Lothian*). Isaacs J concluded that the starting of fire for domestic uses was an ordinary use, so it could not be said to bring an 'increased danger', though a non-natural use of land.[7] Isaacs J also defended the *Rylands* principle by stating that the principle of non-natural use was flexible, ensuring a case-by-case consideration of whether strict liability would be applied in a given situation, placing questions of liability, in his view, on a less arbitrary and more reasonable footing.[8]

The court considered *Rylands* again in *Hazelwood v Webber*.[9] This case involved the defendant burning stubble on their farm. This was something that farmers, including those in the immediate vicinity, typically did. While engaged in this activity, a tree stump caught fire. A high wind carried that fire to the plaintiff's land, causing damage. The jury had found that the defendant's activity did not amount to negligence. All members of the High Court applied *Rylands* to make the defendant liable to the plaintiff for the damage caused.

The joint reasons noted the reasoning of the Privy Council in *Rickards* to the effect that *Rylands* applied only in cases involving special, non-ordinary use of land carrying with it increased risk to others, and having regard to community benefits. Purporting to apply this to the facts, the joint reasons stated that five factors were relevant considerations, at least in the context of the use of fire in agricultural contexts. These were:

> the benefit obtained by the farmer who (uses it), the frequency of its use by other farmers, … the degree of hazard to others involved in its use, the extensiveness of the damage it is likely to do and the difficulty of actually controlling it.[10]

In so applying the factors, the joint reasons stated that the climate, character of the country and the natural conditions would all be relevant. It concluded that

[5] ibid, 615.
[6] ibid, 618.
[7] ibid, 619.
[8] ibid, 620.
[9] *Hazelwood v Webber* (1934) 52 CLR 268.
[10] ibid, 278 (Gavan Duffy CJ, Rich, Dixon and McTiernan JJ).

the burning of vegetation in Australia was an 'extraordinary, … special use of land involving exceptional danger to others'.[11] Starke J agreed in the outcome, but disagreed that the fact that a large percentage, if not all, of the farmers in the region engaged in the practice made a difference to the application of *Rylands* principles.[12]

The other important issue in the case was relevant legislation which regulated when fires could be lit on premises, and when they would be unlawful. The Act made clear that it was not intended to interfere with an individual's right to claim compensation for damage or injury they suffered through the 'reckless or negligent' use of fire.[13] The court interpreted this provision to have two consequences: (a) that a person injured could only claim compensation for the activity specifically regulated by the legislation upon proof of negligence; but (b) in cases where the legislation did not specifically regulate the activity, the common law (including *Rylands*) would continue to apply. The defendant conceded in this case that their activity did not fall within anything specifically authorised as per (a), thus *Rylands* principles operated on the facts.

The High Court confirmed that the installation of a water supply to business premises would not typically attract the operation of *Rylands v Fletcher* strict liability because this is not generally considered to be a non-natural use carrying a heightened level of danger.[14] Dixon J recognised that to apply 'at their own peril' to situations of that nature would be unreasonable. He referenced the connection of a water supply to premises as being 'so desirable in the interests of the community', in a way that the House of Lords had also (controversially) recognised the social utility of the defendant's conduct in assessing strict liability, before later appearing to recant. However, Dixon J said that it was not in all circumstances involving water supply that *Rylands* would be irrelevant. If the defendant's business involved accumulating water in such a way, or with such volumes or flows, bringing a 'new or increased risk of escape', then *Rylands* liability might be appropriate.[15]

A narrow interpretation of the concept of non-natural user was evident in *Wise Bros Pty Ltd v Commissioner for Railways (NSW)*.[16] There the defendant operated a flour milling business. The defendant had combustible flour dust and fumes on its premises, as well as a portable boiler, fire box and smoke stack. A fire started, though it was not entirely clear from whence it emanated. It damaged the plaintiff's property on premises adjoining that of the defendant. The evidence suggested that at the relevant time, a strong wind was blowing from the defendant's premises towards that of the plaintiff. All members of the court dismissed

[11] ibid, 279.

[12] ibid, 281: 'burning off stubble … is an operation necessarily attended with great danger. And I cannot agree that such an operation is an ordinary or natural or reasonable use or enjoyment of land, even if sixty or seventy percent – or all – of the farmers in the district in which the land is situate take the risk'.

[13] Careless Use of Fire Act 1912 (Vic) s9.

[14] *Torette House Pty Ltd v Berkman* (1939) 62 CLR 637.

[15] ibid, 654–55.

[16] *Wise Bros Pty Ltd v Commissioner for Railways (NSW)* (1947) 75 CLR 59, 68 (Latham CJ), 70 (Starke J), 73 (McTiernan J) and 74 (Williams J).

the *Rylands v Fletcher* claim on the basis that the defendant's use of their premises for the purposes of manufacturing flour was not a non-natural use. Further, Latham CJ stated there was no evidence the defendant started the fire on their premises or brought it to their premises.[17] This seems to suggest that he might have found *Rylands* inapplicable to a situation where a fire started on the defendant's premises *without their volition*, only to then engulf that of the plaintiff.

The High Court did not apply *Rylands v Fletcher* either in *Hargrave v Goldman*.[18] There the defendant owned a 600 acre property. During a thunderstorm lightning struck one of the trees on the property, setting it alight. The defendant arranged to remove the tree. This occurred, and the tree fell to the ground. However, fire travelled from the felled tree onto the plaintiff's neighbouring property, causing him damage. The question was whether the defendant was liable to the plaintiff for his loss. All members of the court found in favour of the plaintiff, but this was on the basis of negligence and/or nuisance. The *Rylands* claim was rejected on the basis that the defendant did not intentionally start the fire or bring it onto his premises.[19] However, the court also confirmed that fire was something likely to do mischief if it escaped, thus *Rylands* could still apply in Australia where a fire had escaped from the defendant's premises onto another, in circumstances where the defendant or someone for whom he was responsible had started it, or brought it there.[20] The Privy Council decision in this case did not address the *Rylands* aspect of the case.[21]

In its next *Rylands* decision the High Court grappled with the question of whether statutory authority precluded such an action. The case, *Benning v Wong*,[22] involved a plaintiff who suffered personal injury as a result of gas which escaped from a gas main laid and used by the defendant company. The company raised the defence that statute authorised them to construct and use the gas main, thus *Rylands* strict liability was not applicable. One of the plaintiff's heads of claim was based on *Rylands* strict liability. The case came to the High Court on a demurrer application, as to whether the *Rylands* claim was based on a recognised cause of action, given the existence of the statute. By a majority of three to two, the High Court found that there was no recognised cause of action based on *Rylands*, and that aspect of the statement of claim was struck out.

In the majority, McTiernan J stated that the relevant legislation authorised the defendant to construct the gas pipes. Further, the legislation provided that where the company was notified of a leak in the pipes, it was required to take steps to take immediate remedial action. From this, McTiernan J concluded that the legislature 'must have had in view that it would be an ordinary incident of carrying on

[17] ibid, 68.
[18] *Hargrave v Goldman* (1963) 110 CLR 40.
[19] ibid, 59 (Windeyer J); the other two judges did not consider the *Rylands* question.
[20] ibid, 72 (Windeyer J).
[21] *Goldman v Hargrave* [1967] AC 645.
[22] *Benning v Wong* (1969) 122 CLR 249.

this gas undertaking that gas would escape'.[23] For McTiernan J, this meant that *Rylands* type liability could not apply. There was no evidence in the legislation that the legislature intended that *Rylands* strict liability should apply. Menzies J agreed that, according to the UK precedent cases, strict liability should not apply where the dangerous thing was brought to the defendant's land pursuant to legislative authority. Owen J took a similar position.

Barwick CJ and Windeyer J dissented on this point. Barwick CJ stated that the mere existence of a statutory authority to do something did not necessarily have the consequence that strict liability was inapplicable. He adopted the well-known principle of statutory interpretation that statutes should not be interpreted in a manner that is invasive of common law rights, in the absence of clear words to the contrary.[24] He said there was nothing in the express terms of the legislation under which the gas main was laid to suggest that Parliament intended to abrogate the existing rights of individuals to bring action in the event they were injured by the laying or use of the gas main. To the contrary, section 79 of the relevant legislation made it clear that the defendant company could be held liable in an action from someone who had been injured as a result of the work done.[25] Barwick CJ stated that courts should not search out implications to displace common law rights.

Discussing the UK precedents, he noted that cases had recognised that where an enterprise had been granted statutory authority to perform works, strict *Rylands* liability had been held to be not applicable. However, this exemption was limited. It was limited to things that were necessarily encompassed within the statutory authority. This explained the railway cases, where the court found that it was inevitable that trains did generate sparks, which in some cases might ignite surrounding lands. The UK courts had established that in such cases *Rylands* liability should not apply, and the defendant companies should only be liable in cases where they were shown to have been negligent, as discussed in Chapter 3.

However, Barwick CJ emphasised that this exemption from *Rylands* liability only existed to the extent of activity or risk generated that had the character of necessity, inevitability or unavoidability.[26] This did not apply to the current situation.

[23] ibid, 275.

[24] This was expressed early in the history of Australian law in *Potter v Minahan* (1908) 7 CLR 277, 304 (O'Connor J); see also *R v Secretary of State for the Home Department; Ex Parte Simms* [2000] 2 AC 115, 131–32 (Lord Hoffmann). Gleeson CJ connected the so-called principle of legality with the rule of law in *Electrolux Home Products Pty Ltd v Australian Workers' Union* (2004) 221 CLR 309, 329.

[25] The section provided that 'nothing herein contained shall extend or be construed to extend to prevent any persons from proceeding against the said company or against any of their officers servants or workmen in respect of any works of the said company or the method which shall be employed by them for furnishing such light as aforesaid as a public or private nuisance or for bringing an action against any of the said company or any of their officers or servants or workmen for any injury sustained by them by reasons of any such works or methods of lighting whether such injury shall proceed from the nature of such method of lighting or the carelessness or want of skill of the person or persons employed thereon': *Australian Gas Light Company Act 1837* (NSW) s87.

[26] *Benning v Wong* (1969) 122 CLR 249, 258–61. This result was similar to that in the early High Court decision of *Fullarton v North Melbourne Electric Tramway and Lighting Co Ltd* (1916) 21 CLR 181, where Griffith CJ referred to a defence applying in cases where activity cannot be carried on without

He found there was no evidence before the court that the laying of gas mains would inevitably and of necessity lead to gas leaks of the kind which occurred. Thus, for Barwick CJ the existence of the statute here did not necessarily exempt the defendant from *Rylands* type liability.

Windeyer J adopted a similar position. In his view, the mere fact that statute had authorised a particular activity did not necessarily lead to the conclusion that no *Rylands* liability could apply. He noted that the activity of constructing the reservoir in *Rylands* itself was a lawful activity; clearly, this did not preclude application of strict liability principles.[27] He noted it would be a question of statutory construction in each case as to whether Parliament intended to abrogate the pre-existing common law rules that would otherwise govern a particular factual scenario. He also agreed with Barwick CJ that a major distinction had been drawn in the cases between accidents that were seen to be inevitable consequences of the activity authorised by Parliament, and those that were not. In the former case, it would be much more readily concluded that strict liability should not apply. He found that the present situation was in the latter category of case – it was not inevitable that the construction and use of a gas main would be accompanied by leaks. Thus he concluded that the plaintiff did have a viable cause of action on the basis of *Rylands*.[28] The case was also notable because a majority found that a *Rylands* action was available for a case of personal injuries.[29]

Then came the landmark decision in *Burnie Port Authority v General Jones Pty Ltd*.[30] The plaintiff owned a building. It gave a licence to General Jones Pty Ltd to occupy part of the building. Relevantly, General Jones stored large quantities of frozen vegetables in the building. Burnie Port Authority was undertaking renovation of another part of the building of which they retained occupation, doing some of the work themselves, and engaging contractors to do some of it. At the time of particular work being done, a large quantity of insulation was stored in cardboard boxes nearby. As a result of welding work being done, sparks or molten metal fell onto the cardboard boxes, igniting them and the insulation which they housed. The fire spread to that part of the building occupied by General Jones, destroying their frozen vegetables. They brought legal action against Burnie Port Authority in respect of this loss, including an action based on *Rylands v Fletcher*. This action was successful at State Supreme Court level.

In the landmark decision, the High Court of Australia, by a majority of five to two, effectively subsumed the *Rylands v Fletcher* principle into the law of negligence, for the purposes of Australian law. In other words, it converted what had been an action seen as involving strict liability into an action requiring proof of fault.

creating a nuisance (187) being exempt from strict liability principles, as did Barton J (192). Barton J added that in cases where the relevant legislation conferred a discretion, it should be assumed that Parliament did not intend that the exercise of the discretion should abrogate common law rights (193).

[27] *Benning v Wong* (1969) 122 CLR 249, 307.

[28] ibid, 311–12.

[29] ibid, Barwick CJ (274), Menzies J (277) and Windeyer J (318).

[30] *Burnie Port Authority v General Jones Pty Ltd* (1994) 179 CLR 520.

This represented a sharp reform of Australian law, setting it on quite a different path to that of the United Kingdom. It was seen in Chapter 3 that the UK courts had determined that the *Rylands* principle was a sub-species of the tort of private nuisance. On the other hand, the High Court's reform enjoyed some support in the academic literature.[31]

The joint reasons[32] noted that the 'true rule' espoused by Blackburn J in *Rylands* was no longer authoritative or valid. Its reference to the defendant bringing something onto land 'for their own purposes' was generally not applied. The reference to the defendant bringing something onto 'their land' was no longer valid because it had been applied to support a plaintiff bringing an action under its principles although they were a mere occupier, rather than owner, of land. The reference to 'collects and keeps' was not accurate; as applied, the conjunction 'or' was more correct. Further, in *Rylands* itself, the evidence suggested the defendant had not 'brought anything on' to their land – the water in the reservoir had gathered naturally.

The High Court noted that Blackburn J seemed to be aware that the principle which he espoused in that case could lead to the imposition of liability that was 'too wide'. He attempted to rein in the doctrine with qualifiers, that it applied to things that were 'likely to do mischief if (they) escape' and things that were 'not naturally there'. However, subsequent decisions, commencing in the House of Lords decision in *Rylands* itself, cast a different meaning on these exceptions, with the 'likely to do mischief' phrase reinterpreted to mean 'dangerous', and things that were 'not naturally there' converted into 'ordinary use'.[33] The requirement that the defendant 'knows' the thing is likely to be mischievous was subsequently converted into a reasonable foreseeability requirement, which may be different from that originally intended by Blackburn J. It was not entirely clear what 'escape' meant, whether it meant escape from the defendant's land, or any occasion on which the defendant lost control of something. It could easily lead to arbitrariness. The High Court pointed out possible anomalies with two plaintiffs seeking to enter the defendant's premises when they were injured by an explosion on those premises.

[31] W Friedmann, 'Modern Trends in the Law of Torts' (1937) 1 *Modern Law Review* 39, who stated that developments in the application of *Rylands v Fletcher* had brought the action 'near to negligence' (57), and suggested *Rylands* was superfluous given acceptance of the generalised duty of care in negligence (62). Donal Nolan, 'The Distinctiveness of *Rylands v Fletcher*' (2005) 121 *Law Quarterly Review* 421, 450–51, stated that 'sometimes it is better simply to extinguish the flickering flame that remains when legal developments leave past doctrines behind. In the case of *Rylands v Fletcher*, the reluctance to take this step may be down in part to legal sentimentalism … the new orthodoxy [speaking of its reinterpretation as a principle of private nuisance in the United Kingdom] has left the rule in *Rylands v Fletcher* a shadow of its former self, lacking either rationale or practical significance, and hedged about with arcane and indefensible restrictions … would not putting this poor creature down have been more merciful than leaving it in the legal equivalent of a persistent vegetative state?'

[32] *Burnie Port Authority v General Jones Pty Ltd* (1994) 179 CLR 520, Mason CJ, Deane, Dawson, Toohey and Gaudron JJ.

[33] The reasons noted such conversion (from the Court of Exchequer Chamber speech of Blackburn J to the decision in the same case in the House of Lords) may have been 'inadvertent', ibid, 544.

The rights of the plaintiff who had crossed the threshold of the door and entered the property would not be governed by *Rylands*, while the rights of the other, who technically remained outside those premises, would be. The High Court criticised these kinds of arbitrary results as unacceptable.[34]

The joint reasons honed in on the 'critical obscurity' caused by the twin requirements of 'dangerousness' and 'non-natural use'.[35] It noted that if water could be regarded as 'dangerous', as *Rylands* itself found, it became difficult to identify anything that, if gathered in sufficient quantities, could not be held to meet the description.

In relation to what was meant by non-natural use, the High Court noted the decision in *Rickards v Lothian*, which sought to define such a use as one bringing with it increased danger to others, as opposed to an ordinary use for community benefit. This had been accepted and applied in previous Australian High Court decisions. However, the court noted that this test had been interpreted so as to require consideration of the manner and nature of the use of land. It converted *Rylands* into a doctrine which required all of the circumstances surrounding the introduction or maintenance of the material on the given land. In this way, effectively notions of 'reasonable care' had entered the equation in terms of considering application of the *Rylands* principle to given facts.[36] The defences to which courts had regard in these cases, including consent, plaintiff's default, and Act of God, had come to closely approximate those considering whether in effect the defendant was at fault for the plaintiff's loss.[37] Where the defence of statutory authority applied, as noted earlier, these cases had usually effectively been converted into pure negligence cases.[38] At least in Australia, differences between damages available for *Rylands* actions and ordinary negligence actions had disappeared, in particular with the acceptance that personal injuries were recoverable under *Rylands* principles in *Benning v Wong*.[39]

The High Court criticised the state of the law in this area, denying that the cases discerned any objective basis for determining the requirements of dangerousness and non-natural use. It said that the law had degenerated into 'an essentially unprincipled and ad hoc subjective determination of whether the particular facts of the case fall within undefined notions of what is special or not ordinary'. It found

[34] ibid, 548–49.

[35] ibid, 537.

[36] ibid, 539; see to like effect *Attorney-General v Cory Brothers* [1921] 1 AC 521, 536: 'the line of demarcation between proof of negligence and the proof of what is necessary to bring such a case [as the present case] within this well-known principle of *Rylands v Fletcher* is but a faint one' (Viscount Haldane). This had also been earlier noted by David Williams, 'Non-Natural Use of Land' (1973) 32 *Cambridge Law Journal* 310, 315: 'when some object or substance is brought on to land, and the object or substance is likely to do mischief if it escapes, then the use of the land will be regarded as non-natural if the object or substance is dealt with on the land in a negligent fashion … judges will in practice equate the two concepts of negligence and non-natural use'.

[37] *Burnie Port Authority v General Jones Pty Ltd* (1994) 179 CLR 520, 545.

[38] eg *Manchester Corporation v Farnworth* [1930] AC 171.

[39] *Burnie Port Authority v General Jones Pty Ltd* (1994) 179 CLR 520, 545–46.

the courts had so far made 'spectacularly unsatisfactory efforts' to resolve ambiguities in the content and application of the *Rylands* rule.[40] These concepts were a product of great confusion, with highly variable decisions regarding whether simple items such as trees, water, gas, electricity, fire and explosives were, or were not, within the rule.[41]

It viewed the House of Lords decision in *Read v Lyons* this way, criticising that decision for suggesting that the use of property for munitions manufacture could be seen to be a 'natural use', thereby excluding the circumstances from strict liability.[42] The High Court referred to this as an example of the *Rylands* principle being 'progressively weakened and confined from within'. It had also been weakened and confined from without, given the acceptance of the generalised duty of care in negligence.[43] The judges contrasted the generalised duty of care in negligence, represented in the landmark judgment of *Donoghue v Stevenson*,[44] as a unifying principle and general conceptual explanation for liability for unintended injury, with the unattractive *Rylands* principle, hopelessly confused by the concepts of 'non-natural use' and 'dangerousness'. They noted it was the confusion caused by the former principle that might have animated, and justified, the prescient observation of Sir Frederick Pollock that the *Rylands* principle would become an example of a case authority 'that [is] followed only in the letter … becom[ing] slowly but surely choked and crippled by [judicially imposed] exceptions'.[45] The joint reasons downplayed the extent to which the subsumption of *Rylands* into the law of negligence would practically impact upon plaintiffs, finding that, at least in the vast majority of cases, a plaintiff with a putative action under *Rylands* would also be able to demonstrate that they were owed a duty of care, and that it had been breached.[46]

The joint reasons also developed the concept of a non-delegable duty. They recognised that in some circumstances, the duty of care that a given defendant owed was non-delegable. In other words, though they might employ someone else to perform the relevant task, the legal liability remained with them. It was a duty not merely to take care, but to ensure that care was taken. The High Court of Australia had recognised this concept in some earlier cases,[47] as had UK case law.[48]

[40] ibid, 540.
[41] ibid, 544.
[42] ibid, 541.
[43] ibid, 540–41.
[44] *Donoghue v Stevenson* [1932] AC 562.
[45] *Burnie Port Authority v General Jones Pty Ltd* (1994) 179 CLR 520, 544 (citing Sir Frederick Pollock, *The Law of Fraud, Misrepresentation and Mistake in British India* (Thacker, Spink & Co 1894) 54).
[46] *Burnie Port Authority v General Jones Pty Ltd* (1994) 179 CLR 520, 555. The joint reasons also developed a doctrine of non-delegable duties (550–54), but since this doctrine is not strictly relevant to the question of *Rylands v Fletcher* and because, in any event, subsequent High Court decisions would appear to go cold over the issue of non-delegable duties (*New South Wales v Lepore* (2003) 212 CLR 511, 533–34 (Gleeson CJ), 599–600 (Gummow and Hayne JJ), 608 (Kirby J) and 624 (Callinan J), this aspect of the joint reasons will not be explored further here.
[47] *Kondis v State Transit Authority* (1984) 154 CLR 672.
[48] *Dalton v Angus* (1881) 6 AC 740.

It is difficult to categorise the circumstances in which such a duty is owed. The courts have recognised that they might include hospital and patient, school authority and school, and employer and employee. Though it can be difficult to satisfactorily explain the principles that determine whether or not a non-delegable duty was owed, they typically involved the defendant assuming responsibility and/or control over another person, who was thereby in a vulnerable or dependent position, or in relation to a particular situation. The UK decisions had apparently accepted a non-delegable duty of care in cases involving ultra-hazardous or dangerous situations.[49] However, the High Court of Australia had rejected a suggestion that this was the concept around which non-delegable duties in various factual contexts should coalesce.[50]

The relevance of this in the current context was that the High Court determined that the circumstances in which a *Rylands* action typically arose, for instance neighbouring property owners, or between a property owner and someone nearby, might attract a non-delegable duty. The High Court said that in such cases the property owner was in one of those positions of supervision and control. They controlled what they brought onto their land, and how they used their land. They controlled the danger. This was similar to the escape of something dangerous from land. Accordingly, to the High Court, factual situations mirroring the *Rylands*-type case were really an instance of a non-delegable duty.[51] This becomes particularly important in cases where the defendant has engaged an independent contractor to work on their land, and the contractor in some way contributes to the release of the danger. There remains conjecture as to whether a non-delegable duty is an example of strict liability or not, with support that it is.[52]

This aspect of the judgment can be critiqued, as part of a broader criticism of non-delegable duties in the law.[53] To some extent, it might be seen to muddy the waters of the judgments in *Burnie*. On the one hand, the decision can be read as an adoption of fault-based negligence principles, and an abandonment of the strict liability *Rylands* principles. However, such a conclusion is more difficult once it is borne in mind that the High Court also seemingly embraced, as something of a

[49] ibid, 831 (Lord Watson); *Black v Christchurch Finance Co* [1894] AC 48, 54 (Lord Shand, for the Court).

[50] *Stoneman v Lyons* (1975) 133 CLR 550, 563–65 (Stephen J) and 575 (Mason J); *Stevens v Brodribb Sawmilling Co Pty Ltd* (1986) 160 CLR 16, 29 (Mason J) and 41–42 (Wilson and Dawson JJ).

[51] *Burnie Port Authority v General Jones Pty Ltd* (1994) 179 CLR 520, 550–52.

[52] Jonathan Morgan, 'Liability for Independent Contractors in Contract and Tort: Duties to Ensure That Care is Taken' (2015) 74 *Cambridge Law Journal* 109: 'the defendant (in a non-delegable duty case) must exceptionally ensure that they take reasonable care (or rather, since it is impossible to ensure that contractors are never careless, he must answer for any harm negligently caused'; Peter Cane, 'The Changing Fortunes of Rylands v Fletcher (1994) 24 *University of Western Australia Law Review* 237, 241; Christian Witting, 'Breach of the Non-Delegable Duty: Defending Limited Strict Liability in Tort' (2006) 29 *University of New South Wales Law Journal* 33; *cf* John Murphy, 'The Liability Bases of Common Law Non-Delegable Duties – A Reply to Christian Witting' (2007) 30 *University of New South Wales Law Journal* 86, 86.

[53] Anthony Gray, 'Reinvigorating Non-Delegable Duties in Australia?' (2017) 25 *Tort Law Review* 59.

substitute to *Rylands*, the concept of a non-delegable duty in *Rylands* situations, based on the dangerousness of an activity. This becomes somewhat incoherent and counter-intuitive if it is accepted that a non-delegable duty is an example of strict liability, as some do.[54] In the same case, the High Court criticised *Rylands* and its progeny for use of amorphous concepts such as 'likely to do mischief it is escapes', but arguably did no better in apparently accepting that a non-delegable duty was owed in circumstances of dangerousness.[55]

To some extent, this argument is 'academic' because after initially apparently further supporting the concept of the non-delegable duty,[56] within a decade of *Burnie* a majority of the High Court seemed to turn away from it.[57]

Brennan and McHugh JJ dissented in *Burnie*. Brennan J conceded that in many cases, a plaintiff with a viable *Rylands* action would also have a valid claim in negligence. However, he stated that to subsume the doctrines as the joint reasons had would 'depreciate the duty which *Rylands* … imposes on the occupiers of land and premises and correspondingly to diminish the security which that rule confers on their neighbours'.[58] McHugh J said that the High Court had reached an acceptable understanding of the *Rylands* doctrine and had applied it for many years. While concepts such as non-natural use were to some extent indeterminative, so were key concepts in the law of negligence such as reasonable foreseeability.[59] He said there were substantial numbers of cases where *Rylands* liability would exist but liability in negligence would not, because plaintiffs could not prove that the defendant breached a duty of care.[60] He said the defences that existed under *Rylands* were not analogous to those which existed in negligence because they went to issues of causation. Contributory negligence was not an available defence in *Rylands* cases. McHugh J said that another difference between a *Rylands* action and a negligence one was that, in the latter, the defendant was only liable for reasonably foreseeable harm, but this had not been a limit that (the Australian courts) had placed on a *Rylands* claim, though he noted the different approach in the United Kingdom.[61]

[54] Peter Cane, 'The Changing Fortunes of *Rylands v Fletcher*' (1994) 24 *University of Western Australia Law Review* 237, 242: 'once the concept of dangerousness is made a criterion for the imposition of strict liability through the medium of a non-delegable duty of care, we need to be able to say whether any particular activity is dangerous independently of … [whether] it was conducted with reasonable care … it is … difficult to define the scope of strict liability by reference to the nature of the activities which attract such liability (whether they are dangerous or not)'.

[55] Jeannie Maree Paterson, '*Rylands v Fletcher* into Negligence: *Burnie Port Authority v General Jones Pty Ltd*' (1994) 20 *Monash University Law Review* 317, 327: 'the distinction between the rejected extra-hazardous acts doctrine and the non-delegable duty in *Rylands v Fletcher* circumstances is not clear'.

[56] *Northern Sandblasting Pty Ltd v Harris* (1997) 188 CLR 313.

[57] *New South Wales v Lepore* (2003) 212 CLR 511, 533 (Gleeson CJ), 599–600 (Gummow and Hayne JJ), 608 (Kirby J) and 624 (Callinan J); *Leichhardt Municipal Council v Montgomery* (2007) 230 CLR 22, 34–35 (Gleeson CJ), 54 and 64 (Kirby J), 75 (Hayne J) and 86 (Callinan J), Crennan J agreeing with Gleeson CJ and Hayne J.

[58] *Burnie Port Authority v General Jones Pty Ltd* (1994) 179 CLR 520, 570–71.

[59] ibid, 590.

[60] ibid, 592; similar concerns were noted by John Murphy, 'The Merits of *Rylands v Fletcher*' (2004) 24(4) *Oxford Journal of Legal Studies* 643, 660.

[61] 590–91; *Cambridge Water Co v Eastern Counties Leather Plc* [1994] 2 AC 264.

McHugh J noted that the escape of material including oil, fire, gas, chemicals and radioactive had and continued to cause others substantial damage. He said it was not clear why the common law should abandon strict liability in such cases for the 'indeterminancy of the action for negligence'.[62] He noted strict liability had a long history in the common law.[63] He noted some Law Reform Commissions had advocated strict liability rules in particular areas of social activity which involved dangerous substances[64] and suggested much more analysis, evidence and argument was necessary before the court should take the large step of effectively abolishing the *Rylands* action.[65]

Canada

The *Rylands* precedent has only been lightly considered and applied in the Canadian courts.[66] It was recognised in the Canadian Supreme Court decision *Canadian Southern Railway Co v Phelps*.[67] The exception to it based on statutory authority was also recognised and applied in that early decision.[68] This also occurred in the 1915 decision of *Raffan v Canadian Western Natural Gas Light, Heat and Power Co.*[69] There a difference of opinion emerged as to the interpretation of a statute, permissive in its terms, mirrored on UK versions and without express provision as to whether the defendant company should only be held liable in cases of proven negligence or on a strict liability basis. Two justices specifically held that *Rylands* principles should apply to determine the liability of the defendant company, authorised by statute to assemble a gas main, when gas escaped from it, injuring the plaintiff.[70]

The *Rylands* principle was subsequently applied in a range of cases, including involving the excavation of land pursuant to defence work. The court found the mere fact that the work was defence related did not take it outside of the *Rylands* principle, concluding that the use of the land to conduct excavations was a non-natural use, such that *Rylands* could apply.[71] This decision might be contrasted with that of *Read v Lyons*, which, although decided on other grounds, contained dicta comments suggesting that the fact that land was being utilised for defence

[62] *Burnie Port Authority v General Jones Pty Ltd* (1994) 179 CLR 520, 593.
[63] ibid, 593.
[64] *Royal Commission on Civil Liability and Compensation for Personal Injury* (1978) 7054-1 (United Kingdom).
[65] *Burnie Port Authority v General Jones Pty Ltd* (1994) 179 CLR 520, 594.
[66] *Smith v Inco Limited* [2011] ONCA 628, [68] (Doherty, MacFarland JJA and Hoy J (ad hoc)).
[67] *Canadian Southern Railway Co v Phelps* (1884) 14 SCR 132.
[68] This exception was recognised and discussed by Strong J (144), Henry J (148) and Gwynne J (162).
[69] *Raffan v Canadian Western Natural Gas Light, Heat and Power Co* (1915) 8 Western Weekly Reports 676 (Supreme Court).
[70] ibid, 686 (Idington J) and 689 (Anglin J). A Quebec statute was interpreted to not preclude the imposition of strict liability in *Quebec Railway, Light, Heat and Power Co v Vandry* [1920] AC 662 (PC).
[71] *J P Porter Co v Bell* [1955] 1 DLR 62 (MacDonald J, for the Nova Scotia Court of Appeal).

purposes might be relevant in assessing whether or not strict liability should apply to the activity. It also applied, for example, to construction of a canal,[72] and the deepening of a channel.[73]

Dissatisfaction with the adoption in Canada of the strict liability principles of *Rylands v Fletcher* emerged quite early in the academic literature. In 1923 calls were being made for its subsumption into the law of negligence:

> Without in any way impeaching the authority of the case in *Rylands v Fletcher*, such a course is still open to the courts; it is still possible to dispose of this class of case by applying the general doctrine of liability based on the absence of due care and invoking, where necessary, the supplementary principle of res ipsa loquitur. The adoption of such a course by the courts would render unnecessary the application of an irrational and out of date standard, and the extension of the general theory of liability to instances hitherto regarded as exceptional would result in the removal of the one of the chief obstacles to the development of a logical and symmetrical doctrine of responsibility for torts.[74]

Leading Canadian torts scholar Fridman was also unimpressed with *Rylands v Fletcher*, calling for its assimilation with other torts:

> Even where injuries to or in connection with the enjoyment of land are concerned, there is something to be said for the idea that the law is paying more attention to the fault underlying the defendant's behaviour and is not deciding cases by the application of 'strict' rules of liability. Even if *Rylands v Fletcher* liability is therefore confined to injuries to land, there is strong support for the proposition that it is akin to liability for negligence. It is certainly accepted that *Rylands v Fletcher* liability is often intermingled with or akin to liability for nuisance … *Rylands v Fletcher* liability is not so distinct in modern law, but is often very much like other forms of liability which also include or are forms of negligence liability … whatever may have been said then (at the time of the decision in *Rylands*) it must now be conceded that the barriers between these various kinds of torts are fast vanishing.[75]

The potential anomalies that might be thrown up by the requirement, for *Rylands* to apply, that the dangerous thing 'escaped' were highlighted by a couple of cases involving injury on or near a car racing track. In one, *Rylands* applied because the plaintiff was injured while standing beyond the fence surrounding the track.[76] In the other, a *Rylands* action was dismissed because the plaintiff was injured while on the defendant's premises.[77]

[72] *Pilliterri v Northern Construction Co* [1930] 4 DLR 731. Strict liability for bridge construction was established in *Guelph Worsted Spinning Co v Guelph* (1914) 18 DLR 73, though *Rylands v Fletcher* was not discussed.

[73] *Aikman v Mills and Co* [1934] 4 DLR 264, and this action was maintainable against a sub-contractor because they had a right to occupy the premises from which the dangerous thing escaped (applying *Charing Cross Electricity Supply Co v Hydraulic Power Co* [1914] 3 KB 772).

[74] Vincent Macdonald, 'The Rule in *Rylands v Fletcher* and its Limitations' [1923] *Canadian Bar Review* 140.

[75] GHL Fridman, 'The Rise and Fall of *Rylands v Fletcher*' (1956) 34 *Canadian Bar Review* 810, 823.

[76] *Aldridge and O'Brien v Von Patter, Martin and Western Fair Association* [1952] OR 595.

[77] *Deyo v Kingston Speedway Limited* [1954] OR 223.

Despite these substantial jurisprudential comments disfavouring the retention of *Rylands v Fletcher* as a stand-alone principle of strict liability, its existence as part of Canadian tort law was confirmed by the Supreme Court of Canada in *Tock v St John's Metropolitan Area Board*,[78] though no member of the Supreme Court applied it in that case. The case involved damage to the plaintiff's premises caused by an overflowing storm sewer for which the defendants were responsible. All members of the Supreme Court found that the *Rylands* principle was not applicable on the facts since on no view could the use of premises to convey a sewer be viewed as non-natural.

La Forest J, with whom Dickson CJ agreed, was the only justice to consider *Rylands* in any detail, and the consideration was brief. He observed that the vast increase in town planning provision over the years had placed a new light on the meaning of concepts such as non-natural use. Here the provision of public sewerage and draining systems had become a necessity of urban life, and this particular system had been installed as part of town planning work. As such, it was impossible to find that the use was non-natural. La Forest J added that it was for the benefit of the community.

The main controversy in the *Tock* case was over the question of statutory authority. As was discussed in Chapter 1, a series of decisions in the late nineteenth and early twentieth centuries determined that where Parliament had required or, on one view, authorised a public body to undertake works, then the ordinary common law principles of tort liability, including the *Rylands v Fletcher* principle and ordinary rules of nuisance, did not apply. The courts did note, though, that in such an event, the public authority could be held liable for any breach of duty of care, or according to the terms of the statute pursuant to which the work had been done. As was noted in Chapter 1, the way in which courts interpreted these statutes diminished the scope of strict liability principles such as *Rylands* and nuisance, and gave further momentum, whether by inadvertence or by design, to the idea that liability was (or should be) fault based.

La Forest J, with whom Dickson CJ agreed, stated that circumstances had changed significantly since those times. He said there was much less acceptance today than was evident in the late nineteenth and early twentieth centuries that public authorities should be able to conduct operations without being held to be subject to the ordinary law, including common law liability rules. He agreed with scholarly observations that past immunities accorded to public authorities were now in a state of 'contraction and decay'.[79] He seemed to suggest that courts had been too ready to imply an intent to immunise public bodies from liability:

> The truth is that there is an air of unreality and contrivedness to the defence of statutory authority in this context … where the statute in question does not expressly exempt a body for damages in nuisance, or … does not provide for a compensation scheme

[78] *Tock v St John's Metropolitan Area Board* [1989] 2 SCR 1181.

[79] Allen Linden, 'Strict Liability, Nuisance and Legislative Authorisation' (1966) 4 *Osgoode Hall Law Journal* 196, 202.

> of its own or contain other clear legislative indications, I doubt that divination of an unexpressed intent of the legislature can shed much light on the question whether the person who has suffered damage should be denied compensation.[80]

La Forest J disagreed with the UK precedents that had presumed a parliamentary intent to abolish common law rights (in particular those imposing strict liability) in cases where the damage to injured parties from the conduct authorised or mandated by statute was 'inevitable'. He said the public authority should be held financially responsible for damage it caused whether or not it was inevitable, except where the legislation clearly stated that a person injured or who suffered other damage from the activity did not have a right to exercise ordinary common law rights.[81]

The other justices took a different view. Wilson J delivered a judgment with which Lamer and L'Heureux-Dube JJ agreed. Wilson J essentially adopted the position of the UK decisions. This distinguished between occasions where work has merely authorised, and where it was directed, whether the legislation was specific or more general. This was summarised in three principles:

(a) if the legislation imposed a duty and the nuisance was the inevitable consequence of discharging it, the nuisance was authorised and common law rights were extinguished, except if there was negligence;
(b) if the legislation authorised the conduct of an activity but was specific in terms of how and/or where activity would occur, and nuisance was the inevitable consequence of conducting the activity in that way or in that location, the nuisance was authorised and common law rights were extinguished, except if there was negligence; and
(c) if the legislation confers an authority and provides discretion, common law rights will apply.[82]

The Ontario Court of Appeal considered *Rylands* in *Smith v Inco Limited*.[83] There the plaintiff alleged that nickel particles from the defendant's factory had deposited on their land, causing a reduction in the value of their property. The trial judge had found in the plaintiff's favour on the basis that *Rylands* principles governed the case. The Court of Appeal unanimously disagreed. It rejected the trial judge's approach that treated *Rylands* as standing for a general principle of liability for extra-hazardous activities.[84] The House of Lords had made clear in *Read v Lyons* that *Rylands* was not to be interpreted in this way, a position with which the Court of Appeal agreed.[85] If the law should adopt such a general principle, it was best

[80] *Tock v St John's Metropolitan Area Board* [1989] 2 SCR 1181, 1198.
[81] ibid, 1201.
[82] ibid, 1214; Sopinka J disagreed that a distinction should be made between cases where work was required, as opposed to merely authorised (1226).
[83] *Smith v Inco Limited* [2011] ONCA 628.
[84] ibid, [78].
[85] ibid, [86].

implemented by Parliament, in the court's view, rather than judicial fiat.[86] In any event, the court found that the defendant's activities, pursuant to and in accordance with government-issued permits, could not be said to be extra-hazardous.

The Court of Appeal considered the troubled concept of 'non-natural use' or non-ordinary use. Consistently with the UK authorities, it noted that various factors would be relevant, including the location, the time when the use is made, and how it occurs. Planning legislation would be relevant, as would whether the community benefitted. The court noted here it was similar to the give-and-take principle evident in the law of nuisance, where the courts would typically weigh up the impositions on property interests that the community might reasonably have to accept as opposed to those which the person creating the nuisance might be expected to incur.[87] The court did not apply concepts of 'general benefit of the community' because it believed the phrase was more appropriate in the case of public authorities as opposed to private companies.[88] It found that this use of land was not 'non-natural'. This is where the evolution of Blackburn J's test has become particularly important. If his concept of 'not naturally there' is applied, the facts would meet the requirement. Clearly a factory is not naturally on property. However, as it has evolved, it has become more about the particular area, how long the activity has been conducted, timing and manner of use of the land. As a result, cases that once would have fallen within the *Rylands* rule now fall outside of it, as the facts in this case demonstrate.[89] It applied a similar approach to that of the United Kingdom in *Cambridge Water* by limiting *Rylands* actions to circumstances where the kind of loss the plaintiff suffered was reasonably foreseeable.[90]

In two respects, the Ontario Court of Appeal departed from UK authorities. First, it determined that *Rylands* liability could 'probably' apply where the plaintiff complained of personal injury,[91] contrary to the House of Lords decision in *Read v Lyons*.[92] And secondly, it determined that *Rylands* liability applied both to one-off and continuing escapes,[93] where the House of Lords held in *Cambridge Water* it would be better to see *Rylands* as being confined to one-off escapes[94] (there, on the

[86] ibid, [87].

[87] ibid, [98].

[88] ibid, [104].

[89] Tim Wood, 'Sticks and Carrots: *Rylands v Fletcher*, CSR and Accountability for Environmental Harm in Common Law Jurisdictions' (2012) 91 *Canadian Bar Review* 275, 286: 'this narrowing of non-natural use has been criticised by Canadian commentators. Nothing inherent in the original language of *Rylands*, as articulated at either instance, requires such a restrictive construction'.

[90] This has been criticised: Lynda Collins and Laura Freitag, 'Rescuing *Rylands*: Strict Liability and Environmental Protection in Canada' (2013) 23 *Tort Law Review* 85, 93; John Eekelaar, 'Nuisance and Strict Liability' (1973) 8 *Irish Jurist* 191, 192.

[91] *Smith v Inco Limited* [2011] ONCA 628, [68].

[92] *Read v Lyons* [1947] AC 156.

[93] *Smith v Inco Limited* [2011] ONCA 628, [111]. An example is *Bower v Richardson Construction Co Ltd* [1938] Can LII 111 (ONCA) per Bower J (continuing vibration from a pile-driver); *cf Barrette et al v Franki Compressed Pile Company of Canada Ltd* [1955] OR 413–30 (Schroeder J).

[94] *Cambridge Water Co v Eastern Counties Leather Plc* [1994] 2 AC 264, 306; *Transco Plc v Stockport MBC* [2004] 2 AC 1, 15 (Lord Hoffmann).

basis, however, that *Rylands* should be seen as a sub-species of the tort of private nuisance, with that tort applying to cases of continuing nuisance).

Rylands-type liability was further considered by the Nova Scotia Court of Appeal in *Canada (Attorney-General) v Macqueen*.[95] There the plaintiff complained about release of hazardous contaminants from a steel works that had been operating within a particular area for nearly 100 years. The Court of Appeal rejected a *Rylands* argument in the present case. This was for two reasons. First, the court found that *Rylands* did not apply in cases of *intentional* escape of materials from the defendant's land.[96] Here any emissions from the relevant factory were intentional, thus *Rylands* had no application.[97] Secondly, the court found that the requirement of a non-natural use could not be satisfied. The court took into account that the site had been utilised for the purposes of steel making for many years.[98] It also agreed with earlier decisions that *Rylands* did not represent a general cause of action based on notions of dangerousness or ultra-hazardous activity.[99]

United States

Of each of the jurisdictions studied, the United States generally has accepted the basis, if not the letter, of *Rylands v Fletcher* most of all. It has accepted a generalised principle of strict liability, in some cases, based on broad notions of dangerousness.[100] Before continuing, two preliminary points must be made. The first is that care must be taken in espousing any general 'United States legal position'. The common law is a matter for each state. The United States is robustly federal in this way, in sharp contrast to the other jurisdictions considered.[101] There is no uniform American common law, in contrast to the position in Australia[102] and in Canada. There is a common law of the United Kingdom, with some recognised exceptions, including Scots law. Secondly, and partly as a result of the first point, the Restatements published by the American Law Institute play a particular

[95] *Canada (Attorney-General) v Macqueen* [2013] NSCA 143.

[96] It has been observed that this moves *Rylands* outside the realm of strict liability and towards the negligence standard. Traditionally, negligence imports unintentional injury to another. Collins and Freitag say this is anomalous and counter-intuitive because it essentially protects the intentional tortfeasor, but not the unintentional tortfeasor, from strict liability, whereas intentional wrongdoing would typically be viewed as more serious than non-intentional wrongdoing: Lynda Collins and Laura Freitag, 'Rescuing *Rylands*: Strict Liability and Environmental Protection in Canada' (2015) 23 *Tort Law Review* 85, 96.

[97] *Smith v Inco Limited* [2011] ONCA 628, [79]–[80].

[98] ibid, [68].

[99] ibid, [74].

[100] Oliver Wendell Holmes Jr had observed that the *Rylands* precedent was based 'on the principle that it is politic to make those who go into extra-hazardous employments take the risk on their own shoulders': 'The Theory of Torts' (1873) 7 *American Law Review* 652, 653.

[101] *Erie Railroad v Tompkins* 304 US 64, 78–79 (1938).

[102] *Lange v Australian Broadcasting Corporation* (1997) 189 CLR 520, 563–64 (all members of the Court).

role in attempting to determine the American legal position on matters of non-constitutional law. There is no obligation on states, of course, to adopt the position of the relevant Restatement on any particular matter, but they are influential, and their content to some extent will reflect the existing legal position in a range of jurisdictions, and will likely provide impetus for other jurisdictions to adopt the position of the relevant Restatement.

An early example is *Shipley v Fifty Assocs.*[103] There the defendants owned a building in Boston. During winter, a large quantity of snow accumulated on their roof. As the plaintiff was walking past, some snow fell from the roof and onto the plaintiff, injuring her. The Supreme Court of Massachusetts found for the plaintiff, explicitly referring to and applying the *Rylands* principle of strict liability. It noted that no one had a right, by creating an artificial structure on their land, to cause water to pool and then eventually discharge onto others. The water was 'not naturally there'. It was irrelevant that the defendant might have taken all reasonable precautions in the construction and management of their roof. The court specifically engaged the ancient phrase of 'at peril' strict liability, concluding the defendant

> must at his peril keep the ice or the snow that collects upon his own roof, within his own limits, and is responsible for all damages, if the shape of the roof is such as to throw them upon his neighbour's land, in the same manner as he would be if he threw them there himself.[104]

A similar approach was subsequently taken by the Supreme Judicial Court of Massachusetts.[105] Interestingly, the judgment was written by Oliver Wendell Holmes Jr, later to join the US Supreme Court. The case concerned the escape of water from a pipe on the defendant's premises onto a sidewalk. The water subsequently froze and the plaintiff slipped on it. Holmes J, for the Court, stated that

> when knowledge of the damage done or threatened to the public is established, the strict rule of *Rylands v Fletcher* is not in question. The general principles of tort establish liability unless some special privilege can be made out … if the defendant knew that his gutter or spout created a nuisance, he was absolutely answerable for the harm it did.[106]

However, in his extra-judicial writings, Oliver Wendell Holmes Jr was far less enamoured with strict liability, denouncing the 'coarse and impolitic principle that a man always acts at his peril'.[107] He refers to the general principle that liability only exists in cases of fault.[108] Interestingly, he makes only two minor references to *Rylands* in the body of *The Common Law*, a highly influential source. *Rylands* seems to be completely at odds with Holmes' strongly worded preference for

[103] *Shipley v Fifty Assocs* 106 Mass. 194 (1870).
[104] ibid, 199–200 (Ames J).
[105] *Davis v Rich* 180 Mass. 235 (1902).
[106] ibid, 237–38 (Holmes CJ, for the Court).
[107] Oliver Wendell Holmes, *The Common Law* (Little, Brown & Co, 1881) 102.
[108] ibid, 66.

fault-based liability, yet his book all but ignores it, and he subsequently writes judgments which expressly affirm and purportedly apply it.

The New York courts would take a very different attitude to *Rylands v Fletcher*. One example is the Court of Appeals decision in *Losee v Buchanan*.[109] There the court denied that the owner of a steam boiler was liable when the boiler exploded, causing others injury. There was no suggestion that explosion was caused by any negligence on the defendant's part. The Court of Appeals disagreed with a major premise of the reasoning of Blackburn J in *Rylands*, which had sought to deduce a major premise from the strict liability applicable when animals caused injury to be applied to damage caused by property owners. It denied that there was a sufficient analogy.[110] Earl J said that *Rylands* 'was in direct conflict with the law as settled in this *country*' (emphasis added).[111] Earl J offered a social contract rationale for this position:

> By becoming a member of civilized society, I am compelled to give up many of my natural rights, but I receive more than a compensation from the surrender by every other man of the same rights, and the security, advantage and protection which the laws give me … the general rules that I may have the exclusive and undisturbed use and possession of my real estate … are much modified by the exigencies of the social state. We must have factories, machinery, dams, canals and railroads. They are demanded by the manifold wants of mankind and lay at the basis of all our civilization … I am not responsible for any damage they accidentally and unavoidably do to my neighbour. He receives his compensation for such damage by the general good in which he shares … most of the rights of property … in the social state are not absolute but relative and they must be so arranged and modified, not unnecessarily infringing upon natural rights, as upon the whole to promote the general welfare.[112]

Shortly afterwards, the New Hampshire Supreme Court savagely attacked the *Rylands* precedent,[113] claiming it penalised attempts to 'rise above a condition of barbarism', recognised 'peculiar rights of savage life in a wilderness (and) ignores the rights growing out of a civilized state of society'. It criticised *Rylands* for its extreme breadth:

> This is going back a long way for a standard of legal rights, and adopting an arbitrary test of responsibility that confounds all degrees of danger, pays no heed to the essential elements of actual fault, puts a clog on the reasonable and necessary uses of matter, and tends to embarrass and obstruct much of the work which it seems to be man's duty carefully to do.[114]

[109] *Losee v Buchanan* 51 NY 476 (1873).
[110] ibid, 483.
[111] ibid, 486–87.
[112] ibid, 484–85.
[113] *Brown v Collins* 53 NH 442 (1873).
[114] ibid, 448; see similarly *Pennsylvania Coal Co v Sanderson* 113 Pa. 126 (1886) where that State's Supreme Court stated that *Rylands* 'has not been generally received in this country' (150), denouncing the 'arbitrary and absolute rule of responsibility it declares' (154) and stating that 'a rule which casts upon an innocent person the responsibility of an insurer is a hard one at best' (150).

As has been noted above, at least to some extent[115] some American courts were initially not receptive to *Rylands v Fletcher* strict liability principles.[116] There are various explanations for this. Concern with industrial development, and how a zealous strict liability rule might crimp it, is clearly evident in the above case law. So is a kind of utilitarian thought, that individual rights must and should be ceded for the greater economic good. Leading scholars were against it, arguing that the explosive growth of the tort of negligence rendered it redundant.[117]

Further, it might be that the culture of the United States was markedly different from that of the United Kingdom.[118] In the latter jurisdiction, the law traditionally strongly protected property interests. Property interests were of very long-standing status. Large-scale industrial activity was somewhat new at the time these rules were being determined. In contrast, the United States from its inception was a society heavily based on capitalistic activity. Property interests did not enjoy the kind of reverence accorded to them in the United Kingdom. They were seen as something to be exploited for material gain:

> The first [that of the United Kingdom] is the view natural in a country whose development, gradual and slow, is substantially complete. It is the natural attitude of an aristocracy more concerned with land as a possession, a domain, under their exclusive occupation and dominion, rather than its development as a commercial asset. The latter is the view natural to a new settled country urgently requiring development even at the cost of some apparent injustice or of some entailment of individual rights. It is the attitude of a commercial people as distinguished from landowning aristocracy.[119]

In this context, American resistance to the idea of imposing strict, no-fault liability on enterprise is readily explicable.

[115] Obviously, space precludes a fuller treatment. It is argued that despite its rejection in north-eastern jurisdictions, *Rylands* was applied in a range of other States: Jed Handelsman Shugerman, 'The Floodgates of Strict Liability: Bursting Reservoirs and the Adoption of *Fletcher v Rylands* in the Gilded Age' (2000) 110 *Yale Law Journal* 333, 342–46.

[116] Francis Bohlen, 'Rule in *Rylands v Fletcher*' (1911) 59 *University of Pennsylvania Law Review* 298, 313; Francis Bohlen, 'Rule in *Rylands v Fletcher* II' (1911) 59 *University of Pennsylvania Law Review* 373, 388, noted the 'violent and indignant opposition' to it.

[117] Ezra Ripley Thayer, 'Liability Without Fault' (1916) 29 *Harvard Law Review* 801, 814: 'such a result as *Rylands v Fletcher* produces in our system is intolerable, and those courts have done well who have flatly refused to have anything to do with it … the law of negligence in its present development is a very modern affair, rendering obsolete much that went before it'; Jeremiah Smith, 'Tort and Absolute Liability – Suggested Changes in Classification' (1917) 30 *Harvard Law Review* 409, 414.

[118] Francis Bohlen, 'Rule in *Rylands v Fletcher*' (1911) 59 *University of Pennsylvania Law Review* 298, 315–19.

[119] Francis Bohlen, 'Rule in *Rylands v Fletcher* II' (1911) 59 *University of Pennsylvania Law Review* 373, 386; Wex Malone, 'Ruminations on Group Interests and the Law of Torts' (1959) 13 *Rutgers Law Review* 565, 572, stating that the transition that took place in the Industrial Revolution 'was not entirely precipitous for old values retained their traditional hold. But in America, which from the beginning had little in the way of indigenous values except the universal passion for pioneering and exploitation of new resources, the values of industry and transportation were quickly identified with the meaning of life itself … it followed that the flexible formulas [*sic*] of private nuisance and negligence were eagerly seized upon by the American courts, and Rylands v Fletcher was largely rejected. Live and let live was the only motto appropriate for the solution of this group struggle'; Clarence Morris, 'Hazardous Enterprises and Risk Bearing Capacity' (1952) 61 *Yale Law Journal* 1172, 1175–76.

Where American states did embrace *Rylands*, they often sought to limit its ambit by restricting it to highly dangerous activity potentially raising circumstances of exceptional peril.[120] This is clearly much narrower than the original formulation 'likely to do mischief if it escapes' and would pre-date later attempts by the UK courts in cases such as *Read v Lyons* to restrict it in the same way. This strand of reasoning is evident through the subsequent Restatements. Differentiation on this basis has been the subject of criticism in the United Kingdom.[121]

Though American law was originally sceptical regarding strict liability, it clearly eventually embraced it to some extent, as reflected in the Restatements. There are some theories on this. Shugerman refers to disasters such as the Johnstown Flood, which killed 2,000 people,[122] as pivotal in the same way to US law as the dam failures in England were explained above by Simpson to have been pivotal to the decision in *Rylands*.[123] Briefly, new owners took possession of a very large dam above the town of Johnstown. After purchasing it, they made some repairs without consulting engineers. They were warned that the dam was vulnerable to failure. Eventually the dam failed and 20 million tons of water was released, overwhelming the town and causing mass deaths. Legal action against the owners failed. Shugerman says a perception arose that it was fault-based liability rules that made recovery difficult. This case captured very strong public interest. Shugerman says it triggered a renewed interest in strict liability principles in the cases. This trend was strengthened by the fact that, in the United States, unlike the other jurisdictions studied in this book, many judicial positions are voted by the people, rather than government appointed. This in turn made judges unusually sensitive to public opinion on legal matters and caused a rethink on fault-based rules versus strict liability. He also notes that, at the time, the *American Law Review* was extremely influential in legal thought, with very eminent editors including Oliver Wendell Holmes Jr. The *Review* was supportive of *Rylands* strict liability, particularly after the Johnstown disaster.

The other explanation is that American society had changed. While in the late nineteenth century it was undergoing a rapid period of industrialisation and social change, and courts were loath to interfere with this by imposing strict liability, by the early to mid-twentieth century the country's economic ascendancy was firmly

[120] Francis Bohlen, 'Rule in *Rylands v Fletcher* III' (1911) 59 *University of Pennsylvania Law Review* 423, 440.

[121] *Hodge & Sons v Anglo-American Oil Co* (1922) 12 Lloyd's Law Reports 183, 187: 'personally, I do not understand the difference between a thing dangerous in itself, as poison, and a thing not dangerous as a class, but by negligent construction dangerous as a particular thing. The latter, if anything, seems the more dangerous of the two; it is a wolf in sheep's clothing instead of an obvious wolf' (per Scrutton LJ). This passage was cited with evident approval by Lord Atkin in his pivotal judgment in *Donoghue v Stevenson* [1932] AC 562, 595–96.

[122] Jed Handelsman Shugerman, 'The Floodgates of Strict Liability: Bursting Reservoirs and the Adoption of *Fletcher v Rylands* in the Gilded Age' (2000) 110 *Yale Law Journal* 333, 358–72.

[123] AWB Simpson, 'Legal Liability for Bursting Reservoirs: The Historical Context of *Rylands v Fletcher*' (1984) 13 *Journal of Legal Studies* 209.

established, and the need to 'subsidise' industry by withholding strict liability, at least for dangerous or hazardous activity, had subsided.[124]

Perhaps one example of this is the California Supreme Court decision in *Green v General Petroleum Corp*.[125] The defendant had drilled a deep well, in compliance with the environmental conditions under which it operated. Nevertheless, the well exploded, causing damage to the plaintiff's property nearby. It was known that sometimes wells would do this, given the pressure from the gas. The court found the defendant had not been negligent. The court found for the plaintiff, referring to principles of 'absolute liability' for accidents:

> It ought to be, and we are of the view that it is the rule that, where an injury arises out of, or is caused directly and proximately by the contemplated act or thing in question, without the interposition of any external or independent agency which was not or could not be foreseen, there is an absolute liability for the consequential damage, regardless of any element of negligence either in the doing of the act or in the construction, use or maintenance of the object or instrumentality that may have caused the injury.

It was not entirely clear how, if at all, this decision fitted in with broad-scale acceptance of fault basis of liability in the United States by the early twentieth century. The court did not rely on *Rylands* to reach its conclusion. Nor did the court specifically base its decision on notions of extra-hazardous or ultra-dangerous activity. However, subsequent decisions would expressly be based on the dangerousness of the defendant's activity, in making them liable for non-negligent injury caused to others. One example here is *Exner v Sherman Power Const Co*,[126] where the defendant stored explosives on their premises. Judge Hand said in such circumstances the defendant was an insurer, absolutely liable if injury were caused to a third party as a result. He specifically found that the liability of the defendant 'is not founded on illegal storage or on negligence, which was not proved, but upon the ground that the use of dynamite is so dangerous that it ought to be at the owner's risk'. Judge Hand specifically noted that *Rylands* had not generally been adopted in the United States, but noted that in so-called cases of blasting, resulting in explosions on the defendant's premises which then damaged the plaintiff's, absolute liability had been applied. This case and others of its ilk would prove important since the *First Restatement*, to be discussed below, issued seven years after this decision, would adopt a principle of strict liability for ultra-hazardous activity, as Judge Hand had done in *Exner*. And subsequently, the court would explain that the decision in *Green v General Petroleum Corp* was based on the fact that the particular activity was extra-hazardous.[127]

[124] Jed Handelsman Shugerman, 'The Floodgates of Strict Liability: Bursting Reservoirs and the Adoption of *Fletcher v Rylands* in the Gilded Age' (2000) 110 *Yale Law Journal* 333, 372.

[125] *Green v General Petroleum Corp* 205 Cal 328, 334; 270 Pac. 952, 955 (1928).

[126] *Exner v Sherman Power Const Co* 54 F. 2d. 510 (Second Circuit, 1931).

[127] *Luthringer v Moore* 31 Cal. 2d 489, 500, 190 Pac. 2d 1, 8 (1948): 'the case *Green v General Petroleum Corp* enunciated a principle of absolute liability which is applicable to the present case [pest control gases escaping and injuring the plaintiff neighbour] … the important factor is that certain activities

The American Law Institute has published three *Restatements on Torts* to date. Each of them provide for strict liability based on the perceived dangerousness of a particular activity, in general terms, and also specific terms, for instance relating to product liability. The general provisions have been expressly linked with the *Rylands v Fletcher* precedent,[128] though it has been noted that it has not been explained why the Restatements focused on the hazardous nature of an activity as a significant determinant of the relevant approach to be applied to resolution of a dispute.[129] Others have attempted a rationalisation.[130] Understandings of how it is to be determined whether or not an activity is to be considered ultra-hazardous or extra-dangerous seem to vary.[131] The use of such concepts to control the principles applicable to determining liability are also open to strong criticism:

> It is a bit incongruous that those very activities which cause most of our injuries are not deemed extra-hazardous, even though substantial resource readjustments would occur if they were included, and although loss spreading would certainly favour their inclusion. Continuation of a narrow definition of extra-hazardous activities must necessarily find what justification it has in factors outside (law and economics theory).[132]

The *Restatement (First) of Torts*[133] imposed strict liability for ultra-hazardous activity. This was defined in s520 as activity that necessarily involved the risk of serious harm that could not be avoided by the taking of reasonable care, and was not a matter of 'common usage'. Liability for such activity was limited to plaintiffs

under certain conditions may be so hazardous to the public generally, and of such relative infrequent occurrence, that it may well call for strict liability as the best public policy'; see for discussion Charles Gregory, 'Trespass to Negligence to Absolute Liability' (1951) 37 *Virginia Law Review* 359.

[128] William Landes and Richard Posner, 'The Positive Economic Theory of Tort Law' (1981) 15 *Georgia Law Review* 851, 908: 'The general principle of *Rylands*, that of strict liability for non-natural land uses, was absorbed into the American law as an element in the definition of an ultrahazardous activity'.

[129] George Fletcher, 'Fairness and Utility in Tort Theory' (1972) 85 *Harvard Law Review* 537, 541: 'it is never made clear by the Restatement why extra-hazardous risks warrant strict liability while ordinarily hazardous risks do not'.

[130] Robert Leflar, 'Negligence in Name Only' (1952) 27 *New York University Law Review* 564, 573, who suggested that the judges 'agreed that some types of activity were so dangerous that ordinary care, or even higher degrees of care than ordinary, could not with any assurance guard innocent persons from harm, yet these activities were so necessary, or desirable, in a civilized society … [that] they should not be prohibited … they were 'good' enterprises; our technology had merely failed to invent safety devices to control them. The enterprises [that] satisfied society's demands by undertaking the dangerous activity could not be blamed for failing to employ uninvented safety devices, therefore negligence could not easily be charged to [them] … they concluded generally that if an activity was so ultrahazardous that normal standards of care could not guard against normal injuries from it, and at the same time not so common in occurrence that people were accustomed to its risks in everyday life, [strict] liability would be imposed for injuries caused by it … the dangerous activity in that manner can pay its own way'.

[131] For example, Guido Calabresi, 'Some Thoughts on Risk Distribution and the Law of Torts' (1961) 70 *Yale Law Journal* 499, states that 'the typical extra-hazardous activity is one in which a substantial chance of substantial damage exists' (541), and 'in order to be extra-hazardous an activity requires more than the mathematical certainty that harm will occasionally occur. It is necessary that there be great likelihood that the harm will occur frequently as a result of that activity' (542). With respect, these interpretations are not entirely reflected in the *First* and *Third Restatements*, and only partially reflected in the *Second*, in the author's view.

[132] ibid, 543.

[133] *American Law Institute* (1938).

(or categories of plaintiff) that the defendant should have recognised would likely be harmed by the activity. Reflecting uncertainty (or perhaps unresolved disagreement) about the status of *Rylands* in American law, the *First Restatement* specifically left open whether the storage of water in large quantities was considered to be an 'ultrahazardous' activity.

The *Restatement (Second) of Torts*[134] provided for strict liability in cases where an activity was abnormally dangerous, either because of its inherent danger, or the manner in which it was carried out, regardless of whether or not the defendant who conducted it exercised a high degree of care (s519). In other words, it is strict, not fault-based, liability. Section 520 stated six factors that should be utilised to determine whether or not activity should be regarded as abnormally dangerous:

(a) the existence of a high degree of risk of harm to the person, land or chattels of another;
(b) the likelihood that the harm that results from it will be significant;
(c) whether the risk could have been eliminated by exercising reasonable care;
(d) the extent to which the activity is not a matter of common usage;
(e) whether the activity is appropriate given where it is conducted; and
(f) the extent to which its value to the community is outweighed by its dangerous features.

An abnormally dangerous activity is one that 'arises from activities that are in themselves unusual, or from unusual risks created by more usual activities under particular circumstances'.

Section 20(a) of the *Restatement (Third) of Torts*[135] states that a person who engages in an abnormally dangerous activity is subject to strict liability to the extent that physical damage results from it. Section 20(b) defines an abnormally dangerous activity as one creating a 'foreseeable and highly significant risk of physical harm when reasonable care is exercised by all actors', where the activity is not one of common usage.[136] This liability is subject to exceptions set out in section 24.[137]

It has been observed that these provisions have, in practice, been applied only in a very limited number of cases.[138] This is for two reasons – first, because only

[134] *American Law Institute* (1977).
[135] *American Law Institute* (2009).
[136] As to how notions of 'common usage' have been applied, see Frank Woodside, Mark Silbersack, Travis Fliehman and Douglas Feichtner, 'Why Absolute Liability Under *Rylands v Fletcher* is Absolutely Wrong' (2003) 29 *University of Dayton Law Review* 1, 22–25.
[137] These relate to non-characteristic risks of the dangerous activity, where the injury results from the actions of a third party, where the plaintiff is a trespasser on the defendant's premises, where the plaintiff comes into proximity to the dangerous activity in order to secure a benefit, or where the activity occurs pursuant to law or a legal order.
[138] Kenneth Simons, 'The Restatement (Third) of Torts and Traditional Strict Liability Doctrine: Robust Rationales, Slender Outcomes' (2009) 44 *Wake Forest Law Review* 1355; Kenneth Simons, 'The Restatement (Third) of Torts and Traditional Strict Liability: Robust Rationales, Slender Doctrines' (2009) 44 *Wake Forest Law Review* 1355, 1376: 'very few activities have been found to be abnormally dangerous under the Restatement (Second) test, and the Restatement (Third) test is unlikely to change this result'.

a relatively small number of activities have been deemed to be ultra-hazardous or abnormally dangerous and, secondly, because of the 'common usage' exception.[139] There is criticism that, to the extent that the Restatements in this area seem to accept a utilitarian-type reasoning, it is contrary to what courts were doing prior to their issue and since that time. It is said to be a somewhat rare example of a situation where a Restatement does not accurately reflect the law at the time and which has had limited impact on the law since its issue. It has been pointed out that Judge Learned Hand was one of the founders of the American Law Institute, which publishes the Restatements.[140] In a famous American torts case, he articulated the test for negligence in a highly utilitarian manner.[141] Again, criticism of that was that it did not reflect what was actually occurring in American courts, despite claims to the contrary,[142] and still does not.[143]

Some key differences between the American position and that pertaining elsewhere are immediately apparent. First, these Restatements accept that dangerousness, whatever the precise term used, is a term around which the imposition of strict liability might coalesce.[144] This is arguably what Blackburn J or the House of Lords in *Rylands* might have hoped, but it was knocked on the head in the United Kingdom in *Read v Lyons*, and has not been so accepted in Australia or Canada either. Secondly, it is apparent that none of the Restatements in this area have ever required, as a condition of the imposition of strict liability, that there be an escape of something, unlike the principle in *Rylands* does. Thirdly, the provisions seem to encompass a broad range of potential damage that might attract them. Liability for personal injury is not excluded, as has occurred with *Rylands* in the United Kingdom. Fourthly, the third iteration, but not the first two, consider foreseeability of harm as being relevant, as the United Kingdom accepted in *Cambridge Water*. Fifthly, the American position differs from that in Canada by not requiring that the acts complained of be unintentional in order that strict liability can be applied.

Unlike each of the other jurisdictions, the American law, at least on its face in the Restatements, does not take into account that the activity complained of might have been conducted pursuant to statute.[145] As has been seen, this may operate as a defence in the United Kingdom, Canada and Australia. There is no express equivalent in the Restatements. The *Second Restatement*, however, and in particular factors (e) and (f), might involve such considerations. Further, there is

[139] Gary T Schwartz, 'The Vitality of Negligence and the Ethics of Strict Liability' (1981) 15 *Georgia Law Review* 963, 971.

[140] Richard Wright, 'Hand, Posner and the Myth of the Hand Formula' (2003) 4 *Theoretical Inquiries in Law* 145, 149.

[141] *United States v Carroll Towing Co* 159 F. 2d 169 (Second Circuit, 1947).

[142] Richard Posner, 'A Theory of Negligence' (1972) 1 *Journal of Legal Studies* 29, 73.

[143] Richard Wright, 'Hand, Posner and the Myth of the Hand Formula' (2003) 4 *Theoretical Inquiries in Law* 145, 148: 'the aggregate-risk-utility test (of the kind contained in the Restatements) is infrequently mentioned in the courts, almost never included in jury instructions, rarely actually employed in judicial opinions, and almost never explains the actual results reached by the courts'.

[144] *Cambridge Water Co v Eastern Counties Leather Plc* [1994] 2 AC 264, 304–05 (Lord Goff, for the Court).

[145] Although, for an early example see *Bellinger v New York CRR Co* 23 NY 42 (1861).

no defence, as courts in the United Kingdom and Australia have recognised, of actions of a third party and/or Act of God-type considerations.

Each of the iterations refer to 'common usage' as an exception to application of the principle. This is similar to the defence of 'ordinary user' as became accepted in the UK case law, though clearly different from Blackburn J's original formulation of 'not naturally there'. This exception has been significant, effectively precluding the application of strict liability to vast areas of accident liability, including that relating to motor vehicle accidents and accidents involving railways.[146]

Somewhat perversely in a provision apparently imposing strict liability, factor (c) in the *Second Restatement* considers whether or not the risk to the plaintiff might have been avoided by the defendant taking reasonable care. Most would say that strict liability is imposed in circumstances where the taking of reasonable care is irrelevant. And the other factors are also typically taken into account in determining whether a particular wrong is actionable in negligence.[147] Considering both the notionally strict abnormally dangerous provisions and the notionally strict product liability provisions of the Restatements, Schwartz says that in practice, as applied, they are relatively similar to a negligence standard.[148]

Conclusion

Rylands v Fletcher has had a chequered reception in comparable common law jurisdictions to that of the United Kingdom. After initially being embraced in Australia, the High Court eventually rebelled against it, in a judgment of unusually scathing criticism of the decision and the complexities and confusion engendered by it. In Canada, the doctrine lives on, but has been progressively limited and pretensions of its reflecting a broad-scale, generalised principle of liability denied, just as in the United Kingdom. After initial resistance in the United States, it would find a home there, but the way in which the various Restatements express the principle, and exceptions to it, confine its practical operation.

The controversy over *Rylands v Fletcher* strict liability in the United States had the benefit of spawning a very large quantity of academic literature on the debate between strict liability and fault in the law of torts. Part III of the book embarks on a review of this very rich intellectual debate. Serious attempts have been made to try to craft the intellectual ballast that would support general application of a strict liability regime, primarily through the enterprise risk model of liability. Part III will reflect on these attempts and provide a critique of attempts to justify strict liability in the law of torts.

[146] Virginia E Nolan and Edmund Ursin, 'The Revitalization of Hazardous Activity Strict Liability' (1987) 65 *North Carolina Law Review* 257, 267.

[147] Elspeth Reid, 'Liability for Dangerous Activities: A Comparative Analysis' (1999) 48 *International and Comparative Law Quarterly* 731, 737.

[148] Gary T Schwartz, 'The Vitality of Negligence and the Ethics of Strict Liability' (1981) 15 *Georgia Law Review* 963, 971.

PART III

The Theoretical Debate: Strict Liability and Fault-based Liability

5

Summary of the Theoretical Debate: Strict Liability and Fault-based Liability

Introduction

The twentieth and twenty-first centuries have seen a range of theories developed that are said to support the recognition of strict liability in particular cases. Much of this intellectual thought is of course not evident in the plethora of legal cases described in Parts I and II of the book, many of which imposed what we would now regard as strict liability. Earlier chapters have documented the shift away from concepts of strict liability towards a fault-based system of liability. By a process which began perhaps in the late seventeenth century, and had become virtually complete by the end of the nineteenth century, fault had become the dominant form of liability, strict liability having been largely discredited and maligned. In this light, there is some curiosity about the fact of the surge in intellectual support for strict liability doctrine, particularly in the United States, commencing in the early twentieth century, and its appearance in limited contexts within the law of torts.

Prior to commencing this discussion, it is important to reiterate the intended meaning of terms used in the discussion. I take strict liability to mean liability imposed in the absence of 'fault'. When I use the word 'fault', I mean a failure to live up to objectively determined standards of conduct. Strict liability is distinct from absolute liability,[1] and fault could have a range of meanings.[2] I have indicated my intended meaning in this context.

[1] As indicated in Chapter 1, absolute liability is the imposition of liability in a given situation without exceptions such as defences. Strict liability, in contrast, recognises the availability of defences.

[2] Some have suggested that fault should involve the question of personal fault on the part of the defendant. This might imply that a subjective standard be applied – eg, what the law might expect of a person given their individual circumstances and characteristics. This view became untenable after *Vaughan v Menlove* (1837) 3 Bing. NC 468; 132 ER 490. Alternatively, others such as Ehrenzweig appear to view it as a question of whether the defendant voluntarily chose to engage in the activity that caused the plaintiff loss. This is not a generally accepted meaning of fault and will not be used here. For discussion of the various approaches see Allan Beever, *A Theory of Tort Liability* (Hart Publishing, 2016) 29–37.

Jeremiah Smith

Jeremiah Smith's articles on workers' compensation statutes were pivotal in the intellectual movement in support of strict liability.[3] Smith discussed the introduction of workers' compensation statutes in the United Kingdom in 1897, providing compensation for workers injured while at work in the absence of any evidence that an employer was at fault in causing the injuries. These statutes were a reaction to the so-called unholy trinity of tort doctrines in the employment context, namely the doctrine of common employment preventing an employee injured at work from obtaining compensation against their employer if they were injured while in the company of another employee,[4] and the strictness with which defences of *volenti non fit injuria* and contributory negligence applied.[5] These principles crippled the ability of employees injured at work to successfully bring a case against their employer. He noted that, initially, the UK workers' compensation legislation had applied only to those working in particularly dangerous industries, however within a decade it had been expanded to include all industries.[6] He noted it had been estimated that in nearly half of the cases in which an employee had been injured at work, it was not possible for them to prove that their injuries were the fault of the employer. It was often due to dangers 'inherent in the method of work and the damaging results may be viewed as inevitable'. It will be recalled from an earlier chapter that, in the past, the defence of 'inevitable accident' was available as a defence to an action for personal injuries.

Interestingly, Smith considered a theory said to underlie the imposition of liability upon employers for injuries suffered by employees at work:

> It is argued that a part (at least) of the damage happening to workmen in a business without fault on the part of any one, should be borne by the owner of the business, because the latter initiated the undertaking with a view to his own benefit, and because he will reap the net profit of the business if any should accrue. Indeed the assumption seems to be that the owner is to get all the benefits of the business, and that hence it would not be unjust to require him to bear all the risks encountered by the workmen and to make full compensation for the entire damage suffered by the workmen. The incorrectness of this assumption has been pointed out … the owner or master 'in no proper sense gets all the benefits of the business'. Ordinarily the master is not the only one who receives benefit. 'Being employed may be just as great a benefit to the servant as the employment of him may be to his master'.[7]

[3] Jeremiah Smith, 'Sequel to Workmen's Compensation Acts' (1914) 27 *Harvard Law Review* 235, 344.

[4] *Priestley v Fowler* (1837) 3 M & W 1; 150 ER 1030.

[5] *Butterfield v Forrester* (1809) 11 East 60; 103 ER 926; *Smith v Baker and Sons* [1891] AC 325.

[6] Jeremiah Smith, 'Sequel to Workmen's Compensation Acts' (1914) 27 *Harvard Law Review* 235, 344–45.

[7] ibid, 252. The quotes are from a work by Floyd Mechem, 'Employers' Liability' (1910) 44 *American University Law Review* 221, 227 and 241–42.

In other words, he rejected the suggestion that the employers should in fairness be financially accountable to employees injured at work (whether through a legislated system of workers' compensation or otherwise) because the employers obtained the gains of the employees' labour. Interestingly, this was an old basis for the imposition of vicarious liability upon employers.[8] It would later find support in the so-called 'enterprise risk' theory of liability, which will be discussed below.

Smith then pointed out the conflict between the philosophical basis of the workers' compensation legislation and that of the common law of tort, the former being based on a system of no-fault liability and the other being fault based (by the time Smith wrote in the early twentieth century, the common law had primarily adopted a fault-based system of liability): 'the theory underlying the statute … is in direct conflict with the fundamental doctrine of the modern common law of torts. The statute shows a distinct revulsion from the conception that fault is essential to liability'.[9]

He suggested that the law had to resolve this incongruity, where it apparently simultaneously accepted a no-fault and fault-based system of liability. He opined the public would agitate for further change to the law 'to put outsiders, when damaged by the non-culpable conduct of a business, upon an equality with workmen employed in that business'.[10] Though Smith maintained he had an open mind as to how this conflict would or should be resolved,[11] it seems clear from the tenor of his article, including the statement just quoted and his assumption that the outcomes achieved under the workers' compensation schemes were 'fair', that he favoured the spread of the no-fault principle of liability to instances beyond workers' compensation.[12]

Smith's arguments for the extension of strict liability principles beyond the context of workers' compensation would find some favour, at least to an extent. Each of the three *Restatements* (*Torts*) discussed in the previous chapter, recognises

[8] *Turberville v Stampe* (1698) 1 Ld. Raym. 264, 265; 91 ER 1072, 1073: 'the master shall be liable … for it shall be intended that the servant had authority from his master, it being for his master's benefit' (Holt CJ); see Anthony Gray, *Vicarious Liability: Critique and Reform* (Hart Publishing, 2018).

[9] Jeremiah Smith, 'Sequel to Workmen's Compensation Acts' (1914) 27 *Harvard Law Review* 235, 246.

[10] ibid, 362.

[11] ibid, 367: 'the aim has been to bring out distinctly the exact question, and to show that it must be met and cannot be evaded. How it should be answered is a matter not to be dealt with here' (367); *cf* a statement on the same page: 'justice to certain persons other than workmen must also require similar legislation for their benefit … the common law of AD 1900 is wrong in principle and ought to be repudiated'.

[12] Smith said 'there may be an attempt to induce judges to repudiate the fundamental doctrine of the modern common law of torts that fault is generally requisite to liability, and to go back to the ancient common law doctrine that an innocent actor must answer for harm caused by his non-culpable conduct' (365). As Gary Schwartz pointed out, there were particular issues with the ability of employees to sue for work-related injuries that on one view might have justified the introduction of no-fault workers' compensation schemes. Those particular issues may not be replicated in relation to other types of accident: 'Hidden and Fundamental Issue of Employer Vicarious Liability' (1996) 69 *Southern California Law Review* 1739, 1771: 'because tort law as applied to workers' injuries was peculiarly ungenerous, unsatisfying and administratively costly, it proved vulnerable to challenge and to eventual displacement'.

strict liability in the context of extra-hazardous or ultra-dangerous activity. The law of product liability has generally accepted strict liability principles.[13] However, fault remains the predominant theory of tort liability in the United States.

Young Smith

Young Smith adopted a similar position. He sought to understand and explain the principle of vicarious liability, making employers liable for injuries that employees caused to others, at least within the scope of employment. He used the enterprise risk theory in order to do so. He appeared to agree with a 'characteristic risks' approach to the imposition of such liability:

> It may be argued that it is a matter of common knowledge that servants employed to drive automobiles frequently do make short excursions or errands of their own which they would not have made but for the fact that they had been sent on an errand for the master. Such conduct on the part of servants must, therefore, be regarded as a probable result of employing servants to drive automobiles: just as probable as that they will drive with a reckless speed. Accordingly the undertaking of an enterprise involving the employment of chauffeurs must necessarily expose third parties to a risk of injury from such excursions as well as expressly authorized acts and should, therefore, be borne by the enterprise which caused the risk.[14]

Young Smith sought to draw inferences from the position of Jeremiah Smith on workers' compensation, to explain notions of vicarious liability, and perhaps provide the impetus for an even broader reform of the law of torts:

> A reason which occurs to the writer is that which has been offered in justification of workmen's compensation statutes. In substance it is the belief that it is socially more expedient to spread or distribute among a large group of the community the losses which experience has taught are inevitable in the carrying on of industry, than to cast the loss upon a few … if it is socially expedient to spread and distribute throughout the community the inevitable losses occasioned by injuries to employees engaged in industry, is it not also socially expedient to spread and distribute the losses due to injuries to third persons which are equally inevitable? Surprising as it may seem, by means of [vicarious liability] the common law has partially accomplished in the latter case what workmen's compensation statutes have accomplished in the former.[15]

Some examples of the acceptance of these notions of loss spreading as a specific goal of the law of torts appear in the case law.[16]

[13] *Henningsen v Bloomfield Motors Inc* 32 N.J 358, 161 A. 2d 69 (1960); *Greenman v Yuba Power Products Inc* 59 Cal. 2d 57, 377 P. 2d. 897, 27 Cal. Rptr 697 (1963); *Restatement (Second) of Torts* s402A, *Restatement (Third) Law of Torts* (1998).

[14] Young Smith, 'Frolic and Detour' (1923) 23 *Columbia Law Review* 716, 724.

[15] 'Frolic and Detour' (1923) 23 *Columbia Law Review* 444, 456–57.

[16] *Sieger v Kuhlman* 502 P. 2d. 1181, 1188 (1972): 'a good reason to apply [strict liability] principles … is that the commercial transporter can spread the loss among his customers – who benefit from this

Fleming James

Fleming James advocated that tort law should impose absolute liability, quite independently of fault.[17] He conducted research on the notion that some individuals were more prone to suffer personal injury than others. He found that often accidents that occurred were not related to, and quite distinct from, any fault or blame on the part of any possible defendant.[18] He saw an incongruence between the reality that personal injuries often occurred independently of fault, and the fact that the law of personal injury was heavily based on fault. He recommended that the law should deal with this incongruence by moving towards a system of absolute liability for injuries caused to another. He also noted that 'large units, such as transportation companies, government and insurance companies, are in a strategic position to reduce accidents'.[19] He found that since workers' compensation statutes had been introduced, the level of accidents had reduced, pointing to the fact that the imposition of absolute liability upon defendants would likely lead to a reduction in the level of accidents.[20] He found that it was pointless to impose norms of behaviour on those who were vulnerable to being injured by another because they were often unaware of their proneness to accidents and/or unaware of how to make activities safer.[21] James's work was particularly significant in convincing a strict liability approach to product liability cases, on the basis of unequal bargaining power between customer and business, the need for businesses to internalise costs their activities generate, and the ability of businesses to spread their losses through insurance.[22]

extrahazardous use of the highways. Also, if the defect which caused the substance to escape was one of manufacture, the owner is in the best position to hold the manufacturer to account'; *Lubin v Iowa City* 131 N.W 2d 765, 770 (Iowa, 1964): 'the risks of such a method of operation should be borne by the water supplier who is in a position to spread the cost among the consumers who are in fact the true beneficiaries of this practice'.

[17] Fleming James and John Dickinson, 'Accident Proneness and Accident Law' (1950) 63 *Harvard Law Review* 769, 780; Fleming James, 'Tort Law in Midstream: Its Challenge to the Judicial Process' (1959) 8 *Buffalo Law Review* 315, 337: 'I should like to see courts maintain and extend existing areas of strict liability'. George Priest, 'The Invention of Enterprise Liability: A Critical History of the Intellectual Foundations of Modern Tort Law' (1985) 14 *Journal of Legal Studies* 461, 470: 'from his earliest articles, James promoted one principle – risk distribution – above all others. Every other consideration that might be thought relevant to the resolution of a tort dispute, James ruthlessly devalued or ignored'; 'James' scholarship after 1940 represents a calculated program aimed at achieving the complete overturn of the fault system and the substitution of a general accident compensation plan' (475).

[18] Fleming James and John Dickinson, 'Accident Proneness and Accident Law' (1950) 63 *Harvard Law Review* 769, 780, 775.

[19] ibid, 780.

[20] Fleming James, 'Tort Law in Midstream: Its Challenge to the Judicial Process' (1959) 8 *Buffalo Law Review* 315, 331.

[21] ibid, 330.

[22] George Priest, 'The Invention of Enterprise Liability: A Critical History of the Intellectual Foundations of Modern Tort Law' (1985) 14 *Journal of Legal Studies* 461, 517.

Gregory Keating

More recently, Gregory Keating has articulated a strong defence of the imposition of strict liability. He essentially uses the concept of fairness to impose strict liability upon businesses:

> The idea of fairness implies that the tort law of accidents is and should be concerned with the fair distribution of the burdens and benefits of mutually beneficial but harmful activities. Fairness requires – presumptively, that those who impose risks bear the accident costs that issue from those risk impositions … this conception of fairness gives rise to a presumption in favour of strict liability. Because those who impose risks normally reap the benefits that flow from their risk impositions, injurers should generally be strictly liable to those they accidentally injure unless those they injure are already compensated 'in kind' for bearing their loss.[23]

Keating favoured the idea that businesses should absorb the costs associated with risk, or harm, that is 'characteristic' of its activities, regardless of fault. This has come to be known as the enterprise risk notion of liability. It is commonly utilised to impose strict liability upon business enterprises, including vicarious liability.

He articulates the fairness basis of support of strict liability upon business for 'characteristic' risks as follows:

> Fairness requires a just distribution of burdens and benefits. It therefore gives rise to a presumption that the costs of the accidental physical injuries characteristic of an activity should be borne by those who benefit from the activity, whether or not they are culpably responsible for precipitating the injuries at issue.[24]

He connects this notion of enterprise risk with historical strict liability principles as follows:

> Enterprise liability is a general and distinctively modern theory of strict liability. Whereas traditional strict liability expressed the maxim that those who act do so as their own peril, enterprise liability expresses the maxim that those who profit from the imposition of risk should bear the costs of the accidents that are a price of their profits.[25]

He traces the enterprise risk theory to that underlying the workers' compensation statutes, as discussed by Smith.[26] Keating believed that the doctrine of enterprise risk provides the basis for a general principle of strict liability. He criticises the position of the *Third Restatement*, which exceptionally imposes strict liability.

[23] Gregory Keating, 'Distributive and Corrective Justice in the Tort Law of Accidents' (2000) 74 *Southern California Law Review* 193, 200.

[24] Gregory Keating, 'The Theory of Enterprise Liability and Common Law Strict Liability' (2001) 54 *Vanderbilt Law Review* 1285, 1286–87.

[25] ibid, 1287. He notes that 'enterprise liability came to unify and infuse much of traditional common law strict liability' (1288).

[26] ibid, 1287: 'the theory of enterprise liability originated outside the law of torts, in a distinctly modern piece of legislation – the workers' compensation schemes enacted in England and the United States around the turn of the twentieth century'.

His view is that this falls well short of what is required – he argues that strict liability is not exceptional in the law of tort, which is what the *Third Restatement* implies, but rather a general organising principle supporting the general imposition of strict liability, 'enabling legal scholars and judges to reconceive and reconfigure the common law of torts'.[27]

As he acknowledges, such an approach reflects a distributive theory of the law of torts – seeking to distribute the burden and benefit of socially useful, if risky, activity fairly, irrespective of moral blame.[28]

As with Young Smith, Keating lauds the loss-spreading potential of the doctrine of enterprise risk:

> If enterprise liability is capable of spreading the costs of accidental harm across those who benefit from the creation of the relevant risks, then it may be fair and just – not just efficient or humane – to shift the costs of accidents arising out of reciprocal risks onto those who imposed the risks.[29]

Keating claims that

> when an activity is large enough, the accidental harm associated with its conduct is predictable and the cost of that harm can be foreseen and priced into that activity … when enterprises themselves are actuarially large, they tend to engender non-negligent accidents in a regular and calculable way, and the costs of these accidents can be factored into the costs of conducting the enterprise.[30]

Evidence of judicial acceptance of such an approach includes *Ira S Bushey and Sons v United States*.[31] The case involved a drunken sailor. As he walked towards his ship, which was in dry dock at the time, he turned three large wheels many times. This had the effect of flooding the dry dock, and the ship damaged the dock. The question was the liability of the sailor's employer vicariously for what he did. On appeal, Judge Friendly found for the plaintiff. However, this was on the basis that businesses should in fairness be held liable for 'accidents which may fairly be said to be characteristic of (their activities)'.[32] Judge Friendly determined that 'characteristic' accidents were those 'that flow from an (enterprise's) long-run activity in spite of all reasonable precautions on (its) part'.[33] According to the court, this would lead

[27] ibid, 1329.

[28] ibid, 1330.

[29] Gregory Keating, 'The Idea of Fairness in the Law of Enterprise Liability' (1997) 95 *Michigan Law Review* 1266, 1329. See to like effect Howard Klemme, 'The Enterprise Liability Theory of Torts' (1976) 47 *University of Colorado Law Review* 153, 179 stating one of the criteria as 'who is probably in the most effective position to cause the costs of such preventive action, or in the alternative, the costs of insurance, to be passed on more efficiently, economically, to the consuming purchasers or other economic beneficiaries of the enterprise which failed to meet normal expectations'; see also George Priest, 'The Invention of Enterprise Liability: A Critical History of the Intellectual Foundations of Modern Tort Law' (1985) 14 *Journal of Legal Studies* 461, 464.

[30] Gregory Keating, 'The Idea of Fairness in the Law of Enterprise Liability' (1997) 95 *Michigan Law Review* 1266, 1333.

[31] *Ira S Bushey and Sons v United States* 398 F. 2d. 167 (Second Circuit, 1968).

[32] ibid, 171.

[33] ibid, 171.

to a fair allocation of the burden of the costs of accidents. Another example is found in *Green v General Petroleum Corp*, where it is stated that

> [w]here one, in the conduct and maintenance of an enterprise … deliberately does an act under known conditions, and with knowledge that injury may result to another, proceeds, and injury is done to the other as the direct and proximate consequence of the act, however carefully done, the one who does the act and causes the injury should, in all fairness, be required to compensate the other for the injury done.[34]

Both Keating and Fletcher strongly emphasise the concept of reciprocal risk.[35] Essentially, they posit that where plaintiffs and defendants impose risks upon each other that are roughly equivalent, the law of negligence is the optimal way to deal with accidents. However, in cases where one class of individuals, defendants, impose non-reciprocal risks on plaintiffs, in other words they impose risks and costs on others which the others do not generally impose back, strict liability principles should apply. This theory is said to rest on notions of social contract – that when it can be said that all parties have relinquished broadly equivalent rights, then it might be said they give up the 'right' to obtain compensation for injury they suffered that was not caused through negligence. However, they do not give up that right unilaterally – if the imposition of this rule upon certain categories of individual is unfair and unequal, because it is not imposed, or not imposed to roughly the same extent on others, then they should not be taken to have given up that right at all.[36]

George Fletcher opines that

> [t]he general principle expressed in all of these situations governed by diverse doctrinal standards is that a victim has a right to recover for injuries caused by a risk greater in degree and different in order from those created by the victim and imposed on the defendant – in short, for injuries resulting from non-reciprocal risks. Cases of liability are those in which the defendant generates a disproportionate, excessive risk of harm, relative to the victim's risk-creating activity … conversely cases of non-liability are those of reciprocal risks, namely those in which the victim and the defendant subject each other to roughly the same degree of risk.[37]

[34] *Green v General Petroleum Corp* 205 Cal. 328, 333–34, 270 P. 952, 955 (1928) (California Supreme Court).

[35] George Fletcher, 'Fairness and Utility in Tort Theory' (1972) 85 *Harvard Law Review* 537; Gregory Keating, 'The Idea of Fairness in the Law of Enterprise Liability' (1997) 95 *Michigan Law Review* 1266, 1310–12; Virginia E Nolan and Edmund Ursin, 'The Revitalization of Hazardous Activity Strict Liability' (1987) 65 *North Carolina Law Review* 257, 290–91. It also finds support in Keith Hylton, 'The Theory of Tort Doctrine and the Restatement (Third) of Torts (2001) 54 *Vanderbilt Law Review* 1413. It is referred to in the *Third Restatement* as one of the accepted rationales for the imposition of strict liability.

[36] Gregory Keating, 'The Idea of Fairness in the Law of Enterprise Liability' (1997) 95 *Michigan Law Review* 1266, 1317–18: 'the general justification that we have for bearing risks imposed by others lies in our reciprocal right to expose others to equal risks … when mutuality of benefit is fully realized, no-one's life or limb is sacrificed to the greater good of others … for mutuality of benefit to be fully realized, risks must, first, be reciprocal in a qualitative [not quantitative] way; they must be equal in probability and magnitude, and be imposed for equally good reason [and] … the reasons must be sufficiently good'.

[37] George Fletcher, 'Fairness and Utility in Tort Theory' (1972) 85 *Harvard Law Review* 537, 542. Fletcher claims that *Rylands v Fletcher* is in fact an example of non-reciprocal risk – the defendant who constructed the reservoir 'sought to use his land for a purpose at odds with the use of land then

Fletcher seeks to explain the focus of the Restatements on notions of extra-dangerous or ultra-hazardous activity. He claims that they are really based on non-reciprocal risk.[38] He maintains this leads to fair outcomes: 'if the defendant creates a risk that exceeds those to which he is reciprocally subject, it seems fair to hold him liable for the results of his aberrant indulgence'.[39]

Later Keating states that reciprocity of risk can only be a 'master organizing idea' rather than a 'master test' of the choice between negligence and strict liability because reciprocity of risk is an ideal, it is abstract and is of uncertain meaning and application.[40] He also excludes what is within the concept of 'background risks' from the analysis of whether or not risks are reciprocal.[41] Keating would let losses flowing from background risks lie where they fell.[42] He also states that 'the rise of liability insurance … undermines the case for dividing tort liability in accordance with the presence or absence of reciprocal risk'[43] and seems to eschew strict liability in cases of 'unusually high level(s) of risk'.[44]

Other scholars sought to explain the American focus on ultra-hazardous activity as a basis for the imposition of strict liability in a different way. For example, Leflar stated that the judges

> concluded generally that if an activity was so ultrahazardous that normal standards of care could not guard against normal injuries from it, and at the same time not so common in occurrence that people were accustomed to its risks in everyday life, [absolute] liability would be imposed for injuries caused by it.[45]

Utilitarian Support for Strict Liability: Jeremy Bentham

Jeremy Bentham's utilitarianism can be used to support strict liability. If the law should be about providing the greatest happiness to the greatest number,[46] where

prevailing in the community … the critical feature … is that the defendant created a risk of harm to the plaintiff … different from the risks that the plaintiff imposed on the defendant. Without the factor of non-reciprocal risk-creation … (the case) would have been decided differently' (545–46).

[38] ibid, 547: 'the uncommon, ultra-hazardous activities pinpointed by the Restatement are readily subsumed under the rationale of non-reciprocal risk-taking … dangerous activities like blasting, fumigating and crop dusting stand out as distinct, non-reciprocal risks in the community'.

[39] ibid, 548.

[40] Gregory Keating, 'The Idea of Fairness in the Law of Enterprise Liability' (1997) 95 *Michigan Law Review* 1266, 1325.

[41] Gregory Keating, 'Distributive and Corrective Justice in the Tort Law of Accidents' (2000) 74 *Southern California Law Review* 193, 210.

[42] ibid, 211.

[43] ibid, 214.

[44] ibid, 218. This is clearly contrary to the position in each of the Torts Restatements.

[45] Robert Leflar, 'Negligence in Name Only' (1952) 27 *New York University Law Review* 564, 573.

[46] James Barr Ames, 'Law and Morals' (1908) 22 *Harvard Law Review* 97, 110: 'the law is utilitarian. It exists for the realization of the reasonable needs of the community. If the interests of the individual runs counter to this chief object of the law, it must be sacrificed'. Of course, it is not entirely clear how happiness is to be measured and judged: Richard Posner, 'Utilitarianism, Economics and Legal Theory' (1979) 8 *Journal of Legal Studies* 103, 114: 'some utilitarians have faith in the eventual discovery of a psychological metric that will enable happiness to be measured and compared across persons … but in

benefits are aggregated, it becomes important to weigh up the benefit of a particular activity compared with its costs. Only activities where the marginal benefit (to the public) exceed the marginal cost to individuals should be permitted.[47]

An apparent example of utilitarian reasoning, though not identified as such by its author, to support strict liability appears in judgments of Baron Bramwell in the mid to late nineteenth century. It is very rare to specifically see such reasoning in the case law. As was noted above, Baron Bramwell was a long-term supporter of strict liability. He favoured it in *Rylands v Fletcher* in the original decision, and in other cases. So, for example, in *Bamford v Turnley*[48] Baron Bramwell notes that

> [t]he public consists of all the individuals of it, and a thing in only for the public benefit when it is productive of good to those individuals on the balance of loss and gain to all. So that if all the loss and all the gain were borne and received by one individual, he on the whole would be a gainer .... But whenever a thing is for the public benefit ... the loss to the individuals of the public who will lose bear compensation out of the gains of those who gain.

In this way, Baron Bramwell utilised utilitarian reasoning in order to justify the strict liability he favoured.

Richard Epstein

Richard Epstein also purports to provide some intellectual ballast for the imposition of strict liability. His focus is simply upon causation. He argues that if it is shown that the defendant's activity caused harm to the plaintiff, the plaintiff is prima facie entitled to compensation from the defendant, unless the plaintiff can demonstrate an excuse or justification for what they did.[49] This theory would take the common law back prior to the late seventeenth century when fault really began to take hold in the common law in this area, though exceptionally it finds some support in the House of Lords decision in *Rylands v Fletcher*.[50]

the two centuries that have elapsed since Bentham announced the felicific calculus no progress towards the discovery of such a metric has been made'.

[47] *Powell v Fall* (1880) 5 QBD 597, 601 (CA): 'it is just and reasonable that if a person uses a dangerous machine, he should pay for the damage which it occasions; if the reward which he gains for the use of the machine will not pay for the damage, it is mischievous to the public and ought to be suppressed, for the loss ought not to be borne by the community or the injured person. If the use of the machine is profitable, the owner ought to pay compensation for the damage' (Baron Bramwell, with whom Baggallay and Thesiger LLJ agreed).

[48] (1862) 3 B & S 66; 122 ER 27, 33.

[49] Richard Epstein, 'A Theory of Strict Liability' (1973) 2 *Journal of Legal Studies* 151, 189: 'rules of liability should be based upon the harm in fact caused and not upon any subsequent determination of the reasonableness of the defendant's conduct', and 'proof of the proposition that A hit B should be sufficient to establish a prima facie case of liability' (168).

[50] *Rylands v Fletcher* (1866) LR 3 HL 330, 341: 'in considering whether a defendant is liable to a plaintiff for damage which the plaintiff may have sustained, the question in general is not whether the defendant has acted with due care and caution, but whether his acts have occasioned the damage' (Lord Cranworth).

Epstein takes issue with cases decided on the basis of negligence. One example he uses is the classic case of *Bolton v Stone*.[51] The well-known facts involved the plaintiff being injured by a cricket ball which had been hit outside of the cricket ground. Such an incident was extremely rare. The House of Lords found that the cricket club was not liable in negligence, given that the probability that the events that transpired would in fact occur was extremely low.[52]

On the basis of his causation analysis, Epstein says the legal result was wrong. In his view, the result should have been that the defendant was liable. He says that '*Bolton v Stone* is an easy case under the rules of strict liability. The plaintiff's conduct provides no defence for the defendant, once the prima facie case A hit B is proved'.[53] Epstein frames his disagreement with the negligence standard in the following terms:

> Once a defendant is allowed to excuse himself on the grounds that he acted with due regard for the plaintiff, it follows that he will be able to keep for himself the benefits of his own actions even as he imposes their costs upon a stranger. The crucial question is whether or not the defendant should be allowed to force (and here the words should be taken literally) others to bear his costs because prior to the accident he made a decision that was rational in the case. The major premise of the theory of strict liability is that, prima facie, he should not be allowed to help himself by taking or destroying the plaintiff's person or property.[54]

While the fact that a defendant applied force with volition and caused injury to the plaintiff is one way in which Epstein finds that his requirement of causation is satisfied, he discusses another based on notions of 'dangerous conditions'. In effect, a defendant is liable, according to Epstein, if they created 'dangerous conditions' as a result of which the plaintiff was injured. By so doing, the theory goes, the defendant will have caused the plaintiff injury.[55]

Howard Klemme

Another advocate of enterprise liability, Howard Klemme, bases enterprise risk strict liability on various factors, including the most likely cost-distributor, which

[51] *Bolton v Stone* [1951] AC 850.

[52] 'In the crowded conditions of modern life even the most careful person cannot avoid creating some risks and accepting others. What a man must not do and what … a careful man tries not to do, is create a risk which is substantial … in my judgment the test to be applied here is whether the risk of damage to a person on the road was so small that a reasonable man in the position of the appellants, considering the matter from the point of view of safety, would have thought it right to refrain from taking steps to prevent the danger. In considering that matter I think that it would be right to take into account not only how remote is the chance that a person might be struck but also how serious the consequences are likely to be if a person is struck' (867) (Lord Reid).

[53] Richard Epstein, 'A Theory of Strict Liability' (1973) 2 *Journal of Legal Studies* 151, 171. I will ignore for present purposes the fact that it was not the defendant who was sued in the case who actually hit the cricket ball, such that it is not accurate to say that liability is easy in the case once the fact that 'A hit B' is proved. In that scenario, it would be the batsman who struck the ball, not the cricket club, which would be liable for what occurred.

[54] Richard Epstein, 'Intentional Harms' (1975) 4 *Journal of Legal Studies* 391, 398.

[55] Richard Epstein, 'A Theory of Strict Liability' (1973) 2 *Journal of Legal Studies* 151, 177–189.

has already been discussed above.[56] He also seeks to justify enterprise risk on the basis of the defendant not meeting 'normal expectations'. This appears in the following passage:

> The enterprise liability theory starts with the proposition that as people go about living their ordinary lives they ought to be permitted and encouraged to rely on their normal expectations as to how their activities and those of others will or may interrelate. One of the most basic of these normal expectations is that all enterprises or activities will be carried on in a manner which will not disrupt the normally expected status quo by causing tort-like losses which will in turn frustrate the realization of other normal expectations community members may have … (thus) the ultimate burden of an otherwise compensable tort is assignable to that particular enterprise which … failed to function as most people would normally have expected, and which thereby disturbed the normally to be expected status quo.[57]

Klemme connects this with economic concepts by holding that in order for a person to make rational decisions about the most efficient utilisation of their resources, they must be able to rely on others to act in accordance with expected norms of behaviour.[58] He acknowledges that distortions are possible in the system he favours, where the enterprise cannot effectively distribute costs to others, and/or cannot accurately determine the costs of prevention.[59]

Albert Ehrenzweig

Albert Ehrenzweig sought to understand the circumstances in which a defendant could be strictly liable, or as he terms it, liable in 'negligence without fault', and what, if anything, brought those categories of case together.[60] He developed the notion of 'inevitable consequences' of activity. He first observes that

> [f]requently railways and automobile operators are, under the negligence rule, 'really' not held (liable) for a particular 'fault' occurring in their operations, but, as under rules of strict liability, for the inevitable consequences of their dangerous activities which, but for their being tolerated because of a superior interest, would be 'negligent' because of being foreseeably harmful.

I put to one aside the immediate response that the mere fact that particular harm is foreseeable does not (and should not) lead to the immediate conclusion that the

[56] Howard Klemme, 'The Enterprise Liability Theory of Torts' (1976) 47 *University of Colorado Law Review* 153, 180.
[57] ibid, 180.
[58] ibid, 184–85.
[59] ibid, 188.
[60] Albert Ehrenzweig, 'Negligence Without Fault' (1966) 54 *California Law Review* 1422. Elsewhere he noted 'the underlying idea [is] that to start a hazardous activity, though being aware that it would inevitably cause damage, is itself negligence': 'A Psychoanalysis of Negligence' (1953) 47 *Northwestern University Law Review* 855, 863.

defendant was liable in negligence. All it shows is that a duty of care was owed; it says nothing about breach.

Ehrenzweig says that

> [w]hat the law wants to know is whether liability can be fairly imposed on the railroad in those cases because the harm was typical for its activities, and thus calculable and reasonably insurable. This typicality test is the one adopted in the law of strict liability.[61]

He then gives an example of the liability of the charterer of a ship, in a case where a spark drops onto the ship's hold, causing fire. Ehrenzweig says that, in such a case, the liability of the charterer is not based (or should not be based) on the question of whether the charterer was negligent, but 'on the consideration that a charterer can calculate as typical (and can insure against) the loss by fire of a petrol cargo'.[62] He says liability for the consequences of dangerous activities should be based on the fact that, given such consequences are typical for that industry, they could have been reasonably foreseen.[63] In other words, he favours liability, in terms of the world of negligence, where the reasonable foreseeability element is satisfied, and the causation element is satisfied, but without the need to demonstrate the breach of any duty of care.

Ehrenzweig eschews a fault-based imposition of liability. He claims it has a primitive basis: 'it is this barbaric system of revenge, in its more refined form of retaliation, which lies at the root of our fault rule'.[64] He also urges acceptance of enterprise liability principles based on 'treat[ing] insurance … as by far the most important factor' in determining liability.[65]

Christine Beuermann

Christine Beuermann has articulated a limited support of strict liability in particular situations.[66] She does not attempt a general defence of strict liability. However, she defends it in particular exceptional categories of case involving making one person liable for the torts of another, in particular vicarious liability of an employer for acts of employees (including school environments), and in relation to agents. She embraces the concept of 'conferred authority strict liability', defending strict

[61] Albert Ehrenzweig, 'Negligence Without Fault' (1966) 54 *California Law Review* 1422, 1457.

[62] ibid, 1458.

[63] ibid, 1459.

[64] Albert Ehrenzweig, 'A Psychoanalysis of Negligence' (1953) 47 *Northwestern University Law Review* 855, 866. He adds that 'we must finally recognize and acknowledge that, when we compel litigants in "negligence" cases to prove and disprove guilt and innocence as causes of what are in truth inevitable incidents of our hazardous activity, we are repeating a procedure not greatly superior to the trial by battle or the ordeal by water or fire' (871).

[65] ibid, 869: 'it is high time to abandon what has aptly been called an undignified game of "hide and seek" and to treat insurance as what it is and should be ie by far the most important factor in the development of enterprise liability'.

[66] Christine Beuermann, *Reconceptualising Strict Liability for the Tort of Another* (2019).

liability in those limited instances on the concept of authority. It arises where one party (an employer, a school) has conferred authority over another (employee or student). It is this relationship that, for Beuermann, justifies the imposition of strict liability, primarily via the mechanism of vicarious liability. I have written elsewhere at length about vicarious liability and have been highly critical of the strict liability it imposes upon employers, including for employee activity that was not authorised, and employee activity that was criminal in nature.[67] My view was, and remains, that an employer should only be liable for actions of an employee that were authorised and for the benefit of the employer. Broad, strict liability on an employer for anything an employee does if (tenuously) related to employment, typically justified by an enterprise risk model, was not supported.

Argument for Strict Liability based on Difficulties of Proof

Some who defend and support strict liability do so on the basis that it may on occasion be difficult for a plaintiff to prove on the balance of probabilities what they would typically need to show in order to claim in negligence, and in particular that the accident occurred due to a breach of the duty of care that the defendant owed the plaintiff, and (perhaps) causation, though it is likely that causation would also need to be demonstrated in a strict liability action.

John Murphy, in a defence of *Rylands v Fletcher*, points to such evidentiary difficulties:

> To allow the rule in *Rylands v Fletcher* to be swallowed up by the law of negligence would mean that in some cases claimants would face insurmountable evidentiary burdens, burdens indeed, that may be thought inappropriate as a matter of policy and justice. If we assume … that large factories and other industrial enterprises are the most likely sources of escapes … it is highly improbable that a relatively impecunious claimant would be able to establish the necessary lack of reasonable care for the purposes of a negligence action … it [would] be an almost impossible task in relation to the activities of a specialist industrial enterprise [to prove lack of reasonable care] … [this would be] daunting and unmanageable to a relative man of straw'.[68]

[67] Anthony Gray, *Vicarious Liability: Critique and Reform* (Hart Publishing, 2018).

[68] John Murphy, 'The Merits of Rylands v Fletcher' (2004) 24(4) *Oxford Journal of Legal Studies* 643, 659–60. See to like effect Cornelius Peck, 'Negligence and Liability Without Fault in Tort Law' (1971) 46 *Washington Law Review* 225, 240: 'disasters caused by those who engage in abnormally dangerous or extra-hazardous activities frequently destroy all evidence of what in fact occurred'. On the other hand, as Thayer responds, the common law doctrine of *res ipsa loquitur* can be of assistance in such cases: Ezra Ripley Thayer, 'Liability Without Fault' (1916) 29 *Harvard Law Review* 801, 807. Friedmann said such an observation was fully proven in the case of the English cases: 'Modern Trends in the Law of Torts' (1937) 1 *Modern Law Review* 39, 61.

Law and Economics: Guido Calabresi and Others

There is, or has been, substantial support from law and economics scholars for notions of enterprise risk theory as it supports the imposition of strict liability. Leading law and economics scholar Guido Calabresi stated that 'Activities should bear the costs they engender. It is only fair that an industry should pay for the injuries it causes. Enterprise liability – the notion that losses should be borne by the doer, the enterprise, rather than distributed on the basis of fault – is usually explained in such terms'.[69] Calabresi argued that efficient resource allocation was implicated in these tort rules. Unless costs were accurately allocated to the activities which created them, an excessive level of those activities would be conducted. Conversely, if too many costs were allocated to a particular function, where these were not closely related to that activity in the sense of being caused by them, that function would occur less often than was optimal.[70] Calabresi's comments purported to apply across the law of tort; they were not confined, as those of Jeremiah and Young Smith had been, to instances of workers' compensation and vicarious liability respectively.

Calabresi defines torts in terms of economics. So he states the principle of negligence in terms of comparing the cost that the defendant would have incurred in avoiding the accident with the cost of the accident, having regard to the probability that it occurred. If the former is less than the latter, negligence is proven and the plaintiff is entitled to recover.[71] Thus, it is not surprising that he casts strict liability in a similar fashion. His essential point is that the law should follow either negligence or strict liability principles, depending on 'which of the parties to the accident is in the best position to make the cost-benefit analysis between accident costs and accident avoidance costs and to act on that decision once it is made'.[72] According to Calabresi, if the defendant were in the better position to do so, they are strictly liable for the accident, regardless of fault. He seeks to explain case decisions, including *Rylands v Fletcher* as well as other cases such as liability for animals.[73] He specifically names that case and claims that the courts, in using concepts such as 'unnatural use',

> [w]ere in effect expressing judgments as to whether the injurer or the victim could better decide the advantages of avoidance as against accident costs. Both limits suggest

[69] Guido Calabresi, 'Some Thoughts on Risk Distribution and the Law of Torts' (1961) 70 *Yale Law Journal* 499, 500.

[70] ibid, 514. This theory built on the work of Pigou, who distinguished between private costs and social costs. Pigou states that, typically, only private costs were allocated to relevant parties. A way had to be found to apply the social costs of the activities parties engaged in to such parties in order to ensure an optimal level of such activity occurred. Pigou's solution was a tax on the activity equivalent to the social costs it engendered: Arthur Pigou, *The Economics of Welfare* (Macmillan, 1932). See also Ronald Coase, 'The Problem of Social Cost' (1960) 3 *Journal of Law and Economics* 1.

[71] Guido Calabresi, 'Towards a Test for Strict Liability in Torts' (1972) 81 *Yale Law Journal* 1055, 1057.

[72] ibid, 1060.

[73] Calabresi appears to be mistaken, with respect, in his discussion of *Rylands v Fletcher*. After referring to that case and other factual scenarios, he states that one limitation on liability considered 'had the victim engaged in an "unnatural" use of his land'? In fact, the concept of whether a use of land was natural or not was applied to the defendant's use of their land, not that of the plaintiff.

> questions such as who has the greater knowledge of the risk involved and who is better able to choose to avoid that risk by altering behaviour should the risk appear too great.[74]

He acknowledges limitations and difficulties with the enterprise risk theory. Specifically, he acknowledges that arguments about internalisation of costs depend on a multitude of variables, including the extent to which the industry in which the relevant firms operate is competitive or monopolistic in nature, the substitutability of other resources whose accident costs are lower, and alternative uses for the resources substituted or discarded. Its effectiveness would also depend on variables such as whether or not there are high barriers to exiting the industry, and the general state of the economy at the time.[75] He also concludes that 'though as a system of loss-spreading enterprise liability has some merits, it is still relatively inefficient'.[76]

He also notes that loss spreading is not, and cannot be, a goal in itself of tort law:

> If spreading of injury losses were the only goal of tort law, there would be no point at all in requiring, as a prerequisite to liability, a causal link between an act or activity and the injury. The fact that some acts or activities increase the chances that an injury will occur in the future, while others do not, indicates nothing about the ability of either injurer or victim to spread injury costs that have occurred. A prediction of the likelihood of future accidents resulting from particular behaviour has no relation to ability to spread past injury costs. Hence, causal link between an action and an injury would be irrelevant to liability.[77]

Calabresi did not find that enterprise risk theory was particularly efficient.[78]

Another law and economics scholar, Richard Posner, explained his theory of strict liability in *Indiana Harbour Belt RR v American Cyanamid Co.*[79] To be clear, he did not write in support of strict liability in principle. As will be seen below, he was primarily devoted to a defence of negligence. However, he recognised the efficacy of a limited number of cases where strict liability principles would be applied:

> The baseline common law regime of tort liability is negligence. When it is a workable regime, because the hazards of an activity can be avoided by being careful (which is to say non-negligent), there is no need to switch to strict liability. Sometimes, however, a particular type of accident cannot be prevented by taking care but can be avoided, or

[74] Guido Calabresi, 'Towards a Test for Strict Liability in Torts' (1972) 81 *Yale Law Journal* 1055, 1072.

[75] Guido Calabresi, 'Some Thoughts on Risk Distribution and the Law of Torts' (1961) 70 *Yale Law Journal* 499, 519–24.

[76] 529.

[77] Guido Calabresi, 'Concerning Cause and the Law of Torts: An Essay for Harry Kalven' (1975) 43 *University of Chicago Law Review* 69, 73–74.

[78] Guido Calabresi, 'Some Thoughts on Risk Distribution and the Law of Torts' (1961) 70 *Yale Law Journal* 499, 529–30; see similarly Gregory Keating, 'The Idea of Fairness in the Law of Enterprise Liability' (1997) 95 *Michigan Law Review* 1266, 1308.

[79] *Indiana Harbour Belt RR v American Cyanamid Co* 916 F. 2d 1174 (1990).

> its consequences minimized, by shifting the activity in which the accident occurs to another locale, where the risk of harm of an accident will be less, or by reducing the scale of the activity in order to minimize the number of accidents caused by it … by making the actor strictly liable – by denying him in other words an excuse based on his inability to avoid accidents by being more careful – we give him an incentive, missing in a negligence regime, to experiment with methods of preventing accidents that involve not greater exertions of care, assumed to be futile, but instead relocating, changing, or reducing (perhaps to the vanishing point) the activity giving rise to the accident.[80]

Landis and Posner made some important contributions to this debate.[81] One of their insights is that it is difficult to draw an easy conclusion as to whether negligence or strict liability standards will be more efficient. On one level, negligence is less efficient because of the adjudication costs incurred in determining whether or not a given defendant met the reasonable care standard (what they call information costs). On another level, strict liability is less efficient. Because it will induce more claims, there are increased costs of processing and collecting the claim in strict liability as compared to negligence. Causation and loss and other issues must still be demonstrated (which they call claim costs). They claim that in areas of known liability determination, information costs will be less than in less developed areas. Thus, in those cases a negligence standard rather than strict liability standard might be more efficient. In contrast, in relation to novel claims, a strict liability standard would be more efficient. It is possible that a given area of law might shift over time from a strict liability standard to a negligence standard, as claims become more common, and their resolution more predictable.[82]

Another of Landes and Posner's insights is that courts might also consider a broader range of considerations in determining these kinds of cases. Traditionally, a case brought in negligence will consider the extent to which the defendant took precautions against given risks. However, it typically does not consider whether the defendant might have reduced the level at which a particular activity is conducted, or whether it should even have been conducted at all. They see strict liability as advantageous in this regard, forcing would-be defendants to consider the live option of reducing activity levels, including to zero, which negligence typically does not consider.[83] This is complicated, however, by the question of the plaintiff's activity levels, and what, if any, impact liability rules will have on that.

[80] He explained strict liability being applied to 'those … activities where unavoidable accident costs are greater, and therefore where one is most likely to find that an alternative method of achieving the same result (for example, digging rather than blasting) is cheaper when unavoidable accident costs are taken into account. A rule of strict liability – the rule applied to activities classified as ultrahazardous – compels them to be taken into account': Richard Posner, 'A Theory of Negligence' (1972) 1 *Journal of Legal Studies* 29, 76.

[81] William Landes and Richard Posner, 'The Positive Economic Theory of Tort Law' (1981) 15 *Georgia Law Review* 851.

[82] ibid, 875.

[83] ibid, 876.

Taking this into account, they conclude that

> [i]f a change in the plaintiff's activity is unlikely to be an efficient method of accident avoidance, but a change in the defendant's activity is likely to be an efficient method, strict liability is an attractive rule. It will deter many accidents, and what we have called the claim cost of strict liability will be reduced. However, where greater care rather than less activity is the optimal method of accident avoidance by potential injurers, the case for negligence is strengthened, for now the claim costs of strict liability are likely to be high relative to its allocative effect, compared to negligence.[84]

In other words, they concluded that strict liability was preferred in cases where optimal accident avoidance involved altering the levels of the defendant's activity, not the extent to which they take care, and not the level of the plaintiff's activity nor the extent to which they take care.[85]

Landes and Posner seem to favour the imposition of strict liability when accidents are inevitable. This is because, in such cases, they want to encourage the defendant to reduce their levels of activity. The examples they use involve animals.[86] They say, for instance, that this is why strict liability applies in the case of a defendant who keeps dangerous animals. They say strict liability should apply there because it is inevitable that such an animal will injure others. The taking of reasonable care will not prevent this. As a result, they say it is right to impose strict liability upon the owner of such an animal, because the law is encouraging them to reconsider owning such an animal (in other words, to reduce activity levels). This is in contrast with keeping an animal not known to be dangerous – they say a negligence standard is appropriate there, because it is not inevitable the animals will injure others. The taking of reasonable care could realistically reduce the chance it will injure others. The law is not seeking to discourage the owning of such animals. They apply the same rule to the context of farm animals, such as cattle and sheep. They say it is inevitable that stock will stray, and no amount of reasonable care will prevent this – it is in the nature of the animals, and fences cannot be kept in good repair at all times. Fencing is also costly. Thus, they say the imposition of strict liability for straying animals is appropriate in such cases, given the inevitability of such events. The taking of reasonable care will not prevent this. By imposing strict liability upon stock owners, Landes and Posner say this will cause the farm owner to reconsider relocating the farm elsewhere, or reducing their herd (in other words, reducing activity levels).

Landes and Posner question what they view as the orthodox view that strict liability will lead to defendants being more careful than they would be under principles of negligence liability.[87] Posner concluded that the level of safety would

[84] ibid, 877.
[85] ibid, 904.
[86] ibid, 905–06.
[87] ibid, 874: 'conventional legal scholars long have assumed that strict liability would induce potential injurers to be more careful than they would be under a negligence standard; economic analysis suggests that their analysis is superficial'.

be unaffected, at least in the short term, regardless of whether a strict liability or negligence rule were applied. And in the long term, he disagreed that strict liability encouraged higher levels of safety.[88]

Steven Shavell also approached the question of strict liability versus negligence through the prism of law and economics principles.[89] He studied two paradigms – so-called unilateral cases (where the victim's actions could not affect the probability of severity of losses, ie where contributory negligence was irrelevant), and the bilateral cases, where the victim can influence the probability or magnitude of accident losses by their decisions concerning the level of care and/or level of activity.

In relation to unilateral cases, Shavell found that negligence rules were relatively inefficient because they merely required a defendant to take reasonable care. They did not require a defendant to consider their level of activity, including whether they should engage in the activity at all. For this reason, Shavell said that, in relation to accidents between strangers, negligence rules had the effect that defendants chose levels of activity that were higher than was optimal.[90] He said that, in contrast, where a defendant was subject to rules of strict liability, they would consider whether or not to engage in the activity at all, and if so, at what levels. Shavell argued this meant the defendant would make 'efficient' decisions as to levels of activity.[91]

In relation to accidents between sellers and customers or employees, again Shavell found that negligence rules would be inefficient because sellers would only take reasonable care.[92] As a result, the costs associated with losses caused by non-negligent activity would not be priced into the activity, meaning it would occur at higher than optimal levels. The only exception to this would be where customers or employees could correctly perceive the risks associated with the product or activity. In such cases, they could price in themselves that risk. However, strict liability principles were more efficient, whether or not customers and employees could correctly perceive risk.

Regarding bilateral cases, where the victim's choices could influence the likelihood or severity of injury, negligence principles would again be inefficient (in both stranger and stranger cases, and those involving sellers and strangers). Because not all of the costs associated with the risk of the activity are allocated to the defendant, again they will 'overproduce'. However, considering the plaintiff's position, in a strict liability with defence case, if contributory negligence applies, all they need to do is to take reasonable care. Thus, they are similarly under-incentivised to reduce activity levels. Thus, in Shavell's view neither negligence nor strict liability is efficient here. He concluded that in such a situation, 'Strict liability with the

[88] Richard Posner, 'Strict Liability: A Comment' (1973) 2 *Journal of Legal Studies* 205, 209.
[89] Steven Shavell, 'Strict Liability Versus Negligence' (1980) 9 *Journal of Legal Studies* 1.
[90] ibid, 2.
[91] ibid, 3.
[92] ibid, 4.

defence will be superior to the negligence rule when it is more important that injurers be given an incentive through a liability rule to reduce their activity level than that victims be given a similar incentive'.[93] He concludes his study by stating that 'strict liability is preferable if it is more desirable to control injurers' activity than victims'.[94]

Judicial Consideration of these Rationales in the Context of Strict Liability

It is somewhat rare for judges to engage in this broad philosophical debate regarding the merits or otherwise of adoption of strict liability principles. Understandably, they are focused on the immediate dispute in front of them and its resolution, among a large case load. They may not have the time for this kind of philosophical reflection, as a general rule.

One rare example is provided by the Supreme Court of Canada in *Bazley v Curry*.[95] The case primarily concerned the question of vicarious liability. However, the court used the concept of 'enterprise risk' to justify the imposition of vicarious liability upon the employer. It is trite to observe that vicarious liability is seen as a prime example of strict liability. Thus, although in a different context, what the Supreme Court of Canada said there about enterprise risk theory is considered to be highly relevant to the current context.

In *Bazley*, McLachlin J (as she then was), delivering the judgment of the court, provided three reasons why the employer in that case should be held vicariously liable for abuse committed by one of its employees. These reasons were that it was fair, and that it would (or may) provide an employer with sufficient 'deterrence'. McLachlin J stated that imposition of (strict) liability upon the employer was fair on the facts because

> [t]he employer puts in the community an enterprise, which carries with it certain risks. When those risks materialize and cause injury to a member of the public despite the employer's reasonable efforts, it is fair that the organization that creates the enterprise and hence the risk should bear the loss. This accords with the notion that it is right and just that the person who creates a risk bears the loss when the risk ripens into harm.[96]

This is close to Keating's argument about the fairness of imposing strict liability upon a defendant for creating risks, independently of the question of negligence, and Epstein's argument about causation, in that it can be said that the defendant's activity caused the plaintiff injury.

[93] ibid, 7.
[94] ibid, 24.
[95] *Bazley v Curry* [1999] 2 SCR 534.
[96] ibid, 554.

McLachlin J also seeks to make an economic argument for the imposition of strict liability (via vicarious liability) in that case: 'The employer is often in the best position to spread the losses through mechanisms like insurance and higher prices, thus minimizing the dislocative effect of the tort within society'.[97]

The third reason that McLachlin J gave for the imposition of strict liability via vicarious liability in that case was that of deterrence. This is not a rationale for strict liability that has been canvassed in the literature above. McLachlin J stated that a major policy consideration underlying vicarious liability (an exemplar of strict liability)

> [i]s deterrence of future harm. Fixing the employer with responsibility for the employee's wrongful act, even where the employer is not negligent, may have a deterrent effect. Employers are often in a position to reduce accidents and intentional wrongs by efficient organisation and supervision. Failure to take such measures may not suffice to establish a case of tortious negligence directly against the employer. Perhaps the harm cannot be shown to have been foreseeable under negligence law. Perhaps the employer can avail themselves of the defence of compliance with the industry standard. Or perhaps the employer [complied] with the standard of reasonable care … [however] beyond the narrow band of employer conduct that attracts direct liability in negligence lies a vast area where imaginative and efficient administration and supervision can reduce the risk that the employer has introduced into the community. Holding the [defendant liable] may … encourage [them] to take such steps, and thus to reduce the risk of future harm.[98]

The UK courts' attitude towards this enterprise risk theory of strict liability (in the form of vicarious liability) has been somewhat ambivalent. In *Lister v Hesley Hall*,[99] one member of the House of Lords adopted it,[100] but two Lords expressly did not.[101] However, subsequent decisions of the House of Lords and then the Supreme Court pointedly embraced the enterprise risk theory,[102] with the possible exception of the reasoning regarding its deterrent effect.[103] After initially apparently accepting the enterprise risk approach,[104] the Australian High Court began to criticise it,[105] and now ignores it.[106]

[97] ibid, 554. Another example appears in the judgment of La Forest J in *Tock v St John's Metropolitan Area Board* [1989] 2 SCR 1181, 1202, referring to a public authority being 'in a position to defray the cost (of a nuisance) by spreading it among all subscribers to the system'.

[98] *Bazley v Curry* [1999] 2 SCR 534, 554–55.

[99] *Lister v Hesley Hall* [2002] 1 AC 215.

[100] ibid, 244 (Lord Millett).

[101] ibid, 230 (Lord Steyn) and 242 (Lord Hobhouse).

[102] *Dubai Aluminium Co v Salaam* [2003] 2 AC 366, 377 (Lord Nicholls, with whom Lords Slynn and Hutton agreed); *Various Claimants v Catholic Child Welfare Society* [2013] 2 AC 1, 15 (Lord Phillips, for the Court); *Mohamud v Wm Morrison Supermarkets Plc* [2016] AC 677; *Cox v Ministry of Justice* [2016] 660, 670 (Lord Reed, with whom Lord Neuberger, Baroness Hale, Lord Dyson and Lord Toulson agreed); *Armes v Nottinghamshire County Council* [2018] AC 355, 381 (Lord Reed, with whom Lady Hale, Lord Kerr and Lord Clarke agreed).

[103] *Armes v Nottinghamshire County Council* [2018] AC 355, 381.

[104] *Hollis v Vabu* (2001) 207 CLR 21, 40 (Gleeson CJ, Gaudron, Gummow, Kirby and Hayne JJ).

[105] *State of New South Wales v Lepore* (2003) 212 CLR 511, 543 (Gleeson CJ), 587 (Gummow and Hayne JJ).

[106] *Prince Alfred College Inc v ADC* (2016) 258 CLR 134. No member of the Court referred to it.

Another example appears in the judgment of the Supreme Court of California in *Greenman*. There Traynor CJ for the court noted that the purpose of imposing strict liability 'is to ensure that the costs of injuries resulting from defective products are borne by the manufacturers that put such products on the market rather than by the injured persons who are powerless to protect themselves'.[107]

Theories against Strict Liability

Alan Schwartz

The weakest aspect of the law and economics reasoning said to support the imposition of strict liability is the assumptions upon which it relies. So, for instance, the above theories postulated that a defendant could calculate the likely costs associated with the realisation of 'inevitable risks' and price them into the cost of their product accordingly. Yet that assumption may be seriously questioned. Alan Schwartz does so, stating that one reason

> [t]o object to strict liability is that the efficiency case for it is weak … firms are required to compensate all consumer losses, but cannot estimate those losses, including non-pecuniary losses, with any degree of precision. As a consequence, strict liability probably does not induce the optimal provision of safety.[108]

Stephen Perry

Stephen Perry wrote a significant critique on the work of Richard Epstein.[109] One of the issues he takes with Epstein's work is that Epstein appears to assume an active/passive paradigm, with the plaintiff cast in a passive role, and the defendant in an active role. It is the defendant's actions which inflict damage, injury or loss upon the plaintiff. In Epstein's model it is because the defendant voluntarily chose to engage in the given activity that they should be liable for the damage caused by that activity, regardless of negligence. Perry states that Epstein's view on this point is central to his argument.[110]

[107] *Greenman v Yuba Power Products Inc* 59 Cal. 2d 57, 63, 377 P 2d. 900, 901 (1963).

[108] Alan Schwartz, 'The Case Against Strict Liability' (1992) 60 *Fordham Law Review* 819, 834.

[109] Stephen Perry, 'The Impossibility of General Strict Liability' (1988) 1 *Canadian Journal of Law and Jurisprudence* 147.

[110] Perry cites Epstein's comment (discussed above) that 'once a defendant is allowed to excuse himself on the grounds that he acted with due regard for the plaintiff, it follows that he will be able to keep the benefits of his own actions even as he imposes their costs upon a stranger'. He says this sentiment lies 'at the heart of (Epstein's) position': Stephen Perry, 'The Impossibility of General Strict Liability' (1988) 1 *Canadian Journal of Law and Jurisprudence* 147, 154.

Perry points out that this assumption is not, in fact, correct in many cases.[111] In many situations, with the typical motor vehicle accident being a typical one, both the plaintiff and the defendant are engaged in activity. Both have chosen to conduct activities. He says that the law must properly consider the conduct, actions and decisions made by both the plaintiff *and* the defendant.[112] It would be arbitrary to simply consider those of the defendant, as he argues that Epstein's view requires.[113] And he wonders why, even in cases where only the defendant has acted, the fact they acted is apparently the trigger for liability.[114] Perry states:

> There is no such thing as a passive bystander. Consider … the situation in which both the plaintiff and the defendant are active at the moment that the former is injured: an example would be an accident on the highway in which two vehicles collide while both are moving and under the control of their respective drivers … no distinction can be drawn between one party's activity and the other's passivity which would permit the justification for strict liability being considered here to take hold, and in this sort of case it would be impossible to apply a pure standard of strict liability in any event. Neither party alone could be said to have 'caused' whatever injury might have resulted.[115]

As a result, he concludes there is no moral argument for strict liability because

> the only plausible argument in moral terms for a standard of strict liability rests upon the very distinction between the activity of the defendant and the passivity of the plaintiff which it does not seem possible to draw … interactions … [are] in general the result of choices to act that were made by both parties, where each can be assumed to have engaged in the pursuit of his own individual interest. The simple idea that one party is benefiting from, while the other is bearing at least some of the costs of, a single action or series of actions performed by the former is thus a completely misleading picture of the relationship between them.[116]

Perry is also critical of Epstein's use of concepts of 'dangerous conditions' as a basis for demonstrating the causation necessary, in Epstein's view, to attract at least prima facie liability. He notes that there is no justification for determining that the existence of 'dangerous conditions', however determined, establishes causation in a way that 'normal conditions' do not. Perry says that in order to determine whether or not conditions are 'dangerous' a range of factors should be considered, including the level of knowledge that the defendant had at the time. He says these factors

[111] 'The interaction between the plaintiff and the defendant which gave rise to injury to the (plaintiff) … is always (except in anomalous cases) the result of choices to act which were made by both parties', ibid, 156.

[112] William Jones, 'Strict Liability for Hazardous Enterprise' (1992) 92 *Columbia Law Review* 1705, 1714, makes a similar point: 'imposing strict liability upon an injurer tends to reduce the incentives for victims to take care'.

[113] Stephen Perry, 'The Impossibility of General Strict Liability' (1988) 1 *Canadian Journal of Law and Jurisprudence* 147, 156.

[114] ibid, 156: 'there is no principled distinction to be drawn between cases involving an active plaintiff and those in which the plaintiff is supposedly passive'.

[115] ibid, 155.

[116] ibid, 157.

are better viewed in terms of personal responsibility and fault, rather than being connected with causation.[117]

Perry also denies that courts typically in fact apply a utilitarian, cost-benefit analysis in resolving torts cases.[118]

Oliver Wendell Holmes Jr

Oliver Wendell Holmes Jr stated his general position that the loss resulting from an accident should lie where it falls. If a position were taken that the loss should not lie where it falls, but be transferred to another party, there would have to be strong justification for it.[119] He rejects the supposed causation basis of strict liability:

> The undertaking to redistribute losses simply on the ground that they resulted from the defendant's act would not only be open to these objections [lack of public benefit] but … to the still graver one of offending the sense of justice. Unless my act is of a nature to threaten others, unless under the circumstances a prudent man would have foreseen the possibility of harm, it is no more justifiable to make me indemnify my neighbour against the consequences than to make me do the same thing if I had fallen upon him in a fit, or to compel me to insure him against lightning.[120]

Holmes favoured a general principle of tort liability based on the notion of reasonable care:

> Be the exceptions more or less numerous, the general purpose of the law of torts is to secure a man indemnity against certain forms of harm to person, reputation or estate, at the hands of his neighbours, not because they are wrong, but because they are harms. The true explanation of the reference of liability to a moral standard, in the sense which has been explained, is not that it is for the purpose of improving men's hearts, but that it is to give a man a fair chance to avoid doing the harm before he is held responsible for it. It is intended to reconcile the policy of letting accidents lie where they fall, and the reasonable freedom of others with the protection of the individual from injury.[121]

[117] ibid, 163: 'the normative question of whether or not [the defendant] should have possessed the relevant information, and if so, whether the probability of harm was sufficiently great that he should not have [done what he did because it was 'dangerous'] seem most naturally described as issues of personal responsibility rather than as issues of causation'; see for similar criticism that strict liability theory tends to embrace fault-like considerations, while purporting to deny their utility, in Gary Schwartz, 'The Vitality of Negligence and the Ethics of Strict Liability' (1981) 15 *Georgia Law Review* 963, 1003.

[118] Stephen Perry, 'Cost-Benefit Analysis and the Negligence Standard' (2001) 54 *Vanderbilt Law Review* 893, 895.

[119] To like effect Robert Keeton, 'Conditional Fault in the Law of Torts' (1959) 72 *Harvard Law Review* 401, 401–02: 'the usual starting point for explaining bases of liability in tort is the assertion that the machinery of adjudication will not be set in motion without good reason. Its operation is costly. From the community point of view, its use to shift a loss is not worth the price unless the loss shifting serves some good purpose … in modern Anglo-American tort law, fault has been considered the one generally acceptable reason for such loss-shifting'.

[120] Oliver Wendell Holmes, *The Common Law* (Little, Brown & Co, 1881) 60; see also Warren Seaver, 'Mr Justice Cardozo and the Law of Torts' (1939) 52 *Harvard Law Review* 372.

[121] Oliver Wendell Holmes Jr, *The Common Law* (Little, Brown & Co, 1881) 90.

Relatedly, Schwartz concludes that

> [t]he negligence concept … does a reasonably good job of identifying that conduct which the public morality would regard as wrongful. And that the distinction between proper and improper conduct should have a major bearing on attitudes towards civil responsibility is hardly surprising. Ethically regarded, the idea of liability for harm caused by one's unexcused errors and mistakes is both straightforward and intuitive. By comparison, the purely ethical arguments in favour of strict liability seem frequently to encounter difficulties that encourage their supporters to seek the assurance of negligence-like positions.[122]

Robert Morris

Robert Morris challenges that aspect of enterprise risk theory that is premised on the ability of the enterprises subject to it to distribute the risk via insurance, on the basis that the insurance premiums charged to those businesses will reflect the notion that the 'proper costs' of the enterprise will be properly attributed to it, which promises to mean that an efficient level of goods or services will be produced or provided by the enterprise.[123]

Morris disagrees with the premise that the insurance premiums that an individual enterprise pays will be based on an individualised assessment of the risks generated by such enterprise. He considers the practicalities of insurance in some detail. He points out that when insurers price the risk associated with a particular policy, they are likely to do so based on generalised assessments of claims within a particular industry, usually involving large numbers of entrepreneurs. This may be based on a particular territory. It will be based on accident and claim rates of previous years. It will also be subject to a risk factor based on an even wider range of enterprises. He refers then to 'zone of risk theories'. He has earlier stated that the 'zone of risk approach is premised only upon the insurance and risk-spreading function of enterprise liability'.[124] He says that 'turning to zone of risk theories, it can easily be seen that their concept of risk has little in common with the quantum of risk discovered by actuarial techniques'.[125] Further, the entrepreneur's estimate of their zone of risk is likely to differ substantially from that of the insurer. Morris concludes:

> These zone of risk theories of enterprise liability overlook the actuarial realities of the administration of risk. They rely upon an entrepreneur's hypothetical estimate of the risk in the light of his foresight, rather than upon the actuary's estimate of the risk based

[122] Robert T Schwartz, 'The Vitality of Negligence and the Ethics of Strict Liability' (1981) 15 *Georgia Law Review* 963, 1003.
[123] Robert Morris, 'Enterprise Liability and the Actuarial Process – The Insignificance of Foresight' (1961) 70 *Yale Law Journal* 554.
[124] ibid, 554.
[125] ibid, 574.

> upon hindsight. Furthermore, they assume that certain factors increase the quantum of risk, which may be contrary to fact, or at least, not measurably true.[126]

Morris alludes to difficulties with interpreting some of the concepts said to underpin the enterprise risk model. It seeks to allocate 'typical' costs to an enterprise, but there is often lack of agreement as to what such typical costs are. He notes it is not a term that actuaries actually use. It embraces concepts of 'inevitable risks', which again lacks precision.[127]

He says, as have others noted earlier, that concepts said to be part of a strict liability doctrine in fact sound a lot like negligence and fault. For instance, he suggests that a 'typical' cost is analogous to a cost associated with a 'foreseeable risk', a concept generally associated with fault-based negligence.[128] Similarly on insurance, he says that businesses can only be expected to insure against costs based on risks that are 'foreseeable'.[129] Again, the question of insurance is more congruent with fault-based negligence, in his view, than strict liability.

He also points out that enterprise risk theory makes assumptions about the ability of organisations to distribute costs elsewhere, including to customers, suppliers and employees. Specifically, it cannot simply be said that an enterprise can pass increased costs on to consumers. Before reaching such a conclusion, it would be necessary to know the dynamics of the market into which the business is supplying, for instance how many competitors there were in that market, the extent to which there are high barriers to entry or exit, and the market share or dominance enjoyed by the relevant firm. There would need to be consideration given to the 'elasticity' of the demand for that particular good or service. In other words, how responsive demand for it was to changes in price. Similar issues would arise in relation to suppliers – do suppliers have ready alternative customers to which they could switch, if a given firm were now paying them less for goods or services? What is the parties' relative bargaining power in this situation? In relation to employees, we would need to take into account the extent to which labour rates in a particular field were flexible, or not flexible. Depending on the industry, industrial awards may protect workers from changes in pay and conditions. Similarly, an enterprise agreement or legislation might do so. Thus, it could not be assumed that an enterprise could respond to increased costs by reducing its labour costs. Thus, Morris says it is a complex, fact-specific determination as to the extent to which a given enterprise might be able to spread risks to its stakeholders. Bald assumptions that enterprise liability theory makes as to the extent to which a firm can do so are misplaced.

Morris concludes on this point:

> The ultimate distribution of the enterprise liability burden cannot be the subject of easy generalizations. Assuming for the moment that the burden is significant,

[126] ibid, 581.
[127] ibid, 584.
[128] ibid, 596–97.
[129] ibid, 556.

> so that entrepreneurs react to it rather than suffer it unnoticed, all that can be said is that entrepreneurs probably bear part of it themselves, that they spread part of it to their employees, creditors, suppliers and customers, and that the members of each of those groups spread it, in turn, to those with whom they have important economic relations.[130]

To some extent, this criticism also applies to assumptions that enterprises can spread their risk by insuring. There may be some risks for which insurance is not available. Often, insurance contracts contain clauses limiting the extent to which the insurer must pay out on a claim.

Relatedly, it has been pointed out that an enterprise might generate positive externalities which it is unable to capture for itself.[131] In theory, such externalities would need to be factored in when determining the 'optimal' level at which a given organisation should conduct its activity. However, if a strict cost approach were taken, they would not be factored in. There may be good reason for society to provide a 'subsidy' for such activities.

Law and Economics and Negligence

The judgment of Learned Hand in *United States v Carroll Towing Co*[132] is often seen as the prime example of the application of economics concepts to explain the law of negligence. The case involved the question whether the owner of a barge owed a duty of care to the owner of the dock at which the barge was hitched. Judge Learned Hand sought to explain the relevant principles through the prism of economics:

> Since there are occasions when every vessel will break from her moorings and since, if she does, she becomes a menace to those about her … the owner's duty, as in other similar situations, to provide against resulting injuries is a function of three variables: (1) the probability that she will break away; (2) the gravity of the resulting injury, if she did; and (3) the burden of adequate precautions … if the probability be called (P); the injury (L) and the burden (B), liability depends upon whether B is less than L multiplied by P.[133]

This approach suggests that when B is less than LP, it would have been 'efficient' for the defendant to have taken steps to prevent the materialisation of the risk. They should have done so. However, if B is greater than LP, such behaviour would have been inefficient, and so the law should not expect the defendant to have done it.

[130] ibid, 585–86; see for a similar conclusion PS Atiyah, *Vicarious Liability in the Law of Torts* (Butterworths, 1967) 25.

[131] William Jones, 'Strict Liability for Hazardous Enterprise' (1992) 92 *Columbia Law Review* 1705, 1712.

[132] *United States v Carroll Towing Co* 159 F. 2d. 169 (2nd Circuit, 1947).

[133] ibid, 173.

In other words, the expected social cost of the accident would be less than the expected social cost of taking precautions to prevent it from occurring.[134]

Richard Posner suggested that 'perhaps … the dominant function of the fault system is to generate rules of liability that, it followed, will bring about, at least approximately, the efficient – the cost-justified – level of accidents and safety'.[135] After reading hundreds of cases decided across the United States in the late nineteenth century and early twentieth, he concludes that 'the rules of liability seem to have been broadly designed to bring about the efficient (cost-justified) level of accidents and safety',[136] at least approximately.

Somewhat problematically, however, he equates wealth maximisation with morality: 'because we do not like to see resources squandered, a judgment of negligence has inescapable overtones of moral disapproval, for it implies that there was a cheaper alternative to the accident'.[137] The problem with this sentiment is the word 'for', and the suggestion that moral disapproval occurs *because of* inappropriate resource allocation. Most scholars would view moral disapproval through a corrective justice, rather than a distributive justice, lens. Moral disapproval would typically be established because the defendant's conduct is viewed as objectively wrong by the standards and mores of society, not because it is economically inefficient.[138]

Posner was relatively neutral as between negligence and strict liability on the question of efficiency, where a defence of contributory negligence was available. Where it was not available, he said that a negligent standard was more efficient.[139] He also concluded that 'a negligence standard of liability, properly administered, is broadly consistent with an optimum investment in accident prevention by the enterprises subject to the standard'.[140]

Other researchers have concluded that most US courts do not in fact apply the *Carroll Towing* formula in rendering decisions in this area of the law.[141]

Ernest Weinrib

Ernest Weinrib has made a significant contribution to torts literature over many years.[142] One of the theories for which he is known is that of corrective

[134] Allan Beever, *A Theory of Tort Liability* (Hart Publishing, 2016) 187.

[135] Richard Posner, 'A Theory of Negligence' (1972) 1 *Journal of Legal Studies* 29, 33.

[136] ibid, 73.

[137] ibid, 33; Richard Posner, 'Utilitarianism, Economics and Legal Theory' (1979) 8 *Journal of Legal Studies* 103, 119.

[138] Ernest Weinrib, 'Utilitarianism, Economics and Legal Theory' (1980) 30 *University of Toronto Law Journal* 307, 311: 'it is difficult to see how wealth, taken in itself, can constitute … what is morally good'.

[139] Richard Posner, 'Strict Liability: A Comment' (1973) 2 *Journal of Legal Studies* 205, 221.

[140] Richard Posner, 'A Theory of Negligence' (1971) 1 *Journal of Legal Studies* 29, 30.

[141] Richard Wright, 'Justice and Reasonable Care in Negligence Law' (2002) 47 *American Journal of Jurisprudence* 143; Richard Wright, 'Hand, Posner and the Myth of the "Hand Formula"' (2003) 4 *Theoretical Inquiries in Law* 145; Richard Wright, 'Negligence in the Courts: Introduction and Commentary' (2002) 77 *Chicago-Kent Law Review* 425.

[142] Ernest Weinrib, *The Idea of Private Law* (Harvard University Press, 1995); Ernest Weinrib, 'Towards a Moral Theory of Negligence Law' (1983) 2(1) *Law and Philosophy* 37; Ernest Weinrib,

justice, arguing that tort law should be based on principles of corrective justice – identifying and correcting 'wrongs', as opposed to questions of distributive justice, or efficient allocation of losses among various possible parties.[143] In his corrective justice approach he adopts Aristotle, who discussed corrective justice in his classic work *Nichomachean Ethics*. Aristotle distinguished corrective justice from distributive justice, without preferring either, and without giving substantive content to either.[144] Here individuals are viewed as equals. Where an individual defendant has obtained a gain at the expense of the plaintiff, they are required to provide compensation and/or restitution for the gain acquired. The defendant should have taken the interests of individuals such as the plaintiff into account in deciding on a proposed course of action. Their failure to do so, or to adequately do so, attracts a legal remedy.

A practical consequence of the idea that parties are equals is the application of an objective standard of care, rather than a subjective standard.[145] Weinrib states that if a subjective view were taken, the defendant would effectively determine the extent of the plaintiff's rights – if the test of the defendant's liability was whether they honestly believed they had taken sufficient care, the plaintiff would have no remedy. Weinrib says such a conclusion is inconsistent with the fundamental rule of the equality of rights among individuals.[146] This means that an objective test must be applied. This was the argument that occurred in *Vaughan v Menlove*,[147] with an objective view winning the court's favour. To the extent that it has been argued that nuisance law contemplates a subjective approach (discussed in Chapter 7), it would be open to similar objections.

Weinrib says that tort law reflects corrective justice and not distributive justice.[148] Thus, he regards as irrelevant discussion of which of the parties in dispute could more easily spread the relevant loss, and which was in the better position to anticipate and insure against it. For this reason, he is fundamentally opposed to the work of Calabresi and the instrumentalist approach it favours. He says tort law is concerned with 'the propriety, rather than the price, of activity'.[149]

He also disagrees with the view of negligence through an economics prism of the kind espoused by Richard Posner. He does not agree with the idea of wealth maximisation that he views as underpinning Posner's position. He is opposed

'Utilitarianism, Economics and Legal Theory' (1980) 30 *University of Toronto Law Journal* 307; Ernest Weinrib, 'Corrective Justice' (1992) 77 *Iowa Law Review* 403; Ernest Weinrib, 'The Gains and Losses of Corrective Justice' (1995) 44 *Duke Law Review* 277.

[143] Ernest Weinrib, 'Towards a Moral Theory of Negligence Law' (1983) 2(1) *Law and Philosophy* 37, 38.

[144] ibid, 38–40.

[145] Ernest Weinrib, 'The Monsanto Lectures: Understanding Tort Law' (1989) 23 *Valparaiso University Law Review* 485, 519.

[146] Ernest Weinrib, 'Towards a Moral Theory of Negligence Law' (1983) 2(1) *Law and Philosophy* 37, 51–52.

[147] *Vaughan v Menlove* (1837) 3 Bing. NC 468; 132 ER 490.

[148] Ernest Weinrib, 'Towards a Moral Theory of Negligence Law' (1983) 2(1) *Law and Philosophy* 37, 38: 'tort law embodies corrective and not distributive justice'.

[149] Ernest Weinrib, 'The Special Morality of Tort Law' (1989) 34 *McGill Law Journal* 403, 404.

to the kind of aggregation of interests that is at the heart of utilitarian theory. He disagrees with both Posner and the utilitarians because, in his view, they give insufficient emphasis to the wrong done to the individual plaintiff, focused as they are on efficient loss distribution and aggregate happiness.[150] He says that tort law is focused, and properly focused, on justice as between the two relevant individuals involved in a factual scenario, and that it is a mistake to interpose further ideas into it, such as deterrence, efficient loss distribution or other goals.[151]

Weinrib then focuses particularly on the choice that a legal system makes between fault-based liability and no-fault, strict liability. Weinrib distils the differences between them as involving, in the former case, a focus on conduct at the point of action and, in the latter case, the results of the defendant's behaviour.[152] He favours negligence because he says that it can accommodate aspects of the particular defendant, including whether they acted on their own free will. He says result-oriented theories like those of strict liability struggle to take into account concepts such as non-voluntary behaviour. He also favours negligence because he says it provides a positive reason to shift losses in accordance with assessments of the propriety of behaviour. The defendant's actions are judged according to whether they violated the equality they ought to have accorded to the plaintiff, and whether they preferred their own interests to those of the plaintiff. Negligence describes the level of wrongfulness where the court's intervention to correct this violation of equality is warranted, in the view of Weinrib. He says that, in contrast, strict liability cannot provide a reason. It is simply focused on the result of the defendant's behaviour. In his view, this is not sufficient to justify the machinery of the state transferring resources from the plaintiff to the defendant.[153] He says that negligence principles better reflect the riskiness inherent in any behaviour. He disfavours strict liability because it effectively treats every act as implicitly a wrong, denying the legitimacy of action. Further, in his view the materialisation of risk into injury is not, in itself, a wrong.[154]

Weinrib conceives of the law of tort as essentially a branch of private law. Its principles and rules aim to resolve primarily a private dispute between individuals and/or organisations. These individuals and/or organisations act for their own purposes.

[150] Ernest Weinrib, 'Towards a Moral Theory of Negligence Law' (1983) 2(1) *Law and Philosophy* 37, 54–55.

[151] 'When this wrong materializes into injury the plaintiff's standing to sue derives from his being wronged and not from his being strategically situated for the imposition of incentives for wealth maximization': ibid, 54.

[152] ibid, 57–58.

[153] 'If corrective justice is regarded as operating against a baseline of equality of result, there must be some positive reason for restoring the status quo ante beside the fact that it is the status quo ante … there seems to be no way to extract from political theory a positive argument for strict liability … the positive argument for strict liability remains to be made': ibid, 60, 62.

[154] Ernest Weinrib, 'The Monsanto Lectures: Understanding Tort Law' (1989) 23 *Valparaiso University Law Review* 485, 519–20.

The law of tort focuses on a particular dispute[155] between parties that are equals. When one of them violates this equality, for instance by being negligent or intentionally harming the other, tort law responds. Weinrib says anything else, such as notions of efficient loss distribution, least cost avoider etc force 'alien' concepts into the law of tort and make it a form of quasi-public law, which it was never designed to be. Thus, he rejects instrumentalist approaches to the law of tort. He says concepts such as deterrence and compensation are examples of such alien concepts. Weinrib views this intrusion as ill-advised.[156]

He contrasts corrective justice, with its focus on righting a wrong between two individuals, with a utilitarian view of seeking the greatest happiness for the greatest number, which implies the value of efficient loss distribution and least cost avoider theory. He says it is inappropriate for a court to attempt to make an assessment of which outcome would facilitate the greatest aggregate utility in society, because only two different parties are represented at the hearing of the case.[157] Judges are not typically expected to, and even if so inclined would typically lack the time to, independently research aspects of the case themselves. The parties' representatives will typically and understandably make submissions based on their clients' best interests. They are unlikely to canvas broader arguments about societal goods. And judges will typically lack the expertise to carefully assess such evidence as there might be on the question, even if they did have the time and/or inclination to pursue such a line of enquiry.

Allan Beever

Similarly, Allan Beever questions the applicability of economic concepts to solve legal problems. He states that law and economics is 'structurally inconsistent' with features of tort law, the logic of economics and law substantially differ, and economics cannot explain or support the reasons given in cases for legal decisions.[158]

Beever is most critical of the movement in tort law towards a focus on loss, as is implicit in law and economics theory, and virtually all of the theories said to support strict liability, which focus on the fact that the plaintiff suffered loss caused by the defendant. He is highly critical of the loss model of tort law:

> The loss model [assumes] that the causing of loss is wrongful, at least prima facie, and that is how the model operates in the Commonwealth … the model maintains that tort

[155] 'Because the normative dimension is intrinsic to the doing and suffering, the tort relationship is not a means to an end. Rather, each harm done and suffered is the core of a single transaction that relates this doer to this sufferer, and each such transaction is a discrete unit of normative significance': Ernest Weinrib, 'The Special Morality of Tort Law' (1989) 34 *McGill Law Journal* 403, 408.

[156] Ernest Weinrib, 'The Insurance Justification and Private Law' (1985) 14 *Journal of Legal Studies* 681.

[157] Ernest Weinrib, 'Towards a Moral Theory of Negligence Law' (1983) 2(1) *Law and Philosophy* 37, 41.

[158] Allan Beever, *A Theory of Tort Liability* (Hart Publishing, 2016) 16–17.

> law is most fundamentally concerned with loss … of course, practicalities demand that not all losses can be compensated. Thus, control mechanisms must be introduced to constrain liability. There is a deep problem with this view, far deeper than its inability to provide an adequate account of the law … the problem is that the loss model is based on notions inconsistent with the reality of the human condition. Given human nature and the world in which we find ourselves, causing loss to others is a fact of life … building into one's understanding of law the notion that things are even prima facie unjust unless they are otherwise is, frankly, otherworldly. It is reality denyingly utopian; the result of failing to look the human condition in the eye. If loss is an evil, then life itself is evil and living a life with one's eyes open to the consequences is an act of intentional evil … the loss model is not merely wrong; it is pathology.[159]

Conclusion

Many different arguments have been made purporting to explain and rationalise strict liability, including arguments about efficient loss distribution, efficient allocation of resources, utilitarian theory, least cost avoider, imposition of non-reciprocal risk, causation, fairness, those relating to the availability of insurance, deterrence, and concerns around the difficulty of proving negligence. On the other hand, others have subjected strict liability rationales to serious criticism, including that it is not the role of torts to efficiently distribute losses but rather to correct wrongful behaviour, challenging arguments that enterprise receives all the 'benefits' of its activity, that insurance is relevant to tort issues at all, and questioning some of the assumptions underlying the supposed economic rationale for strict liability. Many have lauded negligence and reasonable care on the basis of fairness, reflecting community attitudes reasonably well regarding liability. Chapter 6 will now reflect on this literature and several of the arguments contained therein.

[159] ibid, 18.

6

Critical Reflections on the Justifications for Strict Liability

This chapter considers in more depth the arguments presented in the previous chapter said to favour strict liability. It will be seen that there are serious problems with many of these arguments and their appropriateness to the common law legal system as it actually operates.

Inappropriateness of Taking into Account Loss Spreading and 'Efficiency' when Making Judicial Decisions

After referring to arguments about insurance and loss spreading in a case where negligence was alleged, Stephen J of the High Court of Australia noted:

> I have myself avoided reference to either of these factors and I should explain my reasons for doing so. If loss-inflicting consequences of an act are reasonably foreseeable and the necessary proximity is shown to exist, the present state of the law of torts, unreformed by any fundamental departure from fault liability, suggests no reason why the tortfeasor should not bear the consequences of [their] conduct. The task of the courts remains that of loss fixing rather than loss spreading and if this is to be altered it is, in my view, a matter for direct legislative action rather than for the courts. It should be undertaken, if at all, openly and after adequate public inquiry and parliamentary debate, and not worked towards covertly, in the course of judicial decision, by the adoption of policy factors which assume its desirability as a goal and operate to further its attainment … an opposing view [is that] … loss should … be spread by recourse to the relatively efficient device of loss insurance … may have much to be said for it … but there is … no justification for the courts, when deciding actions in tort between private litigants, to make use of such views as policy determinants in the absence of any independent opportunity to test their soundness and without parliamentary sanction for the departure from pre-existing goals of the law of torts which their espousal involves.[1]

[1] *Caltex Oil (Australia) Pty Ltd v The Dredge 'Willemstad'* (1976) 136 CLR 529, 580–81; to like effect Warren Seavey, 'Mr Justice Cardozo and the Law of Torts' (1939) 52 *Harvard Law Review* 372, 373; Richard Wright, 'Justice and Reasonable Care in Negligence Law' (2002) 47 *American Journal of Jurisprudence* 143, 163, states that 'the basic principle of utilitarianism (and of its modern offshoot,

As Stephen J points out, it is not typically a part of the judicial function to decide cases, including tort cases, based on notions such as efficient loss distribution and/or which of the parties was in a 'better' position to avoid the loss. Renowned torts scholar John Fleming makes the same point.[2] It is orthodox in tort law that the availability of insurance does not, and should not, determine liability issues.[3] Insurance follows the law; it does not lead it.[4] This is not to deny that, on occasion, decisions are apparently being made (expressly) on the basis that a defendant is insured.[5]

economic efficiency theory) … directly conflicts with the basic principles of justice'. See in contrast WG Friedmann, 'Social Insurance and the Principles of Tort Liability' (1949) 63 *Harvard Law Review* 241, 261–62: 'the main function of the law of tort is the reasonable adjustment of economic risks in a capitalist … society and not the expression of absolute moral principles … the law of tort [is] a set of rules designed to distribute economic harm according to changing principles of public policy … the law of tort … has steadily moved closer towards a social insurance principle'.

[2] John Fleming, *The Law of Torts* (8th edn, Law Book Co, 1992) 119: 'negligence cannot be reduced to a purely economic equation … in general judicial opinions do not make much of the cost factor (of eliminating the risk) and for good reasons. For one thing, our legal tradition in torts has strong roots in an individualistic morality with its focus primarily on interpersonal equity rather than broader social policy … the calculus of negligence includes some important non-economic values, like health and life, freedom and privacy, which defy comparison with competing economic values. Negligence is not just a matter of calculating the point at which the cost of injury to victims (that is the damages payable) exceeds that of providing safety precautions … the reasonable man is by no means a caricature cold blooded, calculating Economic Man'; Fowler Harper, Fleming James Jr and Oscar Gray, 3 *The Law of Torts* (2nd edn, Wolters Kluwer, 1986) 477–78 (an American text): 'it should not … be thought that in the evaluation of precautions, the common law's standard of reasonableness turns on rigorous cost-benefit analyses. The tone of the common law's approach has been more moral than economic. The emphasis has been not so much on the prevention of (economic) waste as on the blameworthiness of a failure to take precautions deemed reasonable by the community, and within generous limits juries are given latitude in deciding precisely how to balance costs against risks for purposes of making this moral judgment'; Robert Keeton, 'Conditional Fault in the Law of Torts' (1959) 72 *Harvard Law Review* 401, 408–09. At 444, Keeton refers to a liability basis in conditional fault 'offer[ing] some reassurance against the spectre of runaway social engineering with ill-considered emphasis on risk-spreading capacity'.

[3] *Lister v Romford Ice and Cold Storage Co Ltd* [1957] AC 555, 576–77: 'as a general proposition it has not, I think, been questioned for nearly 200 years that in determining the rights inter se of A and B, the fact that one or other of them is insured is to be disregarded'; Jane Stapleton, 'Tort, Insurance and Ideology' (1995) 58(6) *Modern Law Review* 820, 829; *cf Woodland v Swimming Teachers' Association* [2014] AC 537, 590; *cf* Albert Ehrenzweig, 'A Psychoanalysis of Negligence' (1953) 47 *Northwestern University Law Review* 855, 869, who claims that insurance 'is and should be … by far the most important factor in the development of enterprise liability'.

[4] *Cox v Ministry of Justice* [2016] AC 660, 669; Paula Giliker, *Vicarious Liability in Tort: A Comparative Perspective* (Cambridge University Press, 2010) 193–94.

[5] *Woodland v Swimming Teachers' Association* [2014] AC 537, 590 noting, in seeking to explain the existence of a non-delegable duty upon certain categories of defendant, and why it might not be wise to place the obligation on an organisation to which the defendant had delegated tasks, that 'large organisations may well outsource their responsibilities to much poorer or un or underinsured contractors' (Baroness Hale, with whom Lords Clarke, Wilson and Toulson agreed). This passage seems to suggest that the fact that a contractor is or may be 'poor', 'poorer', 'uninsured' or 'underinsured' is a reason for finding that someone or some other organisation should as a matter of policy be liable; see also *Escola v Coca-Cola Bottling Co* 24 Cal. 2d 453, 462, 150 P. 2d 436, 441 (1944) where Traynor J justified making the defendant liable for an exploding Coke bottle on the basis that 'the risk of injury can be insured by the manufacturer and distributed among the public as a cost of doing business'. Dean Pound described Traynor J's observations as 'specious' and 'a variant of a Marxian axiom': 'Law in the Service State' (1950) *American Bar Association Journal* 977, 981, 1050; see also WG Friedmann, 'Social Insurance and the Principles of Tort Liability' (1949) 63 *Harvard Law Review* 241.

It may seem trite to make these observations about the common law. However, it is considered necessary to make them, given some quite extreme comments made about the common law. As discussed above, McLachlin J for the Supreme Court of Canada argued in favour of enterprise risk theory, partly on the basis that employers were in the better position to spread the relevant loss through higher prices or insurance.[6]

Examples also appear in the work of Posner, and Posner and Landes. Posner boldly claims that the common law 'is best (not perfectly) explained as a system for maximising the wealth of society'.[7] Posner and Landes claim that 'the common law of torts is best explained as if the judges who created the law through decisions operating as precedents in later cases were trying to promote efficient resource allocation'.[8] And Calabresi claimed that *Rylands v Fletcher* was really an assessment of which of the parties could make a better decision as to the costs of avoiding a particular accident as compared with expected accident costs. It should be acknowledged that Calabresi stated that, of itself, loss spreading was not a goal of tort law. Further, he acknowledged that strict liability was not a particularly efficient way to determine liability issues.

With respect, these views about the supposed underlying basis of actual tort law cases are fundamentally wrong and misleading. There is a strong element of retro-fitting involved in these sweeping assessments. It is considered quite obvious that this is not in fact how the vast majority of judges actually decide cases, including torts cases.[9] So, for instance, to take a couple of classic negligence cases, there is no discussion in *Donoghue v Stevenson* of the probability that a snail would end up in a bottle of ginger beer, and would stay there long enough to cause injury to a person consuming the bottle, or how much it would have cost the defendant to have taken precautions to prevent the event from occurring, or what the likely extent of injury to a plaintiff might be. Similarly, in *Bolton v Stone* there is no discussion of comparing the costs of taking precautions to prevent a cricket ball from being hit out of the stadium, an assessment of the probability this would occur, or a weighing up of the likely cost of the injuries that would result. Further, there is no evidence in *Rylands v Fletcher* that the courts were actually (consciously) doing what Calabresi claimed almost a century later they were doing. Any theory stands and falls on the question of evidence. Evidence is conspicuously lacking in this instance.

[6] *Bazley v Curry* [1999] 2 SCR 534, 554; Virginia E Nolan and Edmund Ursin, 'The Revitalization of Hazardous Activity Strict Liability' (1987) 65 *North Carolina Law Review* 257, 297: 'increasingly, courts have viewed the loss spreading capacity of enterprises engaged in particular activities as an important factor in determining whether to impose strict liability'.

[7] Richard Posner, *Economic Analysis of the Law* (4th edn, Little, Brown, 1992) 23.

[8] William Landes and Richard Posner, *The Economic Structure of Tort Law* (Harvard University Press, 1987) 1.

[9] Allan Beever, *A Theory of Tort Liability* (Hart Publishing, 2016) 17: 'economics cannot explain or justify the law in the sense that it cannot support the reasons given in law for legal decisions'.

While Learned Hand might have done this in one decision, it is a gross mistake to claim that this is somehow what has been going on in torts cases for centuries. This is most certainly the position in the United Kingdom, Canada and Australia, the case law with which I am most familiar. I am less familiar with all of the American precedent. Yet, even here, other scholars have pointed out that the Learned Hand formula does not reflect reality. This is apparent from two observations by Richard Wright.[10] Wright states that '[Judge Learned Hand] wrote a series of opinions from 1938 through 1949 in which … he set forth and purported to apply an aggregate-risk-utility definition of negligence'.[11] He also states that 'the aggregate-risk-utility test, although pervasive in the secondary literature and mentioned by a small minority of courts, is almost never used by the courts to decide whether particular conduct was negligent'.[12]

It is submitted that, for the vast majority of judges, the judicial role is to decide cases in a way that does justice according to the law. It is just that Learned Hand articulated the judicial role in a radically different way. The correct position is surely that judges typically do not undertake the kind of analysis favoured by law and economics scholars in deciding torts cases, as Stephen J said in *Caltex Oil*, and the approach of Learned Hand was very much the exception. Judges might be surprised to learn that, according to some, their purpose is not to do justice to the parties before them according to the law, but to engage in efficient loss distribution. Judges would typically see their role in tort cases through the prism of corrective justice, as Weinrib prefers, and not distributive justice. And this is not surprising. They are not economists, and nor are the advocates who present the arguments to the court. As a result, a focus on legal principle, in which both have been trained and in which both obviously have significant experience, is entirely expected. It is of course one thing to advocate that the law should take a particular position, or adopt a particular approach. It is quite a different matter to simply assert that the judges have in fact been doing so. The evidence for such a large claim is simply non-existent.[13]

Having established that the claim that economics principles best explain the common law is fundamentally wrong, I should now consider the normative claim that law and economic principles such as which of the parties is the least-cost avoider, which is in the better position to distribute costs associated with risks,

[10] Richard Wright, 'Justice and Reasonable Care in Negligence Law' (2002) 47 *American Journal of Jurisprudence* 143.

[11] ibid 156.

[12] ibid 145; and Richard Wright, 'Hand, Posner and the Myth of the "Hand Formula"' (2003) 4 *Theoretical Inquiries in Law* 145, 148: 'recent analyses of American and British court decisions have found that the aggregate-risk-utility test is infrequently mentioned by the courts, almost never included in jury instructions, rarely actually employed in judicial opinions, and almost never explains the actual decisions reached by the courts'.

[13] After referring to Judge Posner's views in *Indiana Harbour Belt* concerning when strict liability and fault-based liability are appropriate, and the confinement of strict liability to extra-hazardous activity, William Jones concludes that 'Judge Posner's position cannot be reconciled with reality': 'Strict Liability for Hazardous Enterprise' (1992) 92 *Columbia Law Review* 1705, 1753.

or which is in the better position to compare expected accident costs with costs involved in accident prevention, *should* determine tort law cases. These are the arguments of Young Smith, Keating, Klemme and Calabresi as summarised above. It should be acknowledged that these arguments have to some extent been accepted by American courts in particular, for instance in relation to strict liability for defective products,[14] and accidents involving corporations.[15] There is also the argument by Posner that the goal of the law should be wealth maximisation, and that this objective should guide judges in resolving disputes in tort.

The first problem with this type of reasoning as an ideal is that it runs up against practical difficulties in the real world. First, it is dangerous to make any assumptions about the ability of any organisation to distribute the costs associated with risks.[16] In order to properly assess this possibility, there would have to be particular analysis of a particular defendant. No a priori assumptions could be made. Yet, the whole grain of the common law is the development of legal principles and precedent that can then be applied to a broad range of cases. It is completely contrary to this system to use principles in it that simply cannot be universally applied, because they are so situation specific.

Specifically, before it could be concluded that a given organisation could distribute the costs of the risks it generates to its customers, there would need to be detailed consideration of the market/s into which the organisation supplies. The structure and dynamics of that market would be important. Basic economics would suggest that it cannot be assumed that an organisation can simply raise its prices to cover new costs. One would need to consider the elasticity of demand for the product – how sensitive customers in that industry are (or would be) to changes in price. Whether or not the given organisation has substantial market share would be relevant. If it has substantial market share, other things being equal, it would have more scope to increase prices than if it were a small player. Similarly, the number of organisations currently serving that market would be an important consideration. If there are a small number of participants, this might permit the given organisation greater scope to increase prices; the opposite would be the case if there were many participants. The question of high barriers to entry would also be important – if there are high barriers to entry into that market, an organisation would have greater scope to increase prices.

[14] *Greenman v Yuba Power Products Inc* 59 Cal. 2d. 57; 377 P. 2d 897, 27 Cal. Rptr 697 (1962) (Traynor J); Section 402A *Restatement (Second) of Torts* (1965).

[15] *Siegler v Kuhlman* 81 Wash. 2d. 448, 460; 502 P. 2d. 1181, 1188 (1972) (Rosellini J); *Chavez v Southern Pacific Transportation* Co 413 F. Supp. 1203, 1208 (E.D, Cal., 1976).

[16] Clarence Morris, 'Hazardous Enterprises and Risk Bearing Capacity' (1952) 61 *Yale Law Journal* 1172, 1176, refers to the 'dubious assumptions and oversimplifications' involved in arguments about loss spreading in support of enterprise liability theories. He points out that courts typically do not receive evidence from parties in this regard. Further, enterprises would need to be able to guess as to the likely cost of the damage they might cause (1178), in order to properly price those costs in to the goods and/or services they provide. He concludes those engaged in dangerous activities 'sometimes are and sometimes are not' better risk bearers than those injured by those activities (1179).

Similarly, before it could be concluded that a given organisation could distribute the costs of the risks it generates to its employees, there would need to be detailed consideration of the existing regulation of the employment relationship. To what extent are the working conditions of workers regulated, for example by an industrial award or enterprise agreement? There may be protections in place limiting the ability of an organisation to reduce employee wages, for example in response to increased costs. There may be limits on the extent to which employers can reduce staffing costs by dismissing or standing down workers, and these activities may themselves lead to further costs.

Then it is said that the business can distribute the costs associated with these risks through the prism of insurance. However, again assumptions are being made that insurance is available in that particular field, and on reasonable terms. As Morris has noted, this may not be possible. Further, even if it is available, exclusion clauses in insurance contracts might mean the organisation does not have coverage. Further, it is an error to assume that insurance companies make individual assessments of a particular would-be insured when determining the terms upon which they might be given insurance. It is largely an industry-wide and geographically based assessment. This weakens the argument of those who suggest that insurance can be utilised to properly allocate costs to those creating particular risks.

Henderson notes that any system of strict liability requires that losses be insurable. In turn, this means that the risks against which insurance is sought must be ascertainable and quantifiable in advance. He says that given insurers tend to charge uniform premiums to policy holders in particular categories, 'either the risks contributed by insureds must be uniform or the choice of whether to be covered must not be within individual insureds' control'.[17] Because he says neither condition is likely met, strict liability based on an enterprise risk theory is not viable.

Another error is to suggest, as Keating did, that the loss can be spread because the relevant organisation can readily calculate the costs of accidental harm, before spreading these costs, whether to customers, employees, to others who are insured, or a combination of these. This assumption should be scrutinized. Can the costs of accidental harm be so readily calculated? Consider the example of an accidental gas explosion from a burst underground pipe. How can the expected costs of such an accident be readily determined? Much would depend on precisely where along the pipe it occurs – if it occurs in a remote rural setting, losses might be minimal, but if it occurs in the centre of a city, losses might be substantial. It might depend on the time of day, the time of year etc. This is a simple example, but it tends to undercut these assumptions that an organisation could typically readily calculate the expected costs of accidental harms. I respectfully strongly disagree.[18]

[17] James Henderson, 'Why Negligence Dominates Tort' (2002) 50 *UCLA Law Review* 377, 392–93.

[18] Alan Schwartz, 'The Case Against Strict Liability' (1992) 60 *Fordham Law Review* 819, 834: 'firms are required to compensate all consumer losses, but cannot estimate those losses, including non-pecuniary losses, with any degree of precision'.

Finally, to the extent that it is considered necessary that there be a (re)distribution of society's resources, whether on the grounds of efficiency, equity or some other basis, there are alternative levers through which this can occur, for example through a government's taxation policies, or other policies which reward some behaviour and seek to discourage others. Governments have a legitimate role in distributing and redistributing a society's resources. No one would argue with that fact; argument would tend to be about the extent to which such distribution is laudable, trade-offs between efficiency and equity. These need not concern us here. But the point is that it is a legitimate role for government to enter into these kinds of considerations. Governments are democratically accountable at regular intervals for these kinds of decisions.

The legitimacy of a court embarking on such an exercise, in a context in which they have been asked to resolve a specific dispute between specific parties, is much more open to question. They are not politically accountable for the decisions they might make in this regard. Weinrib was right to describe questions of efficient loss distribution and wealth maximisation as material that is extraneous and foreign to the law of tort. As explained above, of course Weinrib was a corrective justice scholar,[19] and this debate occurs in the broader context of whether the proper goals of the law of torts should reflect a system of corrective justice or distributive justice. This debate was first identified in Aristotle's *Nichomachean Ethics*. Weinrib pointed out that a negligence system was more attuned to a corrective justice system, while a strict liability system was more attuned to a distributive justice system.

The possible distributive justice aspect of enterprise liability was probably most clearly espoused by George Priest. He said that 'Enterprise liability theory also allowed judges to join the effort to aid the poor. Indeed, the theory conceived of courts as possessing unique powers to achieve these ends in comparison to alternative branches of government'.[20] In response, respectfully, most would not see it as the role of a court to 'aid the poor'. Courts are not social welfare agencies.[21] Priest did not identify what 'unique powers' courts might have in this regard. It is submitted that, to the extent that a society agrees that it is a good thing to 'aid the poor', this policy objective would be much better placed within the legislative, rather than judicial, branch. Particular parties go to court to have specific disputes resolved, not to permit courts to pursue a social agenda to 'aid the poor'.

Of course, there has been extensive criticism of the kind of aggregation that is at the heart of utilitarian theory, which is typically said to underlie an economic analysis approach to legal problems. Rights tend to be individual, yet utilitarianism

[19] Ernest Weinrib, 'Corrective Justice' (1992) 77 *Iowa Law Review* 403.

[20] George Priest, 'The Invention of Enterprise Liability: A Critical History of the Intellectual Foundations of Modern Tort Law' (1985) 14 *Journal of Legal Studies* 461, 519.

[21] Robert Keeton, 'Conditional Fault in the Law of Torts' (1959) 72 *Harvard Law Review* 401, 444, concluded that a notion of liability based on conditional fault 'offers some reassurance against the spectre of runaway social engineering with ill-considered emphasis on risk-spreading capacity'.

is fundamentally inconsistent with this notion, viewing them in quantitative rather than qualitative terms. Utilitarianism does not take into account the fact that some may weigh particular interests more than others do. Wright concludes that

> [a]lthough it makes no difference under the aggregate-risk-utility test who is getting the benefits and who is suffering the losses, or who is putting whom at risk for whose benefit, it makes a big difference as a matter of common morality and the principles of justice that are a part of that common morality.[22]

It does not describe how courts work.[23]

Posner's wealth maximisation form of utilitarianism is open to the further objection that it treats wealth as a proxy for morality, assumes that everything has a price, and allows for absolutely no non-financial assessment of the behaviour of a particular defendant (or plaintiff).[24] It ignores values such as the equal dignity and autonomy of others that lie at the heart of the work of Weinrib, Aristotle and Kant.[25]

Interestingly, the *Third Restatement of Torts*, which includes a section dealing with the imposition of strict liability, expressly eschews reliance on loss spreading as a justification:

> The appeal of strict liability … does not depend on any notion that the defendant is in a better position than the plaintiff to allocate or distribute the risk of harm: indeed, the defendant may be a small business enterprise; the property damage suffered by the plaintiff may be no more than moderate, and the plaintiff as a property owner may already be insured for the loss that that damage entails.[26]

Inappropriateness of Focus on Deterrence

Another basis on which the Canadian Supreme Court lauded strict liability (via vicarious liability) was on the basis of deterrence. The court claimed that by

[22] Richard Wright, 'Hand, Posner and the Myth of the Hand Formula' (2003) 4 *Theoretical Inquiries in Law* 145, 147.

[23] Robert Stevens, *Torts and Rights* (Oxford University Press, 2007) 94: 'whilst costs and benefits are relevant in a court's determination of negligence, they are not aggregated in the utilitarian manner an economist would employ. Some interests, for example lives and money, are incommensurable. They cannot be weighed in the scales in the manner which a utilitarian approach requires'.

[24] The criticism has been vast. See, for a sample, Ernest Weinrib, 'Utilitarianism, Economics and Legal Theory' (1980) 30 *University of Toronto Law Journal* 307; Richard Wright, 'Justice and Reasonable Care in Negligence Law' (2002) 47 *American Journal of Jurisprudence* 143.

[25] Richard Wright, 'Hand, Posner and the Myth of the Hand Formula' (2003) 4 *Theoretical Inquiries in Law* 145, 147: 'people generally believe that it is not properly respectful of the equal dignity and autonomy of others, and hence not just, for you to create substantial unaccepted foreseeable risks of injury to others' persons or property merely for your own personal benefit, even if your expected gain will exceed their expected loss … [and the law reflects that] … you are not morally required to subject yourself to significant burdens or risks in order to attempt to rescue another from a dangerous situation that you did not create, even if the risk to you seems to be less than the expected utility of the rescue attempt.

[26] *Restatement (Third) of Torts: Liability for Physical Harm* (2005) s20 comment e, as discussed in Kenneth Simons, 'The *Restatement (Third) of Torts* and Traditional Strict Liability: Robust Rationales, Slender Doctrines' (2009) 44 *Wake Forest Law Review* 1355, 1373.

imposing strict liability on organisations, this provided them with an incentive to take steps to reduce the risk that they have introduced to the community.[27] As noted above, Fleming James also lauded strict liability on the basis of its supposed deterrent value.

As discussed above, influential torts scholar Ernest Weinrib was highly critical of any suggestion that the law of tort should be guided by principles of deterrence.[28] Other scholars have taken a similar view,[29] even those who staunchly defend and support the imposition of strict liability on enterprises.[30] Some have concluded that strict liability can lead to over-deterrence of valuable activity.[31] Leaving that to one side, respectfully, reliance on deterrence to justify strict liability is highly problematic. It is not surprising that, although the UK courts have adopted the enterprise risk theory, they apparently will not countenance the supposed deterrence rationale for it[32] on the basis that it is 'empirically untested'. This reticence is justified.

With great respect, the unanimous judgment in *Bazley v Curry*, in the way it relies on deterrence to justify the imposition of strict liability, is internally incoherent. It is incoherent because, on the one hand, it argues that it is fair and reasonable to impose costs associated with an activity upon the enterprise that conducts it, because it will be able to distribute the costs away via higher prices to consumers and/or insurance. But another rationale for it is that it is said to induce the enterprise to engage in risk-preventive practices. With respect, how can a doctrine be lauded (a) on the one hand, because the organisation upon which it imposes the costs will not actually pay them, because they will (presumably) be able to distribute them away; but (b) on the other hand, because, by imposing costs upon them, they will influence its behaviour? With respect, one cannot have it both ways, and most certainly not in the same judgment.

[27] *Bazley v Curry* [1999] 2 SCR 534, 555 (McLachlin J, for the Court): 'beyond the narrow band of employer conduct that attracts direct liability in negligence lies a vast area where imaginative and efficient administration and supervision can reduce the risk that the employer has introduced into the community'.

[28] Ernest Weinrib, 'The Special Morality of Tort Law' (1989) 34 *McGill Law Journal* 403, 408: 'the tort relationship is not morally explicable in terms of deterrence, because deterrence can, without loss of any of its justificatory force, focus on the doer even in the absence of any particular sufferer. If deterrence were the justification for tort law, there would be no need for actual damage, nor for compensation to be paid to the plaintiff, nor for the plaintiff's injury to be the measure of damage'.

[29] Jason Neyers and David Stevens, 'Vicarious Liability in the Charity Sector: An Examination of *Bazley v Curry* and *Re Christian Brothers of Ireland* in Canada' (2005) 42 *Canadian Business Law Journal* 371, 396: 'the deterrence argument is largely incoherent either because it is based on the fault of the employer or it will not work'; see also Izhak Englard, 'The System Builders: A Critical Appraisal of Modern American Tort Theory' (1980) 9 *Journal of Legal Studies* 27, 39: 'we argue that the actual role of market deterrence in primary accident prevention is so limited as to render it all but devoid of practical importance in the framework of a general theory of accident law'.

[30] Albert Ehrenzweig, 'A Psychoanalysis of Negligence' (1953) 47 *Northwestern University Law Review* 855, 865: 'clearly imposition of liability on the manufacturer for harm caused by his defective merchandise to the ultimate consumer despite all possible caution, is not designed to deter him or others from operations otherwise so effectively encouraged by society'.

[31] Peter Huber, *Liability: The Legal Revolution and its Consequences* (Basic Books, 1988) ch 10.

[32] *Armes v Nottinghamshire County Council* [2018] AC 355, 381.

There is a further incoherence with the supposed deterrence rationale for strict liability. If an organisation is aware that it will be liable for accidents arising from its activity, regardless of how much care it took in relation to them, it is suggested that, far from providing it with incentives to take preventive measures, as the Supreme Court of Canada suggests in *Bazley*, it will actually have the opposite effect. Who would rationally take precautions if they would be held liable regardless of what precautions they took?

Now, it is clear enough that the Supreme Court of Canada was not talking in its judgment about activity levels. Some of the law and economics scholars who have lauded strict liability argue for its positive impact on decisions about 'activity levels', which negligence law does not really consider. They say that the imposition of strict liability will cause the enterprise to reduce its activity levels to a more socially optimal level because it knows it will be liable for all of the costs associated with the activity. It is not necessary to engage in this argument here. It suffices to say that this was not the basis of the 'deterrence' argument presented by the Supreme Court in *Bazley* – that court referred to deterrence in terms of 'imaginative and efficient administration and supervision',[33] and said nothing about leading to more efficient decisions about activity levels. And any suggestion that judges should take account of impacts on activity levels in determining liability rules runs up against the objections articulated under the previous heading, including the economic expertise of decision makers in our legal system to make those kinds of judgments and assessments.

Of course, there is no logical connection between notions of deterrence and the restricted application of strict liability to abnormally dangerous or ultra-hazardous activity (in the language of the Restatements), or 'likely to do mischief' in the language of *Rylands v Fletcher*. A goal of deterring activity cannot in logic be confined to activity that is especially dangerous; it must surely apply to any activity that could be dangerous, which of course is most activity.

Use of Terms with Highly Contested Meanings

The problem which many advocates of strict liability have is in trying to place proper boundaries around its use. They generally do not favour it applying to all contexts so seek to limit it, but in doing so then resort to highly ambiguous concepts. There is substantial weight placed on these terms because their meaning is very important in determining liability. If it is the difference between applying strict liability and fault-based liability, it might be the difference between recovery and non-recovery. Yet, it is not obvious that these terms can stand the weight being placed upon them.

[33] *Bazley v Curry* [1999] 2 SCR 534.

With the benefit of hindsight, it is obvious that this was one of the problems with the doctrine of *Rylands v Fletcher*. It was the concept of 'non-natural use' and/or 'not naturally there' (later ordinary use) which would bedevil that precedent, leading to quite unreal situations where the use of land for munitions manufacture is said to be a natural use of land (*Read v Lyons*), and which contributed to the Australian High Court abandoning the doctrine once and for all in *Burnie Port Authority*.

Yet, some do not seem to have learned from this experience. In some jurisdictions the parameters have changed slightly but the same old problem remains. I am talking specifically here about the use of concepts such as 'ultra-hazardous' or 'abnormally dangerous' in various American Restatements to try to express and try to corral the circumstances in which strict liability might apply, derived from the 'likely to do mischief if it escapes' test in *Rylands*. But what is an ultra-hazardous activity? As has been pointed out, virtually any activity might be considered dangerous. Walking across the street, or walking the dog, could be dangerous. When is the line crossed between ordinary activity which contains an element of danger, and something that is 'ultra' or 'extra' dangerous? It is not at all clear.[34]

There is also perhaps the more important question of why? Why should the fact that an activity is very dangerous, even if that can be adequately defined, change the liability rule from that of negligence fault-based liability to that of strict liability? There are few attempts to answer this question, and the answers that are presented are, frankly, unconvincing. Ehrenzweig, as shown above, sought to justify it by explaining it applied to activities which, but for being tolerated, would be negligent because foreseeably harmful. Of course, the mere fact that loss is foreseeably harmful does not automatically lead to a conclusion of negligence. Leflar, in also seeking to justify it, explained that the notion of ultra-hazardous activity applied to those activities that were not so common that people were accustomed to its risks. With respect, ultra-hazardous is not the same as uncommon. And it is not clear why the fact someone is 'accustomed' to a particular risk should bear on their ability to claim compensation if they are injured by it. Being accustomed to a risk is certainly not the same as a voluntary assumption of risk defence. When I drive on the road, I am accustomed to the risk that someone will crash into me. Clearly, this does not mean the voluntary assumption of risk defence will apply.

The uncertainty of meaning is not confined to terms like ultra-hazardous and extra-dangerous. The enterprise risk theory applies in some iterations to what are called 'characteristic' risks of a particular enterprise. This term is used by Keating. Ehrenzweig talks about 'typical' harms relating to particular activity and is probably talking about the same thing that Keating was. Again, it is not clear what a characteristic (or typical) risk is.[35] Is the escape of water from a tailings dam a

[34] Ezra Thayer, 'Liability Without Fault' (1916) 29 *Harvard Law Review* 801, 816.

[35] James Henderson, 'Why Negligence Dominates Tort' (2002) 50 *UCLA Law Review* 377, 395: 'the concept of characteristic risk is too ambiguous and inclusive to serve as an adequate analytical tool with which to sort out the relevant responsibilities'.

characteristic risk of some mining activity? Some of the cases where strict liability has been applied have occurred in the context of abuse of children within educational and/or care environments.[36] It may sound crude and offensive to even ask the question, but is abuse of a child a 'characteristic risk' of running a school, or a system of foster care? And again, even if we can settle upon an acceptable definition of what a 'characteristic risk' is, it is not clear why liability rules should differ according to whether a risk is characteristic of an activity or not. The law of negligence already takes into account foreseeability of a kind of injury in determining whether or not a duty of care is owed, and whether damages might be available for breach.

In the same vein, Klemme seeks to explain the imposition of strict liability on the basis that it should be applied when the defendant has not met 'normal expectations'. Of course, the concept of reasonable care does something very similar, if not identical, in the context of fault-based negligence. It makes sense in the negligence context – a departure from what is typically expected shows that the defendant has not met the standards of conduct that society expected of them; they have failed to act reasonably. The accident that results is their fault. It is less clear how a departure from normal expectations should ground strict liability when it is the departure which creates the fault in the defendant that justifies liability in negligence.[37]

Another interesting term used by those who attempt to justify strict liability is 'inevitable'. Ehrenzweig, for example, would apply strict liability to the 'inevitable consequences' of dangerous activities. So would Landes and Posner. Posner seems to be referring to it in the *Indiana Harbour Belt RR* extract above. There is some judicial support for its use in this context.[38]

However, as will be recalled from Chapter 1, the first thing that can be noted about this concept is that, in historical context, the fact that something was an inevitable accident was a defence that the defendant used to *avoid* otherwise prima facie liability, and historically this liability was often strict.[39] Thus, we have the interesting spectre of something that was in the past utilised to *deny* strict

[36] *Lister and Others v Hesley Hall Ltd* [2002] 1 AC 215; *Bazley v Curry* [1999] 2 SCR 534; *Prince Alfred College v ADC* (2016) 258 CLR 134.

[37] Stephen Perry, 'The Impossibility of General Strict Liability' (1988) 1 *Canadian Journal of Law and Jurisprudence* 147, 167: 'to make liability turn on the expectations that each party did or should have had about how the other would behave is to decide on the basis of a fault standard, not one of strict liability'.

[38] *Tock v St John's Metropolitan Area Board* [1989] 2 SCR 1181, 1201 (Dickson CJ and La Forest J).

[39] For example, *Saddler v South Staffs Tramways Co* (1889) 23 QBD 17, 22, where, in the context of liability for damage caused by a tramcar leaving the tracks, the court found the defendant strictly liable. It then held: 'suppose all the apparatus being in proper order, some miscreant had placed a log across the line unobserved, and in consequence the carriage had run off the rails and injured somebody. Possibly a case of that sort might be one of inevitable accident in which the company might not be responsible, although the injury was caused by their acts'; Oliver Wendell Holmes Jr, *The Common Law* (Little, Brown, & Co, 1881) 95: 'all the cases concede that an injury arising from inevitable accident … is but the misfortune of the sufferer, and lays no foundation for legal responsibility'; Stephen Gilles, 'Inevitable Accident in Classical English Tort Law' (1994) 43 *Emory Law Journal* 575.

liability now being used by some scholars to *justify* application of strict liability principles. Again, the meaning of something being 'inevitable' is not entirely clear. Does this mean the thing will in all cases happen? Or is it sufficient that it is likely to happen? Generally, the word would mean that in all cases it would happen. If the common meaning of the term were applied, it would be a difficult test to satisfy – for instance, it is not inevitable that a train will run off railway tracks, it is not inevitable that a dam will burst or leak, it is not inevitable there will be an explosion at a power plant. Thus, its use here is both ahistorical and of uncertain meaning. Others have also been critical of it.[40]

Liability for Non-reciprocal Risks

The concept of non-reciprocal risks, championed by Fletcher and Keating as an apparent basis for the imposition of strict liability, suffers from a combination of the problems just described above. First, and most importantly, there is the plain fact that judges do not actually use the concept, even when they are proceeding to apply strict liability standards. Of course, the court in *Rylands v Fletcher* does not discuss that they are applying a strict liability approach because of non-reciprocal risk, it does not appear in any of the relevant Canadian and Australia decisions, and none of the iterations of strict liability in the Restatements refer to the concept.[41] Clearly, there are current and historical examples of strict liability that apply in cases where risks are in fact reciprocal. For example, cattle trespass actions typically apply in rural settings where both the plaintiff and defendant have farms, likely including livestock. This is surely a classic example of a reciprocal risk. Yet liability for cattle trespass is strict. This presents a problem for the non-reciprocal theory.[42]

And further, most individuals who own farms need a water supply for agricultural purposes. This will often lead farmers to construct artificial water structures, such as dams and reservoirs. Surely, again, this is a classic reciprocal risk, yet the classic example of strict liability involves the construction of a reservoir on a farm. The same might be said for dangers posed by fires, again historically a source of strict liability, where it is expected that each of the parties might be in a position to pose this risk to another in a way that broadly approaches the meaning of 'reciprocal'.

Secondly, it is surely necessary to consider the precise circumstances of a situation before determining that one is liable for injury caused to another. So, for

[40] Keith Hylton, 'The Theory of Tort Doctrine and the *Restatement*' (2001) 54 *Vanderbilt Law Review* 1413, 1418, noting that it was impossible to eliminate the risk of an accident, and consequences and risks could always be reduced by shifting and reducing the activity. Thus, the claimed distinction was in Hylton's view meaningless.

[41] It does appear in the notes.

[42] Gary T Schwartz, 'The Vitality of Negligence and the Ethics of Strict Liability' (1981) 15 *Georgia Law Review* 963, 985; Robert Stevens, *Torts and Rights* (Oxford University Press, 2007) 108.

example, a train might strike someone on the railway tracks. The owner of a train clearly imposes non-reciprocal risks upon individuals in society – primarily, the risk of being injured by the train. If a train strikes an individual, causing them serious injury, the logic of the theory of non-reciprocal risk would make the owner of the train legally liable to the injured individual. However, it apparently pays no heed to the individual circumstances – what if the individual fell asleep on the train tracks because they were intoxicated? What if it were a deliberate suicide attempt by the individual? We generally find in law that rules cannot be created in the abstract; we need to understand the specific circumstances before we can hope to craft rules that approach the doing of justice.[43] A non-reciprocal risk approach does not permit this to occur.

Of course, the other issue is the precise meaning of 'reciprocal'. Is it applied in a hypothetical way or a real way? For instance, in the context of the facts in *Rylands*, would it be necessary that the plaintiff had in fact constructed a reservoir on their own property in order to conclude that this was a case of reciprocal risk? Or would it be sufficient that they potentially might do so? And of course, if the former, this might actively discourage farmers from constructing reservoirs on their property, in order to preserve their legal rights. The advantages to society of such behaviour are not entirely clear. Does it matter that the magnitude of the risk in the one case, because one of the parties has a bigger reservoir, has more cattle, has more flammable material on their property, is greater than in the other? And on principle, why should that fact make such a difference in terms of liability? Again, while the concept sounds interesting, it is very difficult to apply in practice due to its uncertain meaning, it does not have a clear intellectual or moral justification, and is not actually used in cases, for good reason.

Who Gets the Benefits?

Some who advocated strict liability did so based on the assumption that the enterprise gets all of the benefit of the activity, so it is fair they should incur the associated costs. There is limited judicial support for such a view.[44] This position was advocated by Keating, among others such as Bohlen,[45] the Reporter of the

[43] Donal Nolan, 'The Distinctiveness of *Rylands v Fletcher*' (2005) 121 *Law Quarterly Review* 421, 449.

[44] For example, *Tock v St John's Metropolitan Area Board* [1989] 2 SCR 1181, 1201: 'the cost of damage that is an inevitable consequence of the provision of services that benefit the public at large should be borne equally by all those who profit from the service' (Dickson CJ and La Forest J); *Bridgeman-Russell v City of Duluth* 158 Minn. 509, 511; 197 N.W. 971, 972 (1924) involving the escape of water from a main. The court concluded that 'in such a case, even though negligence is absent, natural justice would seem to demand that the enterprise, or what is really the same thing, the whole community benefitted by the enterprise, should stand the loss rather than the individual'.

[45] Francis Bohlen, 'The Basis of Affirmative Obligations in the Law of Torts Parts I, II and III' (1905) 53 *American Law Register* 209, 273.

First Restatement (*Torts*). However, with respect, Jeremiah Smith was right to point out that it is simply not correct to argue that an organisation reaps all of the benefits of particular activity. In fact, there are many beneficiaries – the organisation employs people, so all of its employees, and their families, benefit. In turn, those individuals spend money, so all of the providers of the goods and services those individuals also gain. This is the concept of the multiplier effect of economic activity, familiar to all of those who have studied any economics. Of course, the organisation's own clients and customers benefit, by having the choice of a particular product or service. The fact that such an organisation exists and provides such a service might benefit those who purchase goods and services from rival firms because it might provide a more competitive environment in that industry. If the firm leases premises, the property owner benefits. If the organisation pays tax, all of those within the jurisdiction benefit. The government spends such taxation revenue on community services and benefits. I could go on, but the point is the folly in making the simplistic argument that an organisation derives all of the benefit of economic activity, thus it should bear all of the costs. This is demonstrably false and cannot be utilised to justify enterprise risk strict liability.

Further, it will often be the case that the other parties involved in the conflict were engaged in activity because they believed that it was for their benefit. Yet, apparently this fact does not lead to a conclusion that they should 'wear' the consequences of this activity. It is difficult to see then why the fact that an enterprise did so should be sufficient.[46]

Difficulties of Proof

Occasionally, adherents of strict liability such as Murphy, seek to justify it on the basis that, if a plaintiff were required to prove fault, they might not be successful, because it might be difficult to obtain the required evidence. These scholars use this as justification for removing the need for the plaintiff to prove that their injuries were the fault of the defendant.

First, I have never been convinced of an argument that liability rules should be influenced by ease or difficulty of proof. I have encountered this argument in another context, where some seek to argue, in criminal matters, that the burden of proof should be placed on defendants because they can more easily prove their innocence (if they are in fact innocent) than the prosecutor prove the truth of their allegations. Yet, our criminal justice system has steadfastly maintained a presumption of innocence and a requirement that the prosecutor prove all of

[46] Paul Weiler, 'Defamation, Enterprise Liability and Freedom of Speech' (1967) 17 *University of Toronto Law Journal* 278, 304, concluding that an organisation 'should not be uniquely responsible because it is an activity engaged in for the self-interested benefit of the defendant. Not only are all of the other intersecting activities so involved for the same reason but also, probably, the various profitable activities serve substantial social purposes'.

the elements of the offence which they allege the defendant committed, at a level beyond reasonable doubt. I have defended that elsewhere.[47] I have rejected in that publication arguments that the burden should be 'flexible' because prosecutors might struggle to prove suspicions. So much may be accepted. But this is for good reason. The default position of the law is, and should be, to do nothing. It is for the person (or organisation) that seeks for the law to do something to show why it should occur. We presume lack of wrongdoing, not wrongdoing. It is for the one accusing another of wrongdoing to prove it, not the accused to demonstrate innocence.[48] For similar reasons, here in a civil context, though concededly the interests involved are not as strong, it is for a plaintiff seeking compensation from another to demonstrate that the other has committed a wrong. Typically, this is expressed by a fault principle, not simply a causation principle.

Further, as others have pointed out, the *res ipsa loquitur* principle may lessen the burden upon plaintiffs to prove the elements of the tort they claim to have been committed by the defendant.[49] Friedmann concluded that 'the rule of res ipsa loquitur has in many cases operated to shift the burden of evidence on to the defendant and thus to eliminate another difference between actions brought under negligence or under a stricter tort'.[50] At the time of *Rylands v Fletcher*, that doctrine had not been developed.

The Plaintiff's Activity or Behaviour

Another criticism of the strict liability approach is its (sometimes) exclusive focus on the activity or behaviour of the defendant. So, for instance, in the view of Epstein, it is sufficient (or should be sufficient), in order for the plaintiff to recover against the defendant, that it is shown that the defendant caused the plaintiff injury. In this paradigm, there is apparently no room for a consideration of the plaintiff's behaviour. For example, the fact that the plaintiff was guilty of contributory negligence would be irrelevant in this analysis.[51] In this space, in economic terms, it would be

[47] Anthony Gray, *The Presumption of Innocence in Peril: A Comparative Critical Perspective* (Lexington Books, 2017) 101; see also Andrew Ashworth, 'Four Threats to the Presumption of Innocence (2006) 10 *International Journal of Evidence and Proof* 260; Paul Roberts, 'The Presumption of Innocence Brought Home? *Kebilene* Deconstructed' (2002) 118 *Law Quarterly Review* 41, 65.

[48] This was recognised by Lord Bingham, who noted in *R v Director of Public Prosecutions; Ex Parte Kebilene* [2000] 2 AC 326, 345 that the mere fact that an accused would find it easier to lead evidence on a particular matter than the prosecution would was not a reason to jettison the standard position that the onus of proof was on the one accusing another of wrongdoing to prove the truth of their accusation at the required standard.

[49] GHL Fridman, 'The Rise and Fall of *Rylands v Fletcher*' (1956) 34 *Canadian Bar Review* 810, 818; Cornelius Peck, 'Negligence and Liability Without Fault in Tort Law' (1971) 46(2) *Washington Law Review* 225, 240; Ezra Ripley Thayer, 'Liability Without Fault' (1916) 29 *Harvard Law Review* 801, 807.

[50] W Friedmann, 'Nuisance, Negligence and the Overlapping of Torts' (1940) 3 *Modern Law Review* 305, 309.

[51] Richard Posner, 'Strict Liability: A Comment' (1973) 2 *Journal of Legal Studies* 205, 217.

irrelevant that (on the view of Calabresi) the plaintiff was in the better position to make an assessment of the likely costs of the accident occurring versus the likely costs of avoidance, or (in the view of Posner) that total wealth would be maximised if the plaintiff were denied recovery, because it would have been cheaper for the plaintiff to have taken steps to avoid being injured than it would have been for the defendant to take steps to avoid injuring the plaintiff.

Conclusion

Scholars have made serious attempts to justify and rationalise the imposition of strict liability. This has been partly necessary due to general dearth of discussion in the case law as to the rationale for its imposition. However, the arguments have not provided very convincing or coherent reasoning. It is not for a court to engage in efficient loss distribution; it is to do justice according to the law. It is believed that the vast majority of common law judges (with some notable exceptions) do not generally believe it to be their role to engage in such distribution. In any event, the court system is generally ill-fitted for the task, and with no disrespect intended, so are the judges. This is not where their training or expertise lies. To ask a court to engage in efficient loss distribution, 'aid the poor' etc is to confuse the role of a court with the role of a legislator. To the extent that society wishes to efficiently allocate, or reallocate, resources, this is much better left to legislators, not courts.

Even if efficient loss distribution were a laudable pursuit for courts, its practical implementation would face insuperable difficulties. Judges would need much more economic information relevant to the fact than they currently actually receive. They would need to know about features of the relevant market, including things such as elasticity of demand, and aspects of market structure, the industrial relations system relevant to the employer etc. It would end up not looking or feeling much like a justice system any more, frankly. Courts should not make assumptions, for that is all they would be, as to the ability of any particular defendant to distribute their risks elsewhere through insurance. Nor should it be assumed that defendants can easily assess the cost of these risks.

There is internal incoherence in applications of the enterprise risk theory, the main current theory said to support and justify the imposition of strict liability. It is at once lauded on the basis that the defendant does not actually pay the costs because it is able to 'distribute' these costs to others, including suppliers, customers, staff and through insurance, but also that it provides appropriate deterrence to the kind of activities and activity levels the law should seek to promote. There is an internal inconsistency at the heart of a doctrine that is, at once in the same leading case, lauded because it means the defendant does not pay, and then lauded because it means the defendant will be deterred because it does pay.

The efforts to explain and justify the imposition of strict liability have been blighted and crippled by the inevitable resort to principles to try to corral and control this form of extreme liability. Those chosen – things not naturally there, not natural or non-ordinary use, dangerous, ultra-hazardous or extra-hazardous, are chronically uncertain and contested in their meaning. The same could be said for other candidates such as inevitable risk, inevitable accident, and non-reciprocal risk.

Arguments that enterprises should be saddled with the costs their activity generates because they obtain all the benefits of such activity are, frankly, wrong. Businesses provide benefit to a broad range of others, including their suppliers, customers, their staff and families, and to society generally through taxation revenue. Arguments about strict liability usually focus on the defendant's activity and their choice to engage in it, while simultaneously ignoring the plaintiff's choices and decisions.

Finally, I have never been convinced that a legal system should be influenced by the difficulty of one side obtaining sufficient proof. Generally, it is on the one alleging wrongdoing by another to prove it. This is as it should be. The default position of the law must be to 'do nothing'. If someone wants the law to 'do something', it is incumbent on them to demonstrate why. The status quo is and should be the starting position. This applies in the criminal realm, where it is for the prosecutor to demonstrate that another has committed wrong, just as it does in the civil realm. The fact that the one upon whom the burden is placed might legitimately encounter difficulties in proving their allegations of wrongdoing is acknowledged. But it does not, in my view, justify reversal of the burden of proof in criminal cases; nor should it influence legal doctrine in the law of torts. In summary, none of the arguments said to favour strict liability are convincing.

PART IV

Fault in Other Torts

7

The Tort of Nuisance and Fault

History and Early Development

The word nuisance is derived from the Latin word *nocumentum*, which refers to harm and/or annoyance. This clearly contemplates a broad range of circumstances in which recovery might be possible. In this regard, it has unkindly, if not altogether inaccurately, been referred to as having 'mongrel origins'.[1] It has been referred to on more than one occasion as being 'vulnerable', particularly to the tort of negligence.[2]

The tort of nuisance is of ancient vintage, pre-dating by centuries other torts, particularly the tort of negligence, at least as we would today recognise it. There was an assize of novel disseisin recognised in 1166, which encompassed a broad range of harms to land, including those we would today recognise as nuisance claims.[3] Novel disseisin referred to complete deprivations of a person's right to exercise their property rights. The nuisance action is said to have emanated from that,[4] supplanting the assize of nuisance. Nuisance was and remains an action on the case, designed to remedy gaps in the writ system, most especially here the right of trespass. Nuisance evolved into two categories – public nuisance, involving interference with, for example, a public thoroughfare, as a result of which a plaintiff suffered damage; and private nuisance, involving interference with the property rights of the plaintiff.[5] Public nuisance was thought to have sufficient analogies with that part of private nuisance dealing with interferences to (private) rights of way such as easements to justify its recognition as part of the law of nuisance. It was

[1] Conor Gearty, 'The Place of Private Nuisance in a Modern Law of Torts' (1989) 48(2) *Cambridge Law Journal* 214.

[2] Maria Lee, 'What is Private Nuisance?' (2003) 119 *Law Quarterly Review* 298, 325; Conor Gearty, 'The Place of Private Nuisance in a Modern Law of Torts' (1989) 48(2) *Cambridge Law Journal* 214, 215.

[3] JR Spencer, 'Public Nuisance – A Critical Examination' (1989) 48 *Cambridge Law Journal* 55.

[4] Janet Loengard, 'The Assize of Nuisance: Origins of an Action at Common Law' (1978) 37 *Cambridge Law Journal* 144, 158–59; JH Baker, *An Introduction to English Legal History* (Butterworths, 2002) 423. The disseisin claim was limited to situations where a defendant had entered the plaintiff's premises: Percy Winfield, 'Nuisance as a Tort' (1931) 4 *Cambridge Law Journal* 189, 190.

[5] Winfield defines a private nuisance as an 'unlawful interference with a person's use or enjoyment of land, or of some right over, or in connection with it': Percy Winfield 'Nuisance as a Tort' (1931) 4 *Cambridge Law Journal* 189, 190.

originally governed exclusively by the criminal law,[6] before being extended into the civil realm, particularly where the plaintiff could show they suffered damage from that nuisance over and above that suffered by others.[7] On occasion, the same facts could give rise to both a private and a public nuisance. Interestingly, though apparently part of the tort of nuisance, courts permitted damages for personal injuries caused by public nuisance.[8] This is considered strange, in that nuisance was/is seen to be confined to damage to property interests. The significance of this will be discussed further later in the chapter.

In relation to the tort of private nuisance, it is essential for any plaintiff to demonstrate that they possessed property rights, typically ownership[9] or (exclusive) occupation,[10] with which the defendant had interfered.[11] Such interference could be caused by a myriad of activity. Typical were complaints about noise, odour and pollution. It would include physical support of another's premises. It could also include direct physical damage to the property of another.[12] One would have thought that escaping water from a reservoir would be a prime example of an actionable nuisance. This of course was not the basis of the judgment in *Rylands v Fletcher*, and it would take approximately 130 years for the UK court to accept that the *Rylands* action was really a subset of the tort of nuisance. The interference with property rights would need to be substantial or material, as opposed to trivial.[13] The location at which the activity occurs would be relevant in determining whether a given activity amounts to a nuisance or not.[14]

The cases can involve a difficult balancing of competing interests. The exercise of one person's property rights may infringe upon that of another. The question

[6] *Thomas v Sorrell* (1673) Vaugh 330, 340; 124 ER 1098, 1104: 'if a man have particular damage by a foundrous way, he is generally without remedy, though the nuisance is to be punisht [*sic*] by the King' (Vaughan CJ); JR Spencer, 'Public Nuisance – A Critical Examination' (1989) 48 *Cambridge Law Journal* 55, 73.

[7] YB Mich. 27 Hen. VIII, fo. 27, pl. 10 (1535); *Boyce v Paddington Corporation* [1906] AC 1.

[8] *Fowler v Sanders* (1617) Cro. Jac. 446; 79 ER 382.

[9] *Kennaway v Thompson* [1981] QB 88.

[10] *Shelfer v City of London Electric Lighting Go* [1895] 1 Ch 287.

[11] *Hunter v Canary Wharf Ltd* [1997] AC 655, 692 (Lord Goff), 703 (Lord Hoffmann) and 724 (Lord Hope).

[12] *St Helen's Smelting Co v Tipping* (1865) 11 HLC 642; 11 ER 1483. These three examples of private nuisance broadly reflect the three categories of the type of case encompassed by the tort as outlined by Lord Lloyd in *Hunter v Canary Wharf Ltd* [1997] AC 655, 695 of encroachment on a neighbour's land, direct physical injury to the land of another, and interference with the quiet enjoyment of a neighbour's land. John Murphy, *The Law of Nuisance* (Oxford University Press, 2010) 6 criticises Lord Lloyd's three categories, arguing it is incorrect to insist upon a need for 'direct' physical damage (which might amount, in any event to trespass), Lord Lloyd's use of the word 'neighbour' to describe nuisance categories, and his failure to acknowledge that a nuisance action may protect use, not just enjoyment of premises.

[13] *St Helen's Smelting Co v Tipping* (1865) 11 HLC 642, 650–51; 11 ER 1483, 1486; *Walter v Selfe* (1851) 4 De. G & Sm. 315, 322; 64 ER 849, 852 referring to a material interference with ordinary comfort having regard to ordinary notions of English life, as opposed to 'elegant or dainty' modes of life.

[14] *St Helen's Smelting Co v Tipping* (1865) 11 HLC 642, 650; 11 ER 1483, 1486; *Sturges v Bridgman* (1879) 11 Ch 852, 865 (Thesiger J, for the Court of Appeal).

of the reasonableness or otherwise of the defendant's activity, and (on occasion) its social utility, became important.[15] In *Bamford v Turnley*[16] Chief Baron Pollock noted that

> I think that the word 'reasonable' cannot be an improper word, and too vague to be used on this occasion [noting extensive use of it in relation to contract disputes]. If the act complained of be done in a convenient manner so as to give no unnecessary annoyance, and be a reasonable exercise of some apparent right, or a reasonable use of the land, house or property of the party under all the circumstances, in which I include the degree of inconvenience it will produce, then … no action can be sustained, if the jury find that it was reasonable.[17]

In *Andreae v Selfridge and Co Ltd*,[18] Lord Greene MR for the Court of Appeal asked whether the defendant had applied 'all reasonable skill and taking all reasonable precautions not to cause annoyance to its neighbours',[19] in considering a nuisance claim. The courts accepted that some give and take in this area was necessary. Individuals could not be 'too precious' about their property rights, including that of quiet enjoyment. Depending on the locality, they might effectively be required to 'put up' with some interference with those rights, in the name of permitting another to exercise their rights.[20] Relevant factors will include the duration, extent and nature or character of the harm done to the plaintiff's property interests, the nature of the activity in which the defendant is engaged, the extent to which it was practical for the defendant to take steps to avoid the interference, and the motive of the defendant for doing what they did.[21] These are very similar, if not identical,

[15] *Sedleigh-Denfield v Callaghan* [1940] AC 880, 903: 'a useful test is perhaps what is reasonable according to the ordinary usages of mankind living in society, or more correctly a particular society' (Lord Wright); *Kennaway v Thompson* [1981] QB 88, 94 where Lawton LJ for the Court of Appeal stated that the question was whether 'the neighbour is using his property reasonably having regard to the fact he has a neighbour'; whether the interference is 'exceptive and unreasonable' (*Gaunt v Fynney* (1872) 8 Ch App 8, 12); *Tock v St John's Metropolitan Area Board* [1989] 2 SCR 1181, 1205 (Wilson J, for Lamer and L'Heureux-Dube JJ, concluding that the flooding of the defendant's basement 'constituted an unreasonable interference with the appellant's use and enjoyment of the property', thus a prima facie case of nuisance had been established. This sentiment is reflected in WVH Roberts, *Winfield and Jolowicz on Torts* (18th edn, Sweet & Maxwell, 2010) 714: 'the central issue of the whole law of nuisance is the question of reasonableness of the defendant's conduct'; for criticism see Allan Beever, *The Law of Private Nuisance* (Hart Publishing, 2013) 9–12.

[16] *Bamford v Turnley* (1862) 3 B & S 66, 80–81; 122 ER 27, 32.

[17] Williams J (for Erle CJ Keating and Wilde B) stated that 'if (the jury) were of the opinion that the spot where the bricks were burnt was a proper and convenient spot and the burning of them was, under the circumstances, a reasonable use by the defendant of his own land', then they would have been required to find in favour of the defendant (1862) 3 B & S 66, 73–74; 122 ER 27, 29). Baron Pollock referred to the 'common and ordinary use of land' as being a defence to a nuisance action (1862) 3 B & S 66, 83; 122 ER 27, 33.

[18] *Andreae v Selfridge and Co Ltd* [1938] Ch 1.

[19] ibid, 7.

[20] *Bamford v Turnley* (1862) 3 B & S 67, 84; 122 ER 27, 33 where Baron Bramwell spoke of the need for 'give and take, live and let live', at least in relation to 'ordinary' uses of land; *Kennaway v Thompson* [1981] QB 88, 94 (Lawton LJ, for the Court of Appeal).

[21] John Murphy, *The Law of Nuisance* (Oxford University Press, 2010) 40–54.

to the kinds of factors that a court would typically take into account in determining whether or not a duty of care has been breached in the case of a claim in negligence.[22] Reasonable foreseeability that a class of persons including the plaintiff would be injured by the activity is a precondition of liability in both torts, as will be seen.[23] The question of the overlap between nuisance and negligence is particularly important. Negligence is a classic tort of fault-based liability. It is less easy to categorise liability in nuisance. This is clearly of real practical importance. The question of whether liability is fault based or not fault based will be highly significant in determining the legal outcome of a given situation.

There is a line of cases which seem to deny liability in nuisance for things that are naturally occurring on the defendant's premises that escape, causing damage to the plaintiff. One example is *Giles v Walker*,[24] where thistles grew on to the defendant's property once it had been cultivated by a previous owner. The thistles were blown onto the plaintiff's neighbouring property, and the plaintiff sued the defendant for the damage which resulted. Both nuisance and negligence were discussed in the submissions. The court summarily dismissed the action, stating they had never heard of such an action in relation to things 'naturally growing' in the soil.[25] This may have been an attempt to distinguish the case from precedent such as *Rylands v Fletcher*. This approach was adopted by the High Court of Australia in *Sparke v Osborne*,[26] where a noxious weed grew from the defendant's property onto that of the plaintiff. The court denied the plaintiff a remedy in nuisance. The court distinguished between misfeasance and non-feasance. If a defendant had by actively using his land caused material damage to that of the plaintiff, this might be actionable; however, cases of mere failure to stop a noxious weed from spreading

[22] *Council of the Shire of Wyong v Shirt* (1980) 146 CLR 40, 47: 'in deciding whether there has been a breach of the duty of care the [court] must first ask itself whether a reasonable [person] in the defendant's position would have foreseen that [their] conduct involved a risk of injury to the plaintiff or to a class of persons including the plaintiff … [if yes then] the [court must] determine what a reasonable [person] would do by way of response to the risk. The perception of the reasonable [person's] response calls for a consideration of the magnitude of the risk and the degree of the probability of its occurrence, along with the expense, difficulty and inconvenience of taking alleviating action and any other conflicting responsibilities which the defendant may have. It is only when these matters are balanced out that the [court] can confidently assert what is the standard of response to be ascribed to the reasonable [person] placed in the defendant's position' (Mason J, with whom Stephen and Aickin JJ agreed). Factors such as the seriousness of the risk and the probability of its materialising have been applied in determining the content of the standard of care owed in a negligence case: *Paris v Stepney Borough Council* [1951] AC 367, 375–76 (Lord Simonds), 381 (Lord Normand, with whom Lord Oaksey agreed), 365 (Lord Morton) and 390 (Lord MacDermott). The practicality of taking precautions, including the difficulty and cost of doing so, were noted as being of importance in *Overseas Tankships (UK) Ltd v The Miller Steamship Co Pty Ltd (Wagon Mound No 2)* [1967] 1 AC 617, 643–44 (Lord Reid, for the Privy Council).

[23] *Overseas Tankships (UK) Ltd v The Miller Steamship Co Pty Ltd (Wagon Mound No 1)* [1961] AC 388.

[24] *Giles v Walker* (1890) 24 QBD 656.

[25] ibid, 657 (Lord Coleridge CJ, with whom Lord Esher agreed); see also *Neath Rural District Council v Williams* [1951] 1 KB 115.

[26] *Sparke v Osborne* (1907) 7 CLR 51.

were of a different order. The court found there was no precedent for making a property liable to a neighbouring property owner for cases of non-feasance.[27]

It should be noted that these decisions were rendered prior to recognition of a generalised duty of care in negligence in 1932, before the High Court of Australia's rejection of a distinction between liability in misfeasance and nonfeasance, at least in the context of a public authority,[28] and prior to the statement of Megaw LJ for the Court of Appeal in *Leakey v National Trust* that, for the purposes of nuisance, the distinction between misfeasance and nonfeasance was meaningless.[29] These decisions also seem somewhat inconsistent with the views expressed by Scrutton LJ in *Job Edwards Ltd v Birmingham Navigations* that 'a landowner has a duty to take reasonable care not to allow his land to remain a receptacle for a thing which may, if not rendered harmless, cause damage to his neighbours'.[30] For these reasons, it is not clear that these decisions would be decided in the same manner today.

There are apparently examples where the court takes the view that liability for nuisance is strict (or even absolute), and examples where liability for nuisance is not seen as strict. This anomaly in the law has been noted by others:

> [I]t is entirely unclear what standard of liability operates in the law of nuisance. Sometimes the law seems to be strict, sometimes it appears to be fault-based. And when it is fault-based, the operative notion of fault seems to be some free-floating standard, fluctuating somewhere in the space between strict liability and negligence.[31]

I will first explain factual examples where the courts apparently view liability for nuisance as strict, and where courts apparently view nuisance liability as involving some question of fault.

Examples where Courts View Liability in Nuisance as Strict

Cases in this category will tend to focus on the fact of the plaintiff's loss, and whether it was caused by the defendant, as opposed to the question of the culpability or wrongdoing of the accused. An early example appears in the 1702 decision in *Tenant v Goldwin*:

> Every one must so use his own, as not to do damage to another. And as every man is bound so to look to his cattle, as to keep them out of his neighbour's ground, that so

[27] This view also finds support in the decision of Shaw LJ in *Leakey v National Trust* [1980] QB 485, 528, where he asked 'why should a nuisance which has its origin in some natural phenomenon and which manifests itself without any human intervention cast a liability upon a person who has no other connection with that nuisance other than the title to the land on which it chances to originate?'

[28] *Brodie v Singleton Shire Council* (2001) 206 CLR 512.

[29] *Leakey v National Trust* [1980] QB 405, 514.

[30] *Job Edwards Ltd v Birmingham Navigations* [1924] 1 KB 341, 358. Though Scrutton LJ was dissenting in that case, his views were subsequently adopted by the House of Lords in *Sedleigh-Denfield v O'Callaghan* [1940] AC 880.

[31] Allan Beever, *The Law of Private Nuisance* (Hart Publishing, 2013) 9.

> he may receive no damage; so he must keep them in the filth of his house of office, that it may not flow in upon and damnify his neighbour … a man shall not lay his dung so high as to damage his neighbour, and the reason of these cases is, because every man must so use his own as not to damnify another.[32]

Here liability for nuisance appears to be strict in nature. There is no mention of fault or lack of reasonableness in this passage. It is focused on causation.

Another important example of this occurs in some of the judgments in *Tarry v Ashton*.[33] The case involved a plaintiff walking along a public street. A lamp attached to the defendant's premises dislodged and fell on her. She was injured. The defendant was aware that the condition of the lamp was deteriorating. They had engaged repairers prior to the incident. The jury determined that the defendant was not guilty of negligence in the circumstances. All members of the Court determined the case in the plaintiff's favour on the basis of public nuisance. However, there were significant differences in how members of the court expressed the defendant's liability in such circumstances.

For instance, Lush J stated that 'a person who puts up or continues a lamp in that position, puts the public safety in peril, and it is his duty to keep it in such a state as not to be dangerous'.[34] Quain J, in broad agreement, decided that the owner of premises from which a lamp hung onto a public thoroughfare was under an obligation to keep it in such a manner as not to injure the public.[35] These judgments appear to cast a strict liability upon a defendant for such a chain of events, although concepts such as 'duty' and 'neglect' are mentioned. As discussed in Chapter 1, some care must be taken in interpreting these words in older cases, not presuming that they mean the same in their historical context as we understand them today.

Subsequently in *Bamford v Turnley*[36] the court overturned *Hole v Barlow*. This was a case that had taken into account whether the defendant's activity took place in a reasonable and proper manner and place (discussed in the next section). The Court in *Bamford* stated that the decision in *Hole v Barlow* cast too widely in apparently permitting an action to take place if it were proper and convenient to do so, notwithstanding the nuisance caused to neighbouring property owners. Baron Bramwell said that 'those acts necessary for the common and ordinary use and occupation of land and houses' might be done,[37] without risk of legal liability. But an uncommon and unordinary use of land would not be included. There are clearly some parallels here with the use of the concept of non-natural use of land in strict liability *Rylands v Fletcher*. *Bamford* was decided in 1862, just three years prior to the decision of Baron Bramwell in 1865, which applied strict liability to a dangerous thing escaping from land.

[32] *Tenant v Goldwin* (1702) Ld. Raym. 1090, 1092–93; 21 ER 222, 224.
[33] *Tarry v Ashton* (1876) 1 QBD 314.
[34] ibid, 320.
[35] ibid, 320.
[36] *Bamford v Turnley* (1862) 3 B & S 67; 122 ER 27.
[37] ibid, 83; 33.

The courts confirmed that where an activity is authorised by statute, the loss that the activity causes to others in terms of property damage is not actionable in nuisance. This was the holding of cases such as *R v Pease*[38] and *Vaughan v Taff Vale Railway Co.*[39] This is the position unless the plaintiff can show that the defendant was guilty of negligence.[40] This line of cases again appears to confirm that nuisance is a tort of strict liability.

The court distinguished between, on the one hand, a material interference with the property rights of another, which would be actionable as a nuisance and, on the other, causing mere personal discomfort to the plaintiff.[41] In the latter case, the court would consider the specific circumstances, including the question of the reasonableness of the defendant's use of their property given the specific spatial surrounds. Lord Wensleydale stated that 'everything must be looked at from a reasonable point of view'.[42] He accepted that individual rights might need to be sacrificed to the 'means of developing the national wealth'.[43]

The strictness with which the common law viewed liability in nuisance is set out clearly in the judgment of Lindley LJ, for the Court of Appeal, in *Rapier v London Tramways Co*, where he stated that 'at common law, if I am sued for a nuisance, and the nuisance is proved, it is no defence on my part to say, and to prove, that I have taken all reasonable care to prevent it'.[44] A similar approach to liability for a highway nuisance is evident in the judgment of the Court of Appeal in *Ware v Garston Haulage Co Ltd*.[45]

In an action for private nuisance brought in *Midwood and Co v Mayor of Manchester*,[46] the Court of Appeal apparently took the position that the defendant would be liable for damage caused to the plaintiff's property by a gas explosion caused by the defendant's activity, quite apart from any question of negligence.

In an action for public nuisance, all three members of the Court of Appeal found that it was not necessary to bring such an action that the plaintiff demonstrate

[38] *R v Pease* (1832) 4 B & Ad. 30; 110 ER 366.

[39] *Vaughan v Taff Vale Railway Co* (1860) 5 H & N 678; 157 ER 1351.

[40] (1860) 5 H & N 678, 685 (Cockburn CJ), 686 (Williams J and Crompton J) and 688 (Willes Byles and Blackburn LLJ); 157 ER 1351, 1354–55.

[41] *St Helen's Smelting Company v Tipping* (1865) 11 HLC 642; 11 ER 1483.

[42] ibid, 653; 1487–88.

[43] ibid, 653; 1487.

[44] *Rapier v London Tramways Co* [1893] 2 Ch 588, 599–600 (Lindley LJ, with whom Bowen and Kay LLJ agreed). See similarly *Farrell v John Mowlem and Co Ltd* [1954] 1 Lloyd's Rep 437, 440: 'I think the law still is that any person who actually creates a nuisance is liable for it and for the consequences which flow from it whether he is negligent or not' (Lord Devlin).

[45] *Ware v Garston Haulage Co Ltd* [1944] 1 KB 30, 31–32: 'even if the judge was wrong … in thinking that he was entitled to decide this case on the ground of his finding of negligence by the (defendant) … the plaintiff is entitled to hold his judgment on the ground that the facts as proved show that there was a nuisance. There was a dangerous obstruction of the highway and consequently an absolute duty on the defendants to light it or otherwise efficiently guard it to prevent accidents. It is no answer for the defendants to say that the light on the trailer had gone out after they left the vehicles' (Scott LJ, with whom Mackinnon and Goddard LLJ agreed). In other words, it was not to the point that the defendant might have been able to show they had taken reasonable steps to avoid injury to others; they remained liable for causing the (highway) nuisance. Note the language is in terms of absolute liability, even stronger than strict liability.

[46] *Midwood and Co v Mayor of Manchester* [1905] 2 KB 597 (CA).

that the defendant was guilty of negligence.[47] Stephenson LJ added, though, that it would be a rare case where an action in nuisance lay, but not one in negligence.[48] Sachs LJ seemed to reach a similar position.[49]

Dicta comments in *Read v Lyons* appear to confirm the strictness of the liability in nuisance.[50]

Examples where Courts Apply Concepts of Reasonableness and Fault to Nuisance Cases

One example, *Hole v Barlow*,[51] involved the plaintiff's complaint that the defendant had burned bricks on their property, near the boundary with the property of the plaintiff, causing them loss. Willes J decided that although individuals had a right to quiet enjoyment of their property, this was not an absolute right. It was subject to the use by others of their land, to the extent it was 'conducted in a reasonable and proper manner, and in a reasonable and proper place'.[52] Willes J stated that private convenience had to yield to cases of 'public necessity'. This is evidence of notions of 'reasonableness' appearing in cases brought under the tort of nuisance.[53] As explained above, this decision was overturned in *Bamford v Turnley*, which favoured a stricter view of nuisance liability. However, divergence of views on this matter would not end there.

The judgment of Blackburn J in *Tarry v Ashton* is another example. That judge apparently required some fault to be shown on the part of the defendant before liability would arise. He stated (in obiter dicta) that:

> If there were a latent defect in the premises, or something done to them without the knowledge of the owner or occupier by a wrongdoer, such as digging out the coals

[47] *Dymond v Pearce* [1972] 1 QB 496 (Sachs Edmund Davies and Stephenson LLJ).

[48] ibid, 508.

[49] ibid, 503. With respect, Sachs LJ appeared to impermissibly mix issues of causation with issues of negligence. After noting that the accident was caused by the plaintiff's negligence, so the defendant's nuisance did not cause the plaintiff's injuries, Sachs LJ concluded that this finding of causation 'in the vast majority of cases, is an inevitable conclusion once negligence on the part of the [defendant] is negatived' (503). With respect, causation is not the entirety of a negligence action. A person may be deemed to have caused injury to another although they were not negligent. A finding that the defendant was non-negligent should not, if liability in private nuisance is indeed strict as Sachs LJ in the same judgment said it was (502), lead inexorably to the conclusion that the defendant did not cause the plaintiff's injuries. In the next sentence, he then raises the question of foreseeability – 'only rarely will that which was found not to be a foreseeable cause of an accident also be found to be in law the actual cause of it' (503). With respect, the issue of whether something caused something else is independent of, and should not be conflated with, whether it was foreseeable or not. If something caused something else, it did so. Whether or not it was foreseeable is irrelevant. They are independent questions.

[50] *Read v Lyons* [1947] AC 156, 183: 'if a man commits a legal nuisance it is no answer to his injured neighbour that he took the utmost care not to commit it. There the liability is strict' (Lord Simonds).

[51] *Hole v Barlow* (1858) 4 C.B (N.S) 334; 140 ER 1113.

[52] ibid, 345; 1118.

[53] FH Newark 'note(s) an endeavour to introduce the element of reasonableness in *Hole v Barlow*': 'The Boundaries of Nuisance' (1949) 65 *Law Quarterly Review* 480, 487.

> underneath and so leaving a house near the highway in a dangerous condition, I doubt … whether or not the occupier would be liable. But if he did know of the defect, and neglect[ed] to put the premises in order, he would be liable. He would be responsible to this extent, that as soon as he knew of the danger he would be bound to put the premises in repair or pull them down.[54]

Some may see an irony here. The author of the classic strict liability decision in *Rylands v Fletcher* is here applying concepts of fault to a factual scenario traditionally regarded as involving the application of strict-liability nuisance principles, yet Blackburn J is applying concepts of fault and neglect.

In his classic article on nuisance, Newark notes that the decision of Blackburn J in this case seems to place a nuisance claim very close to a negligence one, with its focus on fault, in contrast with the judgments of Lush and Quain JJ, which appear to take a strict liability line, in accord with principles applicable to private nuisance.[55]

As well as the application of negligence, fault-based principles to a tort traditionally considered to be of a strict liability nature, we also see examples of cases that appear to be prime examples of nuisance being decided according to the principles of negligence, with no mention of nuisance at all. A prime example here is *Vaughan v Menlove*.[56] There hay on the defendant's land caught fire, subsequently damaging the plaintiff's house situated nearby. These facts might be suggestive of a case in private nuisance. However, nuisance is not even mentioned in the case. In fact, the jury is asked whether the defendant is liable for negligence. The court does acknowledge the long-standing principle that a landowner must enjoy the property in a way that does not disturb neighbouring owners, but adds that 'the care taken by the prudent man has always been the rule laid down'.[57] It is possible that the case was apparently brought in negligence, rather than nuisance, because sometimes nuisance was seen as involving a continuing, interference with the property of another,[58] although *Hole v Barlow* and *Tarry v Ashton* did not seem to involve continuing nuisances, and the facts of *Rylands v Fletcher*, (at least) later

[54] *Tarry v Ashton* (1876) 1 QBD 314, 319.

[55] FH Newark, 'The Boundaries of Nuisance' (1949) 65 *Law Quarterly Review* 480, 486–87: 'Blackburn J … undoubtedly realised that there had been a long line of authority for deciding cases of this type on the footing of negligence, and accordingly did so. Lush and Quain JJ simply accepted the newer view that these cases were labelled "Nuisance" and involved strict liability. Today this type of case is frankly put on grounds of strict liability'.

[56] *Vaughan v Menlove* (1837) Bing. (NC) 469; 132 ER 490.

[57] ibid, 475; 493 (Tindal CJ, Park J concurring). Vaughan J (477, 494) agrees that the conduct of the prudent person had always been important, but other factors were also of relevance. The judgments refer to the old case of *Turberville v Stampe* (1697) 1 Ld. Raym. 264; 91 ER 1072, where a defendant's liability for a fire which escaped onto a neighbour's land was established. The case did not refer to the concept of a prudent person and is generally seen to be an example of strict liability. Writing of *Vaughan v Menlove*, Gearty describes the language used as 'that of a primitive tort of negligence': 'Private Nuisance in a Modern Law of Torts' (1989) 48(2) *Cambridge Law Journal* 214, 220.

[58] FH Newark, 'The Boundaries of Nuisance' (1949) 65 *Law Quarterly Review* 480, 488: 'though never decisively laid down in any case, there are plenty of dicta scattered through the reports to support the view that the true nuisance must have some permanence about it'.

to be seen in the United Kingdom as a sub-species of private nuisance,[59] did not involve a continuing nuisance, but rather a one-off event.[60] Subsequently, it was accepted that a private nuisance could include a one-off event.[61]

Another example of this is *Caminer and Another v Northern and London Investment Trust Ltd*.[62] There a tree on the defendant's premises fell onto a roadway, injuring the plaintiff. The plaintiff brought action in nuisance and negligence, but the nuisance claim was abandoned, and the appellate decisions in this case focus almost entirely on principles of negligence.

The question subsequently arose as to the liability of a defendant landowner in nuisance for damage or injury caused to another by virtue of something of which the defendant was unaware. This was the factual scenario in *Barker v Herbert*,[63] which essentially involved gaps in the railings that the defendant had constructed to divide his property from the roadway. Others had created the gaps. The plaintiff was injured when he climbed through one of the gaps. The defendant was not aware of the gaps. All members of the Court of Appeal found that the plaintiff was not liable in nuisance. The court found that a defendant was not liable in nuisance unless they either created the nuisance or continued it. There was no suggestion that the defendant created this nuisance; it was created by a third party.[64] A defendant could only be said to have continued a nuisance if they were aware of it (or perhaps should have been aware of it), and failed to act to correct it within a reasonable time. The court rejected a suggestion that the defendant's liability for such accidents was absolute in nature and rejected a suggestion that *Rylands v Fletcher* strict liability should be visited upon defendants in such circumstances.[65] This line of cases seems to suggest that questions of reasonableness impact on the extent to which a defendant will be deemed liable in nuisance, which is said to be a tort of strict liability.

[59] *Cambridge Water Co Ltd v Eastern Counties Leather Co* [1994] 2 AC 264.

[60] Conor Gearty says the *Rylands* decision can be partly explained by the fact that, traditionally, nuisance was seen as involving continuing interferences with the property rights of another, as opposed to one-off interferences: 'Private Nuisance in a Modern Law of Torts' (1989) 48(2) *Cambridge Law Journal* 214, 222; see to like effect John Murphy, *The Law of Nuisance* (Oxford University Press, 2010) 10. An example appears in the judgment of Lord Denning in *Attorney-General v PYA Quarries* [1957] 1 QB 169, 192: 'a private nuisance always involves some degree of repetition and continuance. An isolated act which is over and done with … may give rise to an action in negligence or an action under the rule in Rylands v Fletcher but not an action for nuisance'.

[61] *Midwood and Co v Mayor of Manchester* [1905] 2 KB 597 (CA); *British Celanese Limited v A H Hunt* [1969] 1 WLR 959, 969 (Lawton J).

[62] *Caminer and Another v Northern and London Investment Trust Ltd* [1951] AC 88 (HL); [1949] 2 KB 64 (CA).

[63] *Barker v Herbert* [1911] 2 KB 633.

[64] Of course, it had earlier been established that a defendant could be liable in public nuisance although it had been created by third parties: *Attorney-General v Tod Heatley* [1897] 1 Ch 560.

[65] This decision was followed in *Ilford Urban District Council v Beal and Judd* [1925] 1 KB 671, where the court found that a property owner was not liable for damage that their retaining wall caused to a sewer which crossed their property because they were not aware of the existence of the sewer and could not have become aware of it by the taking of reasonable measures.

The matter was further considered in *Noble v Harrison*.[66] There a branch of a tree on the defendant's property fell onto a nearby highway, injuring the plaintiffs, who were travelling in the area. The tree had a latent defect, which contributed to its falling. The defendant was not aware of it. It was not discoverable by the making of a reasonable inspection. They brought action against the defendant alleging negligence and (public) nuisance. The court explicitly took into account duty, neglect and reasonableness contexts in considering the action in nuisance.

For example, Rowlatt J stated that, in applying *Baker v Herbert* and other cases:

> The result … is that a person is liable for a nuisance constituted by the state of his property (1) if he causes it; (2) if by the neglect of some duty he allowed it to arise; and (3) if, when it has arisen without his own act or default, he omits to remedy it within a reasonable time after he did or ought to have become aware of it.[67]

Rowlatt J then proceeded to discuss the judgments in *Tarry v Ashton* discussed above. He noted the opinion of Lush and Quain JJ to the effect that the defendant was required to prevent the lamp falling 'at his peril'. He said this reasoning 'proceeds really upon the same lines as that in *Rylands v Fletcher*'.[68] Rowlatt J said the reasoning was not applicable here because a tree was not a non-natural use of land. He rejected the suggestion that an owner was to be an insurer of nature. Wright J took a similar position. He expressed a preference for the position of Blackburn J in *Tarry v Ashton*,[69] not Lush and Quain JJ,[70] to the effect that a landowner should not be held liable for latent defects and the injury or damage they cause. Clearly Wright J was concerned that a strict liability approach to such issues would cast the net of liability too widely:

> [I]f the overhanging branch was in itself a nuisance from the mere fact that it overhung the public highway it was a public nuisance … it is startling to contemplate how many such public nuisances add amenity and beauty to our roads … the overhanging branch was not per se a nuisance.[71]

A further example of the apparent intrusion of principles of negligence into the law of nuisance occurred in the facts considered by the House of Lords in *Sedleigh-Denfield v O'Callaghan*.[72] The case involved neighbouring property owners. The defendant's property contained a ditch, along which flowed water. The previous owners had permitted the local council to construct a pipe within the ditch. Once they had done so, they covered it with earth. There was a risk that

[66] *Noble v Harrison* [1926] 2 KB 332.

[67] ibid, 338.

[68] ibid, 338.

[69] ibid, 344.

[70] 'Lush and Quain JJ appear to have held that there was an absolute duty on the defendant to keep the lamp in a safe state of repair … I prefer the reasoning of Blackburn J (that a defendant would not be liable in nuisance for latent defects of which they were unaware) (ibid, 343–44).

[71] ibid, 341.

[72] *Sedleigh-Denfield v O'Callaghan* [1940] AC 880 (HL).

leaves and debris would enter the pipe and eventually clog it up. It was standard practice to construct a grille near the mouth of the pipe to prevent this occurring. The council did not do this. Evidence suggested that in the past the defendant's employees had cleared out the ditch but this had not occurred recently. During a heavy downpour the pipe became clogged with debris and the water entered the ditch instead, flowing onto the plaintiff's property and causing damage. The plaintiff sued the defendants in nuisance. The House of Lords found in their favour.

The court found that the defendants had adopted the nuisance. They were clearly aware of it and failed to take simple measures such as to move the position of the grille, which would have avoided the overflow. The language of the House of Lords is of most interest in explaining why the defendant was liable. Lord Atkin said that a nuisance had been created on the defendant's land. This was because 'an obstruction might reasonably be expected in the pipe from which obstruction flooding of the plaintiff's ground might reasonably be expected to result'.[73] Lord Atkin held that neither a deliberate act nor negligence were essential elements of a nuisance action, but 'a degree of personal responsibility' was required[74] – here it was knowledge of the nuisance, the ability to prevent it, and failure to do so.

Lord Wright cast his explanation of nuisance in terms of reasonable use – 'what is reasonable according to the ordinary usages of mankind living in … a particular society'.[75] He sought to explain the differences (and some similarity) with the torts of nuisance and negligence. He said that this case

> [h]as affinity also with a claim for negligence, because the trouble arose from the negligent fitting of the grid. But the gist of the present action is the unreasonable and unjustified interference by the defendant in the user of his land with the plaintiff's right to enjoy (their) property. Negligence, moreover, is not a necessary condition of a claim for nuisance. What is done may be done deliberately, and in good faith and in genuine belief that it is justified.[76]

He agreed with Court of Appeal judgments in relation to nuisance that a defendant could be held liable for nuisances created without their knowledge and consent, if they knew or should have known about them in time to correct them and so avoid damage to the plaintiff.[77] This is again couched in language similar to that used in

[73] ibid, 895–96.
[74] ibid, 897.
[75] ibid, 903.
[76] ibid, 904. With respect, this attempted differentiation is somewhat unconvincing. Whether or not something is done in the 'genuine belief it is justified' is irrelevant to questions of negligence, which clearly applies an objective, not a subjective, standard: *Vaughan v Menlove* (1837) 3 Bing. (NC) 468; 132 ER 490; *Donoghue v Stevenson* [1932] AC 562. Similarly, the fact that something was done in good faith is irrelevant to a negligence claim. The attempted differentiation based on something being done 'deliberately' requires further clarification – it is not entirely clear whether it means something done with the intention of harming the plaintiff, or in the sense of a voluntary act. If the former, typically negligence is associated with unintentional harm. However, it is not clear that nuisance requires intentional harm, so the attempted differentiation remains unhelpful, in my view.
[77] *Sedleigh-Denfield v O'Callaghan* [1940] AC 880 (HL), 910, including *Job Edwards Ltd v Birmingham Navigation Proprietors* [1924] 1 KB 341, 358 (Scrutton LJ, dissenting).

negligence, in particular 'should have known',[78] 'with ordinary and reasonable care should have become aware of it'.[79] He concluded that 'the liability for a nuisance is not, at least in modern law, a strict or absolute liability'.[80]

Lord Romer agreed that the defendant was liable, because he was aware of the nuisance and failed to 'take reasonable means' to end it.[81] Lord Porter adopted a similar sentiment:

> [T]he occupier of land is liable for a nuisance existing on his property to the extent that he can reasonably abate it, even though he neither created it nor received any benefit from it. It is enough is he permitted it to continue after he knew or ought to have known of its existence … the respondents ought … as reasonable persons to have recognized the probability, or at least the possibility, of a flood occurring.[82]

Gearty describes the case as 'negligence pure and simple, confused by an ill-fitting and woolly disguise of nuisance'.[83] Murphy describes this case, and a later one, as making the law 'so confused that is it impossible to assert with certainty whether these cases are better seen as falling within the scope of private nuisance or the law of negligence'.[84]

Apparent mixing of concepts of negligence into a nuisance claim also appears in the Australian High Court decision in *Torette House Proprietary Limited v Berkman*.[85] There Starke J, in the context of discussing the defendant's possible liability in nuisance, stated in rejecting it that there was not neglect of duty on the part of the defendant.[86] In the same context, Dixon J stated that it was not enough to make occupiers of a building liable for nuisances that pre-existed their occupation, simply because of the fact of occupation: 'some element of fault on their part is necessary'.[87]

Negligence principles also appear to have intruded into consideration of a case brought both in nuisance and negligence in *Slater v Worthington's Cash Stores Ltd*.[88] The facts involved a plaintiff being injured by accumulated ice and snow

[78] *Sedleigh-Denfield v O'Callaghan* [1940] AC 880 (HL), 904.

[79] ibid, 904–05.

[80] ibid, 904.

[81] ibid, 913; see similarly Viscount Maugham (894): 'an occupier continues a nuisance if with knowledge or presumed knowledge or its existence he fails to take any reasonable means to bring it to an end though with ample time to do so'.

[82] ibid, 919–20. Though this language is highly similar to that used in negligence cases Lord Porter also said that the defendants were being held liable in nuisance, and not negligence, though he also said it may be that the defendants had in fact been negligent (920).

[83] Conor Gearty, 'The Place of Private Nuisance in a Modern Law of Torts' (1989) 48(2) *Cambridge Law Journal* 214, 237.

[84] John Murphy, *The Law of Nuisance* (Oxford University Press, 2010) 17.

[85] *Torette House Proprietary Limited v Berkman* (1940) 62 CLR 637.

[86] ibid, 651.

[87] ibid, 659.

[88] *Slater v Worthington's Cash Stores Ltd* [1941] 1 KB 488 (CA). It is conceded that care must be taken with these cases where both negligence and nuisance are alleged, to ensure that when the courts apply concepts such as reasonable care, duty etc, they are in fact talking about the nuisance claim.

falling from the roof of the defendant's premises. The ice and snow had largely been deposited by a snow storm several days prior to the incident in question. While all members of the Court of Appeal found in favour of the plaintiff, the reasoning of the trial judge is of most interest. Oliver J stated:

> In this case it is obvious that the nuisance was not created by the defendants. It was created by the operation of nature, and if, during the course of this great blizzard and before there had been any reasonable opportunity of removing the snow, it had fallen and injured the plaintiff, I would have found for the defendants, but this was not the case. Four days elapsed between the creation of the nuisance and the accident … if this view is right, the question of liability on the ground of negligence becomes academic.[89]

Clearly Oliver J judged the defendant's liability in nuisance based on the reasonableness of their conduct. It was unreasonable of them to have left the ice and snow where it was, appreciating the danger. Had they not had an opportunity to clear the snow, however, he would not have found against them. This clearly suggests fault is being considered. And it is clear that this is being considered in relation to their liability in nuisance. The Court of Appeal curtly dismissed the appeal without delivering a full judgment, indicating their agreement with the decision and reasoning of Oliver J.

Another example appears in *Maitland v Raisbeck and R T and J Hewitt Ltd*.[90] There the plaintiff was injured on the highway when the vehicle in which the plaintiff was travelling struck the defendant's truck. It was a dark night, and the rear light on the defendant's truck had apparently gone out, meaning that the plaintiff could not see the defendant until it was too late. A lower court had found no negligence on the defendant's part in relation to the extinguishment of the truck light. The Court of Appeal rejected the plaintiff's case in public nuisance.

The Court rejected the suggestion that the mere fact that a truck was on the road without being lit at night-time, without more, created an actionable public nuisance. Lord Greene MR, with whom MacKinnon and Luxmoore LLJ agreed, stated:

> Every person who uses the highway must exercise due care, but he has a right to use the highway, and if something happens to him which, in fact, causes an obstruction to the highway, but is in no way referable to his fault, it is wrong to suppose that ipso facto and immediately a nuisance is created. A nuisance will obviously be created if he allows the obstruction to continue for an unreasonable time or in unreasonable circumstances but the mere fact that an obstruction has come into existence cannot turn it into a nuisance.[91]

Obviously, it is entirely unremarkable when they discuss reasonableness and duty of care in the context of the negligence claim, but of most interest for current purposes is their use of concepts traditionally associated with the tort of negligence in considering the tort of nuisance.

[89] ibid, 491–92.

[90] *Maitland v Raisbeck and R T and J Hewitt Ltd* [1944] 1 KB 689.

[91] ibid, 692.

Lord Greene MR said that he disagreed with a possible interpretation of the decision in *Ware v Garston Haulage Co Ltd* (discussed in the previous section) that it reflected a general principle of strict (or near absolute) liability for a public nuisance on the highway. Lord Greene MR noted that accidents frequently occurred on roadways, and if an accident occurred in circumstances where all parties involved had acted reasonably, then anyone suffering injury or damage as a result of the accident had to 'put up with it'.[92] This is a firm establishment of liability in nuisance in principles of fault.

Though the appellate decisions in *Caminer v Northern and London Investment Trust Ltd* focus almost entirely on the negligence part of the claim, the nuisance claim having been abandoned, Lord Porter noted in passing that the defendants 'appear to me to be free from blame whether the case is against them is framed in negligence or nuisance'.[93] Of course, this statement presupposes that blame is as relevant to the nuisance action as it is to the negligence action.

In *Bolton v Stone*, two members of the House of Lords noted the concession of the plaintiff that her claim in nuisance could not proceed in the absence of proof of negligence.[94] The defendant had clearly created the alleged nuisance in this case.

Finally in this section, the comments of Lord Parker CJ in *British Road Services Ltd v Slater* are of note.[95] They are appropriately noted here because they seem to sum up the effects of the numerous cases just discussed: 'I feel that the present tendency of the law is not only to move further and further away from absolute liability, but more and more to assimilate nuisance and negligence'.[96] He expressed agreement with the judgment of Lord Wright in *Sedleigh-Denfield*, that in this context there was no difference between principles applicable to private nuisance and public nuisance. He also agreed with Lord Wright's position that a person could not be held liable for a nuisance created without their knowledge or consent, unless they had knowledge or means of knowledge of the defect, and a reasonable time within which to correct it. He agreed with Lord Wright that the liability for nuisance was not a strict or absolute liability.[97]

[92] ibid, 693.

[93] *Caminer v Northern and London Investment Trust Ltd* [1951] AC 88, 99. And the judge at first instance, Lord Goddard CJ, stated it was 'immaterial whether the cause of action is laid in negligence or nuisance', suggesting that the question of whether the defendant's response to the risk was reasonable was relevant to both causes of action. He actually found the plaintiff entitled to recovery on either negligence or nuisance grounds because he found they should have done more to protect the public from the risk posed by the overhanging tree. Though his conclusion differed from that of Lord Porter, they agreed that the cases in negligence and nuisance both had to consider questions of the defendant's culpability for what occurred. The mere fact that it did occur was clearly not sufficient to attract liability, as it would if the obligation were an absolute one, or (unless a defence applied) if the obligation were a strict one.

[94] *Bolton v Stone* [1951] AC 850, 860 (Lord Porter) and 868 (Lord Reid).

[95] *British Road Services Ltd v Slater* [1964] 1 WLR 498.

[96] ibid, 504.

[97] ibid, 503–04.

At this point it seemed that negligence, or at least principles relevant to negligence cases, such as concepts of reasonableness and fault, were highly relevant in deciding nuisance cases. However, the position seemed to alter somewhat in some Privy Council decisions, a position which has been evident in more recent cases. It is to those developments to which I now turn.

Developments in UK Nuisance Law in the Last 50 Years

The relationship between the torts of nuisance and negligence was considered in some detail in the Privy Council decision in *Overseas Tankship (UK) Ltd v The Miller Steamship Co Pty Ltd (The Wagon Mound No 2)*.[98] The facts involved the appellants polluting a harbour with oil. This oil remained on the top of the water in the harbour. Sparks from the respondents' operations on their vessel, sitting in that harbour, caused the oil on the water to ignite. As a result, the respondent's vessel was seriously damaged. It brought legal action in nuisance and negligence against the appellant.

Two points of importance emerge from the judgment of the Privy Council. The first is that it agreed with the statement of Devlin J in *Farrell v John Mowlem and Co Ltd*,[99] where he said that a person who creates a nuisance is liable for it and the consequences which flow from it irrespective of negligence.[100] The Privy Council stated that negligence was not an essential element in nuisance.[101] It stated that a person who emitted noxious fumes or noise may incur liability for it although they had taken the utmost care in constructing and using the premises. It acknowledged that in many cases, the same facts would establish liability in both nuisance and negligence.[102] It made the interesting observation that 'although negligence may not be necessary, fault of some kind is almost always necessary and fault generally involves foreseeability'.[103]

With respect, it is not entirely clear what is meant by fault of some kind was 'almost always necessary' but negligence was not. On one view, the existence of fault means that the defendant was negligent. Later in the judgment this (obvious)

[98] *Overseas Tankship (UK) Ltd v The Miller Steamship Co Pty Ltd (The Wagon Mound No 2)* [1967] AC 617.

[99] *Farrell v John Mowlem and Co Ltd* [1954] 1 Lloyd's Rep. 437.

[100] *Overseas Tankship (UK) Ltd v The Miller Steamship Co Pty Ltd (The Wagon Mound No 2)* [1967] AC 617, 638 (Lord Reid, for the Court).

[101] ibid, 639.

[102] ibid, 639. The Privy Council took a similar position in *Goldman v Hargrave* [1966] AC 645, where Lord Wilberforce for the Council noted 'the tort of nuisance, uncertain in its boundary, may comprise a wide variety of situations, in some of which negligence plays no part, in others of which it is decisive' (657).

[103] ibid, 639.

connection is acknowledged.[104] Their Lordships did not elaborate on their statement. They could not have meant fault in the sense of mere causation, because earlier in the judgment it is acknowledged that the mere fact that fumes or noise was emitted by the defendant does not necessarily make them liable in nuisance. Thus, respectfully, the precise meaning of 'fault' in the absence of negligence is somewhat elusive.

The second important point to emerge involved the question whether recovery of damages in nuisance required proof that the kind of loss the plaintiff suffered was reasonably foreseeable by the defendant. It had been established in *Overseas Tankship (UK) Ltd v The Miller Steamship Co Pty Ltd (No 1)*[105] that reasonable foreseeability of this nature was essential to recovery in negligence. The Privy Council found that the same requirement should be applied to cases of nuisance.[106]

In the same year, the Privy Council considered an appeal from Australia in *Goldman v Hargrave*, involving the failure of a landowner to put out a fire on his land, which spread to the neighbouring property owned by the plaintiff. The plaintiff's land suffered damage. Action in both nuisance and negligence was brought. The matter was heard both by the High Court of Australia and, by appeal, the Privy Council. After discussing the UK nuisance cases including *Sedleigh-Denfield*, Taylor and Owen JJ in the High Court stated that an occupier with knowledge or presumed knowledge of a nuisance on their land created by another would be liable for damage caused to a third party by the nuisance if by the exercise of reasonable care the damage would have been avoided.[107] Here again, we see reference to negligence concepts in applying the law of nuisance. The court indicated it was of no consequence, in terms of the result in the case, whether the action was brought in nuisance or negligence.[108] The only other judge in the case, Windeyer J, stated the distinction between nuisance and negligence was not clear cut. He noted that negligence was of recent origin, such that many cases in the past that would have been brought on the basis of nuisance would now be brought in negligence.[109] Windeyer J decided the case on grounds of negligence.

[104] 'The present case is one of creating a danger in persons or property in navigable waters … and there it is admitted that fault is essential – in this case the negligent discharge of the oil'.

[105] *Overseas Tankship (UK) Ltd v The Miller Steamship Co Pty Ltd (No 1)* [1961] AC 388.

[106] ibid, 640. An early example of a similar finding occurred in *Chadwick v Trower* (1839) 6 Bing. (N.C) 1 where the Court of Exchequer Chamber held that a property owner could not be held liable for withdrawing support for a structure on a neighbouring property unless it was established he was aware of it. There is also evidence that reasonable foreseeability is a feature of liability in *Rylands v Fletcher*: see *Nichols v Marsland* (1876) 2 Ex. 1, 6 (Court of Appeal); see for discussion David Clarke, *Fault in a Strict Liability Tort: Foreseeability as an Element of the Rule in Rylands v Fletcher*, LLB Honours Thesis, Victoria University of Wellington, 1994. It has been the subject of strident criticism: Allan Beever, *The Law of Private Nuisance* (Hart Publishing, 2013) 111: 'if (liability) is to be strict, then what does it matter that I can foresee the injury?'

[107] *Hargrave v Goldman* (1963) 110 CLR 40, 51.

[108] ibid, 53.

[109] ibid, 61–62. Windeyer J stated that in nuisance liability was founded on a state of affairs created, adopted or continued by the defendant (other than in the reasonable and convenient use of their land) which substantially harmed the plaintiff, an owner or occupier of land, in their enjoyment of same (62).

On appeal to the Privy Council, although the submissions made referred to the nuisance ground, the Council announced that the case involved questions of liability for 'negligence and nothing else',[110] adding whether it fell within or overlapped the boundaries of nuisance was not necessary for the court to determine. And somewhat confusingly, in a case that was apparently to be determined on principles of negligence, where an objective approach would be taken to questions of reasonableness, Lord Wilberforce determined that, at least in some cases, 'the standard ought to be to require of the occupier what is reasonable to expect of him in his individual circumstances'.[111] This is confusing because, at least traditionally, one difference between negligence and nuisance is that the question of reasonableness is typically applied in an objective way in the former tort, and in a subjective way in the latter.

In a case involving the escape of fire lit by trespassers on the defendant's property onto that of the plaintiff's nearby, Lord Goff in the House of Lords, with whom Lord Keith agreed, concluded that in such a case, it was 'difficult to believe … there could be any material difference between liability in nuisance and liability in negligence'.[112]

Negligence principles were involved in determining nuisance claims in relation to the requirement, in the tort of private nuisance, that the interference with property rights be 'unlawful'. In determining whether or not the interference was unlawful, the court has had regard to the question of whether a duty of care existed, and/or was breached, on the facts. In other words, the outcome in the consideration of the tort of negligence is conclusive in determining the outcome in the consideration of the tort of nuisance. An example of this occurred in *Langbrook Properties Limited v Surrey County Council*.[113] There, after determining that the defendant did not owe a duty of care to the plaintiff neighbour in relation to water-based support of his property, Plowman J stated that the action in nuisance 'fare(d) no better', since the action in nuisance required an unlawful interference with the property rights of the plaintiff, and no such interference existed on the facts.[114]

More evidence of the relevance of negligence to a claim in nuisance appears in the decision in *Leakey v National Trust*.[115] There Megaw LJ in the Court of Appeal notes:

> The plaintiff's claim is expressed in the pleadings to be founded on nuisance. There is no express reference to negligence in the statement of claim. But there is an allegation of a breach of duty and the duty asserted is, in effect, a duty to take reasonable care to

[110] *Goldman v Hargrave* [1967] AC 645, 657 (Lord Wilberforce, for the Council).
[111] ibid, 663.
[112] *Smith v Littlewoods Organisation Limited* [1987] AC 241, 274 (Lord Goff), with whom Lord Keith agreed (249).
[113] *Langbrook Properties Limited v Surrey County Council* [1970] 1 WLR 161.
[114] ibid, 178 (Plowman J).
[115] *Leakey v National Trust* [1980] QB 485.

> prevent part of the defendant's land from falling on to the plaintiff's property. I should for myself regard that as being properly described as a claim in nuisance.[116]

The scope of the duty was described in terms of considering a range of factors, including the extent of the risk, the likelihood of damage, what kind of damage was reasonably foreseeable, the practical ability of the defendant to minimise or avoid the damage, and whether there was sufficient time for preventive action to be taken.[117]

Here, members of the Court of Appeal state that a case involving a question of whether the defendant had taken reasonable care to prevent their land from falling onto that of the plaintiff was a case of *nuisance*. Yet the factors that the court went on to describe as being relevant to an assessment of whether or not the relevant duty had been breached are virtually the same as those that would be relevant in assessing whether a duty of care was breached in the context of a negligence claim.[118] Further, the court considered whether the kind of loss the plaintiff suffered was reasonably foreseeable, in a similar way to a negligence action. It should be conceded that the nuisance inquiry differs to some extent from a typical negligence analysis in terms of its subjective approach to the particular defendant, as opposed to an orthodox reasonable person, objective test.[119] The facts in *Leakey v National Trust* involved an encroachment from the property of the defendant to that of the plaintiff. Again, Gearty has criticised this decision for blurring nuisance and negligence.[120]

[116] ibid, 514 (with whom Shaw and Cumming-Bruce LLJ agreed). See to like effect *Stockwell v Victoria* [2001] VSC where Gillard J, after considering cases such as *Leakey* and *Goldman*, noted that 'the modern law of nuisance in cases where the defendant does not create the nuisance is very similar to the modern law of negligence. Indeed, many cases of nuisance also involve liability in common law negligence' ([249]). As to the qualification in the first sentence, though it is similar to that used by Lord Goff for the House of Lords in *Cambridge Water*, it is contrary to the position of Megaw LJ for the Court of Appeal in *Leakey* that in the context of nuisance, there is no relevant distinction between cases of misfeasance and cases of nonfeasance.

[117] *Leakey v National Trust* [1980] QB 485, 524 (Megaw LJ), with whom the other justices agreed.

[118] 'The duty is the duty to do that which is reasonable in all the circumstances, and no more than that, if anything, is reasonable, to prevent or minimize the known risk of damage or injury to one's neighbour or their property … there will fall to be considered the extent of the risk; what, so far as [can reasonably] be foreseen, are the chances that anything untoward will happen or that any damage will be caused? What is to be foreseen as to the possible extent of the damage if the risk becomes a reality? Is it practicable to prevent, or to minimise, the happening of any damage? If it is practical, how simple or difficult are the measures which could be taken, how much and how lengthy work do they involve, and what is the probable cost of such works? Was there sufficient time for preventative action to have been taken, by persons acting reasonably in relation to the known risk, between the time when it became known to, or should have been realised by, the defendant, and the time when the damage occurred? Factors such as these … fall to be weighed in deciding whether the defendant's duty of care requires, or required them, to do anything, and if so what' (524) (Megaw LJ, with whom Shaw and Cumming-Bruce LLJ agreed).

[119] ibid, 526 (Megaw LJ), for the Court of Appeal. However, it should be noted that in other cases involving nuisance, an objective approach has been taken to the question of reasonable user: *Home Brewery Limited v William Davis and Company (Leicester) Ltd* [1987] QB 339, 351 (Piers Ashworth QC).

[120] Conor Gearty, 'The Place of Private Nuisance in a Modern Law of Torts' (1989) 48(2) *Cambridge Law Journal* 214, 240–41, claiming the decision in *Leakey* 'robs the word [nuisance] of any meaning

It was subsequently applied to a case alleging the defendants had not done enough to support the plaintiff's neighbouring property, resulting in a land slip, in *Holbeck Hall Hotel v Scarborough Borough Council*.[121] Again in that case, a cause of action ostensibly based on nuisance was determined in accordance with principles of negligence. The court applied a standard of what was 'fair, just and reasonable' in determining one neighbour's responsibility (in nuisance) to that of another. Obviously, this is the same test that UK law has applied to questions involving a duty of care in negligence.[122] One difference was that, although in a general negligence case it is sufficient that the defendant reasonably foresee the kind of injury suffered by the plaintiff, not its magnitude, in *Holbeck Hall* there are suggestions that in nuisance, liability might be limited to the magnitude of the loss that was reasonably foreseeable.[123]

The *Leakey* precedent was also applied to a case involving interference with the enjoyment of land, without any physical damage.[124] The approach taken in *Leakey v National Trust* was subsequently approved by the House of Lords.[125] Members of the House expressed the duty as being one of taking reasonable steps to prevent their land becoming a source of injury to one's neighbour.[126] The case was brought in nuisance.

In *Delaware Mansions Ltd v Westminster*,[127] Lord Cooke, with whom all other Law Lords agreed,[128] decided a case in nuisance brought in relation to tree roots which had caused property damage to the plaintiff. Lord Cooke referred to the *Wagon Mound* and *Goldman v Hargrave* decisions, stating that the decisions are based on what a reasonable person in the position of the defendant would have done. Lord Cooke stated that 'the label of nuisance or negligence is treated as of no real significance',[129] the question involving 'the fair and just content and incidents of a neighbour's duty rather than affixing a label and inferring the extent of the duty from it'.[130]

until the duty arises – at which point it is turned into a branch of the law of negligence. Like Viscount Maugham and Lord Wright before him, Megaw LJ is talking the language of negligence in what is supposed to be an action in nuisance. The result once more is conceptual confusion'.

[121] *Holbeck Hall Hotel v Scarborough Borough Council* [2000] QB 836 (CA). Another example of this category of case being decided on the basis of negligence principles, with no mention of nuisance whatsoever, is *Ward v Coope* [2015] 1 WLR 4081.

[122] *Caparo Industries Plc v Dickman* [1990] 2 AC 605.

[123] *Holbeck Hall Hotel v Scarborough Borough Council* [2000] QB 836 (CA), 861 (Stuart-Smith LJ, with whom Schiemann and Tuckey LLJ agreed).

[124] *Wandsworth London Borough Council v Railtrack Plc* [2000] QB 756.

[125] *Marcic v Thames Water Facilities Ltd* [2004] 2 AC 42, 57 (Lord Nicholls, with whom Lords Steyn (61), Hope (67) and Scott (71) agreed).

[126] ibid, 64–65 (Lord Hoffmann), with whom Lords Steyn (61) and Scott (71) agreed.

[127] *Delaware Mansions Ltd v Westminster* [2002] 1 AC 321.

[128] ibid, Lords Steyn (324), Browne-Wilkinson (324), Clyde (335) and Hutton (335).

[129] ibid, 333.

[130] ibid, 333. This passage was cited by Jackson LJ (with whom Lord Dyson and Sir Stanley Burton agreed) in *Vernon Knight Associates v Cornwall Council* [2013] EWCA Civ 950 for the proposition that 'in this area of law the defendant's liability in nuisance is effectively the same as his liability in negligence' [48]. It is not precisely clear what 'this area of law' is taken to mean. The precise circumstance in *Vernon Knight Associates* was escape of water from land controlled by the defendant onto that of the

It has been noted by others that cases such as *Sedleigh-Denfield*, *Goldman* and *National Trust v Leakey* seem to involve the application of negligence concepts in the context of an ostensible claim in nuisance:

> In a number of instances, the courts have certainly, whilst calling the action private nuisance, emphasised the importance of the conduct of the defendant, and analysed the issues in the language of negligence, particularly breach of duty and fault … [*Sedleigh*, *Goldman* and *Leakey*] … are the classic examples of cases that suggest a shift to a negligence-type analysis … the argument that negligence-type fault is required in certain cases addressed under private nuisance has apparently been accepted by the courts. Even if the courts describe the question in terms of private nuisance, or say that it does not matter which tort is used, the claim is essentially fault-based, and rests on negligence.[131]

In *Longhurst v Metropolitan Water Board*, Lord Porter, with whom Lords Normand and Morton agreed, stated that 'liability for nuisance without negligence or deliberate act is not readily established apart, of course, from cases of the *Rylands v Fletcher* type'.[132]

The matter was considered again by the House of Lords in *Cambridge Water Co v Eastern Counties Leather Plc*.[133] The case has already been discussed at length above in terms of reinterpreting the *Rylands v Fletcher* action as an extension of the tort of private nuisance to cases of escape of dangerous substances from land.[134] The importance of the case for present purposes, and this may not be completely independent of the point just made, are the court's comments about the strictness of the liability in nuisance. Lord Goff for the House noted:

> Although liability in nuisance has generally been regarded as strict, at least in the case of a defendant who has been responsible for the creation of a nuisance, even so that liability has been kept under control by the principle of reasonable user – the principle of give and take as being neighbouring occupiers of land, under which 'those acts necessary for the common and ordinary use and occupation of land and houses may be done, if conveniently done, without subjecting those who do them to an action' … the effect is that if the user is reasonable, the defendant will not be liable for consequent harm to his neighbour's enjoyment of his land, but if the user is not reasonable, the defendant will be liable, even though he may have exercised reasonable care and skill to avoid it.[135]

plaintiff, due to the failure to keep drainways clear. Jackson LJ summarised the relevant law to include that 'a landowner owes a measured duty in both negligence and nuisance to take reasonable steps to prevent natural occurrences on his land from causing damage to neighbouring properties … in determining the content of the measured duty the court must consider what is fair, just and reasonable as between the two neighbouring landowners. It must have regard to all the circumstances, including the extent of the foreseeable risk, the available preventive measures, the costs of such measures and the resources of both parties' [49].

[131] Maria Lee, 'What Is Private Nuisance?' (2003) 119 *Law Quarterly Review* 298, 303.

[132] *Longhurst v Metropolitan Water Board* [1948] 2 All ER 834, 839.

[133] *Cambridge Water Co v Eastern Counties Leather Plc* [1994] 2 AC 264.

[134] ibid, 306 (Lord Goff, for the Court).

[135] ibid, 299. See to like effect Lord Hope in *Hunter v Canary Wharf* [1997] AC 655, 724: 'the tort of nuisance is a tort of strict liability in the sense that it is no defence to say that the defendant took all reasonable care to prevent it' (Lord Hope). Subsequently it was held that the test of reasonable user

Lord Goff pointed out the 'striking similarity' between this principle of reasonable user in the law of nuisance, and that of 'non-natural' use in *Rylands v Fletcher*. Acknowledging there may be differences between them, he nevertheless noted their similarity in function in terms of control mechanism.

By way of respectful response, it is not entirely correct to state that liability in nuisance has generally been regarded as strict. Cases such as *Hole v Barlow* focus on the reasonableness of the defendant's behaviour. Although it is true that case was overruled in *Bamford v Turnley*, Blackburn J in *Tarry v Ashton* eschewed a strict liability approach to nuisance cases. His views would find favour in later decisions, including *Noble v Harrison*. It is not correct, with respect, to claim or suggest that the strictness of liability in nuisance applies 'at least' in cases where the defendant had created a nuisance. Though this suggestion also appears elsewhere,[136] *Tarry* was a case of alleged creation of a nuisance. The decision of Lord Greene in *Maitland v Raisbeck* clearly took into account the reasonableness of the defendant's behaviour in a case alleging that they created the nuisance. Parker CJ in *British Road Services*, a nuisance case, said that the law was moving away from strict liability. The case of *Leakey v National Trust*, where the claim in nuisance was held by the Court of Appeal to be based on whether the defendant had taken reasonable steps to prevent land subsidence, was one involving an alleged creation of a nuisance. In that case, Megaw LJ in the Court of Appeal, in a judgment with which the other judges concurred, specifically held in the context of a nuisance claim that no distinction should be drawn between cases of non-feasance and cases of misfeasance.[137] It is not entirely correct, with respect, to claim that in cases of defendants alleged to have created a nuisance, a strict liability approach had 'generally' been taken. Nor is it clear, in terms of principle, why liability for creation of a nuisance should be strict, but liability for alleged continuation of a nuisance should not be. Other courts in the past have not made this distinction.

While the concept of 'reasonable user' continues to be applied in nuisance cases, this has been the subject of trenchant academic criticism on the basis it

is to be applied objectively: *Lawrence v Fen Tigers Ltd* [2014] AC 822, 831 (Lord Neuberger) (with whom Lords Sumption, Mance and Clarke agreed), and 868 (Lord Carnwath); or what (objectively) a reasonable person would find it reasonable to have to put up with: *Barr v Biffa Waste Services Ltd* [2013] QB 455, 478 (Carnwath LJ, quoting Tony Weir's *An Introduction to Tort Law* (2nd edn, Oxford University Press, 2006)), not what the plaintiff or defendant thinks to be unreasonable or reasonable, respectively. Lord Carnwath noted the concept of reasonable user was 'not without its problems' and noted strong criticism of it by academics such as Allan Beever, who concluded it could not explain anything: *The Law of Private Nuisance* (Hart Publishing, 2013) 9.

[136] Allan Beever, *The Tort of Private Nuisance* (Hart Publishing, 2013) 69 refers to an 'intermediate view' that 'the tort of nuisance has at least two parts, one strict and one fault-based: the strict form applying when the defendant created the event or activity complained of and the fault-based pertaining when the event or activity was created by another'. Beever calls this the 'intermediate' view of liability for private nuisance. He acknowledges two other views – the traditional view, that a defendant was not liable at all for nuisances that came to them, provided they warned others of the risk upon becoming aware of it, and a modern view, that the law of nuisance was fault based.

[137] *Leakey v National Trust* [1980] QB 485, 514 (CA).

'cannot explain anything'.[138] In *Southwark London Borough Council v Mills*,[139] Lord Miller stated:

> The use of the word reasonable in this context is apt to be misunderstood. It is no answer to an action for nuisance to say that the defendant is only making reasonable use of his land … what is reasonable from the point of view of one party may be completely unreasonable from the point of view of the other. It is not enough for a landowner to act reasonably in his own interest. He must also be considerate of the interests of his neighbour. The governing principle is good neighbourliness, and this involves reciprocity. A landowner must show the same consideration for his neighbour as he would expect his neighbour to show for him.[140]

The similarities between this description of reasonable user in the context of the tort of nuisance, and description of the 'neighbour' principle in the tort of negligence,[141] and obvious and striking.[142] Leading tort textbook writers have suggested that 'total assimilation of nuisance into negligence' may occur.[143]

It is sometimes stated that 'reasonableness' in the context of nuisance does not mean the same as reasonableness in the context of negligence.[144] After citing this, Beever asks what it does in fact mean, insisting 'we are not told. This is no mere oversight. It is the result of the fact that the law operates in accordance with no specific understanding of reasonableness whatsoever'.[145] However there does seem to be some difference in how reasonableness is applied in nuisance, apparently at least at times taking a subjective view of the reasonableness of the defendant's response (if any) to becoming aware of a nuisance, as opposed to the objective view taken in negligence. At other times, reasonable user in nuisance seems to approximate an objective view. One example is in relation to the sensitivity of the claimant. If a defendant uses their property in a way that would not materially affect most people's use of their land, but does impact the particular plaintiff

[138] Allan Beever, *The Law of Private Nuisance* (Hart Publishing, 2013) 9.

[139] *Southwark London Borough Council v Mills* [2001] 1 AC 1; cited with evident approval by Carnwath LJ in *Barr v Biffa Waste Services Ltd* [2013] QB 455, 477 in the course of a criticism of the use of the 'reasonable user' concept (476–78), a criticism which Lord Carnwath continued in *Laurence v Fen Tigers Ltd* [2014] AC 822, 868.

[140] *Southwark London Borough Council v Mills* [2001] 1 AC 1, 20.

[141] *Donoghue v Stevenson* [1932] AC 562, 580: 'the rule that you are to love your neighbour becomes in law, you must not injure your neighbour; and the lawyer's question, Who is my neighbour? receives a restricted reply … the answer seems to be – persons who are so closely and directly affected by my act that I ought reasonably to have them in contemplation as being so affected when I am directing my mind to the acts or omissions which are called into question' (Lord Atkin).

[142] Sir Terence Etherton MR (for the Court of Appeal) in discussing the case law on private nuisance noted that 'the broad unifying principle in this area of law is reasonableness between neighbours (real or figurative)': *Williams v Network Rail Infrastructure Ltd* [2019] QB 601, 615. It was also observed there the pure economic loss is traditionally not actionable under the tort of nuisance, though the claim might be reconceptualised in another way (for example, in that case, loss of amenity) in a way that might effectively circumvent that limitation.

[143] S Deakin, A Johnston and B Markesinis, *Markesinis and Deakin's Tort Law* (6th edn, Oxford University Press, 2008) 528. They add that 'strict liability … is undoubtedly in retreat in this area'.

[144] WVH Rogers, *Winfield and Jolowicz on Torts* (18th edn, Sweet & Maxwell, 2010) 714.

[145] Allan Beever, *The Tort of Private Nuisance* (Hart Publishing, 2013) 11.

because of their unusual sensitivities, the plaintiff will likely not succeed in an action for nuisance.[146]

Further, although Lord Goff stated in *Cambridge Water* that a difference between them was that if the user was unreasonable in the context of a nuisance claim, it would make no difference whether the defendant took reasonable care and skill to avoid it. By way of respectful response, it might be said that the fact that the defendant took reasonable care and skill in the use of their property to avoid damage to the property of another might be evidence that the use of the defendant's property was, in fact, reasonable. Thus, the same evidence could be utilised to defeat an action in nuisance or negligence or, if there were evidence of a lack of such reasonable care and skill, to support liability in both.

Some Australian Authorities

It might be useful at this stage to consider some Australian authorities, particularly in the area of public nuisance. It will be evident that there has been some substantial mixing and overlap between situations of public nuisance and the tort of negligence, at the risk of incoherence, before the High Court of Australia took decisive action on the matter in 2001. Some of the problems in the UK case law have been 'imported' into Australia.

Three early Australian cases will first be discussed. Two observations may be made about them. First, there is evident mixing between principles of (public) nuisance and negligence. And secondly, there is a clear preference among the judges to decide these kinds of cases on the basis of negligence, as opposed to nuisance. And a third observation must be made prior to discussing any of the cases – it is that, again, care must be used with language. Sometimes, judges use the word 'nuisance', but in context it is clear they are not talking about that concept in a legal sense, but in a generic, lay sense. The same observation can also be made sometimes with the use of the word 'negligent' or similar. References to them must be read with care to determine precisely what it is that the courts mean through use of such words.

It is appropriate to commence discussion with *Bathurst v McPherson*, an Australian decision that was appealed to the Privy Council.[147] This case suggests a mixing of nuisance and negligence in the following passage from the judgment of Sir Barnes Peacock for the Council:

> The appellants, by reason of the construction of the drain and their neglect to repair it, whereby the dangerous hole was formed, which was left open and unfenced, caused a nuisance in the highway, for which they are liable to an indictment.[148]

[146] *Rogers v Elliott* 15 NE 768 (1888) (Massachusetts Supreme Court). Allan Beever, *The Tort of Private Nuisance* (Hart Publishing, 2013) 35, notes that 'this aspect of the law of nuisance is the equivalent of the objective approach to the standard of care in the law of negligence'.

[147] *Bathurst v McPherson* (1879) 4 App Cas 256.

[148] ibid 267.

Here is an example of a court taking into account negligence in the commission of a nuisance, or more precisely, using the fact of negligence to buttress a conclusion that an actionable nuisance had been committed. We must be wary of the possibility noted just above of the use of terms in a generic, rather than a legal sense. It occurred to me that the term 'nuisance' in the just-cited passage may be an instance of this. However, the reference to 'indictment' reassures me that the judgment is based on legal nuisance, with public nuisance obviously having the criminal aspect justifying use of the word indictment that would not be applicable to a case decided purely on negligence grounds.[149]

The first consideration of this matter occurred early in the High Court's history in *Miller v McKeon*.[150] The question concerned the liability of a government authority for work it had done on a rural highway. In the course of cutting land to permit a road and bridge through a particular area, it had left some steep embankments at the side of the road. These were not fenced and no warning had been given as to them. The plaintiff was injured when he got out of his car in the area late at night and fell down the embankment. The plaintiff brought an action in both negligence and nuisance.

Mixing of the principles of negligence and nuisance in this context is clearest in the judgment of O'Connor J. He stated that

> [t]he plaintiff rests his case upon two grounds, nuisance and negligence. In my view they come to the same thing. The mere construction of a work by the government upon a public road is not in itself a nuisance, if it is for the more convenient exercise by the public of their right of passage over the road, and if the work is carried out without negligence. If there is any negligence the work is a nuisance, if there is no negligence there is no nuisance.[151]

Griffith CJ, with whom Barton J agreed, simply decided the case on the basis of negligence principles, without considering the nuisance ground. A similar thing occurred in *Woollahra Council v Moody*,[152] where the action was brought in nuisance and negligence for allegedly faulty drain construction, leading to the plaintiff being injured. The judgments merely discuss negligence. It is perhaps idle to speculate as to why the judges (apart from O'Connor J in *Miller*) do not discuss the nuisance claim, basing their judgments on negligence. It is possible that it is the strict liability aspect of the nuisance claim that they find unappealing, preferring to focus their judgments on the question of the defendant's culpability for the plaintiff's loss, as opposed to the mere issue of causation.

The next important case to consider is *Buckle v Bayswater Road Board*.[153] The plaintiff was injured as they walked along a roadway. The defendant had done

[149] It was subsequently confirmed in a later Privy Council decision that the decision in *Bathurst* was based on nuisance: *Municipal Council of Sydney v Mary Jane Bourke* [1895] AC 433, 441 (Lord Chancellor, for the Council).

[150] *Miller v McKeon* (1905) 3 CLR 50.

[151] ibid, 63.

[152] *Woollahra Council v Moody* (1913) 16 CLR 353.

[153] *Buckle v Bayswater Road Board* (1936) 57 CLR 259.

some work in the area, including the construction of a drain. Originally the drain had been an open one, but the defendant had covered it over after laying the drain pipe. The pipe apparently broke, leading to some subsidence in the boggy ground, such that there was a hole in the ground. This was covered over with grass. The plaintiff was injured when he walked into the hole. He brought an action against the defendant in both nuisance and negligence.

Again, there is (with respect) evidence of a mixing of the torts. Of the three judges in the case, Latham CJ stated that 'there can be no doubt in this case that the hole in the drain was a nuisance in the highway and that, if there was a duty to repair, there was a negligent failure to perform that duty'.[154] Dixon J stated:

> A road authority [doing work on the roadway] … must take due care for the safety of those using the highway and is not protected if it creates dangers which reasonable care and skill could avoid. Because the road is under its control, it necessarily has an opportunity denied to others for causing obstructions and dangers in highways. But when it does so, the road authority is liable, not, I think, under any special measure of duty which belongs to it, but upon ordinary principles. These principles include the rule that to render the highway unsafe is to commit a nuisance.[155]

One view of these cases is that they are simply demonstrations of the unremarkable fact that the torts of nuisance and negligence can exist on the one set of circumstances. But it is submitted they demonstrate more than this. They are examples where courts are taking into account whether the defendant has acted with 'due care' (classically a reference to principles of negligence) in determining whether or not the defendant has committed the tort of nuisance (where, traditionally, concepts of due care would be irrelevant, given it is traditionally a tort of strict liability). The judges clearly prefer to judge the defendant's actions by notions of reasonableness and reasonable care, as opposed to principles of strict liability.[156]

Finally, a majority of the High Court in *Brodie v Singleton Shire Council*[157] subsumed the tort of public nuisance into the tort of negligence, at least with respect to 'the highway cases'.[158] It expressly did so 'by parity with the reasoning in *Burnie Port Authority v General Jones Pty Ltd*'.[159] It will be recalled that this was the case where the High Court subsumed the (strict liability) doctrine of *Rylands v Fletcher* into the fault-based tort of negligence. The joint reasons also noted of the previous High Court decision in *Buckle* that it had been decided 'at a time

[154] ibid, 273.
[155] ibid, 283.
[156] 'To speak of the resulting state of the road as a nuisance in the highway may be correct enough. There is, of course, always a risk in applying the word to the physical thing instead of to the act or omission constituting the wrong of nuisance. But apart from that, the question is not whether a nuisance has been caused … when the highway authority acts in that capacity the question is whether, by the negligent exercise of the statutory powers … it has been the active agency in causing the nuisance' (ibid, 292).
[157] *Brodie v Singleton Shire Council* (2001) 206 CLR 512.
[158] ibid, 570 (Gaudron McHugh and Gummow JJ; Kirby J concurring (588).
[159] ibid, 570.

when the tort of negligence had not been extricated from that of nuisance'.[160] The *Buckle* decision was rendered in 1936. With respect, it is not entirely clear when, according to these judges, the tort of negligence was in fact 'extricated' from that of nuisance. Obviously, they could not have been referring to recognition of the generalised duty of care in 1932's *Donoghue v Stevenson*.

Academic Views

FH Newark

FH Newark's views on the tort of nuisance have special significance. It was his observation in his seminal 1949 article 'The Boundaries of Nuisance'[161] which heavily influenced the House of Lords decision in *Cambridge Water* to reinterpret the *Rylands v Fletcher* case as one of private nuisance, rather than a standalone principle,[162] more than a century after the original decision.

Of most significance here are Newark's observations on the boundaries between nuisance and negligence, and their blurring. He lays much of the blame (no pun intended) on dicta comments from Fitzherbert J in an early case,[163] which suggested that if a plaintiff were injured while riding their horse along a public thoroughfare because the defendant had dug a trench across it, an action for public nuisance would lie for the plaintiff against the defendant because the plaintiff had suffered special damage. This was the first recognition that damages for personal injuries might be available for a claim in public nuisance. It was obiter dicta in a dissenting judgment, with the actual decision primarily focused on denying that plaintiffs could bring a civil action for public nuisance. Newark says these obiter comments were picked up and reflected in the 1617 decision in *Fowler v Sanders*,[164] where personal injuries damages were successfully claimed for a public nuisance. He said subsequently many cases emerged involving plaintiffs bringing legal action because they had suffered personal injury due to obstructions on the highway (late eighteenth and early nineteenth centuries). He said that almost all of these cases were decided on the basis of negligence and fault principles.

However, he says a change began to emerge in the 1840s. He says this was caused by one of two reasons, or both of them, in part.[165] First, *Chitty's Pleadings*

[160] ibid, 568.
[161] FH Newark, 'The Boundaries of Nuisance' (1949) 65 *Law Quarterly Review* 480.
[162] *Cambridge Water Co v Eastern Counties Plc* [1994] 2 AC 264, 297–99 (Lord Goff, for the Court).
[163] *Anon* (1536) YB Mich. 27 Hen. 8, fol. 27, pl. 10.
[164] *Fowler v Sanders* (1617) Cro. Jac. 446.
[165] FH Newark, 'The Boundaries of Nuisance' (1949) 65 *Law Quarterly Review* 480, 485; *cf* discussion of the different onus of proof in the actions. Denning LJ in *Southport Corporation v Esso Petroleum Co Ltd* [1954] 2 QB 182, 197 explained that in an action for public nuisance, once the plaintiff shows the existence of a nuisance caused by the defendant, the onus of proof switches to the defendant to justify

categorised these types of injuries cases in terms of nuisance rather than negligence. Secondly, Newark says that by framing the action in nuisance, not negligence, plaintiffs could thereby circumvent defendant arguments that the nuisance was created by independent contractors, so the defendant could not be held responsible in negligence. He gives *Bush v Steinman* as an example of this type of situation.[166] There the owner of a property was held liable for a highway nuisance, though the actual nuisance was caused by an act of a servant of D. D had been sub-contracted by C to provide materials. C had been sub-contracted by B to do the work. The defendant had contracted B to do the work. The court found the property owner liable in nuisance.

Newark says that Fitzherbert's example in 1536 was really a case of negligence 'before its time'.[167] Had the case been determined in the nineteenth century, it certainly would have been dealt with under such principles; however, that was not available to the judges in the sixteenth century. Newark says that, in particular, the courts seemed to treat accidents on public thoroughfares caused by cellar flaps differently from those caused by vehicles. They tended to decide the 'cellar flap' cases as nuisance cases, and motor vehicle cases as negligence cases.[168] The distinction was not defensible and led to 'irreconcilable decisions' such as *Ware v Garston Haulage Co* and *Maitland v Raisbek* (both discussed above). It explained the diverse judgments in *Tarry v Ashton*, with two judges applying strict liability principles to a highway accident involving personal injury, and one judge applying negligence principles.

Newark said that the different rules led to highly anomalous results. He gives one example – if a plaintiff were injured by a defective grating on a highway just outside the boundary of the defendant's property, liability was dealt with according to the strict liability principles of nuisance; however, if it occurred just inside the boundary of the defendant's property, it would be governed by occupiers' liability and negligence principles.[169] Lord Goddard CJ in deciding *Howard v Walker* acknowledged that it would be difficult for a lay person to understand why recovery would be permitted for public nuisance if there were a slip on the highway, but not for the same slip occurring just inside the defendant's premises (because, in the one case, strict liability applied, and the other, fault-based principles applied).[170] There was clear dissatisfaction with this state of affairs evident also in the judgment of the Court of Appeal in *Jacobs v LLC*.[171]

or excuse it. In contrast, the onus of proof remains on the plaintiff. In *Brodie v Singleton Shire Council* (2001) 206 CLR 512, 567 Gaudron McHugh and Gummow JJ suggest this may have been the reason for the change of which Newark speaks.

[166] *Bush v Steinman* (1799) 1 Bos. & Pul. 404; 126 ER 978; see similarly *Gray v Pullen* (1864) 5 B & S. 970; 122 ER 1091.

[167] FH Newark, 'The Boundaries of Nuisance' (1949) 65 *Law Quarterly Review* 480, 485.

[168] ibid, 486.

[169] An example of the former situation was *Howard v Walker and Others* [1947] KB 860. An example of the latter situation was *Jacobs v LCC* [1949] 1 KB 685.

[170] *Howard v Walker and Others* [1947] KB 860, 866–67.

[171] *Jacobs v LCC* [1949] 1 KB 685, 699 (Tucker LJ) and 703 (Singleton LJ).

Further, because cases that had been decided according to negligence principles were now being considered nuisances and subject to strict liability, Newark says that negligence principles began to 'infect' nuisance cases, and principles of negligence were applied to cases that were ostensibly brought on the basis of nuisance. He cites *Hole v Barlow*, discussed above, as an example of this phenomenon. He blames this blurring of the torts and the 'fog' around the boundaries of nuisance for causing the controversial decision in *Rylands*, explaining why it was not decided on the simple basis of nuisance – because, by this time, negligence principles had infected the tort of nuisance, while it was common ground that the defendant in *Rylands* had been guilty of no negligence.

Newark suggested various solutions to this problem. One of them was to effectively subsume the law of public nuisance into the tort of negligence,[172] an idea that was duly implemented by the High Court of Australia in 2001.[173]

JR Spencer

JR Spencer's work relevantly focused on the tort of public nuisance.[174] In relation to it he favoured collapsing it into the tort of negligence, given his findings that almost all cases of public nuisance were highway cases in which the courts would find the same result if negligence principles were applied, subject to two exceptions, one of which he disagreed with, and the other of which remains but is of limited scope in the current context.[175] Given the same result in the cases, apart from these two exceptions, Spencer concluded:

> [T]he case law seems to make liability in public nuisance virtually strict. But … why should this be so? Personal injury claims normally involve proof of fault in the defendant. What is so special about this type of case to justify a different result? We are angry with such a defendant, and instinctively feel that he should pay, but surely this is because we feel that people with roadside property are blameworthy if they let it fall into disrepair. If that is the case, we could and should be holding them liable for negligence.[176]

[172] 'A person who maintains any thing on, under, above or adjacent to a highway owes a duty to persons lawfully using the highway to prevent damage to their person and chattels. This duty is not higher than a duty to use reasonable care, and the appropriate remedy for a break of such a duty is an action for negligence. Accordingly, those cases of this type where the plaintiffs have recovered for damage to person or chattels on the ground of nuisance … must be regarded as wrongly decided' (FH Newark, 'The Boundaries of Nuisance' (1949) 65 *Law Quarterly Review* 480, 490).

[173] *Brodie and Another v Singleton Shire Council; Ghantous v Hawkesbury City Council* (2001) 206 CLR 512, 570 (Gaudron McHugh and Gummow JJ), 604 (Kirby J).

[174] JR Spencer, 'Public Nuisance – A Critical Examination' (1989) 48 *Cambridge Law Journal* 55.

[175] The first exception related to plaintiffs suffering damage from the collapse of the defendant's buildings into the street. Spencer said that negligence, not strict liability principles, should govern such a situation. The second exception identified was recovery for purely economic loss. There would be few nuisance cases involving purely economic loss.

[176] JR Spencer, 'Public Nuisance – A Critical Examination' (1989) 48 *Cambridge Law Journal* 55, 82.

Percy Winfield

Leading torts writer Percy Winfield sought to defend the boundaries between various torts.[177] For example, he sought to explain how the *Rylands v Fletcher* action was separate from the action in nuisance.[178] As indicated above, the House of Lords in *Cambridge Water* re-conceptualised the *Rylands v Fletcher* action as a subset of the tort of nuisance.

Winfield also sought to explain and defend differences between the action for negligence and that in nuisance.[179] He acknowledged that the word 'negligence' was often used in nuisance cases and unreasonableness was a 'main ingredient' of liability in nuisance. He suggested that, over time, courts were moving to more sharply distinguish the torts.[180] However, he argued that 'reasonableness' here meant something different from what it did in the context of negligence, ie taking proper care. He said that, in the context of nuisance, it meant 'what is legally right as between the parties taking into account all of the circumstances of the case',[181] including those not taken into account in determining what the reasonable person would have done in a given situation, as the law of negligence did. He contrasted what he saw as the simplicity and certainty of negligence ('it is putting a comparatively simple proposition before [a person] to tell [them] … that [they] are liable for negligence if [they] carelessly drive [their] car against another person'.[182] This was in contrast with the law of nuisance:

> [M]aking a noise is a tort only sub modo. Thus it must often be a pure gamble whether I act lawfully in opening a particular business in a street. If I make an error of judgment in deciding whether the business is offensive or not, I shall not escape liability by proving that I took all reasonable care to prevent the business from being a nuisance. This is far short of saying that taking care is irrelevant in liability for nuisance … reasonableness plays an important part in deciding whether there has or has not been a nuisance.[183]

Peter Cane

Peter Cane, another leading torts scholar, focused on the apparent attempt by the House of Lords in *Hunter v Canary Wharf* to reorient the tort of private nuisance

[177] Percy Winfield, 'Nuisance as a Tort' (1931) 4 *Cambridge Law Journal* 189.
[178] ibid, 195–97.
[179] ibid, 197–200.
[180] Percy Winfield, 'The History of Negligence in the Law of Torts' (1926) 42 *Law Quarterly Review* 184, 197–98, talking about recent examples involving a 'hybrid' action of nuisance and negligence, but insisting that courts were now insisting upon a division. With respect, this claim may be contested. I have earlier discussed examples in the case law well after 1926 that demonstrate a continuing mixing of principles of negligence and nuisance within the one factual scenario.
[181] Percy Winfield, 'The History of Negligence in the Law of Torts' (1926) 42 *Law Quarterly Review* 184, 199.
[182] ibid, 199.
[183] ibid, 199.

to damage to property interests.[184] As part of this attempt, several members of the Court downplayed the extension of that tort to cases of personal injuries, over the dissent of Lord Cooke. Cane criticised the majority position on three grounds. First, he said, 'it apparently fails to take into account of the centrality to the tort of nuisance of the fault-based concept of unreasonableness'.[185] Secondly, he said that it did not explain why the law was apparently privileging amenity damage to property (by imposing apparently strict nuisance liability) over liability for personal injuries. Thirdly, he criticised the result of the case – that a person who did not have a proprietary interest in land could bring a claim in negligence for personal injury (and property damage), but not for amenity damage. He feared that strait-jacketing of torts in the old forms of action, with a focus on form as opposed to the substance of the interest sought to be protected.

Conor Gearty

Conor Gearty also acknowledges the growing confusion between the torts of nuisance and negligence.[186] His solution is to separate cases involving physical damage and cases involving non-physical damage. He says that at present, both are, or may be, actionable as nuisance. He would deal with cases of physical damage under the tort of negligence, and deal with cases of non-physical damage under the tort of nuisance. He says this will allow nuisance to do 'what it does best' – to protect occupiers of land from non-physical interference with the enjoyment of their land. Gearty's suggestion has attracted high-level judicial support.[187]

Gearty criticises the current use of the concept of 'reasonableness' in the tort of private nuisance. He says its use has exacerbated confusion in the tort, and how it relates to the tort of negligence. He says it has not been the subject of academic scrutiny. He suggests that its removal from the tort of nuisance is 'both possible and desirable … help[ing] nuisance achieve a clearer definition of itself'.[188] He also blames cases accepting that private nuisances can include one-off events for further muddying the waters between negligence and nuisance.[189] He is highly critical of decisions such as *Sedleigh-Denfield* and *Leakey* on the basis that they, in his view, unacceptably mix the torts of negligence and nuisance.

[184] Peter Cane, 'What a Nuisance!' (1997) 113 *Law Quarterly Review* 515.

[185] ibid, 520.

[186] Conor Gearty, 'The Place of Private Nuisance in a Modern Law of Torts' (1989) 48(2) *Cambridge Law Journal* 214, 216, stating that 'nuisance is both attacked and burdened because it has lost all sense of that for which it stands'.

[187] *Hunter v Canary Wharf Ltd* [1997] AC 655, 692 (Lord Goff); *Hussain v Lancaster City Council* [2000] QB 1, 26 (Hirst LJ).

[188] Conor Gearty, 'The Place of Private Nuisance in a Modern Law of Torts' (1989) 48(2) *Cambridge Law Journal* 214, 218.

[189] ibid, 222.

One weakness of Gearty's article is that he does not explain from a principled basis why the law relating to non-physical damage to property should be governed by strict liability, nuisance principles, while he concedes that the cases involving physical damage to property should be effectively ceded to the law of negligence. It may be that he does this because many of the cases where the blurring has occurred have in fact involved damage to the plaintiff's property. That conceded, it is not clear why, on principle, liability for non-physical damage to property should be governed by the strict liability principles of nuisance, as Gearty claims, while liability for physical damage to property should be governed by the fault-based principles of negligence. Gearty never justifies this highly differential treatment of physical and non-physical damage. It is clear he is trying to preserve an area in which private nuisance, including strict liability, can operate without 'interference' with the law of negligence. It is much less clear that such a differentiation can be defended on an intellectually coherent basis.

Maria Lee

In an important work, Maria Lee states that there are in fact three different torts under the rubric of private nuisance.[190] She states that the first is a fault-based tort involving the intervention of natural events or third parties on the defendant's property.[191] The focus is on property damage. She believes this tort is more appropriately considered to be part of the tort of negligence. She perceives the second as a 'nuisance-style strict liability', where the fact the defendant has taken all reasonable care is no defence. She argues that *Rylands v Fletcher* and private nuisance are basically used interchangeably in this category, but without the restrictions traditionally attached to *Rylands*. She says there is a third category dealing with loss of amenity – noise, dust, pollution-type cases. She says there has been a 'definite and unhelpful' confusion between negligence and nuisance.[192]

[190] Maria Lee, 'What is Private Nuisance?' (2003) 119 *Law Quarterly Review* 298.

[191] 'A fault-based tort has developed within private nuisance in respect of physical damage brought about by the intervention of third parties or natural events … these cases may well fit more comfortably within negligence' (ibid, 308). With respect, there are examples other than those pertaining to property damage involving the intervention of third parties or natural events. For example, *Wandsworth London Borough Council* [2000] QB 756 involved loss of amenity rather than property damage, as did a recent decision (many years after Lee's article) in *Williams v Network Rail Infrastructure Ltd* [2019] QB 601. It is not clear to me why negligence is seen to be appropriate for just this category of private nuisance cases and not others. Clearly negligence principles are also being utilised in factual circumstances typically fitting within the tort of public nuisance, though Lee's article focuses on private nuisance. And as Lee acknowledges, the House of Lords emphasised in *Hunter v Canary Wharf* that the essence of a private nuisance claim is in any event interference with enjoyment of property rights, not property damage per se (308). On this basis, it is difficult to justify the special treatment that Lee suggests for claims for physical damage based on acts of a third party or natural events.

[192] ibid, 300.

There is a strategic purpose behind Lee's three-category approach to existing claims of private nuisance, together with an argument the first should be sloughed off into negligence. She seems to want to preserve the strictness of the other categories of private nuisance: 'Since property damage does not require the flexible balancing approach that is generally taken to amenity harm in nuisance, the common law is able to develop categories of activity that attract liability without fault in private nuisance'.[193] However, she criticises the courts for failing to articulate the rationale for the imposition of strict liability on some activities, and not others.[194] She says that labels such as 'reasonable' (in the context of reasonable user for nuisance) and 'natural' (in the context of non-natural use in the *Rylands* context) 'are problematic if the court is actually identifying a category of activities that should be subject to a stricter form of liability than in negligence … reasonableness turns the lawyer's mind to the … tort of negligence'.[195] She argues there is no rationale for the imposition of strict liability in respect of land use but not, for example, in relation to the transport of dangerous substances. She argues that pockets of strict liability, if seen as desirable, might be better made law by the legislature rather than the courts.[196]

JM Eekelaar

JM Eekelaar is very critical of the confusion in the existing law of nuisance in relation to the question of the strictness of liability:

> There can surely be few more fundamental features to civil litigation than knowing whether liability for the act complained of is strict or not. Yet on no other matter do judicial and academic comments on nuisance betray so much confusion.[197]

Eekelaar's position is that the tort of private nuisance is not a tort of strict liability, having regard to the Privy Council decision in *The Wagon Mound* and other sources.[198] He is not convinced by supposed distinctions between circumstances in which the defendant created the nuisance, and why they 'came to the nuisance'.[199] Eekelaar eventually reaches a position where he favours that a defendant's liability in nuisance should generally be governed by negligence principles, except where the facts involve a 'specially dangerous state of affairs' on the defendant's property.[200] This is a sop to the *Rylands v Fletcher* precedent, prior to a time where it was reconceptualised as a sub-branch of the tort of private nuisance.

[193] ibid, 311.
[194] ibid, 320.
[195] ibid, 320.
[196] ibid, 324.
[197] JM Eekelaar, 'Nuisance and Strict Liability' (1973) 8 *Irish Jurist* 191.
[198] ibid, 201.
[199] ibid, 198.
[200] ibid, 205.

John Murphy

John Murphy states that the question whether liability for nuisance is strict or not is 'the most confusing question in the whole of the law of private nuisance'.[201] He is highly critical of the courts in failing to explain how, if at all, the concept of 'reasonable user' in the tort of nuisance differs from reasonableness in the context of negligence:

> Yet, by insisting that an unreasonable user is central to nuisance liability, Lord Goff [in *Cambridge Water*] merely raises (but fails to answer) the question of how a failure to engage in a reasonable user may be distinguished from a failure to take the degree of care that the law demands from the hypothetical reasonable man … adding to the confusion is Lord Wilberforce's assertion in *Goldman v Hargrave* that 'the tort of nuisance may comprise a wide variety of situations, in some of which negligence plays not part, in others of which it is decisive', and Lord Reid's famous proclamation in *The Wagon Mound No 2* that … 'although negligence may not be necessary [for nuisance actions] fault of some kind is almost always necessary and fault generally involves foreseeability'.[202]

Murphy says these passages indicate the 'less than obvious' role that reasonableness and fault play in the law of private nuisance.[203]

Murphy's way out of the confusion is to state that when judges refer to 'reasonableness' in the context of nuisance, they are talking about the nature of the interference, rather than the defendant's conduct. In other words, the defendant's conduct might be entirely reasonable, but the nature of the interference with the plaintiff's property interests might be judged unreasonable. Murphy cites a couple of cases where, although the defendant's conduct was judged to be reasonable, the interference with the plaintiff's property rights was judged to be unreasonable.

On the other hand, as Murphy himself acknowledges, there might be a sense of artificiality in attempting to distinguish the conduct of the defendant from the interference with the plaintiff's property rights. After all, it is the defendant's conduct that causes the interference. He acknowledges that the question whether the defendant's conduct was unreasonable is in fact relevant in assessing whether the interference was unreasonable.

He then suggests a way out is to consider fault in (at least) two different senses. The traditional sense of fault in the context of negligence is that a breach of a duty of care by the defendant has caused injury or damage to the plaintiff, that the defendant has not met expected norms of behaviour, and this has caused the

[201] John Murphy, *The Law of Nuisance* (Oxford University Press, 2010) 54.
[202] ibid, 55.
[203] ibid, 55.

plaintiff loss. Murphy suggests that the references to 'fault' in what are ostensibly nuisance cases are to a different, narrower, concept of fault. This test of fault would be satisfied on the simple fact that the defendant chose to engage in the relevant activity at all, in circumstances where loss to a class of individuals including the plaintiff was reasonably foreseeable.[204]

It is not entirely clear that the judges did in fact mean fault in this way in the relevant cases described above. It would clearly not impose a very high bar for the relevant defendant to be held liable for a nuisance – it would simply be satisfied on the basis of causation and foreseeable injury to a class including the plaintiff. But this would apparently view as irrelevant the factors that Murphy himself states are relevant to the question of reasonable user – including the degree and nature of interference, the characteristics of the location, and practical ability to avoid the interference. None of these factors would be relevant if 'fault' were constrained to merely considering whether the defendant voluntarily chose to engage in the activity, and caused the plaintiff foreseeable loss. Thus, I do not share Murphy's conclusion that the tort of nuisance is one of 'stricter' liability.

Allan Beever

Allan Beever is strongly critical of existing aspects of the law of nuisance. Most relevantly for current purposes, he fundamentally rejects use of the concept of 'reasonableness' in determining liability for nuisance.[205] Beever strongly criticises the acceptance by the Privy Council in *The Wagon Mound No 2* of the need for reasonable foreseeability of damage or injury in order to succeed in nuisance. He says that it is incompatible with the (traditional) view of the tort as being one of strict liability.[206] He concludes that

> [i]f foreseeability is to be relevant [to nuisance], that can only be because of the connection between foreseeability and negligence. That is, foreseeability can be a coherent element in nuisance liability only if that liability is negligence liability. Accordingly, if foreseeability is to remain a prerequisite to liability in this area, we must come to recognise that liability is fault-based – that is, negligence based … [T]o go down this path ultimately means the assimilation of the law of nuisance to that of negligence.[207]

[204] ibid, 57: 'the fault inheres in knowingly taking the much heightened risk of a road accident by deciding to drive in circumstances known to be perilous. In short, anything voluntarily done in the face of foreseeable harm is capable of being described as a kind of fault'.

[205] Allan Beever, *The Law of Private Nuisance* (Hart Publishing, 2013) 6–12.

[206] '[I]f nuisance is a tort of strict liability, it is odd that it requires foreseeability. As we have seen, liability in negligence requires foreseeability because, in that context, foreseeability is linked to negligence … if liability is strict, then there is no reason to insist that the defendant have been able to foresee the claimant's injury' (ibid, 100–01).

[207] ibid, 105.

W Friedmann

W Friedmann studied a range of cases said to involve nuisance, said to involve negligence, and said to involve *Rylands v Fletcher*. He concluded that

> [t]he traditional analytical distinctions have lost much if not all of their former importance … these torts frequently overlap and rationalisation seems desirable [he pointed out a case where it was impossible to tell upon which basis the court determined the case] … in other cases the courts had to resist attempts to plead exactly the same facts supported by identical arguments, first in nuisance, then in negligence. Practitioners and teachers of law are bound to feel increasing difficulty in maintaining distinctions which have lost most of their legal as well as their social significance. The basic difficulty appears to result from the fact that the modern judicial tests for negligent conduct and strict liability are, under the pressure of modern social and industrial developments, substantially the same [he referred to the decision in *Wringe v Cohen*, which he used as an example of a case raising doubt as to any difference between negligent conduct and strict liability] … [which] consequently ma[kes] it difficult to decide whether nuisance demands proof of negligent conduct or not [after citing *Wilchich v Marks* [1934] 2 KB 56, he says that, again] the present writer has never been able to find out whether it was decided as a case of public nuisance or under the rule in *Donoghue v Stevenson*. The duty was derived from proximity, but textbooks appear to treat it as a case of nuisance, and that is further evidence for the proposition that the actions are now practically interchangeable.[208]

Friedmann's solution was to abandon the distinction between strict liability and fault-based liability. He argued that social developments had made the distinction redundant. He favoured

> [c]o-ordinating the various torts in a common principle, infinitely desirable for the practice as well as the learning of the law … it would seem to be easy to unite this group of torts, comprising probably negligence, trespass on and off the highway, statutory duties, nuisance, *Rylands v Fletcher*, liability for animals, for fire, and the various aspects of liability for dangerous things or premises, under a common formula. *Rylands v Fletcher* could today be decided as a case of negligence … there is no reason why the scienter rule should be anything but an aspect of negligence in regard to the keeping of animals.[209]

Other Views

Another leading torts scholar has observed the large degree of overlap between use of the concepts of reasonableness in the torts of nuisance and negligence: 'The test of unreasonable user in nuisance is structurally very similar to the concept of unreasonableness in the tort of negligence – both are standards of conduct based

[208] W Friedmann, 'Nuisance, Negligence, and the Overlapping of Torts' (1939) 3 *Modern Law Review* 305, 305 and 308.

[209] ibid, 309. He claimed that 'modern liability is, to a large extent, no longer based on individual fault, but on a standard of conduct which is a corollary of social responsibility'.

on the balancing of personal and social interests'.[210] Tony Weir concluded that the 'intrusion of negligence into nuisance law now appears nearly complete'.[211]

Reflections

It has been demonstrated that the law in this area is highly unsatisfactory. The supposed boundaries between the torts of nuisance and negligence have become increasingly blurred. This has occurred to the extent that it is sometimes difficult to determine whether the case is actually being determined according to principles of negligence or nuisance.[212] The courts have stated that liability for one of the torts determines liability for the other.

The courts have used principles of negligence, including duty of care, in determining whether a defendant is liable in nuisance. A key example of this has been an insistence that, in order to be successful in a nuisance action, damage or injury to the plaintiff must be reasonably foreseeable. This is a classic negligence principle. Beever is correct to say that while reasonable foreseeability makes eminent sense in relation to a fault-based tort such as negligence, it makes no sense to use it in relation to a tort like nuisance, which has traditionally been regarded as a tort of strict liability. (Nor, of course, does it make any sense in the context of strict-liability *Rylands v Fletcher*).[213] The point of reasonable foreseeability is that it supports a conclusion that the defendant should have done something to avoid the risk of injury to the plaintiff. The 'should have done something' irredeemably points to a breach of the duty of care that the defendant owed to the plaintiff. But in a strict liability paradigm, where the fact that the defendant caused the plaintiff injury or loss is the gist of the action, it is not clear why that loss should be foreseeable. There, causation, not foreseeability, is surely the gist of the action.

There is also confusion in terms of the standards of behaviour to be applied. In negligence cases, it is quite clear that an objective, reasonable person test is to be applied. There has been confusion in nuisance cases, where at times a subjective and, at times, an objective test seems to have been applied in making a judgment about the defendant's behaviour.

Most unsatisfactory of all, we do not have a clear idea of what seems to be a simple question – whether liability in nuisance is strict or fault based.

[210] Peter Handford, 'Mens Rea in Tort Law' (2000) 20(4) *Oxford Journal of Legal Studies* 533, 549.

[211] Tony Weir, 'The Staggering March of Negligence' in Peter Cane and Jane Stapleton (eds), *The Law of Obligations: Essays in Honour of John Fleming* (Clarendon, 1998) 103.

[212] Percy Winfield, 'The History of Negligence in Torts' (1926) 42 *Law Quarterly Review* 184, 197–98.

[213] *Rylands v Fletcher* (1866) LR 2 Ex. 265, 280 where Blackburn J for the Court of Exchequer Chamber claimed that a defendant from whose property something dangerous escapes should be held liable for the foreseeable consequences: 'it seems just that he should at his peril keep it there so that no mischief may accrue, or answer for the *natural and anticipated consequences*' (emphasis added); Allan Beever, *The Law of Private Nuisance* (Hart Publishing, 2013) 111.

Clearly, there are cases supporting both positions. Many commentators have pointed out this defect at the heart of the law as it presently stands. It is surely unsatisfactory in relation to a tort that has existed for many centuries, one of the oldest torts, that there is no agreement as to its essential nature. It does no credit to the law to have uncertainty about such a fundamental question.

The clearly unsatisfactory state of the current law cannot be cauterised by attempts to divide up the cases by imposing boundaries that are themselves questionable. It is not correct to try to cling on to strict liability aspects of nuisance, and to get around all of the cases where negligence has been considered in a notional case of nuisance, by claiming that strict liability applies to nuisances *created* by the defendant, while fault-based liability applies to nuisances *continued* by the defendant. There are inconvenient precedents in the way, where a defendant who has clearly 'created' a nuisance is judged in a nuisance case by principles of negligence.

More importantly, it is not clear why a tort should be given a bipolar nature, alternatively adopting a strict liability or a fault-based liability nature according to whether the defendant 'created it' or merely 'continued it'. That distinction could not bear the weight that would be placed upon it. Sometimes, it would be difficult to determine whether a defendant 'created' a nuisance or merely 'continued' it. Should it matter so much, in terms of the factual scenario in *Tarry v Ashton*, for example, whether the defendant bought the lamp that fell onto the plaintiff (creating the nuisance), or merely bought the property containing the lamp (continuing the nuisance), perhaps with knowledge? For analogous reasons, attempts to subdivide between cases of non-feasance (which might in most cases map adopting a nuisance in any event) and cases of misfeasance (which might in most cases map creating a nuisance) are unconvincing. Such a distinction has been removed in other areas of tort law, as explained above.

Donal Nolan made the point, in the context of *Rylands v Fletcher*, that it was 'indefensible' for the law to privilege property interests over personal interests. He was correct. This led him to suggest abandoning the strict liability principle of *Rylands v Fletcher*. However, the same point can be made in relation to the tort of nuisance. To the extent that it is, or should be as some suggest, a tort of strict liability, it is hard to defend. Why is interference with property interests to be governed by a strict liability standard, whereas liability for personal injuries requires proof of intent or breach of duty of care? It suggests an anachronistic preferencing of property interests over interests of bodily integrity, which should have no place in modern tort law.

The tort of nuisance made sense at a time when the tort of negligence did not exist. As the tort of negligence has taken off, the raison d'etre of the tort of nuisance has become increasingly thin. The beauty of the common law is its capacity to adapt, to change shape as the society that it regulates changes. Yet, sometimes the fact that a legal principle has existed for many centuries can make change to that doctrine extremely difficult. Sometimes, there is suspicion that we hang on to principles for reasons of 'sentimentality' or that they have been in existence for many centuries. There is no room in the law for sentimentality, particularly where the relevant doctrine is the subject of so much uncertainty and confusion in the law. While legal history can make our understanding of the law much richer and deeper, it must not shackle us to the past. Understanding our history does not mean an abiding allegiance to all that has gone before. Boldness is sometimes required to recalibrate principle, where past principles have been 'overtaken by events'. This is the situation with the tort of nuisance.

Some purists maintain that there is a difference between negligence and nuisance, that the concept of 'reasonable user' is different from the concept of reasonable care in the law of negligence. However, as Beever has pointed out, the difference is usually not well articulated. It is said that a defendant can be liable in nuisance where their use of their property is unreasonable, even when they took all reasonable care in relation to it.

Writing nearly a century ago, and prior to recognition of the generalised duty of care principle in *Donoghue v Stevenson*, Winfield argued that the torts of nuisance and negligence were distinct.[214] He acknowledged the importance of the concept of 'reasonableness' in the law of nuisance. Yet, he made some unflattering comparisons of the law of nuisance with the law of negligence. It is appropriate, given the importance of the question, to quote Winfield at length here:

> In negligence, assuming the duty to take care has been proved, the vital question is [whether] the defendant [took] reasonable care. But in nuisance it does not in the least follow that the defendant is quit of liability even if he has taken reasonable care … unreasonableness is a main ingredient of liability in nuisance. But her 'reasonableness' means something more than merely 'taking proper care'. It signifies what is legally right as between the parties taking into account all of the circumstances of the case, and some of these circumstances are often such as a man on the Clapham omnibus could not fully appreciate [a reference to a negligence reasonably foreseeability standard]. It is putting a comparatively simply proposition before him to tell him that he is liable for negligence if he carelessly drives his car against another person, but it is not so simple to tell him that, while he can make some noise on his premises, he must not make too much, or he will be liable in nuisance … thus it must often be a pure gamble whether I act lawfully in opening a particular business in a street. If I make an error of judgment in deciding whether the business is offensive or not, I shall not escape liability by proving that I took all reasonable care to prevent the business from being a nuisance. This is far short of saying that taking care is irrelevant in liability for nuisance. If the defendant has conducted his trade or business in a proper manner, ie as a reasonable man would conduct such a trade or business, he has gone some of the way towards making out a defence, but only some of the way; and conversely he will be in danger of losing his case if he has taken no such reasonable care. But even where he has given proof of it, he will still be liable if there has been a sensible [ie unreasonable] amount of damage caused to

[214] Percy Winfield, 'Nuisance as a Tort' (1931) 4 *Cambridge Law Journal* 189, 198.

> the plaintiff. So will he be if he has taken over from another person property on which existed a nuisance, though he will not be liable for the act of a trespasser in creating the nuisance unless he could reasonably have known of it, and here again reasonable care is a relevant matter. Reasonableness thus plays an important part in deciding whether there has or has not been a nuisance.[215]

Perhaps this position is just no longer tenable. Certainly, Winfield's suggestion that reasonable foreseeability in negligence applies in a different way in the law of nuisance is no longer tenable after *The Wagon Mound No 2* (obviously decided several decades after he wrote). Further, it may not be desirable. The uncertainty surrounding whether or not a defendant will be held liable in nuisance can hardly be an argument in favour of its retention as a stand-alone doctrine. Winfield states that negligence principles are more easily understood by the average person than are nuisance principles. If this is true, and it is acknowledged that the concept of 'reasonable care' is attended by some uncertainty, again it is not easy to defend why nuisance should be retained as a stand-alone doctrine.

The main argument that is apparently being made to separate the torts is that in nuisance it is not sufficient, to avoid liability, that the defendant has taken all reasonable care to avoid injury or damage to the plaintiff, if the defendant's use of their premises is 'unreasonable'. It does not seem to be much of a leap in legal principle to determine that, where the defendant's use of their premises is 'unreasonable', they will be regarded as having breached their duty of care to the plaintiff. By definition, then, if their use of the property is unreasonable, they will not be held to have exercised 'all reasonable care' to prevent injury or damage to the plaintiff. The supposed demarcation boundary is hardly insurmountable and struggles for logic in any event.

To the extent that nuisance is defended and contrasted with negligence on the basis it is and should remain a principle of strict liability, as was pointed out in Chapter 6, it is increasingly difficult to summon a convincing rationale any more for imposing strict liability upon anyone. This includes property owners. Strict liability has become increasingly isolated in the law of obligations. As it has become more isolated, the need for it to be rationalised and justified becomes even more pressing. Yet, no convincing arguments are made.

It is sometimes sought to distinguish the torts of negligence and nuisance on the basis that, in the former, it is necessary to establish that the defendant owes the plaintiff a duty of care, and that this is not necessary in the case of nuisance.[216] While this may be true, of course subsequently to when Winfield wrote, the landmark *Donoghue v Stevenson* was decided. In developing the generalised duty of care, Lord Atkin said that it was a duty not to injure one's 'neighbour'. A neighbour was there defined as someone who ought to have been in contemplation

[215] ibid, 199–200.
[216] ibid, 198.

of the defendant as someone liable to be affected by their action or omission.[217] Clearly, there is a very close analogy with Lord Atkin's figurative 'neighbour' principle, establishing that a duty of care exists, and the literal 'neighbour' relationship reflected in most cases of nuisance. The gist of the action is unreasonable interference with the property rights of another, and the overwhelming majority of these cases in private nuisance involve neighbouring property owners (or occupiers). This also serves to bring the torts into an ever-closer orbit.

It is submitted that, in the vast majority of cases, the actual result would not differ greatly if the principles of negligence were applied instead of the principles of nuisance. It can be readily accepted that, in most cases where there is an 'unreasonable use' of the defendant's land, the defendant will have breached the duty of care that they owed to individuals such as the plaintiff. In applying a negligence standard to property owners, the court would take into account the circumstances of the alleged 'nuisance'. It would be relevant to determine whether the defendant was aware, or ought to have been aware, of the nuisance. It would be considered how the nuisance came about. It may be that the court would view somewhat differently situations where the defendant created the nuisance, and situations where they 'inherited' it. This might be relevant to what, if anything, the defendant should have done by way of response to the nuisance of which they were aware or ought to have been aware. This is of course quite different to the suggestion some have made that strict liability should apply to situations where the defendant created the nuisance, and fault-based liability should apply to situations where the defendant 'inherited' the nuisance.

I should acknowledge that the result in some cases may be different, if negligence were applied rather than nuisance. I am thinking particularly of that line of nuisance cases where the court found that the defendant did not have to do anything about naturally occurring 'nuisances' on their property, such as *Sparke v Osborne* involving the noxious weed (known to the defendant) growing from their property onto that of the plaintiff, causing them damage, and similarly *Giles v Walker*. As indicated above, the reasoning in those cases, in particular the emphasis on the 'natural' nature of the nuisance, may have been infected by the judgment in *Rylands v Fletcher*. The judges in *Sparke* and *Giles* may have been attempting to avoid *Rylands* strict liability by distinguishing the natural nuisance in those cases from the 'non-natural' one in *Rylands*. Further, the cases were decided at a time when the generalised duty of care in negligence had not yet been recognised. Thus, it is considered highly likely that they would be decided differently if the cases were brought today. Most would surely consider it to be negligent to stand by and permit a noxious weed to grow from your premises onto that of a neighbour, causing them loss. The same point might be taken about thistle, depending on the extent of the defendant's awareness of the risks to neighbours. In sum, no great injustice is likely to occur if cases previously decided on the basis of nuisance principles are in future governed simply by the tort of negligence.

[217] *Donoghue v Stevenson* [1932] AC 562, 580.

Conclusion

The tort of nuisance is incoherent. It presents as a strict liability tort, but the consideration of fault-based principles has become extremely prevalent in the case law. Reasonable foreseeability is a requirement of both. The question of the reasonableness of the defendant's interference with the property interests of the plaintiff assumes great importance. Attempts to argue that reasonableness in the context of the tort of nuisance means something different from what it means in the tort of negligence wear somewhat thin. Claims that would on traditional analysis be nuisance cases are being dealt with via principles of negligence, with no explanation as to why. Respectfully, some judges point out there is a difference between them, but appear to be reluctant to defend it. It is said that in a nuisance case, fault of some kind will 'almost always' be relevant. This is hardly a satisfactory state of affairs. Academic writing has been highly critical of the uncertain nature of the tort of nuisance, betraying its strict liability origins at times, but increasingly being overwhelmed by the negligence juggernaut.

Given that in the vast majority of cases, the legal result of the specific factual scenario would be no different in nuisance than it would be in negligence, it becomes more difficult in the twenty-first century to justify why interference with property interests should be dealt with under an ostensibly strict liability basis, while interference with the person is dealt with on a fault basis (whether intentional or negligent). The law's past clear tendency to reify property interests over other interests is now rightly regarded as an anachronism, yet it still props up the argument for strict liability in nuisance in a fault-dominated world. Strict liability nuisance looks increasingly isolated within the torts family.

8

Strict Liability in the Law of Defamation

Introduction to Freedom of Speech

Prior to discussing the specific law relating to defamation, and in particular its strictness, it is necessary to say something of the broader context in which the law operated on speech throughout English legal history. Defamation law as it currently exists has been subject to trenchant criticism and highly unflattering description.[1] In this context, it is important to understand how it came to be so.

Essentially, traditionally the English law has not been strongly supportive of free speech. Evidence of this includes the *Scandalum Magnatum* (1275), creating a capital offence of 'spreading fake news' about the monarch or other nobility in society. These laws were more focused on seditious and treasonous-type activity, as opposed to what we would today regard as defamation. They were enacted primarily in order to preserve stability and peace in society, rather than to preserve reputations per se.[2]

[1] Van Vechten Veeder, 'The History and Theory of the Law of Defamation' (1903) 3 *Columbia Law Review* 546, 546, referred to its 'doubts and difficulties, its meaningless and grotesque anomalies. It is, as a whole, absurd in theory, and very often mischievous in its practical operation'; Robert Leflar, 'Radio and TV Defamation: "Fault" or Strict Liability?' (1954) 15 *Ohio State Law Journal* 252, 253: 'it is doubtful if any major segment of the common law is more medieval in its point of view, more beset by circuitous fictions and uncertain vagaries, than is the law of libel and slander'; Allan Beever, *A Theory of Tort Liability* (Hart Publishing, 2016) 195 described it as a 'discordant attempt to present its divergent themes as one moment'; Tony Weir, *A Casebooks on Tort* (8th edn, Sweet & Maxwell, 1996) 519: 'defamation is odd at its very core … the plaintiff can get damages for a statement made to others without showing that the statement was untrue, without showing that the statement did him the slightest harm, and without showing that the defendant was in any way wrong to make it (much less that the defendant owed him any duty of any kind). Are we still in the law of tort?'; WP Keaton et al, *Prosser and Keeton on the Law of Torts* (5th edn, West Publishing Co, 1984) 771: 'there is a great deal of the law of defamation which makes no sense. It contains anomalies and absurdities for which no legal writer ever has had a kind word, and it is a curious compound of strict liability imposed on innocent defendants, as rigid and extreme as anything found in the law, with a blind and almost perverse refusal to compensate the plaintiff for real and very serious harm'. Matthew Collins in *Collins on Defamation* (Oxford University Press, 2014) ix, said that it resembled 'Frankenstein's monster'. The Supreme Court of the United States noted that 'the common law of defamation is an oddity of tort law, for it allows recovery of purportedly compensatory damages without evidence of actual loss': *Gertz v Robert Welch Inc* 418 US 323, 349 (Powell J, with whom Stewart Marshall Blackmun and Rehnquist JJ agreed).

[2] John Lassiter, 'Defamation of Peers: The Rise and Decline of the Action for Scandalum Magnatum 1497–1773' (1978) 22 *American Journal of Legal History* 216, 217.

Criticism of the courts was dangerous. In a 1344 decision, De Northampton was punished for the offence of 'scandalising the court' for criticising a decision of the King's Bench. The Statute of Treason of 1352 prohibited and punished the levying of war against the monarch, 'adhering' to the king's enemies, and imagining the death of the monarch.

The ecclesiastical courts enforced religious orthodoxy, with the weapon of the offence of blasphemy and others at its disposal. Originally, it was the ecclesiastical courts that also enforced laws that today we would recognise as defamation, as will be seen shortly.

The introduction of the printing press to England in 1476 by William Caxton inevitably ramped up the conflict between citizens wishing to speak their mind, and insecure rulers seeking to shut such conversations down at all costs. In the guise of providing protection for intellectual property through a royalty scheme, the Crown sought to take control over what was published, requiring that all publications be approved prior to publication by the Archbishop of Canterbury or London. Anyone publishing unapproved publications could be punished by being whipped, pilloried or jailed. This position was justified, even by the courts, on the basis that 'to print or publish any newspaper or pamphlet of news whatsoever is illegal; that it is a manifest intent to a breach of the peace'.[3] Any unauthorised material taken to be seditious or slanderous of the government could result in the mutilation or death of the relevant publisher.[4]

The licensing system lapsed in 1641 when the Star Chamber was abolished, but a new Board of Licensors was convened in 1643. A maximum of 20 publishers was permitted. This system of 'prior restraint' only lapsed in 1694. In the eighteenth century, scholars such as Blackstone conceived of the freedom of the press, but it was in narrow terms – it meant freedom from prior restraint, according to Blackstone, but was no broader than that:

> The liberty of the press is indeed essential to the nature of a free state: but this consists in laying on previous restraints upon publication, and not in freedom from censure from criminal matter when published. Every free man has an undoubted right to lay what sentiments he pleases before the public; to forbid this is to destroy the freedom of the press; but if he publishes what is improper, mischievous or illegal, he must take the consequences of his own temerity … to punish … any dangerous or offensive writings which [are] … of a pernicious tendency is necessary for the preservation of peace and good order.[5]

Over time, as a Hobbesian view of the need for strong government was replaced by the social contract model favoured by Locke and others, and as a fear of overthrow of the government by outside forces subsided, the law began to more strongly

[3] *R v Carr* (1680) 7 St. Tr. 1114 (Scroggs CJ).

[4] RC, Donnelly, 'History of Defamation' [1949] *Wisconsin Law Review* 99, 117.

[5] Sir William Blackstone, *Commentaries on the Laws of England 1765–1769* (Clarendon Press, 1769) 152.

protect freedom of speech generally. Prosecutions for seditious libel,[6] a common law offence created in 1606 (see below), and involving criticism of members of the government, decreased and were largely non-existent by the 1830s.[7] Lord Campbell's Act of 1843 finally made truth a defence to a libel action. By 1868 English courts were espousing the fundamental value of free speech:

> Our law of libel has, in many respects, only gradually developed itself into anything like a satisfactory and settled form. The full liberty of public writers to comment on the conduct and motives of public men has only in very recent times been recognised. Comments on government, on ministers and officers or state, on members of both Houses of Parliament, on judges and other public functionaries are now made every day, which half a century ago would have been the subject of actions or ex officio informations, and would have brought down fine and imprisonment on publishers and authors. Yet who can doubt that the public are gainers by the change, and that though injustice may often be done, and though public men may often have to smart under the keen sense of wrong inflicted by hostile criticism, the nation profits by public opinion being thus freely brought to bear on the discharge of public duties.[8]

By now, the value of free speech has been extensively documented in the literature. John Stuart Mill's classic *On Liberty* espoused the value of free speech, including assisting in the search for truth,[9] and assisting in an individual's development and self-actualisation.[10] Alexander Meiklejohn and others emphasise the importance of free speech in the political realm, particularly for a democratic self-government model,[11] and Oliver Wendell Holmes Jr memorably coined the 'marketplace of ideas' concept to buttress freedom of speech as a fundamental constitutional value.[12] The United Kingdom's commitment to freedom of speech is reflected most

[6] Examples include *R v Bear* (1698) 2 Salkeld 417; 90 ER 1132, 91 ER 1175 (KB) and *R v Tutchin* (1704) 10 State Trials (OS) 1096; Philip Hamburger, 'The Development of the Law of Seditious Libel and the Control of the Press' (1985) 37 *Stanford Law Review* 740.

[7] James Fitzjames Stephen, *A History of the Criminal Law of England* (Macmillan, 1904) 373.

[8] *Wason v Waller* (1868) LR 4 QB 73, 93 (Cockburn CJ).

[9] Geraint Williams (ed), *Utilitarianism, On Liberty, Considerations on Representative Government* (Everyman, 1910) 85: 'the peculiar evil of silencing the expression of an opinion is that it is robbing the human race, posterity as well as the existing generation, those who dissent from the opinion, still more than those who hold it. If the opinion is right, they are deprived of the opportunity of exchanging error for truth. If wrong, they lose, what is almost as great a benefit, the clearer perception and livelier impressin of truth, produced by its collision with error … we can never be sure that the opinion we are endeavouring to stifle is a false opinion, and if we were sure, stifling it would be an evil still'.

[10] ibid, 88, stating that a person whose judgment is worthy of confidence 'has kept [their] mind open to criticism of [their] opinions and conduct. Because it has been [their] practice to listen to all that could be said against [them]; to profit by as much of it as was just, and expound to [themselves] and upon occasion to others, the fallacy of what was fallacious … the only way in which a human being can make some approach to knowing the whole of a subject is by hearing what can be said about it by persons of every variety of opinion, and studying all modes in which it can be looked at by every character of mind. No wise [person] ever acquired [their] wisdom in any mode but this'.

[11] Alexander Meiklejohn, *Free Speech and its Relation to Self-Government* (Harper Bros, 1948); 'The *First Amendment* is an Absolute' [1961] *Supreme Court Review* 245; Anthony Gray, *Freedom of Speech in the Western World* (Lexington, 2019).

[12] *Abrams v United States* 250 US 616, 630 (1919) (Holmes J, dissenting).

importantly in the implementation into domestic law of the European Convention on Human Rights[13] through the Human Rights Act 1998 (UK).

Development of Law of Defamation

Early Roman law recognised that spoken words could damage another's reputation. The gist of the action was the personal insult, and was part of the notion of *injuria*, rather than any pecuniary loss that could be quantified. A common example of defamation in this time was a libellous song or chant. This was recognised as wrong and severely punished in the *Twelve Tables*. In respect of public statements that were defamatory, truth was not a defence. Defamation was primarily a civil claim for which compensation was payable, but later developed a criminal aspect, in the so-called *libelli famosi*. These were mainly epigrams (witticisms) and pasquinades (satire or lampoon, typically public). Again, these were severely punished, and truth was irrelevant. In contrast, privately made defamatory statements were dealt with lightly. At this point the law distinguished between cases based on the manner and extent of the publication of the material. No distinction was made between the spoken and the written word.

In England, defamation was originally heard in the ecclesiastical courts. This was because defamation was initially regarded as being sinful. Not surprisingly in that context, there is evidence that it was essential for this court to find that the defendant had acted with malice, or *maliciose*. Where no malice was found, the action for defamation was dismissed.[14] The court would lack jurisdiction.[15] Obviously, malice is some kind of proxy for fault-based considerations. However, the court was very prepared to imply malicious intent, if the material was defamatory.[16] This would even occur if there was clear factual evidence to the contrary.[17] If malice were established, the only available remedy for defamation in the ecclesiastical courts was for the defendant to make penance for their wrongdoing. No financial remedy was available. Truth was a defence.[18] Low-level insult could also be dealt

[13] Article 10 contains the right to freedom of expression.

[14] *Brook v Sir Henry Montague, Recorder of London* (1605) Cro. Jac. 90, 91; 79 ER 77, 78, where the Court referred to an example in *Greenwood v Prick* Cro. Jac. 91 where a clergyman recounted a story where an individual, Greenwood, had committed great sin, including perjury and persecution of individuals, was struck down with plague and then killed by the hand of God. In fact, Greenwood was alive and well, and in the audience. His claim for defamation against the clergyman failed on the basis the latter did not act maliciously.

[15] Van Vechten Veeder, 'History and Theory of the Law of Defamation' (1904) 4 *Columbia Law Review* 33, 35.

[16] Paul Mitchell, 'Duties, Interests and Motives: Privileged Occasions in Defamation' (1998) 18 *Oxford Journal of Legal Studies* 381, 383.

[17] Van Vechten Veeder, 'History and Theory of the Law of Defamation' (1904) 4 *Columbia Law Review* 33, 35.

[18] Chris Dent, 'The Local of Defamation Law Since the Constitution of Oxford' (2018) 44 *Monash University Law Review* 491, 496.

with in the local courts. Originally, the common law courts refused to hear matters involving defamation.[19]

Partly due to the introduction of the printing press, the volume of complaints about allegedly defamatory words grew exponentially. By this time the ecclesiastical courts had entered into some decay.

The Star Chamber began to hear libel cases. That Chamber took its role of preserving the peace very seriously and viewed enforcement of defamation law as a key tool in achieving this. It viewed any criticism of the government very dimly and was concerned to preserve the peace at all costs. It saw defamation law as an important tool at its disposal in this regard. Its major interest was in the criminal realm for alleged written defamation (libel). Truth was not a defence in the Star Chamber.[20] Further, publication of the defamatory material to a third person was not necessary in Star Chamber proceedings. It extended its reach over non-political matters on the basis that these could also effectively risk breach of the peace. Damages were available and fines could be levied against wrongdoers.

The common law courts also began to hear defamation matters. They offered plaintiffs a much broader range of remedies than the ecclesiastical courts could, including money damages. Libel was actionable per se if the plaintiff was exposed to ridicule, contempt or hatred by the defendant's written words. The common law courts also considered particular types of defamation that overlapped with other common law matters. Examples include allegations that a person committed a crime. This involved the criminal law, with which the common law was interested, so the common law courts would hear a slander case that occurred in that context. Similarly, they would hear verbal allegations that a person had an infectious disease or was unfit to practice their chosen profession or trade, or where actual damage could be proven.[21] If it were proven that these types of statements were made, they were actionable per se, without the need to prove special damage.[22] In other words, they were treated as if they were libel, not slander, cases. By 1583, the common law courts had moved to limit the jurisdiction of the ecclesiastical courts in defamation cases.[23]

[19] RC Connelly, 'History of Defamation' (1949) *Wisconsin Law Review* 99, 106, refers to a 1295 decision to this effect.

[20] Colin Rhys Lovell, 'The Reception of Defamation by the Common Law' (1962) 15 *Vanderbilt Law Review* 1051, 1062–63: 'Star Chamber gave short shrift to truth as a defense'.

[21] Van Vechten Veeder, 'History and Theory of the Law of Defamation' (1903) 3 *Columbia Law Review* 546, 571. The category of allegations of unchastity was added by statute. However, s14 of the Defamation Act 2013 (UK) removed that category, and that pertaining to the infectious diseases claim, from that category of slander that was actionable without proof of damage.

[22] William Holdsworth, 'Defamation in the Sixteenth and Seventeenth Centuries' (1924) 40 *Law Quarterly Review* 397, 398; *Lachaux v Independent Print Ltd* [2020] AC 612, 620 (Lord Sumption, with whom Lords Kerr, Wilson, Hodge and Briggs agreed).

[23] In *Palmer and Thorpe's Case* (1583) 4 Co. Rep. 20a, Coke stated that ecclesiastical courts would hear defamation cases involving spiritual matters (eg, alleging that a person was a 'heretic', 'adulterer' or 'fornicator') only, not related to the common law, and re-confirmed that ecclesiastical courts could not order damages.

The common law courts adopted some of the doctrine that had been applied in the ecclesiastical courts. In particular, it required proof that the defendant was guilty of malice in publishing the defamatory material.[24] As indicated, this made sense in the ecclesiastical courts due to the connection with morality, but it was transferred over and applied in the common law courts as well,[25] though it made less sense in that context. Again, malice is some kind of proxy for fault. It partly betrays the criminal nature of the libel jurisdiction in the Star Chamber.[26] Again, the law became very willing to imply malice from the fact that the defamation actually occurred.[27] As it did so, the element of fault became less important.

The Star Chamber was abolished in 1641, after which the volume of defamation cases in the common law courts naturally increased. The common law adapted some of the practices of the Star Chamber. Truth became a defence,[28] and publication of the defamatory material to a third person became necessary.[29] It required that the plaintiff demonstrate they had suffered damage.[30] It began to distinguish certain types of defamation from others. In a case in 1670 the distinction between defamation via the spoken word (slander) and via the written word (libel) is recognised. The court took the position that the latter was more serious because it was thought to reflect more malice.[31] It was actionable without the need to prove special damage, which was implied. This aided in the goal of censorship.[32] Slander was not generally actionable per se and developed as an action on the case. In slander cases in categories other than those mentioned above, proof of damage was required in order to obtain compensation.

[24] So, for example, in *Peacock v Reynal* (1612) 2 Brownl & Golds 151 the court considered an allegation of defamation involving a letter being sent by the defendant to an elderly man containing negative comments about the man's heir. The court differentiated a case where such letter 'had been directed to a father for reformation', it would not be considered defamatory. The court in *Crawford v Middleton* (1662) 1 Lev. 82 stated that statements made in 'grief and sorrow' would not be actionable defamation. Further, the court in *Greenwood v Prick* (a precedent cited in *Brook v Montague* (1605) Cro. Jac. 90)) involved a parson making false assertions that a sinner had been visited by plague and had died, as a result of wrongdoing. The 'sinner' was alive and well and in attendance at the sermon. The parson was held not liable in defamation because he lacked malicious intent.

[25] Van Vechten Veeder, 'History and Theory of the Law of Defamation' (1904) 4 *Columbia Law Review* 33, 36. As indicated above, an example occurred in *Greenwood v Prick* Cro. Jac. 91 where the royal courts dismissed an action for slander against a clergyman on the basis that he had not spoken with malice.

[26] William Holdsworth, 'Defamation in the Sixteenth and Seventeenth Centuries III' (1925) 41 *Law Quarterly Review* 13, 28.

[27] *Mercer v Sparks* (1586) Owen, 51; William Holdsworth, 'Defamation in the Sixteenth and Seventeenth Centuries III' (1925) 41 *Law Quarterly Review* 13, 24.

[28] *Legat v Bull* (Trinity Term, 1533) (KB); *M'Pherson v Daniels* (1829) 10 B & C 263, 272; Colin Rhys Lovell, 'The Reception of Defamation by the Common Law' (1962) 15 *Vanderbilt Law Review* 1051, 1065: 'completely different from the libel doctrines of Star Chamber, and like the canon law of ecclesiastical courts, the common law gave the defendant the complete defence of truth'.

[29] RC Donnelly, 'The History of Defamation [1949] *Wisconsin Law Review* 99, 115.

[30] Colin Rhys Lovell, 'The Reception of Defamation by the Common Law' (1962) 15 *Vanderbilt Law Review* 1051, 1064.

[31] *King v Lake* (1670) Hardres 470; Skinner 124.

[32] RC Donnelly, 'History of Defamation' [1949] *Wisconsin Law Review* 99, 121.

Exceptions that we would today recognise as qualified privilege began to be recognised. In 1585 the court recognised that material filed pursuant to a court action could not be the subject of an action for defamation.[33] However, in *Brook v Montague*[34] an exception to this was recognised. It was held there that if a barrister were to introduce 'scandalous' and irrelevant material to the hearing of a matter, they were required to demonstrate its truth. If they could not, it would be deemed to have been intended to be spoken maliciously and without cause. In such cases, the barrister was liable to a successful action for defamation against them. This case reflects the idea that what would otherwise be a privileged communication might lose that status, and become defamatory, if malice were shown. Similarly, a 1597 case contains glimmers of privilege, concluding that defamation was not actionable when involving advice to the recipient in relation to a particular matter.[35]

The approach to the question of malice morphed. Originally, the common law required that the plaintiff plead and prove the existence of malice, just as the ecclesiastical courts had done. However, that requirement became a formality because the common law courts adopted the practice of the ecclesiastical courts in presuming the existence of malice from the fact of publication.[36]

While at one time it was presumed to exist, in some situations it was possible for the defendant to show they had not acted with malice and thus would escape liability. For example, the defendant might be able to show they had spoken in 'grief and sorrow',[37] or that they were trying to assist another to make a good decision by making their comments.[38] There was some pressure to provide a defence for employers who had made derogatory comments about an ex-employee to a would-be employer of the person.[39]

These situations evolved into two defences in the English law. The first was fair comment on a matter of public interest in circumstances where a duty to comment arose.[40] The second involved qualified privilege, attaching to a range of publication types where the law recognises the special value of the particular speech. As well as the example of court records discussed above, other examples of factual scenarios where privilege applied included reports of parliamentary or court proceedings,

[33] *Cutler v Dixon* (1591) 4 Co. Rep. 14b, 76 ER 886.

[34] *Brook v Montague* (1606) Cro. Jac. 90.

[35] *Vanspike v Cloyson*, Cro. Eliz. 541.

[36] Jeremiah Smith notes the courts might have been more transparent here, frankly acknowledging they were making a substantive change to the law in effectively discarding a requirement of malice, but cloaking it in an apparent rule of evidence: '*Jones v Hulton*: Three Conflicting Judicial Views as to a Question of Defamation' (1912) 60 *University of Pennsylvania Law Review* 365, 371 and 461, 464–66.

[37] *Crawford v Middleton* (1662) 1 Lev. 82.

[38] *Herver v Dowson* (1765); Francis Buller, *An Introduction to the Law Relative to Trials at Nisi Prius* (1772) 8.

[39] *Edmondson v Stevenson* (1766); Francis Buller, *An Introduction to the Law Relative to Trials at Nisi Prius* (1772) 8. In such cases, exceptionally the plaintiff would have to demonstrate malice on the part of the defendant.

[40] *Toogood v Spyring* (1834) 1 CM & R 181, 193; *Campbell v Spottiswoode* (1863) 3 B & S 769.

employment references,[41] and reports of suspected criminal activity. In such cases, the law presumed the absence of malice, subject to the plaintiff proving to the contrary.[42] It was not easy for a plaintiff to prove the existence of malice. Proof that the defendant acted with an improper purpose in publishing the material would assist,[43] as would evidence that the defendant knew the material they published was false.[44] Reckless indifference as to their truth may be sufficient.[45] The mere fact that the defendant was careless, impulsive, used strong language or demonstrated prejudice was not sufficient.[46] Courts were (and still are) reluctant to find that malice exists.[47]

The struggle for the law was to articulate the kinds of occasion when this qualified privilege might arise. One view was that it occurred in circumstances where the defendant could demonstrate that they did not intend to harm the plaintiff,[48] although there was some circularity involved in that reasoning.

In an important decision, the court eventually placed qualified privilege into a context of duty and interest. In *Toogood v Spyring* the court stated:

> In general, an action lies for the malicious publication of statements which are false in fact, and injurious to the character of another … and the law considers such publications as malicious, unless it is fairly made by a person in the discharge of some public or private duty, whether legal or moral, or in the conduct of his own affairs, in matters where his interest is concerned. In such cases, the occasion prevents the inference of malice, which the law draws from unauthorized communications, and affords a qualified defence depending upon the absence of actual malice. If fairly warranted by any reasonable occasion or exigency, and honestly made, such communications are protected for the common convenience and welfare of society.[49]

Subsequent decisions would flit between apparent reversion to the question of whether or not the defendant had acted with malice or for altruistic reasons, on the one hand, or whether the defendant could be said to have had a duty to communicate the material to a person with a particular interest in it. However, in the late nineteenth century, the English court settled upon a duty–interest analysis.[50]

[41] *Edmondson v Stevenson* (1776) (Buller's *Nisi Prius* 8, where Lord Mansfield stated, in the context of an allegedly defamatory reference for an ex-servant, that 'this is not to be considered as an action in the common way for defamation by words; but that the gist of it must be malice, which is not implied from the occasion of speaking, but should be directly proved'.

[42] *Reynolds v Times Newspapers Ltd* [2001] 2 AC 127, 229 (Lord Hope).

[43] *Horrocks v Lowe* [1975] AC 135, 149 (Lord Diplock) (with whom Lords Wilberforce, Hodson and Kilbrandon agreed).

[44] ibid, 145 (Viscount Dilhorne), 149–50 (Lord Diplock).

[45] ibid, 145 (Viscount Dilhorne), 150 (Lord Diplock).

[46] ibid, 145–46 (Viscount Dilhorne) and 150 (Lord Diplock).

[47] ibid, 150 (Lord Diplock); Matthew Collins, *Collins on Defamation* (Oxford University Press, 2014) 244.

[48] *Bromage v Prosser* (1824) 1 C & P 475; (1825) 4 B & C 247; 1 C & P 673.

[49] *Toogood v Spyring* (1834) 1 CM & R 181, 193; 149 ER 1044 (Baron Parke).

[50] *Pullman v Walter Hill & Co* [1891] 1 QB 524, 528: 'an occasion is privileged when the person who makes the communication has a moral duty to make it to the person to whom he does make it, and the person who receives it has an interest in hearing it. Both these conditions must exist in order that the

This was particularly problematic for defendants involved in mass communication, traditionally newspapers and broadcasters. This is because it was virtually impossible for them to demonstrate that their readers, listeners and/or viewers had the requisite interest to satisfy this requirement.[51] They would effectively be left with truth as their sole defence in the vast majority of cases.

Early Examples of the Strictness with which Liability Attached for Defamation

As was noted in previous chapters, one of the historical explanations and justifications for the imposition of strict liability was that the law was seeking to avoid the blood feud. In order to maximise the potential of a regulated system of law to dissuade resort to physical vengeance, it had to be relatively easy to obtain a remedy. Individuals were prone to resorting to physical vengeance if they believed their reputations had been harmed. Thus, the felt need to provide a remedy for those aggrieved by such behaviour was even stronger here than elsewhere in the law of tort.

That this fact buttressed the strict liability in the law of defamation in early times is evident in a famous defamation case, *De Libellis Famosis*, in 1606.[52] It was in this case that the common law first recognised an action for seditious libel. There Coke LJ noted that 'in a state of government, the party ought to complain for every injury done him in an ordinary course of law, and not by any means to revenge himself, either by the odious course of libelling, or otherwise'.[53] The attempt by the court to dissuade and discourage vengeance and self-help for perceived slights and wrongs is clear.

The court also confirmed that, in such cases, it was irrelevant whether or not the material was true. This is impossible to defend and seems incongruous to today's eyes. It might be explained historically by the importance placed in defamation law on preserving the peace. In such a context, the likelihood that a given defamation would tend to a breach of the peace, rather than its actual truth, was critical.[54]

occasion may be privileged' (Lord Esher); *London Association for Protection of Trade v Greenlands Ltd* [1916] 2 AC 15, 35–36 (Lord Atkinson) and 42 (Lord Parker); Paul Mitchell, *The Making of the Modern Law of Defamation* (Hart Publishing, 2005) 162.

[51] Eric Descheemaeker, '"A Man Must Take Care Not to Defame His Neighbour": The Origins and Significance of the Defence of Responsible Publication' (2015) 34 *University of Queensland Law Journal* 239, 251.

[52] *De Libellis Famosis* (1606) 5 Co. Rep. 125; 77 ER 250; likewise *Buckley v Wood* (1591) 4 Co. Rep. 14b.

[53] For another example of this point, see *Merest v Harvey* (1814) 5 Taunt 442, 444; 128 ER 761: 'it goes to prevent the practice of dualling, if juries are permitted to punish insult'.

[54] This was finally overturned in Lord Campbell's Act 1843 (UK). Fox's Libel Act was also important, in giving juries, rather than judges, the power to determine the important factual issues in a defamation trial.

At this time, the courts were not recognising the public benefit that would or might occur through a robust discussion of important issues.

The law of defamation did require proof of malice on the part of the defendant. Though this was applied in the Court of Star Chamber and the common law courts once they took over jurisdiction for defamation matters, the requirement of malice in practice largely fell away. Another way of thinking about malice is to view it as a kind of intentional fault. When it was required to be proven, defamation had some fault basis. However, the common law courts began to imply malice from the fact that the material had been published. Its existence no longer needed to be separately proven by the plaintiff. It was presumed, and (sometimes) conclusively presumed. This effectively made liability in defamation strict in nature.[55] It was not necessary that the defendant was at fault in publishing the defamatory material, or that they intended to harm the plaintiff.[56] An important change in the nature of the tort of defamation had occurred, making it less fault based. As Smith notes, this placed the tort on a path diametrically opposed to the path on which other aspects of the law of tort had traversed.[57] It moved defamation close to a strict liability tort,[58] although this was somewhat ameliorated by development of defences such as qualified privilege. If this were shown, proof of actual malice was required. The existence of actual malice might also impact on the level of damages available, including punitive and/or aggravated damages.

A classic example appears in the judgment of Lord Mansfield in *R v Woodfall*: 'whatever a man publishes he publishes *at his peril*: for there is no entering into the secret thoughts of a man's heart' (emphasis added).[59] Obviously, the phrase 'at peril' is the par excellence expression of a strict liability. A further example appears in *Day v Bream*.[60] There the court decided that a person who personally delivered a handbill which contained defamatory material could be held liable in defamation, unless they could make out a defence. The fact that the defendant did not know of the fact the material was defamatory was regarded as being irrelevant.

[55] Eric Descheemaeker, 'Protecting Reputation: Defamation and Negligence' (2009) 29 *Oxford Journal of Legal Studies* 603, 626.

[56] Patrick McNulty, 'The Gertz Fault Standard and the Common Law of Defamation: An Argument for Predictability of Result and Certainty of Expectation' (1985) 35 *Drake Law Review* 51, 59.

[57] Jeremiah Smith, 'Jones v Hulton: Three Conflicting Judicial Views as to a Question of Defamation' (1912) 60 *University of Pennsylvania Law Review* 461, 470–71: 'while the judicial movement, in cases of physical damage, has been from imposing absolute liability toward requiring culpability, the movement as to defamation has been the reverse. In early times, wrong intent or wrong motive was considered necessary to a recovery for defamation. This … was largely due to the theory as to the basis of jurisdiction in the ecclesiastical courts … after the higher secular courts took jurisdiction in such suits, they gradually came to regard wrong mental attitude as unessential and … practically treated the action for defamation as belonging under (a class) where a defendant does certain acts at his peril'.

[58] Van Vechter Veeder, 'History and Theory of the Law of Defamation' (1904) 4 *Columbia Law Review* 33, 37 n 2: 'the doctrine of implied malice is merely a roundabout way of saying that a person makes defamatory statements at his peril. To say that malice is implied is equivalent to saying that the law will not look into the motive at all'.

[59] *R v Woodfall* (1770) 5 Burr. 2776.

[60] *Day v Bream* (1837) 2 M & R 54.

It was sufficient that the defendant had 'published' the material, and the fact that the defendant was innocent of any conscious wrongdoing or negligence in so doing was irrelevant to that fact.

In *Capital and Counties Bank v Henty and Sons*,[61] a majority of the House of Lords found that it was the tendency of the material to injure the plaintiff's reputation that mattered, not the defendant's intention in publishing it.[62] However, some limits were placed on this. Lord Blackburn said that if the defendant, 'without excuse or justification, did what he knew *or ought to have known was calculated* [meaning likely in this context] to injure the plaintiff, he must [at least civilly] be responsible for the consequences' (emphasis added).[63] In the Court of Appeal decision in this case, Brett LJ railed against finding a defendant liable in defamation where they 'had no reason to suppose' what they published would injure anyone. Further, he indicated that in cases of defamation based on secondary meanings, it would have to be something that the defendant and recipient would reasonably have regarded as defamatory given what they knew. Both the decision of Lord Blackburn and that of Brett LJ seem to contain aspects of fault in how they view the liability position of a defendant in a defamation case.[64] This was also evident in some of the other defamation decisions of this era, for instance those involving innocent distributors of material found to be defamatory,[65] or inadvertent publication to a third party.[66]

But the strictness of the tort of defamation was re-confirmed in the controversial decision in *E Hulton & Co v Jones*.[67] The defendant wrote a witty poem about a supposedly fictional character, Artemis Jones. In fact, a person with that very name existed. That person successfully sued the defendant for defaming him through publication of the poem. The Court of Appeal noted the strictness of the liability of the defendant in such cases:

> It makes no difference whether the writer of the article inserted the name or description unintentionally, by accident, or believing that no person existed corresponding with the name or answering the description. If upon the evidence the jury is of the opinion that ordinary sensible readers, knowing the plaintiff, would be of the opinion that the article referred to him, the plaintiff's case is made out.[68]

[61] *Capital and Counties Bank v Henty and Sons* (1882) 7 App Cas 741.

[62] ibid, Lord Penzance (768), Lord Blackburn (772), Lord Watson (788) and Lord Bramwell (790); in dissent Lord Selborne LC found that an intention to injure the plaintiff was required (749).

[63] ibid, 772.

[64] Paul Mitchell, *The Making of the Modern Law of Defamation* (Hart Publishing, 2005) 109.

[65] *Emmens v Pottle* (1885) 16 QBD 354 (permitting a reasonable care defence in such situations).

[66] *Speight v Gosnay* (1891) 16 QBD 354 (only where publication to the third party was a natural (foreseeable?) consequence of the initial publication).

[67] *E Hulton & Co v Jones* [1909] 2 KB 444. The decision has been extensively criticised. See, for example, Paul Mitchell, *The Making of the Modern Law of Defamation* (Hart Publishing, 2005), who suggests the decision should be overturned (120–22).

[68] *E Hulton & Co v Jones* [1909] 2 KB 444, 454 (Alverstone CJ). Farwell LJ in the Court of Appeal seemed to adopt a slightly stricter standard, requiring that the defendant in a defamation case had to show an 'intention to libel the plaintiff'. This could be shown where the defendant clearly did intend to libel and damage the plaintiff, or alternatively was reckless, not caring whether or not the plaintiff

The House of Lords agreed. Lord Loreburn LC, with whom the other Law Lords agreed, noted:

> [A] person charged with libel cannot defend himself by showing that he intended in his own heart not to defame, or that he intended not to defame the plaintiff, if in fact he did both … a man in good faith may publish a libel, believing it to be true, and it may be found by the jury that he acted in good faith, believing it to be true, and reasonably believing it to be true, but that in fact the statement was false. Under those circumstances, he has no defence to the action, however excellent his intention.[69]

This decision seems somewhat to the contrary of the position of Farwell LJ in the Court of Appeal. That judge had emphasised that an action for defamation lay in cases where the defendant intended to defame the plaintiff, or was reckless as to the effect of his conduct on the plaintiff's reputation (reckless here meaning something more than negligence, in the sense of *Derry v Peek*). This is significant because two of the judges in the House of Lords, Atkinson and Gorell, expressly *agreed* with the position of Farwell LJ in the Court of Appeal.[70] Yet, they also expressed agreement with the judgment of Lord Loreburn LC in the case, a position opposed to that of Farwell LJ in finding liability without fault.

The defendant's intention would be implied from their acts, without the need to be proven. This precedent was later extended to cases where the general population would not be aware that the material referred to the plaintiff, but a third party armed with special knowledge (of which the defendant was unaware and ought not to have been aware) would know it so referred.[71]

This case deepened the attachment of the law of defamation to notions of strict liability.[72] Previous cases had determined that it was not necessary to prove that the defendant intended to publish material that was defamatory in nature. In *Jones*, the House of Lords accepted it was not necessary either to show that the defendant intended to defame the particular plaintiff concerned. This extension of the

would be ridiculed as a result (482–83). This clearly bears some comparison with the 'reckless' standard applied to the tort of deceit in *Derry v Peek* (1889) LR 14 App Cas 337, to which Farwell LJ referred in his judgment. Negligence is not sufficient to meet this requirement.

[69] *E Hulton & Co v Jones* [1910] AC 20, 23–24. For criticism of this passage see Allan Beever, *A Theory of Tort Liability* (Hart Publishing, 2016) 208: 'this is at least dangerously close to absolute liability. Lord Loreburn appears to have said that the fact that the plaintiff was injured is in itself decisive. That cannot be accepted … it is inappropriate to deal with this conflict by imposing strict liability'.

[70] *E Hulton & Co v Jones* [1910] AC 20, 25 (House of Lords); see Jeremiah Smith, '*Jones v Hulton*: Three Conflicting Judicial Views as to a Question of Defamation' (1912) 60 *University of Pennsylvania Law Review* 365.

[71] *Cassidy v Daily Mirror Newspapers Ltd* [1929] 2 KB 331, 354.

[72] Eric Descheemaeker, 'Protecting Reputation: Defamation and Negligence' (2009) 29 *Oxford Journal of Legal Studies* 603, 629: 'liability based on conclusively presumed malice really is strict liability: reference to fault is merely decorative because its presence or absence is immaterial. *Hulton v Jones* became authority for the proposition that liability in ordinary defamation (ie in situations not covered by privilege) is independent of malice, and generally of fault'.

strictness of the law of defamation has been criticised.[73] It was not justified in the judgments.[74]

Clearly, the development of the defences of absolute and qualified privilege served to ameliorate the strictness of the liability for defamation, as will be discussed below. However, another thing that tended to buttress the strictness of the liability was the insistence by the courts that in relation to qualified privilege, it was necessary for the defendant to show they had a duty to publish what they did, and the recipient/s an interest in receiving such information. This provided a viable defence for cases of individual defendants, but it proved to be very difficult for defendant media outlets to meet this test. It was irrelevant they had taken all reasonable care prior to the publication. As a result, their defences were extremely limited, which served to reinforce the strictness to which they were liable for publishing defamatory matter.[75]

Still today in the defamation law of the United Kingdom, it is not necessary for the plaintiff to show that the defendant was aware of the falsity of what was published, or was reckless or negligent with respect to its truth.[76] This is in sharp contrast to the position in the United States,[77] to be discussed below.

In Part III of the book, I considered the main rationales said to justify the imposition of strict liability. Most prominent of these is the so-called theory of enterprise risk, that the costs involved in an activity must be properly allocated to it, in order that the most efficient quantity of that activity will be produced. Thus, it was argued that when risks inherent in a particular activity materialise and cause loss or injury to others, the one who engaged in that activity should bear those costs, as part of the true costs of participating in that activity.

I have subjected that theory to considerable criticism in Chapter 6 and do not repeat that criticism here. In relation to defamation, the enterprise risk

[73] William Holdsworth, 'A Chapter of Accidents in the Law of Libel' (1951) 57 *Law Quarterly Review* 74, 84, concluding that the decision in *Jones* was wrong in not requiring proof that the defendant intended to defame the plaintiff.

[74] Paul Mitchell, *The Making of the Modern Law of Defamation* (Hart Publishing, 2005) 113: 'if there was a coherent rationale for the transition to strict liability [in *Hulton*] it did not appear in the cases'. I must respectfully disagree that *Hulton* changed the law as radically as might be suggested. I have discussed cases prior to *Hulton* that had apparently taken a strict liability view of defamation.

[75] Eric Descheemaeker, 'Three Errors in the *Defamation Act* 2013' (2015) 6 *Journal of European Tort Law* 24, 34.

[76] *E Hulton and Co v Jones* [1910] AC 20; Tony Weir, 'The Staggering March of Negligence' in Peter Cane and Jane Stapleton (eds), *The Law of Obligations: Essays in Celebration of John Fleming* (Clarendon, 1998) 115.

[77] Tony Weir, 'The Staggering March of Negligence' in Peter Cane and Jane Stapleton (eds), *The Law of Obligations: Essays in Celebration of John Fleming* (Clarendon, 1998) 115: 'it is actionable in [the United Kingdom] to say something disobliging about someone else although you reasonably believe it to be true and it causes no provable harm'; Vincent Johnson, 'Comparative Defamation Law: England and the United States' (2016) 24 *University of Miami International and Comparative Law Review* 1, 27. Section 1(1) of the Defamation Act 1996 (UK) provides for defences in some cases for those other than the author, editor or publisher of the defamatory material, as discussed below.

theory might be applied in particular to defendants that are media organisations (obviously, it would be more difficult to apply it in the case of an individual defendant). So, it might be argued that a media company publishes news and information to the public as part of its business. It is inherent in that model that, on occasion, it will damage the reputation of a person. The enterprise risk model would view this as a 'cost' of that business, which the media enterprise ought to bear, to ensure the most efficient level of media will be produced.

A major difficulty with any attempt to apply the enterprise risk model to media defendants in the defamation area is the common problem in economic theory of externalities. Simply, an externality in this context means a consequence of the events being considered that happens to those other than the immediate parties being considered. It is simply not the case, as the enterprise risk model would have it, that the media company should bear all the costs of producing the material because they obtain all of the benefits. This is incorrect – positive externalities are produced. Even more so than in the context discussed in Chapter 5 with enterprise generally, media enterprise activity (typically the focus of a defamation action) generates significant positive externalities. We all benefit from what media/entertainment companies do, in the production and dispersal of information and knowledge. They provide the essence for the kind of truth seeking, democratic self-government and self-actualisation theorised by Mill and others.[78] It is difficult, if not impossible, for an enterprise risk model (which supports the application of strict liability) to take account of these positive externalities. Freedom of speech is an essential public good.[79]

Strict Liability Elsewhere in the Common Law World

A range of positions is evident in the Australian law. This is partly explicable by the fact that, until 1963, the Australian High Court considered itself bound by decisions of the House of Lords.[80]

Initially, the position was taken that a defendant could not be liable for a defamation that occurred 'by accident'.[81] The example given was where the defendant made a statement intending to refer to one person, but some who heard it

[78] This was recognised in *Goodwin v United Kingdom* [1996] ECHR 16, [40] (Grand Chamber); see Anthony Gray, 'The Punishment of Journalists for Contempt for Refusing to Reveal Their Sources in Court' (2019) 29(2) *Journal of Judicial Administration* 60.

[79] See for discussion Paul Weiler, 'Defamation, Enterprise Liability and Freedom of Speech' (1967) 17 *University of Toronto Law Journal* 278, 310: 'if we attempt to utilize a theory of enterprise liability to justify strict liability in the law of defamation, then the resulting legal regime will exact its costs mainly from the domain of freedom of speech'. Weiler concludes that strict liability in defamation is unfair because it 'requires particular individuals to pay for the cost of preserving … social interests. They are singled out to bear this liability merely because they have done something society wants them to do, which is to engage in the process of self-governing via public debate and discussion (330).

[80] *Parker v The Queen* (1963) 110 CLR 610.

[81] *Godhard v James Inglis & Co Ltd* (1902) 2 CLR 79, 87.

understood it to be a reference to another person with the same name – in other words, a factual scenario very similar to that which was the subject of actual litigation in *Hulton v Jones*. In the Australian context, Griffith CJ for the High Court opined (in dicta) that no action for defamation would lie.

However, a different position was adopted in *Lee v Wilson and Mackinnon*.[82] Following the tenor of the House of Lords decision in *Hulton*, the court found that a defendant could be held liable in defamation although they did not intend to defame the plaintiff, instead intending to refer to another person with the same name. The defendant newspaper had published corruption allegations against 'Detective Lee'. There were other police officers with the last name Lee who argued they had been defamed. The High Court found in their favour, although there was no evidence the newspaper proprietor intended to refer to them in the publication.

The continuing strictness of liability for defamation was confirmed by the High Court of Australia in *Dow Jones and Co Inc v Gutnick*:

> The tort of defamation, at least as understood in Australia, focuses upon publications causing damage to reputation. It is a tort of strict liability in the sense that the defendant may be liable even though no injury to reputation was intended and the defendant acted with reasonable care.[83]

On the other hand, the High Court of Australia also recognised a defence of qualified privilege in relation to political communication, including communication about political matters, participants in political life etc.[84] In relation to that defence, the court stated that the defendant would have to demonstrate that publication of the particular matter was reasonable in the circumstances.[85] Relevant to that issue would be questions such as the extent to which the defendant took steps, prior to publication, to verify the accuracy of what it published, had reasonable grounds for believing the truth of what was published, and did not believe the imputation was untrue. It would also be relevant whether the publisher sought to approach the plaintiff for their response to the story, and gave the plaintiff a chance to respond after it was published.[86] To that extent, fault considerations could be relevant to an action based on allegedly defamatory statements.

There is a lengthy history of defamation legislation in Australia. The first instance is the Defamation Act 1889 (Qld). Section 16 contains an 'excuse' for

[82] *Lee v Wilson and Mackinnon* (1934) 51 CLR 276.

[83] *Dow Jones and Co Inc v Gutnick* (2002) 210 CLR 575, 600 (Gleeson CJ McHugh Gummow and Hayne JJ); Patrick George, *Defamation Law in Australia* (2nd edn, LexisNexis Butterworths, 2012) 411: 'it has since been generally accepted as a matter of principle that liability is imposed strictly without fault, whether or not the words are defamatory on their face. It has been no defence at common law that the defendant did not intend to injure the plaintiff's reputation and acted with reasonable care'.

[84] *Theophanous v Herald and Weekly Times Ltd* (1994) 182 CLR 104; *Lange v Australian Broadcasting Corporation* (1997) 189 CLR 520.

[85] *Theophanous v Herald and Weekly Times Ltd* (1994) 182 CLR 104, 137 (Mason CJ, Toohey and Gaudron JJ), with whom Deane J agreed (188); *Lange v Australian Broadcasting Corporation* (1997) 189 CLR 520, 573 (all members of the Court).

[86] *Lange v Australian Broadcasting Corporation* (1997) 189 CLR 520, 574 (all members of the Court).

defamatory matter. This excuse applied in various situations of publication in good faith. Most importantly, s16(e) provided an excuse for publication made in good faith for the purposes of providing information to the person to whom it was made where the publisher reasonably believes the recipient has an interest in that subject matter. According to the section, this would make publication 'reasonable' in the circumstances, and not actionable. Section 16(2) states that publication will be in good faith if it is 'reasonably sufficient for the occasion', not actuated by ill-will or other improper motive, and not where the publisher believes the material published is false. This model was subsequently adapted by other Australian states. The reasonableness of the publisher's conduct was defined to include consideration of whether they took reasonable care to check the veracity of sources. The extent of this defence based on the 'reasonableness' of the publication has existed in some form since 1889 in Australian statute law.[87]

In Canada, the Supreme Court has also recognised a defence of responsible journalism. In *Grant v Torstar* the court emphasised the importance in such cases of the defendant demonstrating the extent to which they took reasonable steps to verify the truth of what they published prior to doing so.[88] The Canadian Supreme Court has also taken the position that it is possible that a negligence action could arise for conduct involving the making of allegedly defamatory statements.[89] In other words, the boundary between the torts of defamation and negligence was not watertight.

Fault Considerations in UK Defamation Law

> If there is one tort which would have benefited from the introduction of the rules of negligence, it is defamation.[90]

Notwithstanding the significant evidence of strictness of liability for defamation, this began to be undercut. This occurred primarily through the recognition of defences, known as privilege, in defamation law. Many of these had a basis in something approaching lack of fault, or blameworthiness. Thus, the tort is unusual in being premised on a strict liability basis (malice being required, but readily implied, and presumed against the defendant), but which permits defences largely based on the fact that the defendant is not morally blameworthy for what occurred.

[87] Eric Descheemaeker, '"A Man Must Take Care Not to Defame His Neighbour": The Origins and Significance of the Defence of Responsible Publication' (2015) 34(2) *University of Queensland Law Journal* 239, 254–58.

[88] *Peter Grant v Torstar Corporation* [2009] 3 SCR 640.

[89] *Young v Bella* [2006] 1 SCR 108, 134 (McLachlin CJ and Binnie J, for the Court). New Zealand courts have taken a contrary position: *Bell-Booth Group v Attorney-General* [1989] 3 NZLR 148 (CA); *Balfour v Attorney-General* [1991] 1 NZLR 519 (CA); *Midland Metals Overseas Pty Ltd v Christchurch Press Co Ltd* [2002] NZLR 289 (CA).

[90] Tony Weir, 'The Staggering March of Negligence' in Peter Cane and Jane Stapleton (eds), *The Law of Obligations: Essays in Celebration of John Fleming* (Clarendon, 1998) 115.

This makes it somewhat difficult to classify defamation as a strict liability tort, as the High Court of Australia did in *Dow Jones*. It is better described as a somewhat unsatisfactory hybrid of strict liability and fault-based principles currently coexisting in the same tort.[91]

In an extremely enlightening and important work, Descheemaeker identifies five examples in UK law where fault-based considerations 'intruded' on the apparently strict liability tort of defamation.[92] He applauds this development. He views the existing position of the tort of defamation as somewhat anomalous in its (part) strict liability position. This has the effect of unjustifiably reifying reputation interests above other interests, in his view. He says that

> [i]f we consider unintentional fault to be the default minimum threshold for redress when a right has been infringed – which is observably true, not simply in modern English law but historically across the divide between the civilian tradition and the common law – then the same standard should apply, at least prima facie, to reputation.[93]

I gratefully adopt his examples for the purposes of discussion here. I should clarify that despite the examples discussed below, it is still accurate to describe the UK law of defamation as primarily strict in nature.[94]

Innocent Dissemination Defence

The court in *Emmens v Pottle*[95] had to determine the question of the liability of the seller of a newspaper for a defamatory article which appeared in it. The plaintiff sought to make the defendant liable. The Court of Appeal disagreed. Lord Esher MR stated that the defendants did not know that the article contained defamatory material, and there was nothing which ought to have made them aware of that fact, had they exercised reasonable care. Lord Esher MR said it would be unjust and unreasonable to find a defendant liable in such a situation.[96] This case would form the basis of an innocent dissemination defence in the law of the United Kingdom.[97] Now a person has a defence if they can show that they are not the author, editor

[91] Paul Mitchell, *The Making of the Modern Law of Defamation* (Hart Publishing, 2005) 101: 'the function of fault in the modern law of defamation … is fragmentary and unprincipled'.

[92] Eric Descheemaeker, 'Protecting Reputation: Defamation and Negligence' (2009) 29 *Oxford Journal of Legal Studies* 603, 627–39.

[93] Eric Descheemaeker, '"A Man Must Take Care Not to Defame His Neighbour": The Origins and Significance of the Defence of Responsible Publication' (2015) 34 *University of Queensland Law Journal* 239, 263. As evidence of the civilian tradition, he cites Article 1382 of the French Civil Code, which uses fault as the general basis of liability to another.

[94] Paul Mitchell, *The Making of the Modern Law of Defamation* (Hart Publishing, 2005) 120.

[95] *Emmens v Pottle* (1885) 16 QBD 354. Cotton LJ concurred, and Bowen LJ expressed very similar sentiments.

[96] ibid, 357.

[97] Defamation Act 1996 (UK), s1(1), protecting a person who took reasonable care in relation to publication of the defamatory material, and did not know or have reason to believe the material was defamatory. The defence does not apply to an 'author, editor or publisher' of the relevant material, but the s1(3) definition of publisher makes it clear that a person who merely prints, produces, distributes or

or publisher of the relevant statement, took reasonable care in relation to its publication, and had no reason to believe that the material was defamatory. There are obvious and close analogies with the law of negligence here.

Offer to Make Amends

Another way in which the apparent strictness of the law of defamation was ameliorated was the introduction of the offer to make amends process found in s4 of the Defamation Act 1952 (UK). This legislation applies where the defendant argues that they published the defamatory material innocently. Descheemaeker describes s4 as 'an excellent example of the imposition of a negligence standard of liability on the law of defamation, in an area from where it had previously been absent'.[98] The Defamation Act 1996 (UK), ss2–4, expand the offer to make amends process, applicable to any occasion on which an allegedly false statement was published. Section 4 states that where the offer to make amends is refused, this is a defence to the defamation action. An exception to this applies where the defendant knew or had reason to believe that the material was both false and defamatory. However, the law presumes that this is not the case, unless the plaintiff can prove otherwise. Again, the phrase 'had reason to believe' clearly alludes to fault.[99] Descheemaeker says that two enactments 'provide, through the recognition of a fault-shaped defence, another very clear illustration of the infiltration of ideas of negligence in an area previously dominated by strict liability'.[100]

Liability for Repetition of Defamation

A question has arisen as to the liability, if any, of a defendant for subsequent repetition of defamation they originally published. In the nineteenth century, this liability was described in terms of whether such repetition was a 'natural consequence'

sells something containing the defamatory material is not, for that reason, to be considered a 'publisher' in this context. To like effect, see s32(1) of the Defamation Act 2005 (NSW). Australia has a system of uniform defamation laws, with states and territories agreeing to pass uniform laws. Thus, (unusually) a reference to the statutory defamation law in one state can be taken as indicative of the law in Australia. Section 32 states that a defendant is not liable as a 'subordinate distributor' where it neither knew nor reasonably ought to have known that the material published was defamatory, and their lack of knowledge was not due to negligence on their part. Difficulties have arisen with questions as to whether tech companies can avail themselves of these defences: see Anthony Gray, 'The Liability of Search Engines and Tech Companies in Defamation Law' (2019) 27 *Tort Law Review* 18 for a discussion of the relevant UK and Australian decisions.

[98] Eric Descheemaeker, 'Protecting Reputation: Defamation and Negligence' (2009) 29 *Oxford Journal of Legal Studies* 603, 630.

[99] Descheemaeker, ibid, 631, states that this provision means the defendant 'will escape liability if [they] cannot be shown to have reached a certain degree of fault in respect of the ingredients of [their] prima facie liability'.

[100] ibid, 632.

of the defendant's actions.[101] This is clearly somewhat analogous to a reasonable foreseeability fault-based standard used in negligence. In more recent decisions involving this area, the court has expressed liability in such circumstances in terms of negligence.[102] Descheemaeker describes the latter case as 'another apparent illustration of the way the rules of negligence have been interfering with the tort of defamation'.[103]

Negligent Defamation

At one time, English courts had shown real reluctance to breach the boundaries separating the tort of defamation from other torts.[104] However, a different approach was taken in the House of Lords decision in *Spring v Guardian Assurance Plc*.[105] The plaintiff had previously worked for the defendant. When the plaintiff sought to obtain employment elsewhere, their would-be new employer asked the defendant for a reference about the plaintiff. The defendant provided such a reference but it contained suggestions that the plaintiff had been dishonest, which were not true. The plan to offer the plaintiff employment fell through. The plaintiff discovered the content of the reference and brought legal action against the defendant alleging defamation, negligence and other causes of action. It was established that the defamation action was not viable because the circumstances of the communication attracted qualified privilege, and there was no suggestion the defendant had acted in malice. This made the question of the possible action in negligence very important, in terms of the practical ability of the plaintiff to obtain a remedy for the incorrect reference.

At the time, English law applied a two-stage test in determining whether a duty of care was owed in negligence. The first stage was based on the concept of reasonable foreseeability – whether the defendant could have reasonably foreseen damage or injury to the plaintiff as a likely or possible result of their activity. The second stage was a policy question – whether the potential duty of care established in stage one should be negatived due to reasons of public policy.[106] The House of

[101] *Speight v Gosnay* (1891) 60 LJQB 231, 232 (Lopes LJ).

[102] *Slipper v BBC* [1991] 1 QB 283, 295 (Stocker LJ) and 298 (Bingham LJ).

[103] Eric Descheemaeker, 'Protecting Reputation: Defamation and Negligence' (2009) 29 *Oxford Journal of Legal Studies* 603, 634.

[104] *Lonrho Plc and Others v Fayed and Others (No 5)* [1991] 1 WLR 1489, 1495: 'the established rules in defamation as to privilege and fair comment could not be side-stepped by pleading the case in negligence and asserting a duty of care to speak the truth when making a statement' (Dillon LJ); 1509 (Evans LJ) (CA).

[105] *Spring v Guardian Assurance Plc* [1995] 2 AC 296.

[106] *Anns v Merton London Borough Council* [1978] AC 728, 752 (Lord Wilberforce). Subsequently a three-stage approach to questions of duty of care would arise, considering (a) whether the injury to the plaintiff was reasonably foreseeable; (b) whether a relationship of neighbourhood or proximity existed between plaintiff and defendant; and (c) whether it was fair and just that the law should impose a duty of care upon the defendant in such circumstances: *Caparo Industries v Dickman* [1990] 2 AC 605, 617–18.

Lords had accepted that a duty of care arose in respect of statements that resulted in economic loss to another, at least in circumstances where the defendant had assumed a responsibility to provide particular information or advice, where the plaintiff had relied on such advice to their detriment.[107] In *Spring*, a majority of the court, Lord Keith dissenting, found that the first stage had been satisfied in the current case, and no policy reasons existed to deny the duty of care existed.

Most importantly for current purposes, a majority of the court found there was no public policy reason for denying that an employer asked to provide a reference for a former employee owed a duty of care to the employee in doing so. It was not relevant that, if an inaccurate and damaging reference was provided, the plaintiff might not have a remedy in defamation, due to the qualified privilege defence. The majority in *Spring* held that the position in the tort of defamation was irrelevant to the question of the position in the tort of negligence.[108] The court expressly countenanced the possibility that the tort of defamation may become less important over time, as negligence continued to expand in scope.[109]

The other noticeable aspect of the judgments is the recognition of the advantage of the tort of negligence in such cases, as opposed to the tort of defamation. The judges clearly believed that to deny the plaintiff a remedy, in circumstances where an inaccurate and highly damaging reference had been provided about them by the defendant, would be substantially unjust. Yet, according to the qualified privilege defence as it stood at the time, the plaintiff would be denied a remedy because they could not demonstrate that the defendant's actions were malicious. The judges were clearly uncomfortable with this result and saw that the tort of negligence could provide a practical remedy for the plaintiff wronged in such a way, in a way that the tort of defamation could not.

An example of this reasoning appears in the judgment of Lord Woolf:

> Because of the defence of qualified privilege, before an action for defamation can succeed … it is necessary to establish malice. In my judgment the result of this requirement is that an action for defamation provides a wholly inadequate remedy for an employee who is caused damage by a reference which due to negligence is inaccurate. This is because it places a wholly disproportionate burden on the employee. Malice is extremely difficult to establish … without an action for negligence the employee may, therefore, be left with no practical prospect of redress, even though the reference may have permanently prevented him from obtaining employment in his chosen vocation. If the law provides a remedy for references which are inaccurate due to carelessness, this would be beneficial.[110]

[107] *Hedley Byrne and Co Ltd v Heller and Partners Ltd* [1964] AC 465.

[108] *Spring v Guardian Assurance Plc* [1995] 2 AC 296, 324 (Lord Goff), 325 (Lord Lowry), 334 (Lord Slynn), 351 (Lord Woolf).

[109] 'It may be that there will be less resort to these torts because a more realistic approach on the basis of a duty of care is adopted' (referring to the torts of defamation and malicious falsehood): ibid, 337 (Lord Slynn).

[110] ibid, 346, to like effect Lord Slynn (337).

Obviously, if the plaintiff were to proceed in negligence, they would need to demonstrate they had suffered loss as a result of a breach of the duty of care, unlike the position in defamation.

Descheemaeker describes the case as a 'perfect example of the law expressing its uneasiness in respect of the "more than ordinary negligence" standard of liability which defamation applies to situations covered by privilege'.[111]

Responsible Journalism

The fifth way in which Descheemaeker describes the law of defamation as moving towards fault principles occurs in the context of responsible journalism. In the past, it had been held that newspapers were not entitled to avail themselves of qualified privilege around publishing matters of public interest.[112] They could not fit within the duty–interest requirement imposed by the courts in respect of qualified privilege. It is possible that UK law could have developed the duty–interest test so that it could apply to cases of mass communication involving the media, providing the media with stronger protection from defamation actions, but it did not so develop.

However, the House of Lords in *Reynolds v Times Newspapers Ltd*[113] developed the concept of a 'right to know'. Lord Nicholls provided 10 factors that would assist in determining whether the defendant publisher could rely on a defence of qualified privilege on this basis.[114] Some of them, including the steps taken to verify the information published, and whether the plaintiff was given an opportunity to comment and/or rebut allegations made, as well as the tone of the article, seem to relate to the question of the reasonableness of the publication of the material.[115] In this way, some of the harshness of the otherwise strict liability of media outlets for publishing defamatory material was diluted through an embrace of fault-based principles in relation to a possible defence to the action.

In *Loutchansky v Times Newspapers (Nos 2–5)*, Lord Phillips (for the Court of Appeal) spoke of the *Reynolds* privilege in terms of responsible journalism.[116]

[111] Eric Descheemaeker, 'Protecting Reputation: Defamation and Negligence' (2009) 29 *Oxford Journal of Legal Studies* 603, 636.

[112] *Blackshaw v Lord* [1984] QB 1, 26: 'no privilege attaches … to a statement on a matter of public interest believed by the publisher to be true in relation to which he has exercised reasonable care'.

[113] *Reynolds v Times Newspapers Ltd* [2001] 2 AC 127.

[114] ibid, 205.

[115] Eric Descheemaeker, '"A Man Must Take Care Not to Defame His Neighbour": The Origins and Significance of the Defence of Responsible Publication' (2015) 34 *University of Queensland Law Journal* 239, 240: 'the underlying idea (of *Reynolds*, and the statutory enactment of a version of it) is clear enough: the defence will operate on condition of reasonableness of conduct. It is a plea of diligence or, to put the same idea differently, of lack of negligence. In recognizing the plea "but it wasn't my fault", the defence recognizes that lack of fault (culpa) operates to – literally – exculpate the defendant'. He sees this as a welcome uniting between torts based around personality (where historically fault concepts were irrelevant) with other areas of tort law, where fault was dominant (241).

[116] *Loutchansky v Times Newspapers (Nos 2–5)* [2002] QB 783.

He indicated the duty to publish could only arise when the publisher had acted responsibly.[117] He found that the existence of 'carelessness, impulsiveness or irrationality' might mean that the qualified privilege defence could not apply.[118]

Descheemaeker concludes on these developments:

> Responsible journalism may, or may not, in this instance, be synonymous with the taking of reasonable care; but it is clear from *Loutchansky* that it cannot be very different. Structurally, the interest of the *Reynolds* defence is that it is entirely fault-shaped … apart from the onus of proof … publications coming within the scope of the Reynolds defence are not subject to an almost pure negligence claim.[119]

Section 4 of the Defamation Act 2013 (UK) would subsequently re-enact a version of this defence, focused on the reasonableness of the belief of the defendant that publication was in the public interest.[120] This is a departure from the early drafts of that legislation, which kept more closely to the iteration of it by Lord Nicholls in *Reynolds*. Noticeably, the reasonableness relates to the belief that publication is in the public interest, not the belief that the material is true. This may be less significant than it sounds.[121] At least in Australia, the High Court has explained that relevant to the issue of the reasonableness of the belief that publication was in the public interest was the question of the reasonableness of the belief that the material was true.[122]

Summarising these developments, Descheemaeker is more emphatic:

> *Reynolds* and its subsequent developments represent … by far the largest and more direct superimposition of an essentially negligence standard of liability onto an area of the law which had always been premised on a different model, that of malice … we have almost completely lost sight of the fact that defamation was meant to be rooted in a different, and higher, form of fault … following *Reynolds* and the *Defamation Act* 2013 (UK) we now have a third standard of liability operating within the law of defamation which is fault-based – in the sense of negligence or culpa … a defence of great practical importance … is rooted in the different paradigm of reasonableness of conduct now sits firmly at the centre of the modern English law of defamation. The foundations of the law have now decisively moved away from its original controlling principle, malicious intent.[123]

[117] ibid, 807.

[118] ibid, 807.

[119] Eric Descheemaeker, 'Protecting Reputation: Defamation and Negligence' (2009) 29 *Oxford Journal of Legal Studies* 603, 639.

[120] *Serafin v Malkiewicz and Others* [2020] 1 WLR 2455.

[121] Eric Descheemaeker, '"A Man Must Take Care Not to Defame His Neighbour": The Origins and Significance of the Defence of Responsible Publication' (2015) 34 *University of Queensland Law Journal* 239, 250.

[122] *Lange v Australian Broadcasting Corporation* (1997) 189 CLR 520, 574 (all members of the Court).

[123] Eric Descheemaeker, '"A Man Must Take Care Not to Defame His Neighbour": The Origins and Significance of the Defence of Responsible Publication' (2015) 34 *University of Queensland Law Journal* 239, 260–61.

More Recent Cases and Statutory Amendment

Since the publication of Descheemaeker's article, there have been further examples of the use of negligence-like concepts in the law of defamation. For example, in *Stocker v Stocker*, in determining whether or not words were defamatory, the court considered how an 'ordinary, reasonable' person would construe the words.[124] This is obviously analogous to the reasonable person in negligence law.

The English Court of Appeal has found that an organisation providing an online platform on which bloggers could place posts was not a publisher of the relevant material for the purposes of the law of defamation.[125] The court has suggested that it may be different if the allegedly defamatory material is brought to the attention of the host provider, and after a reasonable time the provider has not responded satisfactorily – this might be to remove the material, or take steps to determine its veracity.[126] Cases have emphasised that, in order to be considered a 'publisher' for the purposes of defamation law, a mental element is necessary.[127] This is a further step away from imposing strict liability on tech companies who might innocently provide access to material that is argued to be defamatory.

Further, s1(1) of the Defamation Act 2013 (UK) now requires that no action is available for defamation unless the material published has caused or is likely to cause serious harm to the plaintiff's reputation.[128] This moves defamation law somewhat closer to negligence principles again. Clearly, proof of actual loss is essential in a negligence action. In the past, defamation was mostly actionable per se, without the need to prove loss. By amending the law so that now actual harm (or likely harm) is necessary, the law of defamation is closer to requirements in negligence, without being the same.

Considering the first five developments listed here, Descheemaeker concludes that

> [o]ver the course of the past century, the English law of defamation has seen a massive, if typically under-recognized, infiltration of the principles of negligence in a tort which had previously been defined – and whose rules had developed – in isolation from it. This can be taken to reflect the law's growing dissatisfaction with the modern paradigm of defamation. This paradigm is that liability for injuring someone's reputation unjustifiably is ordinarily strict; but in protecting (privileged) situations, the standard of liability is shifted up to malice … there seems to be a gradual convergence towards negligence-culpa as the standard of liability, the main tool for this being the creation or

[124] *Stocker v Stocker* [2020] AC 593, 605 (Lord Kerr, with whom Lord Reed, Lady Black, Lord Briggs and Lord Kitchin agreed).

[125] *Tamiz v Google Inc* [2013] 1 WLR 2151.

[126] This suggestion is based on a possible analogy with the bulletin board notice at issue in *Byrne v Deane* [1937] 1 KB 818. See now s5 Defamation Act 2013 (UK).

[127] *Metropolitan International Schools Ltd v Designtechnica Corp* [2011] 1 WLR 1743, 1745 (Eady J); *Bunt v Tilley* [2007] 1 WLR 1243, 1249 referring to the need for awareness or an assumption of responsibility by the defendant in order to make them liable.

[128] *Lachaux v Independent Print Ltd* [2020] AC 612.

> extension of fault-shaped defences in a wrong which is prima facie situational … the trend is very clear and the exceptional (the taking into account of culpa in defamation actions) less and less exceptional.[129]

Descheemaeker agrees that the 'courts' intuition, which surfaces in many cases, that culpa is – at least prima facie – the right degree of fault to rely on, is correct'.[130]

Mitchell discusses another way in which the law of negligence impacted on the law of defamation.[131] The pivotal period was the late nineteenth century. A central character in these developments was Lord Esher MR. Mitchell points out that in *Heaven v Pender* in 1882,[132] Lord Esher MR (dissenting) constructed a generalised duty of care for the tort of negligence. It would of course find full expression in 1932's *Donoghue v Stevenson*.[133] Its development may have been assisted by the insistence of the House of Lords that in action for the tort of deceit, it was necessary to demonstrate that the defendant knew of, or was reckless as to, the falsity of the statement that they made.[134]

Mitchell says that these developments elsewhere in the law of tort were pivotal in the development of one of the principles of defamation law – the articulation of the basis upon which qualified privilege might exist. There had been different approaches evident earlier in the nineteenth century on this question. Some courts had said that it existed where there was a lack of malice on the defendant's part. Others said it existed when a duty–interest relationship could be established, in terms of a duty on the defendant to communicate what they did, and an interest in the recipient in receiving it. By the late nineteenth century, the court settled upon the latter view in *Pullman v Walter Hill & Co*,[135] including a judgment by Lord Esher MR, who had authored the famous dissent in *Heaven*. Mitchell explains that Esher MR had originally taken the lack of malice view of qualified privilege, before adopting the duty–interest view in *Pullman*. He states that this important change of heart was influenced by developments in negligence:

> At precisely the time when his views about duty in the defence of qualified privilege were changing, Lord Esher MR was formulating a brilliant and original approach to duty in the tort of negligence. This may of course be a coincidence. However, the striking feature about his ideas on a general duty of care in negligence was that it required the courts to say when a duty arose in any given factual situation. The scope of the tort of negligence would be regulated by means of this control device. Similarly, the scope of qualified privilege after *Pullman* … was determined by the court's identification of a duty (or interest). In both cases the duty seems to be based on objective moral considerations. In qualified privilege the defendant's sense of duty is insufficient to found a defence; as

[129] Eric Descheemaeker, 'Protecting Reputation: Defamation and Negligence' (2009) 29 *Oxford Journal of Legal Studies* 603, 639–40.

[130] ibid, 641.

[131] Paul Mitchell, 'Duties, Interests and Motives: Privileged Occasions in Defamation' (1998) 18 *Oxford Journal of Legal Studies* 381.

[132] *Heaven v Pender* (1883) 11 QBD 503.

[133] *Donoghue v Stevenson* [1932] AC 562.

[134] *Derry v Peek* (1889) LR 14 App Cas 337.

[135] *Pullman v Walter Hill & Co* [1891] 1 QB 524.

> for negligence, his Lordship began his discussion in Heaven by asserting that 'every one ought by the universally recognized rules of right and wrong, to think with so much regard for the safety of others who may be jeopardized by his conduct'. These similarities suggest that Lord Esher's assertion of objective duties and interests in *Pullman* … may well have been influenced by his exposition of duty in negligence.[136]

Part of the unsatisfactory nature of the law of defamation as it currently stands is the confusing mix of strict liability and fault principles. While originally it was a strict liability tort, over the course of centuries the law has accepted the need for consideration of fault-like factors. Rather than fundamentally reassessing the actual tort, this has been accommodated by a grafting on to the law of defamation of fault-like principles through the various defences. Various UK statutes have also made piecemeal efforts at reform.[137] The result is an untidy hotch-potch. There is strong academic support for a fundamental reorienting of this tort to reflect its contemporary effective fault basis.[138] The American law has taken some steps in this direction. It is to a consideration of these developments that we now turn.

Introduction of Fault and Negligence Principles to American Defamation Law

There is some early evidence supporting adoption of a position of strict liability for defamation. For example, Holmes J for the Supreme Court quoted with evident approval the statement of Lord Mansfield in *R v Woodfall* (discussed above) that whatever a person publishes, they do so 'at their peril', in the classic language of a strict liability tort.[139] This strictness if also evident in the Restatements.[140]

[136] Paul Mitchell, 'Duties, Interests and Motives: Privileged Occasions in Defamation' (1998) 18 *Oxford Journal of Legal Studies* 381, 406–07.

[137] *Lachaux v Independent Print Ltd* [2020] AC 612, 619 where the word 'piecemeal' is used to describe statutory reforms (Lord Sumption, with whom Lords Kerr, Wilson, Hodge and Briggs agreed).

[138] Allan Beever, *A Theory of Tort Liability* (Hart Publishing, 2016) 210: 'there are three possible torts of defamation: one resembling trespass, one resembling the torts of indirect control and one resembling negligence. The problem is that we have only the first when that is the only one that we should not have. The two that we do not have are the ones that we need. In practice … this difficulty is ameliorated by the fact that the elements of liability for injury are imported into the law through the back door … the result is an incoherent form of liability … liability ought to be determined in accordance with targeting [intention] or fault'; 218: 'the law adopts the wrong form of liability, trespass-like strict liability. This is inappropriate because defamation cases do not involve one person directly exercising control over another … this calls for a major overhaul of the law of defamation'.

[139] *Peck v Tribune Co* 214 US 185, 189 (1909) (for the Court): 'if the publication was libellous the defendant took the risk … as was said of such matters by Lord Mansfield, "whatever a man publishes, he publishes at his own peril" (*R v Woodfall*) … the reason is plain. A libel is harmful on its face. If a man sees fit to publish manifestly hurtful statements concerning an individual, without other justification than exists for an advertisement or a piece of news, the usual principle of tort will make him liable if the statements are false or are true only of someone else'.

[140] *Restatement (First) of Torts* (1938) s580 states that 'one who publishes defamatory matter of another is not relieved of liability because (a) he did not intend the matter so published to be defamatory and neither knew nor by the exercise of every possible precaution could have known that it would be so understood'.

However, there is evidence that some courts took a different path, at least in some instances. For example, in the context of the question of the liability of broadcasters for defamatory material they put to air, the broadcasters argued they were innocent of wrongdoing. Courts in Pennsylvania and New Jersey applied a negligence, fault-based standard to determine questions of their liability in such cases, asking whether the broadcasters could have avoided publishing defamatory material if they had exercised reasonable care.[141] There was evidence of the relevance of the 'reasonableness' of the publication too in earlier decisions. In *Carpenter v Bailey*, it was said that 'when the occasion is proper, one may be excused for stating what proves to be untrue, if he had probable cause to believe it true … [ie] with a belief, founded on reasonable grounds'.[142]

The *Restatement (Second) of Torts* recognised a defence of qualified privilege in relation to statements directed towards the apprehension of those suspected of criminal behaviour, matters of public concern, including relating to honesty in public office and those seeking it, relating to advocacy for social reform,[143] and the interests of the publisher.[144] State defamation laws typically provided for various circumstances of privilege, often reflecting the Restatement. Absolute privilege would typically extend to discussion in the judicial, executive and legislative realm. To the extent that this position was not abrogated by the Supreme Court's subsequent holdings, described below, defamation continues to be regulated by state law, and the states can continue to reflect privilege defences as they see fit.

The US Supreme Court moved the law in a different direction in *New York Times Co v Sullivan*.[145] In this landmark decision, the newspaper published an advertisement which contained serious allegations of wrongdoing against members of the police department. The immediate context was a civil rights demonstration. Though the advertisement did not specifically name the defendant, the defendant submitted that readers would identify him as one of the subjects of the advertisement, since he was one of the three elected police commissioners in the relevant city at the time. Sullivan brought action against the publishers of the newspaper, arguing that the advertisement that they published was defamatory of him. The newspaper raised a constitutional defence. The First Amendment to the United States Constitution guarantees the freedom of the press, and freedom of speech generally, from intrusion.

The Supreme Court reasserted the fundamental importance of free speech in a democracy. It required room for robust discussion of issues. Discussions may on

[141] *Summit Hotel Co v National Broadcasting Co* 336 Pa. 182, 8 A. 2d 302 (1939); *Kelly v Hoffman* 137 N.J.L. 695; 61 A. 2d. 143 (1948); see Robert Leflar, 'Radio and TV Defamation: Fault or Strict Liability' (1954) 15 *Ohio State Law Journal* 252, 255–58.

[142] *Carpenter v Bailey* 53 NH 590 (1873).

[143] *Restatement (Second) of Torts* (1977) s598.

[144] See for discussion Richard Barnes, 'The Constitutional Fault Test of *Gertz v Robert Welch Inc* and the Continued Viability of the Common Law Privilege in the Law of Defamation' (1978) 20 *Arizona Law Review* 799, 810–21.

[145] *New York Times Co v Sullivan* 376 US 254 (1964).

occasion be highly critical, offensive and/or unpleasant. They may be exaggerated in nature and not true, or not entirely true. Nevertheless, they were entitled to constitutional protection. It was irrelevant that the material may not be true, may not be popular or was of questionable social utility. The freedom required breathing space in order to flourish.

The Supreme Court then significantly changed defamation law by creating a special rule around 'public officials'. It stated:

> The constitutional guarantees require, we think, a federal rule that prohibits a public official from recovering damages for a defamatory falsehood relating to his official conduct unless he proves that the statement was made with 'actual malice' – that is, with knowledge that it is false or with reckless disregard of whether it is false or not.[146]

This use of the word 'malice' was different from the previous understanding of the word. Previously, it had been thought to mean something like improper purpose. In *New York Times* the court viewed it as publishing something knowing it was false, or with reckless disregard of that fact.[147]

The court stated that the burden of proof would be on the public official claiming they had been defamed to show malice or fault on the part of the defendant. This enacted a substantial change to defamation law, which had previously required a defendant to make out particular defences, which were in some cases based around 'innocence'. On the facts, the plaintiff lost the case. They could not show that the publishers of the *New York Times* were motivated by malice. No evidence suggested that the publishers were aware of the falsity of the allegations.

Goldberg, Black and Douglas JJ concurred in the joint reasons, but would have gone further. They supported an absolute right (with no exceptions) of an individual to discuss public officials in relation to their public duties. They also suggested that this absolute protection would extend to discussion of 'public affairs', as being critical to the fundamental constitutional notion of self-government.

Many questions remained unanswered by the Supreme Court's decision in *Sullivan*. It was not entirely clear what was meant by 'public officials' and whether the precedent would be expanded to a broader category of would-be plaintiffs.

The *Sullivan* precedent was expanded to discussion of 'public figures', as well as 'public officials', in *Curtis Publishing Co v Butts*.[148] The case involved allegations that a football coach had fixed a game. The court found that the *Sullivan* precedent applied to the coach. He was a 'public figure', being someone who was a 'non-public person who was nevertheless intimately involved in the resolution

[146] ibid, 279–80 (Brennan J, for Warren CJ, Clark, Harlan, Stewart and White JJ); Goldberg, Black and Douglas JJ concurring. Another potentially applicable tort here is that of the intentional infliction of emotional distress. However, that tort has been held to also be subject to a First Amendment-protected speech defence: *Snyder v Phelps* 562 US 443 (2011).

[147] That there is a material difference between the two tests is confirmed in *Greenbelt Co-op Publishing Association Inc v Bresler* 398 US 6, 10 (1970) (Stewart J, for the Court).

[148] *Curtis Publishing Co v Butts* 388 US 130 (1967).

of important public questions, or by reason of their fame, shape events in areas of concern to society at large'.[149]

The *Sullivan* precedent was expanded again to discussions about a private figure, if the statements concerned matters of general or public interest, in *Rosenbloom v Metromedia Inc.*[150] The court rejected the apparently rigid distinction between public and private figures arrived at in *New York Times*. This was partly on the basis that it was believed that public figures would have ready recourse to alternative channels of communication to refute allegations made about them, or negative commentary. These avenues were typically not available to private figures, justifying greater legal protection of their reputation, in the view of the court in *New York Times*. However, this was rejected in *Rosenbloom*. The court there dismissed them as 'unproved and highly improbable generalizations'.[151] According to the court in *Rosenbloom*, all defamation plaintiffs, in cases involving discussion of matters of general or public interest, would have to demonstrate malice, in the *New York Times* sense, in order to obtain a remedy.

Marshall J, with whom Stewart J joined, wrote an important dissenting judgment. He found that states were free to develop their own laws of defamation, provided they did not impose strict liability. He reasoned that, to permit that, would have 'the effect of imposing liability without fault is to place the printed or spoken word with the use of explosives or the keeping of dangerous animals'.[152]

The Supreme Court reconsidered its position in *Gertz v Robert Welsh Inc.*[153] The case involved a family seeking compensation after a police officer had killed their child. They were legally represented by the plaintiff. A magazine published by the defendant published a story which alleged that the plaintiff was attempting to bring communism to the United Sates, was either a communist or socialist, and that he had a criminal record. All of these statements were false. The magazine had made no effort to ascertain whether or not its allegations were true. The plaintiff sued the defendant for defamation. The defendant raised the defence that the plaintiff was a public figure, so the malice requirement applied. The defendant claimed there was no evidence they were actuated by malice.

The Supreme Court in *Gertz* walked back from part of its finding in *Rosenbloom*. Specifically, the court rejected the extension of the *New York Times* principle to private figures. The joint reasons found that there was sense in the distinction between public figures and non-public figures. The former would typically have access to channels of communication to refute untrue allegations or comments made about them.

[149] ibid, 164 (Warren CJ, concurring in the result).
[150] *Rosenbloom v Metromedia Inc* 403 US 29 (1971).
[151] ibid, 63
[152] ibid, 86–87.
[153] *Gertz v Robert Welsh Inc.* 418 US 323 (1974).

The court adopted the views of Marshall J in *Rosenbloom* with respect to strict liability. States were free to develop their own laws of defamation, provided they did not impose strict liability. The court expressed concern that the imposition of such liability upon publishers would unduly 'chill' the freedom of speech that was fundamental to a democracy.[154] Thus, it agreed with Marshall J that states should be free to define for themselves their law of defamation, subject to the baseline requirement that strict liability should not be imposed upon defendants. The imposition of strict liability upon a publisher unless they could demonstrate the truth of their factual assertions would lead to 'intolerable self-censorship'.[155] It added, however, that where states departed from the *New York Times* malice standard, they could not provide for recovery of punitive or aggravated damages. In such cases, recovery would be limited to what could be proven as actual loss.[156] Subsequently, it was clarified that the *Gertz* holding only applies to matters of public concern.[157]

The court has subsequently further clarified that in the context of *New York Times*, the word 'malice' has a special meaning. It is not sufficient to show that the defendant was negligent in publishing what they did. It meant either that the defendant knew the material it published was false, or it was reckless, not caring whether or not what it published was false.[158] This was a higher standard than (mere) negligence.[159] It was subjective, not objective.[160]

Finally, it should be noted that the distinction between public officials and non-public officials has been justified on the presumed ability of the former to access channels of communication to refute negative press about them. While at one time this might have been sensible, of course the media landscape has vastly changed today. The ubiquitous nature of social media has enabled anyone to communicate messages broadly.[161] It may be that at some stage, the US Supreme

[154] ibid, 340 (Powell J, with whom Stewart Marshall Blackmun and Rehnquist JJ agreed).

[155] ibid, 340.

[156] ibid, 350.

[157] *Dun and Bradstreet Inc v Greenmoss Builders Inc* 472 US 749 (1985).

[158] ibid.

[159] For criticism that the concept of 'malice' is inappropriate in the context of the United States, and its presence or otherwise irrelevant to the values that the First Amendment seeks to uphold, see Richard Barnes, 'The Constitutional Fault Test of *Gertz v Robert Welch Inc* and the Continued Viability of the Common Law Privileges in the Law of Defamation' (1978) 20 *Arizona Law Review* 799, 805–06: 'whether society has a legitimate interest in protecting the expression of these ideas should not depend on the motive of their speaker, but on their persuasive character and content. Where the statement is false and the defamer should reasonably have known it to be so, the purpose of promoting free discussion of ideas has been abused to a greater degree than where the statement is made with all reasonable care, but the defamer does not like the person about whom he or she speaks. If what is desired is the opportunity for society to choose knowledgeably from among competing ideas, then the motive of the speaker should not be of as much concern as the factual basis of the idea'.

[160] Vincent Johnson, 'Comparative Defamation Law: England and the United States' (2016) 24 *University of Miami International and Comparative Law Review* 1, 33.

[161] Aaron Perzanowski, 'Relative Access to Corrective Speech: A New Test for Requiring Actual Malice' (2006) 94 *California Law Review* 833.

Court may need to rethink the sharp distinction between public officials and non-public officials as it relates to the law of defamation because the factual basis that underlay this distinction no longer holds.

As indicated, the Supreme Court in *Gertz* permitted states to legislate with respect to defamation in a manner they saw fit, provided they did not legislate a strict liability standard.[162] A majority of states have adopted a simple negligence standard to determine such claims.[163] For example, it might be necessary that the plaintiff in a defamation case demonstrate that the defendant was negligent in publishing because it did not take reasonable steps to ascertain the truth of what it published.[164] Smith argues this area of the law has been undertheorised and suggests a range of factors that should govern the application of negligence principles in the defamation context.[165]

This summary of the US law indicates a complicated web. Fault has intruded into the law of defamation, but only to a limited extent. If the case involves discussion of a public official or public figure, actual malice in the *New York Times* sense is required in order to claim compensation for defamation. If the case does not involve discussion of a public official or public figure, individual states can regulate the matter as they see fit, provided they do not apply strict liability principles. In other words, it will be necessary for the plaintiff to prove some fault on the defendant's part. This will typically be a failure to take reasonable steps to ascertain the truth of what was published. However, as indicated above, provided the state law is consistent with these Supreme Court rulings, state law continues to regulate defamation law, and defamation actions, including the extent of privilege, can be regulated in different ways across the states.

There is substantial academic support for a simplifying of American defamation law, to apply the fault standard. For example, McNulty states that

> [t]he adoption of a fault standard to all defamation actions and the abrogation of conditional privileges would lend much needed uniformity and simplicity to defamation law. Fault is a conventional tort concept with which courts are well-acquainted … the conditional privilege/improper purpose system is a part of the strict liability heritage of the

[162] Dissenting in the result, White J describes the majority decision in *Gertz* as reflecting a 'deep-seated antipathy to liability without fault' (389).

[163] Marc Franklin, 'What Does Negligence Mean in Negligence Cases?' (1983) 6(2) *Hastings Communications and Entertainment Law Journal* 259, 266.

[164] For a fuller discussion of what 'reasonable steps' might entail see Lachland H Bloom Jr, 'Proof of Fault in Media Defamation Litigation' (1985) 38 *Vanderbilt Law Review* 247.

[165] Gerald Smith, 'Of Malice and Men: The Law of Defamation' (1992) 27 *Valparaiso University Law Review* 39, 80–82. He states relevant factors should include the utility of the publication in terms of free speech values, the status of the defendant – a media publisher might be given more leeway than someone simply engaged in gossip, the importance of the information having regard to the public interest and to the likely audience, the magnitude of the foreseeable harm from publication – this would depend on the nature of the allegation, and how widely it was disseminated, and comparing the defendant's actions with how a reasonable person would have acted in the circumstances, including the extent to which they investigated the truth of the material published, and the extent to which it was reasonably possible to do so.

> common law of defamation which a system based on fault effectively replaces. Conditional privileges therefore lose their reason for existence … a fault standard related to falsity more effectively balances the competing interests of reputation and freedom of speech.[166]

Page Keeton takes a similar view:

> If, as a prerequisite to recovery in any case, the law had required some kind of fault with respect to the truth or falsity of the intentional defamation communicated, then there would have been little pressure or need to create the many defences in order to get a proper balance in furthering the two opposing legitimate state interests or protecting reputation and free speech.[167]

Reflections

It may be that a tort such as negligence, with its emphasis on reasonableness of behaviour, is better able to weigh the important competing public policy considerations in this context, such as freedom of speech and a person's reputation, than a strict liability tort of defamation, with defences grafted on to try to ameliorate the resulting harshness and rigidity by introducing essentially fault-based concepts.[168]

Barnes reaches a similar conclusion:

> There are two principal arguments for a uniform negligence system. The first is that adoption of a test giving relief to a person injured by the negligent use of words would lend uniformity to tort law which recognizes liability for physical injury based on negligence. The second reason is that the qualified privilege is an exceptional legal entity, born of the recognition of the harshness of the common law strict liability for defamation. Its origin predates the concept of negligence, and its central reason for existence is no longer present … [the *Gertz* decision] was a reaction against the common law system which restricted the exchange of ideas. This recognition of the value of free

[166] Patrick McNulty, 'The *Gertz* Fault Standard and the Common Law of Defamation: An Argument for Predictability of Result and Certainty of Expectation' (1985) 35 *Drake Law Review* 51, 89–90. He concludes that (100): 'the extension of the fault requirement to other aspects of a defendant's conduct … would complete the modernization of the law of defamation. The tort action would be based, as most other torts are, on the concepts of fault and foreseeability which form the cornerstone of the modern tort system. No longer would scholastic disquisitions on malice be necessary, no longer would burdens of proof shift back and forth; no longer would judicial value judgments on what constitutes a matter of public concern be necessary; no longer would speakers and publishers publish at their peril. Instead, there would be a rule of broad applicability and, concomitantly, predictability of result and certainty of expectation. The fog and fictions which have enveloped the tort of defamation will be lifted, if not dissipated'.

[167] Page Keeton, 'Defamation and Freedom of the Press' (1976) 54 *Texas Law Review* 1221, 1232. See also Paul Weiler, 'Defamation, Enterprise Liability and Freedom of Speech' (1967) 17 *University of Toronto Law Journal* 278, 322: 'a rational system of law delineating liability for defamation in the public sphere would focus on the faulty character of the defendant's conduct'.

[168] Paul Weiler, 'Defamation, Enterprise Liability and Freedom of Speech' (1967) 17 *University of Toronto Law Journal* 278, 285.

> speech led to the elimination of strict liability and the substitution of a new standard of fault to be determined by the states … when the common law of defamation originated, it was logical to see the common law privileges' purpose as the elimination of presumed malice. This alleviated the harshness of strict liability … since that time the United States Supreme Court has begun to phrase the test of liability in terms of due care. Now that *Gertz* has forced the states to impose liability only upon some showing of fault, there exists the opportunity to consider whether the attitude of the defendant should continue to be important in deciding the value of certain communications. *Gertz* has made less harsh the common law of defamation and indicated that society's interests in a free exchange of ideas is greater than the individual's interest in being free from defamation, at least where there is no fault connected with the defamation … [and] an extra step extending this reform to the confusing qualified privilege is desirable.[169]

Paul Mitchell questions whether the decision of the House of Lords in *Jones*, that a defendant can be liable for innocently, unintentionally and non-negligently defaming another, remains appropriate today. He points out that the trend in today's law of tort is to judge professionals by the reasonable care standard, and there is no good reason why journalists (for they and their employers are prime targets of defamation) should be the subject of a different, stricter regime. He continues:

> At the time of the decision in *Jones* … the general principle of liability for negligence had not been acknowledged [this would occur in *Donoghue v Stevenson* in 1932], and recognition that professional liability should be governed by that principle was over thirty years away [citing *Hedley Byrne v Heller and Partners*]. Today, however, there is no good reason why journalists should be treated differently; liability in damages should turn on negligence. In the United States, it already does. The best way to strike the balance between the media and claimants … is to make liability in damages depend on fault; reshaping the law in this way would be doing no more than repeating the balancing process that the courts used in *Jones* … the preferable option [for law reform] would be to formulate a test that … was sensitive to the factual matrix. The standard of reasonable care is admirably suited to this role: assessing whether the defendant has failed to act with reasonable care involves the delicate balancing of a range of factors. For instance, the high degree of harm that is likely to result from widespread publication would call for a higher standard of care than when the publication is to a limited audience, the professional skills and expertise of media defendants would require them to go to greater lengths to verify the accuracy of statements than non-professional speakers … a praiseworthy motive, such as the exposure of corruption, might justify taking an otherwise unjustifiable risk of defaming the claimant. The court could take all relevant factors into account … the position set out in *Jones* no longer deserves support … a standard of reasonable care, by contrast, would be flexible, fair and in line with the level of conduct generally demanded in tort.[170]

[169] Richard Barnes, 'The Constitutional Fault Test of *Gertz v Robert Welch Inc* and the Continued Viability of the Common Law Privileges in the Law of Defamation' (1978) 20 *Arizona Law Review* 799, 822–23.

[170] Paul Mitchell, *The Making of the Modern Law of Defamation* (Hart Publishing, 2005) 121–22.

Conclusion

In some ways, the tort of defamation has followed a path quite familiar in the context of this book. In the common law, it was established as a tort of strict liability, not requiring fault on the part of the defendant publisher. This became more prominent as the need to prove the existence of malice reduced in importance through implications and assumptions. However, over time it was recognised that the strictness of the liability could lead to great injustice. Thus, it was necessary to craft defences into the law of defamation, in the case law and through statute. These exonerated defendants in particular situations. A common theme through these various exceptions are exculpating conditions, based on the reasonableness of the defendant's behaviour, in terms of being an innocent disseminator or a publisher who had made reasonable inquiries as to the truth of what it published, prior to doing so. In addition, cases that involved defamation were also being decided based on the tort of negligence.

It is hard to believe that, if someone sought to design the law of defamation today, they would design this system, with the development of common law principles across various courts involving strict liability, the development of common law fault-based defences to otherwise strict liability, and then various statutory amendments and reforms over the years. Thus, the question whether defamation law is a tort of strict liability or not cannot easily be answered. It is, but then it is not. Negligence, fault-based principles continue to intrude.

From a broad lens, one wonders why it is not better to start again with this tort, recognising the fault of the defendant as one of the prima facie requirements of liability, rather than in a piecemeal way trying to incorporate some aspects through the back door of defences. The American courts provide some kind of example here, drawing the line at the imposition of strict liability on defendants for publishing material found to be defamatory. It is an intellectual commitment to a fault basis of liability that is supported here. As Mitchell says, the existing position, where professional publishers are essentially held to a standard higher than that applicable to other professionals, is anomalous and indefensible.

9

Trespass and Fault

The boundaries between trespass and fault-based negligence are in some ways less troublesome than the boundaries between negligence and nuisance, negligence and defamation, and negligence and *Rylands v Fletcher*. Thus, the discussion in this chapter can be more attenuated. There are fewer cases where problems arise in relation to an acceptable boundary between trespass and negligence. This is largely because trespass is traditionally seen as an intention-based tort, unlike nuisance, defamation or *Rylands v Fletcher* (or negligence).

Obviously, the distinction in the past between trespass and case looms large in this discussion. At one time, the important distinction was between direct injury to another (trespass) and indirect injury to another (case). Plaintiffs could be non-suited if they chose the incorrect form of action. The court began to apply a more flexible attitude to this matter, permitting a plaintiff to proceed with an action on the case regardless of whether the injury was consequential or direct.[1] Further reform followed with the Common Law Procedure Act 1852 (UK), through which plaintiffs were no longer required to specify a particular form of action. Where plaintiffs have a choice, some advantages of trespass remain, including the burden of proof upon the defendant to demonstrate lack of intention and lack of negligence, and the fact it is not necessary to demonstrate that a duty of care was owed, or breached.[2] It is traditionally held that trespass is actionable per se, without any proof of damage necessary,[3] in sharp contrast with an action for negligence, where damage is the gist of the action. Traditionally, whether or not a trespass, if committed, was 'reasonable' or not was irrelevant to liability.

One issue that the law did have to grapple with was whether an action for trespass could exist where there was evidence that the injury that the defendant allegedly caused the plaintiff was unintentional. Cases such as *Weaver v Ward*,[4] *Leame v Bray*[5]

[1] *Williams v Holland* (1833) 10 Bing. 112; 131 ER 848.

[2] Percy Winfield and Arthur Goodhart, 'Trespass and Negligence' (1933) 49 *Law Quarterly Review* 359, 359.

[3] *Ashley v Chief Constable of Sussex Police* [2008] 1 AC 962, 985–86 (Lord Rodger).

[4] *Weaver v Ward* (1617) Hob. 134, 80 ER 234 where the court allowed a defence to a trespass to the person action in cases where the injury to the plaintiff occurred 'utterly without (the defendant's fault'.

[5] *Leame v Bray* (1803) 3 East 593, 599; 102 ER 724, 726 where Lord Ellenborough CJ indicated that provided the injury inflicted was direct, rather than indirect, 'it is immaterial whether the injury be wilful or not'. I will interpret the word 'wilful' to have a meaning analogous to intentional. Grose J agreed, saying the critical factor for a trespass action was the directness of the injury inflicted. It was

and *Underwood v Hewson*[6] suggest that such action could exist in trespass, provided the injury was direct. The question of the defendant's intention was treated in these cases as irrelevant.[7]

However, other decisions appeared to point in a different direction. In *Cole v Turner*, Holt CJ suggested that where a defendant touched the plaintiff in a narrow passage way 'without any violence or design of harm', no action in trespass would lie.[8] In *Williams v Holland* it was held that an action on the case lay for unintentional injury.[9] It remained somewhat unclear whether an action for trespass lay in such cases.

In *Holmes v Mather*[10] the plaintiff was injured in a highway accident in circumstances indicating that the defendant did not intend to harm the plaintiff. The jury found that the defendant had not been negligent. In such circumstances, the court found that no action could lie for trespass. Baron Bramwell indicated that an action for trespass would lie in cases of either wilful (intentional) injury to the plaintiff on the defendant's part, or negligence.[11] He also supported a negligence standard to liability, opining (at least in the highway context) that 'For the convenience of mankind in carrying on the affairs of life, people as they go along roads must expect, or put up with, such mischief as reasonable care on the part of others cannot avoid'.[12] This comment is particularly interesting, coming from one of the judges in *Rylands* most insistent upon application of concepts of strict, no-fault liability in that context.

In *Stanley v Powell*[13] Denman J stated that, in order to successfully bring an action in trespass, the plaintiff would have to show either that the defendant had intentionally harmed them, or were negligent in doing so, in order to succeed. At this point, it is clear that in cases of negligent battery, for example, the plaintiff had the option of proceeding either in trespass or negligence.

In *Fowler v Lanning*,[14] Lord Diplock again considered the matter. He agreed with the position expressed in *Holmes* and *Stanley* and determined that an action for trespass to the person required proof *either* that the defendant intended to

irrelevant whether the injury occurred 'accidentally or by misfortune' (3 East 593, 600; 102 ER 724, 727). Lawrence J agreed that in trespass actions, the 'design' of the defendant was irrelevant to liability (3 East 593, 601; 102 ER 724, 727).

[6] *Underwood v Hewson* (1723) 1 Str. 596; 93 ER 722. The headnote to this case simply states that 'trespass lies for an accidental hurt'.

[7] Christine Beuermann, 'Are The Torts of Trespass to the Person Obsolete? Part I: Historical Development' (2018) 25 *Tort Law Review* 103, 109: 'it can … be seen that, at the very least, whether the defendant intended to interfere with the plaintiff's personal security or intended to harm the plaintiff was not initially a relevant consideration for the courts when imposing liability for trespass to the person'.

[8] *Cole v Turner* (1704) Holt KB 108; 80 ER 958.

[9] *Williams v Holland* (1883) 10 Bing. 112.

[10] *Holmes v Mather* (1875) LR 10 Ex. 261.

[11] ibid, 268–69.

[12] ibid, 267.

[13] *Stanley v Powell* [1891] 1 KB 86.

[14] *Fowler v Lanning* [1959] QB 426.

cause the injury to the plaintiff, *or* that their negligence caused such injury. In *either* event, according to Lord Diplock, a trespass action was available. The distinction between an action in trespass and one in negligence could be practically important in terms of differing onuses of proof, requirements for demonstrated damage, and different limitation periods.

The English Court of Appeal considered the matter in *Letang v Cooper*.[15] Here the distinction was critical because the limitations legislation did in fact prescribe different limitation periods, according to whether the matter was brought in trespass or negligence. Here the court went further than Lord Diplock had done in *Fowler*, providing more clarity of division between the torts. Lord Denning MR, with whom Danckwerts LJ agreed,[16] stated that if the defendant was alleged to have intentionally caused the plaintiff injury, the action was properly in trespass. If the defendant was alleged to have unintentionally caused the plaintiff injury, the action was properly in negligence.[17] Lord Denning simultaneously reinterpreted the long-standing division between the tort of trespass and the tort of negligence. He acknowledged that originally the division was between injury caused to the plaintiff directly (trespass) and that caused indirectly (negligence). However, he said that today, the distinction between trespass and negligence lay not in questions of directness but according to the defendant's intention, trespass being appropriate in cases of allegedly intentional injury to the plaintiff caused by the defendant, and negligence in cases of allegedly unintentional injury to the plaintiff caused by the defendant.

In *Wilson v Pringle*, the Court of Appeal re-confirmed that in cases of unintentional injury to another, the action could only be brought for the tort of negligence, not the tort of trespass.[18]

The law in Australia developed in a partly similar manner to that of the United Kingdom, albeit over a reduced time frame. So in *Williams v Milotin*[19] the facts involved a case brought by the plaintiff after he was struck by a vehicle driven allegedly negligently by the defendant. There was no question that the defendant had deliberately done so. Here, all members of the High Court found that the action was properly brought in trespass, though it could also have been brought in negligence.[20] Further, the court stated that if there were evidence that the defendant had deliberately run the plaintiff down, their only claim would have been in trespass. This was essentially the position taken by Diplock J in *Fowler v Lanning*, permitting an action in trespass where *either* the defendant had intentionally injured the plaintiff *or* where as a result of their negligence, they had done so.

[15] *Letang v Cooper* [1965] QB 232.

[16] The other judge was Lord Diplock, who adhered to his position in *Fowler* to the effect that a plaintiff could bring an action for trespass for unintentional injury, but he said that in such cases, Lord Denning MR was correct in stating that in such cases, the tort of negligence was 'preferred' (ibid, 243).

[17] ibid, 239.

[18] *Wilson v Pringle* [1987] 1 QB 237, 246 (Croom-Johnson J, for the Court).

[19] *Williams v Milotin* (1957) 97 CLR 465.

[20] ibid, 470 (Dixon CJ, McTiernan, Williams, Webb and Kitto J).

A similar position appears in the judgment of Windeyer J in *McHale v Watson*.[21] Thus, the Australian courts have not taken the step taken by the English Court of Appeal in *Letang v Cooper*.[22] Indeed, in *Gray v Motor Accident Commission*, four justices of the High Court of Australia in dicta comments accepted the possibility of a negligence action being based on intentional wrongdoing.[23]

Convergence of Trespass and Negligence – Case Law

Concepts of 'reasonableness' are most readily seen in the law of trespass to the person in relation to the defences available to someone who has prima facie committed a trespass. There is an obvious connection between notions of reasonableness and fault-based negligence liability, as noted by Weir.[24]

One example of this occurs in the context of the defence of self-defence. What would otherwise be an actionable trespass will not be such if the defendant can show they acted in self-defence. The court has framed this defence in terms of whether the defendant honestly *and reasonably believed* that what they did was necessary to protect themselves.[25]

A second example occurs in the context of the defence of 'exigencies of everyday life'.[26] The courts have established that what would otherwise be a trespass to the person is not such if the contact with the defendant was part of common interaction among individuals. Common examples might include touching someone

[21] *McHale v Watson* (1964) 111 CLR 384, 388, Windeyer J stating that in a case of alleged trespass to the person, the defendant would be liable if the evidence demonstrated either that they intended to strike the plaintiff, or that they were negligent in acting as they did.

[22] Peter Handford, 'Intentional Negligence: A Contradiction in Terms? (2010) 32 *Sydney Law Review* 29, 41. He notes that Canada, similarly, has not taken this step. On the Canadian position, see *Cook v Lewis* [1951] 3 SCR 830 (trespass available either for intentional or negligent wrongdoing); Lewis Klar, 'Intentional and Negligent Trespass: It Is Time to Clarify the Law' (2004) 28 *Advocate Quarterly* 410.

[23] *Gray v Motor Accident Commission* (1998) 196 CLR 1, 9: 'there can be cases, framed in negligence, in which the defendant can be shown to have acted consciously in contumelious disregard of the rights of the plaintiff' (Gleeson CJ, McHugh, Gummow, and Hayne JJ); see similarly *New South Wales v Lepore* (2003) 212 CLR 511, 572 (McHugh J), *cf* Gummow and Hayne JJ (602–03); Peter Handford, 'Intentional Negligence: A Contradiction in Terms?' (2010) 32 *Sydney Law Review* 29, 54: 'there is now ample authority, at least in Australia, for saying that the tort of negligence is applicable to harm caused intentionally, whether directly or indirectly, and it has been shown that the roots of this incursion of negligence into the realms of intention go back many years'. This is a reference to acceptance of an action on the case for intentional wrongdoing in *Bird v Holbrook* (1828) 4 Bing. 628, 641–42; 130 ER 911, 916 (Best CJ).

[24] Tony Weir, 'The Staggering March of Negligence' in Peter Cane and Jane Stapleton (eds), *The Law of Obligations: Essays in Celebration of John Fleming* (Clarendon, 1998) 102: 'when we find a modification of the rules of liability so as to impose liability when, and only when, the conduct is unreasonable or the harm foreseeable, we may take it that the tort of negligence is having an influence'.

[25] *Ashley v Chief Constable of Sussex Police* [2008] 1 AC 962, 974 (Lord Scott), 990 (Lord Carswell), 992 (Lord Neuberger).

[26] *Collins v Willock* [1984] 1 WLR 1172, 1177 (Goff LJ).

on the shoulder to get their attention, someone patting another on the back as a recognition of good work or an admonition to 'keep going', or inadvertent touching on public transport. None of these would be actionable trespasses because the courts have recognised that such technical trespasses are, in other words, reasonable. The otherwise strictness of the rules of trespass to the person is tempered by the realities of life, where some give and take is necessary to permit society to function and for people to act as reasonable people do. This defence might explain the reference to the need for an assault or battery to be 'hostile' in order to be actionable.[27] Stevens identifies that this requirement of 'hostility' effectively makes trespass to the person fault based.[28]

A similar principle has been applied to situations where the plaintiff occupies premises near a public thoroughfare and suffers injury or damage through the use of that thoroughfare by the public. Here, the ordinary application of strict liability in trespass or nuisance is again ameliorated. Somewhat ironically, this sentiment appears in the judgment of Blackburn J in *Rylands v Fletcher*:

> Traffic on the highway, whether by land or sea, cannot be conducted without exposing those whose persons or property are near to it some inevitable risk; and that being so, those who go on the highway or have their property adjacent to it may well be held to do so subject to their taking upon themselves the risk of injury from that inevitable danger, and persons who by the licence of the owner pass near to warehouses where goods are being raised or lowered, certainly do so subject to the inevitable risk of accident. In neither case, therefore, can they recover without proof of want of care or skill occasioning the accident, and it is believed that all the cases in which inevitable accident has been held an excuse for what prima facie was a trespass, can be explained on the same principle.[29]

A third example relates to cases of 'necessity'. The House of Lords held that what would otherwise be a claim for trespass or nuisance would be defeated if the defendant could make out a case of 'necessity'. This was held in a case where a ship discharged some of its oil cargo in order to prevent it breaking up and sinking, which may have caused loss of life. The plaintiff's property nearby suffered damage caused by the oil slick. The House of Lords said that a defence of necessity would defeat an action by the plaintiff for trespass or nuisance unless there was evidence that the defendant had acted negligently.[30]

[27] *Wilson v Pringle* [1987] 1 QB 237, 250 (Croom-Johnson LJ, for the Court) (CA).

[28] Robert Stevens, *Torts and Rights* (Oxford University Press, 2007) 101. Stevens is critical of this development.

[29] *Rylands v Fletcher* (1865) LR 2 Ex. 265, 286–87; similar sentiments appear in *River Wear Commissioners v Adamson* (1877) 2 App Cas 743, 767 (Lord Blackburn).

[30] *Southport Corporation v Esso Petroleum Co Ltd* [1953] AC 218, 228 (Devlin J, as the trial judge); confirmed on appeal to the House of Lords, who expressed agreement with the judgment of Devlin J: 235 (Earl Jowitt), 238 (Lord Normand agreeing with the others), 241 (Lord Morton), 242 (Lord Radcliffe) ('since it seems to be conceded that it would be a defence to such a claim to show that the discharge of the oil was reasonably necessary to prevent loss of life in the ship's crew unless the [defendant's] own carelessness had brought about the danger of that loss'). This analysis was applied in *Rigby v Chief Constable of Northamptonshire* [1985] QB 1242, 1253–54 (Taylor J).

First, the defence of consent is a common one. What might otherwise amount to a battery will not do so if there is evidence that it took place with the plaintiff's consent. A common factual scenario in this context is the defendant administering medical treatment to the plaintiff. This would otherwise amount to a battery but the defendant argues that the plaintiff consented to the medical procedure. Often, the conflict between the parties involves the extent to which the defendant made the plaintiff aware of the risks of the medical treatment; in other words, the question of informed consent. In this common situation, there is substantial evidence of the courts preferring to deal with such matters through the principles of the tort of negligence, as opposed to the tort of trespass.[31] In the routine application of the principles of negligence, the question whether the defendant acted in accordance with a respectable body of professional opinion would, of course, be extremely important,[32] as orthodox principles of negligence would typically suggest.

These sentiments have also been applied in the context of trespass to land. The House of Lords has confirmed that what would otherwise amount to a trespass on property is not so where it can be shown that it is a reasonable use of the relevant land which does not unduly restrict public right to egress through the area.[33]

In a trespass to goods action, Diplock LJ reflected on the 'intrusion' of fault principles into trespass to land actions, traditionally considered to involve strict liability:

> The plaintiff's cause of action for interference to their property in goods lies in trespass – a cause of action which traditionally did not necessarily involve blameworthiness on the part of the defendant. The development of the common law in the last thirty years, however, has tended towards equating civil liability with conduct which right-minded men in contemporary society would regard as blameworthy and towards protecting those who act reasonably in intended performance of what right-minded men would deem a duty to their fellow men.[34]

[31] *Reibl v Hughes* [1980] 2 SCR 880, 891–92: 'in situations where the allegation is that attendant risks which should have been disclosed were not communicated to the patient and yet the surgery or other medical treatment carried out was that to which the plaintiff consented … a failure to disclose the attendant risks, however serious, should go to negligence rather than battery' (Laskin CJ, for the Court); *Montgomery v Lancashire Health Board* [2015] AC 1430, 1468 (Baroness Hale); *Rogers v Whitaker* (1992) 175 CLR 479; *Chappell v Hart* (1998) 195 CLR 232.

[32] *Bolam v Friern Hospital Management Committee* [1975] 1 WLR 582; *F v West Berkshire HA* [1990] 2 AC 1, 52 (Lord Bridge): 'the action taken must be such as a reasonable person would in all the circumstances, take, acting in the best interests of the assisted person' (Lord Goff, 75). Lord Jauncey agreed with both judgments (83).

[33] *Director of Public Prosecutions v Jones* [1999] AC 240, 254: 'provided these activities are reasonable, do not involve the commission of a public or private nuisance, and do not amount to an obstruction of the highway unreasonably impeding the primary right of the general public to pass and repass, they should not constitute a trespass' (Lord Irvine), 274 ('an assembly which was not obstructive and which was otherwise lawful [is] a reasonable and usual use of the highway … because the activity was in itself a reasonable one. So it should not be regarded as a trespassory assembly' (Lord Hope), 280 (Lord Clyde), 292–93 (Lord Hutton).

[34] *Chic Fashions (West Wales) v Jones* [1968] 2 QB 299, 315 (CA).

Convergence between Trespass and Negligence – Academic Views

Beuermann's assessment of the development of the tort of trespass is that there is clear evidence of convergence between it and the tort of negligence. She notes that there is evidence that negligence has been incorporated into trespass actions, in particular through defences such as necessity, or that cases that previously would have been considered trespass cases have now been transferred to the negligence column (for instance, cases of 'negligent trespass'). She says that those areas of trespass that have not embraced negligence in either of these ways have been required to 'struggle on with old methods that continue to prove ineffective', citing the defence of 'exigencies of everyday life' as an example.

Beuermann says that the law of trespass has evolved substantially. Historically, it was concerned with the simple fact that the defendant caused the plaintiff injury. However, over time it became more sophisticated, seeking to take into account the totality of the circumstances and to balance the competing interests often involved in such cases. She says that the tort of negligence is better able to manage these competing interests, and this explains the increased use of negligence principles in what would traditionally be regarded as instances of trespass.

She says that, even in cases of intentional injury, apparently the preserve of trespass after the decision in *Williams v Holland*, negligence fault principles have become important. Thus considered, she says there is no longer anything distinct about the trespass action, and declared it obsolete:

> To the extent that the courts have sought to continually improve the balancing techniques employed in the torts of trespass to the person (assault, battery and false imprisonment), it might now be argued that the torts of trespass to the person have been overtaken by the tort of negligence. As with other forms of outdated technology, the torts of trespass to the person are now best viewed as obsolete. It follows that liability for all interferences with personal security should not be determined in accordance with the tort of negligence.[35]

She considers several advantages of such a development. First, it would create certainty and consistency in the law. She indicates that, through the defence to trespass actions of 'exigencies of everyday life', effectively the trespass action has become fault based in any event. She says that although the conduct may be intentional, and thus traditionally dealt with under supposed strict liability principles of trespass, it would be better for any interference with the personal security of another, whether intentional, reckless or negligent, to attract prima facie liability, subject to a balancing of the competing interests involved. She suggests that the

[35] Christine Beuermann, 'Are the Torts of Trespass to the Person Obsolete? Part 2: Continued Evolution' (2018) 26 *Tort Law Review* 6, 17. This was not the first occasion on which such a suggestion had been made: Maurice Millner, 'The Retreat of Trespass' (1965) 18 *Current Legal Problems* 20, 30.

question of intention might remain relevant because the balancing, in the case of intentional wrongdoing, might occur differently from the balancing in cases of (mere) negligence.

She lauds the negligence standard as being the one best able to carry out the necessary balancing. This is because it permits such factors as are relevant to the plaintiff, including the seriousness of the injury and its likelihood, to be balanced against factors relevant to the defendant, including whether they have acted as a reasonable person would, the extent to which it would have been reasonable for them to have taken precautions etc. Beuermann says the negligence standard is superior to the 'exigencies of everyday life' principle in permitting this balancing to occur.[36]

She concedes that it might be thought that introducing intentional conduct under the umbrella of negligence might appear to be a contradiction in terms since negligence is typically seen as involving the defendant unintentionally injuring the plaintiff. However, she says it should be taken more to refer to the kind of balancing of considerations she favours, as opposed to being confined to cases of unintentional conduct.

It should be noted that an example of what Beuermann favours originally appeared in the area of the tort of infliction of emotional injury. There had been an attempt to assimilate this tort,[37] usually considered to require an intention on the defendant's part to inflict such injury, into the law of negligence.[38] However, recently the Supreme Court of the United Kingdom rejected such a move, firmly establishing the tort as an intention-based tort quite separate, in the court's view, from the tort of negligence.[39] The so-called economic torts continue to require an element of intention to establish an actionable tort.[40]

Further support for the convergence theory appears in the judgment of highly regarded McPherson JA in the Supreme Court of Queensland decision of *Carrier v Bonham*:[41]

> Most everyday acts of what we call actionable negligence are in fact wholly or partly a product of intentional conduct. Driving a motor vehicle at high speed through a residential area is an intentional act even if injuring people or property on the way is not a result actually intended. Wilkinson v Downton is an example of that kind … even if [the defendant] did not intend to inflict the harm on [the plaintiff] that followed … he was plainly negligent as regards the result that followed … since the Judicature Act which,

[36] Christine Beuermann, 'Are the Torts of Trespass to the Person Obsolete? Part 2: Continued Evolution' (2018) 26 *Tort Law Review* 6, 14–16.

[37] *Wilkinson v Downton* [1897] 2 QB 57.

[38] *Wainwright v Home Office* [2004] 2 AC 406, 435 (Lord Hoffmann).

[39] *O v Rhodes and Another* [2016] AC 219, 254 (Baroness Hale and Lord Toulson, with whom Lords Clarke and Wilson agreed); 259 (Lord Neuberger, with whom Lord Wilson agreed); Anthony Gray, '*Wilkinson v Downton*: New Work for an Old Tort to Do?' (2015) 23 *Tort Law Review* 127.

[40] *OBG v Allan* [2008] 1 AC 1, 29–31 (Lord Hoffmann), 57 and 62 (Lord Nicholls), 74 (Lord Walker), 86 (Baroness Hale), 91 (Lord Brown); Anthony Gray, 'Change the Rules: Reform of the Economic Torts in Australia' (2020) 21(2) *Flinders Law Journal* 295.

[41] *Carrier v Bonham* [2002] 1 QdR 474.

> in Maitland's famous phrase, buried the forms of action, it no longer matters whether the act was done intentionally or negligently, or partly one and partly the other. What matters is whether the consequences of the conduct, whether foreseen or not, were reasonably foreseeable and are such as should have been averted or avoided. What we really have now is not two distinct torts of trespass and negligence, but a single tort of failing to use reasonable care to avoid damage however caused. Negligence, if narrowly understood, is something of a misnomer.[42]

McPherson JA referred back to the Roman position of *Lex Aquilina*. It embraced the concept of culpa, which he said referred to conduct that was considered blameworthy.[43] This concept did not distinguish between intentional and unintentional acts. It is possible that, at least through today's eyes, the sporadic use of the concept of intention in the law of tort is by and large a throwback to its historical intertwining with crime. Though intention was, and remains, critical in the criminal law, it makes much less sense in the civil law realm and might be better avoided altogether, or at least minimised. These ideas appealed to leading Australian tort scholar Peter Handford.[44] He said that harm-based trespass to the person or trespass to property had been 'effectively subsumed under the rubric of negligence'.[45]

Perhaps it is time to base liability in tort generally around the concept of fault.[46] This is what Article 1382 of the French Civil Code does.[47] Fault might be established by way of demonstrating negligence or by establishing intention. It is useful, to some extent, to retain the distinction between unintentional and intentional conduct in the law of tort. It has a long tradition in the law of tort.[48] It might justify a different level of liability in the law of tort in at least three respects. First, it might justify liability in circumstances where, under the law of negligence, no recovery would be permitted.[49] Examples here include the tort of interference with business relations and the so-called economic torts more generally,[50] the tort of misuse of

[42] ibid, 483–84.

[43] ibid, 484.

[44] Peter Handford, 'Intentional Negligence: A Contradiction in Terms?' (2010) 32 *Sydney Law Review* 29, 61–62: 'the tort of negligence is a valuable addition to the armoury of weapons available for deliberate wrongdoing, one that is superior in many respects to trespass, limited by the confines of directness … a unified principle applicable to all kinds of fault-based harm has a certain attractiveness'.

[45] Peter Handford, 'Mens Rea in Tort Law' (2000) 20(4) *Oxford Journal of Legal Studies* 533, 549. He adds that 'in theory, it is possible to sue for intentional harm to property and to the person, but the difficulties of proving intention and uncertainty about the benefits of doing so have largely robbed this avenue of practical importance'.

[46] Tony Weir, 'The Staggering March of Negligence' in Peter Cane and Jane Stapleton (eds), *The Law of Obligations: Essays in Celebration of John Fleming* (Clarendon, 1998) 137: 'The pull of the negligence principle – pay for the foreseeable harm you are at fault in causing – is immensely strong'.

[47] French Civil Code (1804) Article 1382: 'every act whatever of man which causes damage to another obliges him by whose fault the damage occurred to repair it'. Article 1383 makes clear that a person is liable for damage they caused by their own acts, as well as by negligence or 'imprudence'.

[48] Peter Handford, 'Mens Rea in Tort Law' (2000) 20(4) *Oxford Journal of Legal Studies* 533, 536: 'this line between deliberate and non-deliberate conduct [is one] to which tort law gives prime significance'.

[49] Peter Handford, ibid, 547, refers to this as the 'ancillary' function of intention in tort law.

[50] Anthony Gray, 'Change the Rules: Reform of the Economic Torts in Australia' (2019) 21(2) *Flinders Law Journal* 295.

public office, and the tort of intentional infliction of emotional distress.[51] These torts should still be recognised, and should still require intention as an element to be proven. The fact of intention indicates a more egregious level of behaviour, justifying the imposition of liability in circumstances where mere negligence would typically not. And secondly, it might impact on the level of damages available – damages might be higher in the case of intentional wrongdoing, as compared with unintentional wrongdoing.[52] Thirdly, it might also be relevant in the weighing of the relevant interests – the fact that the defendant has acted deliberately may weigh more heavily against them in the balancing exercise, that if they had acted merely negligently.

Conclusion

This short discussion of the tort of trespass, another strict liability tort, also notes doctrinal confusion. Fault-based considerations have loomed large in the defences available to a trespass action. Where defences of self-defence, exigencies of everyday life, necessity or consent arise, the question of the reasonableness or otherwise of the defendant's behaviour features centrally in the discussion. In other words, fault still looms large, when the court is considering the no-fault, strict liability tort of trespass. Academics, and some judges, have noted this. Perhaps it is time to recalibrate and reorient the law of torts along the 'fault line', with the fault of the defendant being a requirement for the tort to be established, rather than through the back door of defences. Fault here is conceived broadly to include both intentional and negligent wrongdoing. The traditional reference in some parts of the law of torts to the question of the defendant's intention continues to have some utility, but it should be seen as an indicia of the dominant principle of fault, rather than a principle of its own. This will lead to greater coherence in the law of torts, and within individual torts themselves. The current schizophrenic personality of some torts, fault and no-fault at once, including trespass, would disappear.

[51] Anthony Gray, '*Wilkinson v Downton*: New Work for an Old Tort to Do?' (2015) 23(3) *Tort Law Review* 127.

[52] For example, it is said that the test for remoteness of damages is easier in the case of the tort of deceit (an intention- and recklessness-based and non-negligence-based tort): *Derry v Peek* (1889) LR 14 App Cas 337), compared with the tort of negligence: Peter Handford, 'Mens Rea in Tort Law' (2000) 20(4) *Oxford Journal of Legal Studies* 533, 547.

Conclusion

In his brilliant article, Eric Descheemaeker noted that the law of torts had developed in a 'vertical' manner, reflecting the interests with which particular torts were concerned to protect. Cutting across them 'horizontally' was negligence, a principle not dependent on the protection of particular interests, but concerned with standards of behaviour of individuals or organisations and, in particular, where due to fault or wrongdoing, that individual or organisation caused another loss.[1] His immediate focus there was on the relation between the torts of defamation and negligence. He concluded that the latter was acting as a magnet for the other, pushing the standard of liability in the former tort ever closer to the fault sphere of negligence, and that they were on a 'collision course'.

This book has aimed to make that point at a broader level of abstraction, involving the law of defamation, but also the law regarding infringement of property interests, such as nuisance (including *Rylands v Fletcher*), and the law regarding personal injury.

From the viewpoint of a long lens, the law of torts has battled since the beginning with the two seemingly inconsistent arguments – that the defendant should be liable for the simple fact of having caused another injury (subject to exceptions) and that the defendant should only be liable for causing another injury in circumstances where it can be said they were at fault for doing so. While initially the law embraced strict liability, concerned to preserve the peace and discourage the blood feud, it was shown that the law over time moved to a fault-based standard. This occurred through juries (apparently) taking such matters into account, through changes in the forms of action where the action on the case permitted parties to give a fuller account of facts; through legislative changes, which actively demonstrated an intention that liability should only be imposed in cases of fault (in particular areas, such as common carriers and innkeepers), and in relation to government; and through the evolution of court decision and precedent. The Industrial Revolution provided what proved to be the final impetus for such a change.

Notwithstanding these critical developments, strict liability retained its adherents. The classic *Rylands v Fletcher* demonstrates this, as do other decisions involving the law of nuisance, and cases involving defamation.

The abiding difficulty, however, with application of strict liability to precise cases is the injustice caused by inflexible rules that do not readily permit a full

[1] Eric Descheemaeker, 'Protecting Reputation: Defamation and Negligence' (2009) 29(4) *Oxford Journal of Legal Studies* 603, 603.

consideration of the particular factual scenario before the courts. Strict liability, where liability is imposed on defendants who are not at fault, leads to injustice. This has been demonstrated for centuries. Juries deciding cases in the Middle Ages knew it. Parliaments seeking to deny the strict liability of common carriers and innkeepers knew it. And courts seeking to deny strict liability for personal injury, including in *Weaver v Ward*, knew it. Judges faced with the daunting beacon of strict liability in *Rylands v Fletcher* in determining cases factually similar to it knew it, quickly finding ways around its strictness through the interpretation of concepts so as to marginalise and isolate it.

This has been the course of the tort of nuisance and defamation too. Apparently strict in nature, the harshness of such rules was quickly in evidence. Judges slowly but surely permitted defences and exceptions, virtually all of which were fault based. We have almost reached a stage where it is redundant and confusing to call torts such as nuisance and defamation strict, where the prevalence of fault-based defences completely undercut their 'strictness'. The other relic of *Rylands v Fletcher*, redolent of a different era and, as we understand now, an unwelcome throwback to a previous era even in the 1860s, should be put out to pasture, as has occurred elsewhere.

The genius of the common law is its knack of preserving the essence of what has gone before, but being flexible enough to accept new realities and to be applicable to new situations. And the common law has done this, escaping from the confines of strict liability by creating and applying fault-based exceptions to take the harsh edges off, and by painting *Rylands* into a corner from which it is unlikely to 'escape'. However, sometimes something slightly more radical is called for. This is the case here. It is time that the law of torts rebalanced onto a fault axis. The particular interests do not matter so much as an assessment of the defendant's behaviour against the standards of the reasonable person. In such an approach, the nature of the interference with the plaintiff's interests – whether it be personal injury, damage to property interests, damage to reputational interests, all with their own current rules and principles, do not matter so much as the assessment of the defendant's behaviour, given all the circumstances of the case, against reasonable standards of the day. I say something 'slightly more radical' – this is not a totally new idea. More than three centuries ago, Grotius suggested something similar – that the controlling idea of tort ought to be the question of the defendant's fault, that the nature of the plaintiff's interest was not particularly relevant because interests were entitled to equal protection.[2] It has a source in Roman law and reflects the French Civil Code. This is surely better than endless limiting of strict liability *Rylands* so that it is virtually useless, and adoption of a schizophrenic approach to the torts of nuisance, defamation and trespass where they are notionally seen as strict liability torts, but in reality fault plays a large role in the actual determination of disputes through the use of defences.

[2] Hugo Grotius, *On the Law of War and Peace* (1625) 2.17.1, 2.17.2.1.

As this book has documented, try as many scholars might, they have been unable to come up with a settled, convincing rationale for the imposition of strict liability upon individuals and defendants. Advocates of such views invariably make statements that are demonstrably just not true, make wild assumptions that have little relation to reality, or make statements that lack a basis in the actual case law and the process of deciding cases. They often adopt a view of the role of the judiciary that would be foreign to most decision makers, confusing the role of courts with the role of parliaments and/or social welfare agencies.

How might this evolution in the law of torts be practically brought about? Frankly, the judges themselves are typically somewhat reluctant to take the lead. Courts in the United Kingdom have been asked (and refused) to take out *Rylands v Fletcher* once and for all. On occasion, some far-sighted judges have recognised the current inadequate situation, where strict liability torts are infused with fault reasoning, but perhaps do not see it as part of their remit to address the situation. At least in the United States, the Restatement process can herald this kind of change to the law. It might be in the United Kingdom that the Law Commission could lead a review of strict liability in the law, with a view to statutory reform to the structure of existing torts. Specifically, this might mean, for instance, that:

(a) the *Rylands v Fletcher* principle should officially be interred, as discussed in Chapter 3;
(b) the tort of nuisance is effectively subsumed into the law of negligence, as discussed in Chapter 7;
(c) the tort of defamation is either subsumed into the law of negligence or completely re-enacted in statute which makes it clear that the fault of the defendant in publishing is one of the elements of the tort to be proven by the plaintiff, as discussed in Chapter 8; and
(d) the tort of trespass to the person is either subsumed into the law of negligence, or defined in such a way that it must be shown by the plaintiff that the defendant was at fault (either intent or negligence).

Of course, there are many examples where parliaments have redrawn the elements of a tort. Witness the various attempts at statutory reform of the law of defamation in the United Kingdom. During the so-called insurance crisis in Australia in the early years of the twenty-first century, legislatures re-enacted common law principles of some torts in legislative form.

These reforms would simply reflect that the world has moved on from simple causation as a rationale for liability. More is and should be required of anyone seeking compensation from another. And it would end the current dysfunctional and anomalous system whereby the law appears to reify some interests (such as property interests and interests in reputation) over others, in a way that can no longer be justified, if indeed it ever could.

Let the evolution continue.

INDEX

Introductory Note

References such as '178–79' indicate (not necessarily continuous) discussion of a topic across a range of pages. Wherever possible in the case of topics with many references, these have either been divided into sub-topics or only the most significant discussions of the topic are listed. Because the entire work is about the 'strict liability', the use of this term (and certain others which occur constantly throughout the book) as an entry point has been minimised. Information will be found under the corresponding detailed topics.

www.ingramcontent.com/pod-product-compliance
Ingram Content Group UK Ltd.
Pitfield, Milton Keynes, MK11 3LW, UK
UKHW020248290926
15470UKWH00002B/801

9 781509 940998